CAMBRIDGE STUDIES IN NINET
LITERATURE AND CU

General editor
Gillian Beer, *University of Ca.........*

Editorial board
Isobel Armstrong, *Birkbeck College, London*
Leonore Davidoff, *University of Essex*
Terry Eagleton, *University of Manchester*
Catherine Gallagher, *University of California, Berkeley*
D. A. Miller, *Columbia University*
J. Hillis Miller, *University of California, Irvine*
Mary Poovey, *New York University*
Elaine Showalter, *Princeton University*

Nineteenth-century British literature and culture have been rich fields for interdisciplinary studies. Since the turn of the twentieth century, scholars and critics have tracked the intersections and tensions between Victorian literature and the visual arts, politics, social organisation, economic life, technical innovations, scientific thought – in short, culture in its broadest sense. In recent years, theoretical challenges and historiographical shifts have unsettled the assumptions of previous scholarly synthesis and called into question the terms of older debates. Whereas the tendency in much past literary critical interpretation was to use the metaphor of culture as 'background', feminist, Foucauldian, and other analyses have employed more dynamic models that raise questions of power and of circulation. Such developments have reanimated the field.

This series aims to accommodate and promote the most interesting work being undertaken on the frontiers of the field of nineteenth-century literary studies: work which intersects fruitfully with other fields of study such as history, or literary theory, or the history of science. Comparative as well as interdisciplinary approaches are welcomed.

A complete list of titles published will be found at the end of the book.

THE VICTORIAN SUPERNATURAL

The Victorians were haunted by the supernatural, by ghosts and fairies, table-rappings and telepathic encounters, occult religions and the idea of reincarnation, visions of the other world and a reality beyond the everyday. *The Victorian Supernatural* explores the sources of these beliefs in their literary, historical and cultural contexts. The collection brings together essays by scholars from literature, history of art and history of science, which examine the diversity of the Victorians' fascination with the supernatural. The essays show that the supernatural was not simply a reaction to a post-Darwinian loss of faith, but was embedded in virtually every aspect of Victorian culture. This important interdisciplinary study sheds new light on debates surrounding the relationship between high and popular Victorian culture and contemporary notions of the supernatural.

NICOLA BOWN teaches Victorian literature and art at Birkbeck College, University of London. She is the author of *Fairies in Nineteenth-Century Art and Literature* (Cambridge, 2001).

CAROLYN BURDETT is Principal Lecturer in English at London Metropolitan University. She is the author of *Olive Schreiner and the Progress of Feminism: Evolution, Gender, Empire* (2001).

PAMELA THURSCHWELL is a lecturer in English at University College London. She is the author of *Literature, Technology and Magical Thinking 1880–1920* (2001) and *Sigmund Freud* (2000).

THE VICTORIAN
SUPERNATURAL

EDITED BY

NICOLA BOWN

Birkbeck College, University of London

CAROLYN BURDETT

London Metropolitan University

and

PAMELA THURSCHWELL

University College London

CAMBRIDGE
UNIVERSITY PRESS

CAMBRIDGE UNIVERSITY PRESS
Cambridge, New York, Melbourne, Madrid, Cape Town, Singapore, São Paulo, Delhi

Cambridge University Press
The Edinburgh Building, Cambridge CB2 8RU, UK

Published in the United States of America by Cambridge University Press, New York

www.cambridge.org
Information on this title: www.cambridge.org/9780521114646

First published 2004
Reprinted 2005
This digitally printed version 2009

A catalogue record for this publication is available from the British Library

ISBN 978-0-521-81015-9 hardback
ISBN 978-0-521-11464-6 paperback

Contents

Illustrations

Contributors

NICOLA BOWN teaches Victorian literature and art at Birkbeck College, University of London. She is the author of *Fairies in Nineteenth-Century Art and Literature* (2001).

CAROLYN BURDETT is Principal Lecturer in English at London Metropolitan University (formerly University of North London). She has published articles on nineteenth-century imperialism, eugenics and science and is the author of *Olive Schreiner and the Progress of Feminism: Evolution, Gender, Empire* (2001).

STEVEN CONNOR is Professor of Modern Literature and Theory at Birbeck College, London. He is the author of books on Dickens, Beckett, Joyce and post-war British fiction, as well as of *Postmodernist Culture* (1989), *Theory and Cultural Value* (1992), *Dumbstruck: A Cultural History of Ventriloquism* (2000) and *Skin: An Historical Poetics* (2003).

COLIN CRUISE is Senior Lecturer in Art History at the University of Staffordshire. He has published many essays on nineteenth-century art and its relation to literature and religion, notably 'Lovely Devils: Simeon Solomon and a Pre-Raphaelite Version of Masculinity' in *Reframing the Pre-Raphaelites*, ed. Ellen Harding (1996) and 'Wilde's Lily: Oscar Wilde and the Message of Beauty' in *After the Pre-Raphaelites*, ed. Elizabeth Prettejohn (1999).

MICHAELA GIEBELHAUSEN is Lecturer in Art History and Theory at the University of Essex. She has published several essays on prison architecture and on Victorian art. She has recently edited *The Architecture of the Museum: Symbolic Structures, Urban Contexts* (2003) and is currently completing a monograph on Victorian religious painting, entitled *Painting the Bible: Representation and Belief in mid-Victorian England* (2004).

GEOFF GILBERT is Associate Professor and Chair of the Department of Comparative Literature and English at the American University of Paris. He writes and teaches on the culture of modernism, on Scots writing and culture and on questions of sexuality. His book, *Before Modernism Was: Modern History and the Constituency of Writing*, is forthcoming from Palgrave.

LOUISE HENSON completed her PhD on Charles Dickens, Elizabeth Gaskell and Victorian science at the University of Sheffield in 2000, and has published articles on this subject in *Victorian Review, Nineteenth-Century Contexts* and the *Gaskell Society Journal*. She was formerly research associate to the Science in the Nineteenth-Century Periodical project at the Humanities Research Institute, University of Sheffield. She is currently working on an online version of the Old Bailey Proceedings (1670–1834) at the Institute.

ROGER LUCKHURST teaches literature at Birkbeck College, University of London. He is author of *The Invention of Telepathy 1870–1901* (2002) and co-editor of *The Fin de Siècle: A Reader in Cultural History c. 1880–1900* (2000).

EVE M. LYNCH teaches British literature, with a particular interest in Victorian sensation fiction, at California State University, Hayward. Her published essays address various writers, including Charlotte Brontë and Mary Elizabeth Braddon. Her current project is a book-length study on the use of domestic servants in Victorian literature.

RICHARD NOAKES is British Academy–Royal Society Postdoctoral Research Fellow in the History of Science at the Department of History and Philosophy of Science, Cambridge. He has published on science and Spiritualism in Victorian Britain, and the representation of science, technology, and medicine in nineteenth-century generalist periodicals. He is currently preparing a monograph on Victorian physical and psychical sciences.

ADAM ROBERTS is Reader in Nineteenth-Century Literature at Royal Holloway, University of London. He has edited *Browning* (with Daniel Karlin) and *Tennyson* (2000) for the Oxford Authors series, and has published *Robert Browning Revisited* (1997) and *Romantic and Victorian Long Poems: A Guide* (1999) as well as a number of articles and essays on Victorian topics. He is currently editing Browning's Greek Poems (*Balaustion's Adventure, Aristophanes' Apology* and the *Agamemnon*) with

Dr Yopie Prins of Michigan University for the Oxford *Poetical Works of Robert Browning.*

PAMELA THURSCHWELL is a lecturer in English at University College London. She is the author of *Literature, Technology and Magical Thinking 1880–1920* (2001) and *Sigmund Freud* (2000).

Foreword

Gillian Beer

As Orlando reaches 1928, near the end of Virginia Woolf's mock biography, she enters the lift at Marshall and Snelgrove's London department store:

The very fabric of life now, she thought as she rose, is magic. In the eighteenth century we knew how everything was done; but here I rise through the air; I listen to voices in America; I see men flying – but how it's done, I can't even begin to wonder. So my belief in magic returns.

Technology enchants and baffles, suggesting a new kind of supernatural. It also teasingly here persuades belief in improbable fiction, an individual life pursued over centuries. In 1900 Eliza Lynn Linton, in a novel posthumously published, *The Second Youth of Theodora Desanges*, tells as first-person narrative the extraordinary story of a woman who, in her seventies, gradually grows young again. Again, the justification is couched at the outset in terms of the new magic of science and technology, this time in deadly earnest:

With the spectroscope and the phonograph, the germinative force of formic acid, the liquefaction of air, the Röntgen rays, and the new telegraphy, how can we say that any marvel in molecular rearrangement is impossible? . . . until we have stripped the Tree of Knowledge bare to its last leaf, we cannot say that such and such an abnormality is a lie and a figment. (1–2)

The disquieting realisation that all old certainties are now in question both enlarges the scope of the possible and undermines the patterns of the past. This uncertainty bears particularly on the question of the relationship between life and death, and what new possibilities arise in the wake of evolutionary theory and the laws of thermodynamics. Lynn Linton's heroine gains little good from her renewed health and vigour: she is a figure of satiety by the book's end, her pleasure in life sapped by the chronic fatigue of not knowing. For her, and more largely for many actual contemporaries, science offers no synthesis; religion no faith; human love no security. Her status is closer to monster than marvel. Linton's profound pessimism (or, rather, that of her heroine) represents one strong response to the uneven threshold of knowledge in the later nineteenth century. But many people, as this volume makes clear, were both troubled and exhilarated by the fresh routes to perception opened by popular understandings of developmental biology and physics, and by enquiries that questioned the impermeability of the membrane between the living and the dead.

The pioneering mathematician W. K. Clifford, in his discourse 'On Some of the Conditions of Mental Development' delivered at the Royal Institution in 1868, emphasises that it is the capacity to change and respond that marks both individual creativity and successful societies. Even 'the Spirit of the Age' is evidence of the force for change:

This force they call the Spirit of the Age. The spirit, then, which determines all the changes of character that take place, which is, therefore, more persistent than character itself, – is this, at last, a thing absolutely fixed, permanent, free from fluctuations? No: for the entire history of humanity is an account of its gradual changes. It tells how there were great waves of change which spread from country to country, and swept over whole continents, and passed away.

Clifford suggests, indeed, that there 'are actually two new senses, the scientific and the artistic, which the mind is now in the process of forming for itself.' This emphasis on the absolute novelty of human capacities and on the power of radical change bars insight into the future. So does Darwinian evolutionary theory, with its assertion of multiple and diverse variations producing outcomes unforeseeable in advance.

Perhaps this clouding of the relation of the future to the present in part accounts for the lateral drive of so much of the Victorian exploration of the supernatural analysed in this volume: we find spectral messengers, the resuscitation of the dead, second sight, dreams and reincarnation among the topics. Other human beings existing beyond the grave are much imagined, but it is contact with them now, rather than in a future life, that most excites enquiry: telepathy, mesmerism, table-rapping, séances concentrate on the presences just beyond the brink of time and space. And issues of class, empire, and Christianity are given a new turn when set in relation to the debate between fixed natural laws and immanent beings such as apparitions that reach beyond current regularities. As Steven Connor points out, even geometry, with its move to the non-Euclidean, could yield the suggestion that multiple unstable epistemologies are necessary to explanation. All these ideas, sometimes slack or garbled derivations of technical enquiries, sometimes innovative arguments, gave space for thought and enquiry.

The influence of the usually sceptical, sometimes credulous, experiments of the Society for Psychical Research was felt well beyond those who credited the events that occurred at séances. What was at stake, Richard Noakes demonstrates, was not simply science versus Spiritualism but rather 'rival notions of the scientific, the natural and the lawful'. Victorian scientific materialism never quite relinquished the transcendental, as avowedly agnostic writers like John Tyndall demonstrate, despite his irritated distaste for Spiritualist practices. And the instability of information in the further reaches of the empire gave particular potency to uncanny communication, Roger Luckhurst argues. Other writers here point to the submerged worlds of women and the poor and to their sometimes threatening possession of different means of reading evidence.

Not only writers, but artists sought fresh means of tapping into the invisible forces at work in the world. This could happen through the representation of dreams, as Nicola Bown here explores, or through the unexpected juxtaposition of the immortal and the temporal in order to re-imagine Christ, as Michaela Giebelhausen argues was the case for Holman Hunt and William Dyce. For theologians and religious people the claims of history could seem coercive, undermining revealed truth with the demand that documentation and context be provided.

The entire volume brings home the degree to which humdrum life is always perturbed by unwelcome insights and never quite securely closes on itself. This is particularly true in periods of intellectual upheaval such as the later nineteenth century. The writers focus on the formations of feeling, half-belief and recoil so often manifested in the language of those who explored the supernatural within Victorian society, in its various strata. They convincingly demonstrate that it is impossible to divide off scientific enquiry from amateur exploration when the search is on for what remains invisible. The excitement of that search, and its salience still for us, is well communicated by the essays in this collection.

Introduction

Nicola Bown, Carolyn Burdett and Pamela Thurschwell

The Victorians were haunted by the supernatural. They delighted in ghost stories and fairy tales, and in legends of strange gods, demons and spirits; in pantomimes and extravaganzas full of supernatural machinery; in gothic yarns of reanimated corpses and vampires. Even avowedly realist novels were full of dreams, premonitions and second sight. It was not simply a matter of stories and storytelling, though, for the material world they inhabited often seemed somehow supernatural. Disembodied voices over the telephone, the superhuman speed of the railway, near-instantaneous communication through telegraph wires: the collapsing of time and distance achieved by modern technologies that were transforming daily life was often felt to be uncanny. The mysterious powers of electricity, the baffling feats of mesmerists and apparently real communications from the dead elicited by Spiritualist mediums made the world seem as if it were full of invisible, occult forces. Of course, the Victorians also mocked their own fascination with the supernatural in satires and skits directed at the earnest foolishness of believers in supernatural phenomena, and often they indulged their taste for it in fun, getting up table-rapping parties and playing at fortune-telling. In the spirit of scientific enquiry they investigated the supernatural and debated its prevalence, forms and powers, finally setting up the Society for Psychical Research to determine its precise nature. But the Victorians also believed in the supernatural. This belief ranged from the wishful make-believe of many of those who wrote about the fairies and other supernatural figures of folklore, through the circumstantial belief of those visited by true dreams, premonitions and telepathic encounters, to the sometimes unwilling, sometimes eager belief of Spiritualists and Theosophists and the alternately enthusiastic and doubtful faith of Christians of all denominations. The supernatural was both fearful and terrible and ardently desired; it was a spooky sense that there was more to the world than the everyday, and an intimation that reality might be transfigured by something above and beyond.

I

The supernatural was an important aspect of the Victorians' intellectual, spiritual, emotional and imaginative worlds, and took its place in the domestic centre of their daily lives, from the brush with the spirit world at a séance in the parlour, to a serialised adventure story set in the Valley of the Kings, replete with mummies and images of ancient Egyptian deities, and from the weird sensation of looking at the ghostly face of a dead relative staring out of a photograph, to a reproductive engraving of *The Light of the World* on the wall. The supernatural pervaded literature, art and science – to name only three of the most powerful cultural forces – not only because supernatural powers and beings were imagined, explored and investigated through them, but also because the language the Victorians used to represent themselves and their world was saturated with the metaphors of the supernatural.

The essays in this collection attempt to describe and understand the lineaments of this pervasive fascination, looking at supernatural and maybe-supernatural phenomena such as telepathy, ghosts, Spiritualism, second sight, dreams, reincarnation and the divine aspect of Christ. Many of the essays focus on debates over the nature of these phenomena, and show that the ground between natural and supernatural was debatable and the border between the two controversial. The essays look at the supernatural and its metaphors with reference to art, literature and science and show how, for example, thinking about the class system and gender relations, the nature of mind, the bond between the imperial centre and its far-flung margins, the expression of sexual desire and the operation of the housing market were shot through with the language of the supernatural. By bringing together these diverse themes and approaches in this volume of essays, we hope to show that the Victorian supernatural was not merely a reaction to the 'crisis of faith' and the 'challenge of Darwinism', nor a faddish and frankly eccentric residuum of quasi-religious practices and a taste for ghoulish tales left by the 'advancing tide of secularism'. On the contrary, we hope the collection will show that the Victorian supernatural was a complex of images, ideas, beliefs and metaphors that entered into every aspect of life, often in strange and surprising ways.

The contributors to this volume cannot claim, of course, to have discovered the Victorian supernatural. Before we turn, at the end of this introduction, to a brief description of each essay, we discuss some of the ways that important and influential work by literary critics and cultural historians has shaped our understanding of the role the supernatural played in Victorian culture, and suggest how the essays in this volume further that project. However, twentieth-century understandings of the term 'supernatural' are in many respects very different from the meanings of the word current in the nineteenth century. Although all the essays in this volume touch on the ways 'supernatural' was understood, in the main their concerns are with how the supernatural permeated other areas of nineteenth-century thought and culture. It seems important, then, to start this introduction with a brief survey of how the Victorians understood the term 'supernatural' and what, where and who they thought the supernatural was.

In their discussions of the term, it is common for nineteenth-century writers to begin with a robust statement of the universality of belief in the supernatural, such as this one by John Radcliffe, author of *Fiends, Ghosts and Sprites, Including an Account of the Origin and Nature of Belief in the Supernatural* (1854):

A belief in the supernatural has existed in all ages and among all nations. To trace the origin of this belief, the causes of the various modifications it has undergone, and the phases it has assumed is, perhaps, one of the most interesting researches to which the mind can be given, – interesting, inasmuch as we find pervading every part of it the effects of those passions and affections which are most powerful and permanent in our nature.[1]

The importance of the supernatural was matched, however, by the difficulty of speaking about it and by its resistance to definition. John Eagles, metaphorically speaking, throws up his hands on the subject: 'How little, in fact, do we know of the material world, and how much less of the spiritual, and nothing of the connexion between them?'[2] Nevertheless, in spite of the perplexity they faced in trying to define the supernatural, because it was felt to pervade 'those passions and affections which are most powerful and permanent in our nature', writers tried repeatedly to elucidate it. Those who discussed the matter included theologians, Spiritualists, collectors of ghost stories, anthropologists and scientists. Their ideas were by no means uniform, for they defined and used the term in very different ways. They fell into several camps: those who thought of the supernatural as an action, or cause; those who considered it a place, or realm; those who thought of it as an aspect of the human constitution; and those who believed it was an order of non-human beings. There were, however, areas of overlap between these different ideas about the supernatural: seeing the supernatural as a realm did not, for example, prevent writers from thinking of it also as a cause. Opinions also ranged widely on the 'supernaturalness' of the supernatural, with many writers seeking to argue that what was popularly considered supernatural might, in time, be found to be simply another aspect of nature. On the other hand, others were committed to a much more elastic definition of what might be considered supernatural, including in it many phenomena thought by most others to be firmly within the realm of the natural.

A useful starting point is the definition given by the anonymous author of *Footsteps of Spirits: A Collection of Upwards of Seventy Well-Authenticated Stories of Dreams, Impressions, Sounds and Appearances* (1859), who drew a distinction between the 'Praeternatural' ('beside, or out of the usual course of nature') and the 'Supernatural' ('above and beyond the power of natural causes') giving the following example of the difference between the two:

> That a man should walk on water, or that the iron head of an axe should swim upon it, is a supernatural occurrence, which no natural means could effect. That a man should, by angelic ministry or otherwise, obtain a knowledge of what is passing on the other side of the globe at the instant of its occurrence, is praeternatural, because it is more than ordinary natural means could convey, and yet not more than, in other circumstances, time, and a letter, or a messenger could furnish.[3]

In this passage, 'nature' means not only the material world around us, but the immutable laws governing it. Walking on water is contrary to the laws of nature, and therefore could be accomplished only by something or someone outside, and with authority over those laws; knowledge of events on the other side of the world is not, because such knowledge could come from a letter, albeit one that reached its destination extraordinarily fast. The first, therefore, is supernatural, the second, praeternatural. The writer is a Catholic, concerned to argue that – contrary to the prevailing rationalist–Protestant view – the supernatural powers of the deity and his ministering angels are frequently in evidence in the modern world, and that the age of miracles was not confined to the biblical era. Yet his view of the supernatural as an action, or cause, is derived from eighteenth-century Protestant scholastic theology and the Anglican orthodoxy, established by Joseph Butler and William Paley, on the nature of miracles as divine interventions in the laws of nature established by the deity. The laws of nature, they reasoned, were established by the first cause, the deity, who retained the power of intervening in them. The scriptural miracles, they argued, were evidence of this power, although the period of miracles was now over, and the laws of nature unimpeded by supernatural interpositions. Evidence of the supernatural powers of the deity, therefore, had to come from studying the laws, contrivances and design of nature, established by God in the supernatural act of creation. Scholastic and natural theology, therefore, went hand in hand with the understanding of both nature and the supernatural.[4]

This view, however, was becoming superseded by the mid-century, and was attacked head on by Baden Powell in his contribution to *Essays and Reviews* (1860), 'On the Study of the Evidences of Christianity'. Powell argued that credence in all instances of apparent supernatural interventions in nature was dependent on human, fallible testimony; all such happenings could be, and would come to be, explained using the inductive methods of science:

The enlarged critical and inductive study of the natural world cannot but tend powerfully to evince the inconceivableness of imagined interruptions to the natural order, or supposed suspensions of the laws of matter, and of that vast series of dependent causation which constitutes the legitimate field for the investigation of science, whose constancy is the sole warrant for its generalisations, while it forms the substantial basis for the grand conclusions of natural theology. Such would be the grounds on which our convictions would be regulated *as to marvellous events at the present day*; such the rules which we should apply to *the like cases narrated in ordinary history.*[5]

Powell is careful here to reserve judgement on the miracles recorded in Scripture. Nevertheless, the implication of his argument, which was taken up by other liberal theologians, was that even biblical miracles cannot be considered as divine interventions in the order of nature. The supernatural is thus limited to God himself, and to his original act of creation; there are no such things as miracles, and no supernatural occurrences disturb the established laws of nature.

Though this increasingly became the dominant view of liberal theologians, it was hotly contested by numerous evangelical theological controversialists, who continued to restate the view that miracles, supernatural interventions in the laws of nature, had happened and would continue to happen. James M'Cosh, a Scottish Presbyterian minister who eventually became president of Princeton University, is a typical example. In his often-reprinted *The Natural in Relation to the Supernatural* (1862), M'Cosh put forward a trenchant argument for the reality of supernatural intervention in the world:

The beings above this sphere [that is, Nature], and the agents beyond it, though it may be acting on it, we call 'Supernatural'. God, who created the cosmical agencies and set them in operation, is himself supernatural. When a supernatural being or power operates in nature, we call the work supernatural. The effect is among cosmical objects, it is wrought in men's minds or bodies, or in physical nature around them . . . The work of creation is supernatural, it is a work in nature arising from a power above nature. The raising of the dead would be supernatural, for there is no physical or physiological law producing such a result.[6]

Although, as Owen Chadwick remarks, no important theologian continued to argue this view after the mid-1860s, the argument did not die down.[7] Walter Cassels, an amateur biblical scholar, caused a minor controversy in the 1870s with his *Supernatural Religion: An Inquiry into the Reality of Divine Revelation* (1874), in which he aimed to prove through historical evidence that the testimony of the Scriptures to supernatural miracles could not be believed. Ultimately, he argued that if there is no evidence of the supernatural, Christianity as a creed must itself fail:

> On the very threshold of enquiry into the origin or character of Christianity, we are brought face to face with the supernatural ... This religion cannot be accepted without an emphatic belief in supernatural interposition, and it is absurd to imagine that its dogmas can be held, while the miraculous is rejected.[8]

Cassels's scholarship was eventually shown to be flawed, and his radical view of Christianity gained few adherents. Yet the controversy he caused is a measure of how hotly the question of the supernatural was debated in the decades after *Essays and Reviews*, and the tenacity of evangelical theologians in arguing the the supernatural is 'another and higher system, that of spiritual being and government for which nature exists'.[9]

This view was shared by many Spiritualists, especially those, like William Howitt, who managed to combine a belief in Spiritualism with Christian faith. In *The History of the Supernatural* (1863), Howitt argued that miracles are interventions in nature 'as the results of spiritual laws, which in their occasional action subdue, suspend or neutralise the less powerful physical laws, just as a stronger chemical affinity subdues a weaker one'.[10] Howitt's scientific analogy is significant, for many Spiritualists argued that the Spirit world, rather than being supernatural, was an as yet unknown order of nature. Alfred Russel Wallace, for example, contended that an order of 'spiritual beings' existed, 'capable of acting on matter, though they themselves are unrecognisable directly by our senses', and consisting of 'the most diffused and subtle forms of matter'.[11] In *The Scientific Aspect of the Supernatural* (1866), Wallace argued that theological discussions of the supernatural were inadequate to account for the phenomena of Spirit communication, and that the commonly understood demarcation between the natural and the divine could not encompass the existence of Spirit beings, which Spiritualism undeniably proved. Such a view was far from uncommon. In an article on dreams published in 1874, John Rutherford argued that

> Organised bodies – perhaps we might say all bodies – are for ever giving off particles – those at rest, in every direction; those in motion behind them, in one

long stream . . . It requires but a small stretch of the imagination to conceive that the particles thrown off by human feelings bear the impress of their hopes, fears, and expectations – as they exist at the moment of separation.[12]

The view that humans were tripartite beings made up of body, soul and spirit infuses Rutherford's speculations, as well as the beliefs of Spiritualists and others. Spirit beings are sometimes conceived of as unseen presences of the dead among the living, and sometimes as the ethereal aspect of the living person which partially escapes the body in sleep and wholly at death. In some cases, the spirit is thought of as wholly supernatural, for example in the beliefs of Swedenborgians: 'The world of spirits . . . is intermediate between heaven and hell, and is the first receptacle of souls after death. It was chiefly in this intermediate world (in which a man's spirit even whilst living in the body really exists), that [Swedenborg] experienced what he heard and saw.'[13] More often, however, the spirit is viewed as an as yet undiscovered material form, which awaits only new scientific discoveries for its true nature to be revealed. In their efforts to quash the scepticism of the unconverted, followers of Spiritualism frequently had recourse to the argument that 'the time will come, when [Spirit communications and other supernatural phenomena] will be reduced strictly within the bounds of science'.[14]

Yet Spiritualists also commonly conceived of the supernatural as another realm, existing above and beyond the material world. William Howitt invited his readers to 'stroll through the wide corn-fields of the supernatural, or, in modern phrase, of Spiritualism', and his metaphor of the supernatural as a place was widely echoed.[15] Eye-witness accounts of séances commonly described the phenomena as emanating from another realm, as in this example: 'Strange voices – voices not of this world – stole into the room, the gas turned alternately blue and crimson, and the place was suffused with an unearthly glare.'[16] The 'other world' beyond and above the material was thought of as peopled by spirits, whose reality – witnessed by the participants in numerous séances – is 'supernatural, super, superior or above the laws governing the visible elements around us'.[17] The belief of Spiritualists is summed up by John Jones:

SPIRITUALISM is the belief in the existence of SPIRIT AS A PERSON, endowed with mental perceptions and powers of force; by which he can, though invisible, act according to his invisible physical powers, as man can with his visible physical energies.[18]

Jones's terminology illustrates the slippage between the natural and supernatural common in Spiritualist writings, the frequent recourse to the

language of science – powers and forces – to define the supernatural. In
great part, this is due to Spiritualists' need to distinguish their beliefs from
what was thought of as the 'superstition' of the uneducated and ignorant,
whose belief in supernatural beings and events was untouched by the rationalism of educated opinion. Even those who were prepared to admit that
'millions of spirits exist around and among us' were anxious to distance
their belief in the continued existence of the spirit from mere superstition.
Walter Scott, for example, opines:

> These examples of undeniable apparitions . . . fall like the seed of the husbandman,
> into fertile and prepared soil, and are usually followed by a plentiful crop of super-
> stitious figments, which derive their sources from circumstances and enactments
> in sacred and profane history, hastily adopted, and perverted from their genuine
> reading.[19]

In his anthropological study *The Supernatural: Its Origin, Nature and Evolution* (1892), John H. King combines the condemnation of popular superstition with a eugenic view. He sees superstition, and belief in the supernatural
in general, as evidence of the degeneration of the urban and rural working classes, contending that intoxication acting on ignorance produces 'the
wide belief in mystic principles and powers, in ghosts and spirits, in transformation, in the conquest of death and disease . . . and all the spiritual
phenomena of the later world'.[20]

King's view is an extreme one (he believed, for example, that 'there is
not a town in England or in Europe in which witchcraft is not extensively
practised').[21] Yet the prevalence of the supernatural in nineteenth-century
debate, even if not all concerned believed that supernatural phenomena
regularly manifested themselves in nineteenth-century Britain, testifies to
its vital importance in thinking about the nature of the cosmos, of human
beings and their interactions with the unseen world. In her widely read *The
Night-Side of Nature*, Catherine Crowe comments on the 'extreme aversion
to admit the possibility of anything like what is called the Supernatural',
such that 'mere avowal of such a persuasion is enough to discredit one's
understanding with a considerable part of the world'.[22] Yet the several
reprints of her book, and the wide publicity it received, implies that in fact
the Victorians were more susceptible to the supernatural than this suggests.
Perhaps, paradoxically enough, it was because of the slipperiness of the
supernatural, its resistance to definition and its protean quality of being a
cause, a place, a kind of being, a realm, a possibility, a new form of nature,
a hope for the future, that made it so fascinating. Crowe herself admits that

the supernatural is almost impossible to define properly and comments that hardly anyone knows what they really believe about it:

> The truth is, that not one person in a thousand, in the proper sense of the word, believes anything; they only fancy they believe, because they have never seriously considered the meaning of the word and all that it involves. That which the human mind cannot conceive of, is apt to slip from its grasp like water from the hand; and life out of the flesh falls under this category.[23]

The supernatural is like 'water in the hand': a category that defies definition, a realm the human mind cannot conceive. As a writer on 'The Literature of Dreams' put it, 'There may be a class of words unknown to us, the absence of which prevents us forming *precise* ideas of the wondrous phenomena about us, and of comprehending the mystery even of our own being.'[24] The essays in the present volume show how the supernatural in its many forms haunted the Victorians because of its profound yet enigmatic connection with the 'mystery of our own being'. And although in the nineteenth century the supernatural was thought about in ways that seem distant and distinctly odd in hindsight, there are connections to be made between Victorian conceptions and the uses of the supernatural in twentieth-century thought. The metaphor of haunting, of revenants from another place or time, is one such connection, for this idea has been unexpectedly pervasive in recent literary-critical theory and cultural history. Perhaps we are still looking for that 'class of words unknown to us' which will enable us to form 'precise ideas' of the 'mystery of our being'.

'I began with the desire to speak with the dead.'[25] This is Stephen Greenblatt's influential claim for a material and historical literary criticism. But what kind of speech? And which dead? Greenblatt imagines a scene of history in which the people of the past could speak back and be truly heard by a historian who mediumistically channels their voices. New historicism, ideally, is a time machine for speaking to the still living in the past, not a way of listening to ghosts. For critics interested in the supernatural, however, the central question is what kind of conversation one might have with the really dead. In wanting to speak to the dead as if they were living, to listen to and be able to interpret correctly the materially specific traces of history, new historicism finds itself inevitably evoking that desire's impossibility. Paying attention to the forms and meanings of the supernatural shows us that the desire for the full recovery of history can only be expressed as a desire for a supernatural connection.

In Peter Buse's and Andrew Stott's introduction to their collection *Ghosts: Deconstruction, Psychoanalysis, History* they suggest that 'the most sustained engagements this century with the figure of the ghost do not revolve around thinkers attending séances, but rather in the texts of what has come to be called "theory"'.[26] Although there have been major historical and literary considerations of the séance this statement is still a useful place to start in considering the role of the supernatural in recent theory. Certainly it would be difficult to argue with Buse and Stott about the continuing importance of the *figure* of the ghost in contemporary academic writing. Ghosts are repeatedly invoked in the critical work of many late twentieth-century writers who would probably think twice about trying to contact Marx or Freud by means of a Ouija board. The suggestive significance of the supernatural often floats free of its original sources, dispensing with the material forms that give our modern notions of the supernatural shape and heft. In thinking about recent critical uses of the supernatural we should not forget how many of these material forms were put in place during the nineteenth century. But to begin with, let us take a look at the metaphorical supernatural that suffuses recent literary and cultural theory.

The metaphors provided by the supernatural are nothing new. The occult has been a rich source for talking about both individual psychology (the haunted mind) and collective political experience (the sense of being haunted by history). But recently psychoanalytic and deconstructive literary theorists have adopted the metaphors of the supernatural with a ferocity that bears examination. We have crypts and phantoms, 'specters of Marx' and ghosts of modernity.[27] Marx and Freud, for example, are amongst the central practitioners of the 'hermeneutics of suspicion' that has been seen as defining the modern critical attitude, yet along with the sense in their work that there is something hidden behind or underneath the surface that we have come to accept as reality, one can also discern a shared thematics of loss. What is finally uncovered, once the veil is lifted, is often something missing, something that should be there and maybe once (at least in fantasy) was. Losses are often central to these suspicious critical paradigms; the loss of the worker's unreified relationship to their labour or the loss of a sense of infantile plenitude. But these losses are often incomplete and leave a remainder. It is here the supernatural comes into play; the remainder is imagined as a haunting. Theories of both history and the self seem to create ghosts or revenants, leftovers that recent critical theory is quick to seize on and expose as the supplement of history or the psyche.

Freud's essay 'Mourning and Melancholia' evokes ghostliness by suggesting that the process of letting go of the past, of the dead, is often a vexed one.[28] In melancholia the lost object that one cannot completely relinquish returns as an aspect of oneself. Melancholia makes the ghost of the loved (and hated) other inseparable from the self, a part of one's interior being. Psychoanalytic critics such as Nicholas Abraham and Maria Torok take up Freud's Gothic thematics and theorise them as an Edgar Allan Poe story, imagining a psychic formation of walled crypts and phantoms. The process of familial inheritance thus leaves the self embedded with foreign objects and family secrets which must not be known and cannot be exorcised.

Abraham and Torok's extreme use of the supernatural rhetoric of psycho-analysis is at the far end of a rhetorical movement that begins in full force at the end of the eighteenth century: the migration of Gothic horror from the threatening outside world to the inside of the individual's mind. Terry Castle has argued that the nineteenth century is the moment when ghosts retreat into the mind. From dwelling in the outer reaches of Ann Radcliffe's Italian castles they move steadily inwards towards the Englishman's (and woman's) very essence. Eventually they lodge themselves as psychological projections: fears and desires that are anchored in the past and are the ba-sis of our inner selves.[29] Many forms of contemporary nineteenth-century psychology, as well as psychoanalysis, which in part emerges from them, are thus indebted to the uncanny haunted houses of Gothic fiction. The modern self may be pre-occupied.

If the self has become a ghostly projection in recent critical theory, so too has history. A recent critical text that engages with the rhetoric of the supernatural to confront the impossible demands of understanding history is Jacques Derrida's influential *Specters of Marx*. Marx himself relied on haunting. As Derrida reminds us, there is a spectre lying in wait in the first sentence of the *Communist Manifesto*: 'A specter is haunting Europe – the specter of communism.'[30] Or, as Marx wrote even more evocatively in *The Eighteenth Brumaire of Louis Napoleon*: 'Men make their own history, but they do not make it just as they please: they do not make it under circumstances chosen by themselves, but under circumstances directly en-countered, given and transmitted from the past. The tradition of all the dead generations weighs like a nightmare on the brains of the living.'[31] A nightmare is not exactly a ghost, although it may perhaps be supernatural. And that heavy, nightmarish haunting of the present by the brutal eco-nomic conditions and cultural traditions of the past is not identical to the haunting that Derrida evokes, for deconstruction finally bases its critique in narrative and linguistic structures rather than in the more recalcitrant material of history. Derrida implies that a just reading of history should be attentive to the ways in which failed narratives, such as the collapse of communism, reverberate: ghosts will reappear. A loss will be followed by an unexpected return, and predicting the end of history – or the form in which it might come back – is a losing game. For Derrida, history is structurally and necessarily haunted, but where is the supernatural to be found in this kind of haunting? The problem is that the ghost is only one in a series of deconstructive tropes. As Buse and Stott write:

Ghosts are neither dead nor alive, neither corporeal objects nor stern absences. As such, they are the stock-in-trade of the Derridean enterprise, standing in defiance of binary oppositions such as presence and absence, body and spirit, past and present, life and death . . . In the figure of the ghost, we see that past and present cannot be neatly separated from one another, as any idea of the present is always constituted through the difference and deferral of the past, as well as the anticipation of the future.[32]

This use of the supernatural is both evocative and generalising. Along with other recent metaphorical uses of the supernatural, Derrida's work suggests that the supernatural has become a rich rhetorical source for theories of history and the psyche. But such theories unify and flatten out the supernatural: they move too seamlessly over the supernatural into what it signifies. What happens if instead of only looking at what it signifies, we also attend to the ways in which the supernatural signifies differently at different historical moments? The recent 'turn to history' in literary criticism demands a thoroughgoing historical perspective, but this is not easy to achieve. How might we historicise a central aspect of the fascination of the supernatural – the desire to confound history and turn back time, to eschew the material world in favour of an ethereal, magic realm?

One way, of course, is to locate ghosts, fairies and séances in specific times and places and genres. What Gauri Viswanathan has tellingly labelled 'the ordinary business of occultism' is central to recent work on the Victorians' sometimes daily negotiations with various aspects of the other world.[33] In an article on the sound experience of the séance Steven Connor calls for a stricter attention to the various modes of experiencing the Victorian supernatural as it was deeply believed in, scientifically refuted, practised (alone or in groups), played with, dutifully recorded as evidence, fictionalised, worshipped and mocked.[34] As Gillian Beer has recently argued, the invisible was the subject of intense investigation and speculation because of its very invisibility.[35] Groundbreaking works such as Janet Oppenheim's *The Other World: Spiritualism and Psychical Research in England, 1850–1914*, Alex Owen's *The Darkened Room: Women, Power and Spiritualism in Late Victorian England* and Alison Winter's *Mesmerized: Powers of Mind in*

Victorian Britain have put previously sidelined practices such as Spiritualism, psychical research and mesmerism back on the map of nineteenth-century political, religious and cultural history.[36] Such recent cultural histories have shown that in the séance and other arenas of the supernatural powerful dramas of class and gender are played out, and have demonstrated how we need to attend to the practices, beliefs and experiences of the occult to help us understand the 'ordinary business of occultism'. Even this, though, may miss something. What about the dreamer who seems to have dreamt the future? Or the person who feels sure that they have seen a ghost, or that they have lived before? Such experiences evoke the supernaturalness of the supernatural, the fact that it *is* otherworldly, inexplicable and strange. Understanding the Victorian supernatural in all its varieties and manifestations demands a range of approaches because it is otherworldly and strange as well as ordinary and everyday, and because it involves both material practice and metaphorical suggestion. The essays in this collection, taken together, go some way towards demonstrating this diversity.

Richard Noakes's opening essay explores debates about Spiritualism in the mid-Victorian period. A common account of these debates is couched in terms of a struggle between Spiritualists, who sought to secure the authority of scientific law for the range of phenomena displayed in the séance, and their scientific opponents, who viewed Spiritualism as a mess of superstition and charlatans. The capricious, unreproducible and unverifiable happenings of the séance were evidence of supernatural belief, and any definition of science must definitively exclude Spiritualism. As Noakes goes on to demonstrate, however, these commonly understood boundaries between science and pseudo-science, or the natural and the supernatural, were themselves formed from debates about Spiritualism in which scientific claims competed, each vying for authority and legitimacy. Through close examination of two of the most eminent Victorian scientific investigators of Spiritualism – William Crookes and William Benjamin Carpenter – Noakes shows how 'boundaries between natural and supernatural emerged from disputes over spirit manifestations'. The real dispute, he suggests, was not a matter of distinguishing supernatural from natural so much as from competing, and sometimes irreconcilable, versions of what could be taken to be natural.

Dickens's wide-ranging interest in apparitions and spirits, mesmerism, clairvoyance and theories of mind, as well as in collecting, authenticating and telling ghost stories, provides the focus for Louise Henson's exploration of early and mid-Victorian debates about the supernatural. She situates Dickens's popular ghost stories within the context of both scientific and medical writing about apparitions, mesmerism and other ghostly phenomena, and in relation to Dickens's participation in journalistic and other debate about ghosts. Henson shows Dickens as being deeply involved in emerging scientific notions of the mind and its stranger – though still natural – capacities, as well as being sensitive to the ways in which new technologies produced startlingly new ways of understanding mental phenomena. Dickens's ghost stories thus emerge out of his close engagement with early Victorian theories and speculation about the human mind, but his broad definition of the ghost in his journalism and fiction indicates the complexity and diversity of debate about the nature of the ghost in the pre-Spiritualism era.

Eve Lynch's reading of Mary Elizabeth Braddon's ghost stories of the 1860s and 70s sees the supernatural as a means of exploring the 'unknown regions beyond' the visible realm of respectable Victorian society. These 'unknown regions' are the precarious social positions inhabited by women and other dependants, where social status is perilous and financial security absent. The world in which apparitions make themselves seen is the world below stairs from where servants also function as ghostly presences in the respectable Victorian home. Lynch shows Braddon's ghost stories responding to the social reforms of the 1860s and 70s that were to have secured a firmer foundation in liberal and humane values for a successful modernising England. What was often hidden from sight, however, was the misery and dispossession of the many who did not benefit from mid-Victorian economic change or philanthropy. The ghosts of Braddon's stories thus serve as signs of what Victorian society is unwilling to see in and of its own social condition.

Pamela Thurschwell introduces her reading of George Eliot's *Daniel Deronda* with Stuart Cumberland, a minor novelist who made a living and a name for himself by public demonstrations of thought-reading. His insistence that his abilities were entirely explicable in naturalistic terms sets up one of the complex echoes explored by Thurschwell as she turns to examine the ways in which realist fiction manages its own capacity to read unspoken thoughts. In *Daniel Deronda* prophecy and second sight are the point of a splitting in the novel which pits a patriarchal and world-historical stage against a feminine and private one. The Jewish prophet-figure Mordecai's visions are supported by a series of comparisons to scientific and artistic accomplishments, while Gwendolen Harleth's susceptibility to portents is portrayed as atavistic and superstitious. Thurschwell shows how this splitting, the story of two kinds of prophetic transmission, and their fraught relation, is at the heart of what drives Eliot's narrative.

A Christian paradigm of resurrection is one element of Adam Roberts's reading of Browning, a reading which interprets the dramatic monologue as an aesthetics of resuscitation. Browning's poetic form is thus a means of calling forth the dead, having them speak and hearing what they have to say. Despite his antagonism towards the quackery of spirit mediumship, as portrayed in 'Mr Sludge, the "Medium"', Roberts finds in Browning's poetics a productive tension between a purely Christian concept of resurrection and a pagan, and even occult, version of the same. Drawing on contemporary theoretical concepts, particularly as developed by Derrida in his work on haunting, Roberts seeks to understand the complexity of Browning's verbal resuscitations as instances of mourning and as acts of poetic giving. For Roberts the poet's work is giving voice to the dead, and this is a labour of love.

The séance as a narrative device provides the focus for Colin Cruise's reading of the 'Toto' stories of Frederick Rolfe. Rolfe, still a relatively little-known writer, allows Cruise to explore the ways in which images of Italy and of Catholicism coalesce in Rolfe's singular protomodernist texts. Cruise points out that Catholicism – to which Rolfe converted from his dissenting origins – provided Rolfe with a meditative and 'magical' access to experience, an access which Spiritualism affords for the impoverished Protestant. The central story Cruise analyses, 'About These Tales, the Key and Paradise', foregrounds Toto's mediumistic identity, his 'being spoken', in a trance-like state. In substituting for the traditional female medium a beautiful peasant boy, who tells his tales to 'Baron Corvo', Cruise argues Rolfe is able to encode dissident sexual material within a set of 'high' cultural references focused on the boy's paraphrasing of Dante.

John Anster Fitzgerald's 1858 painting *The Stuff That Dreams Are Made Of* prompts Nicola Bown to ask why there are so few pictorial images of dreaming in the Victorian period – especially since dreams were, at the same time, the topic of intense speculation and debate. Images of dreamers and their dreams from the Renaissance through to the Romantic period illustrate the shifting debate about whether dreams are natural or supernatural phenomena. While progressive scientific thinking strives to understand the mind – and thus its stranger night-time outputs – in materialist terms, Bown shows how such thinking is persistently affected by the possibility that dreams may be supernatural in origin. Within the context of developing theories of mind, which sought to understand the stuff of dreams as a key to the stuff of the mind, Bown demonstrates how Fitzgerald's picture insists on the dream's irrepressible strangeness. For Fitzgerald, dreams are truly boundary-defying: both physical and supernatural, material and immaterial, they come from beyond and within the dreamer's mind. His paintings thus reflect and represent the deep uncertainty about the nature of dreams among his Victorian contemporaries.

Michaela Giebelhausen sets Holman Hunt's *The Finding of the Saviour in the Temple* and William Dyce's *The Man of Sorrows* in the context of the theological controversy generated by *Essays and Reviews* to show why, and how, the representation of Christ was so problematic for these artists. *Essays and Reviews* stripped away the supernatural aspects of the biblical narrative, but was silent about the supernatural aspect of Christ; however, for these artists seeking to paint Christ the question of how to represent his human and divine manifestations could not be fudged. Giebelhausen argues that Hunt's strategy of historical reconstruction produces proliferating significations and leaves puzzling ambiguities in the picture: his commitment to realism prevents the communication of the divine. Dyce, on the other hand, eschews the unbroken historicity of Hunt's image, juxtaposing an iconographically traditional Christ with a locally specific, realistically depicted landscape. Through this radical disjunction, Giebelhausen argues, Dyce's picture allows the viewer to perceive the mystical and wondrous: a vision of the living Christ as God.

Roger Luckhurst begins with the Society for Psychical Research's 'quotidian archive of occult experiences' – that is, the accounts of strange experiences lodged by correspondents to the Society, many of them from far-flung reaches of the empire. Luckhurst finds there certain repeated themes and concerns. These he sees as revealing the ways in which semi-legitimate knowledges find a way into the culture precisely because they are not able to be sanctioned through authoritative channels: they act instead like rumour. Luckhurst shows how these strange knowledges operate on the imperial margin, where sanctioned ideas and less legitimate beliefs become blurred; magical thinking was part of colonial rule. Thus, as modern communications systems supposedly stamped out native superstition, Luckhurst shows how occult forms – such as the Hindu Secret Mail – nevertheless compete and sometimes take over. He then turns to illustrate these permeable boundaries of authority and knowledge via a detailed case study of Andrew Lang, the literary critic, folklorist and anthropologist who exemplifies the complex ways in which colonial contexts inform the categories of psychical research.

Carolyn Burdett focuses on the four works by Henry Rider Haggard that feature 'She', the immortal white queen who rules in Africa. All contain extensive reference to reincarnation and to occult phenomena. Burdett shows how these themes, and their treatment in Haggard's adventure fiction, can be illuminated by examining the movement in Britain most associated with reincarnation, namely Theosophy. Alongside its emphasis on the pursuit of a universal brotherhood of man, Theosophy also espoused hierarchy based on the existence of elites. These elites were the 'Masters' and adepts who hold access to esoteric knowledge of the occult laws. Although Haggard often portrayed 'primitive' superstition, which is usually resisted by sceptical and rational Englishmen-heroes, he also confounded these men with the esoteric occult powers associated especially with Ayesha. Burdett argues that the contrary trends in Theosophical doctrine allow Haggard both a means of criticising the spiritual blight he associates with modern life, and provide him with a model of hierarchy with which to withstand the vulgar and destructive forces unleashed by democratisation.

In the collection's final chapter Geoffrey Gilbert looks past the historical ending of the Victorian period to the origins of modernism – and sees that origin as intimately connected to property and ghosts. Virginia Woolf identifies modernism's origins in the 'smashing and crashing' of an Edwardian literary world-view capable of rendering personhood only through its external trappings. In seeking to secure the autonomy of the person and of the work of art, Gilbert argues, modernism must disavow these outer trappings, including the fact of what it means to make money out of writing. What results is a form of haunting which Gilbert explores via Henry James's ghost story, 'The Jolly Corner'. The problem with Victorian haunted houses, as the Society for Psychical Research discovered, was that ghosts damaged property values. By contrast, the modernist house is haunted by its own disavowals of money, property and literary value.

NOTES

1 John Netten Radcliffe, *Fiends, Ghosts and Sprites, Including an Account of the Origin and Nature of Belief in the Supernatural* (London: Richard Bentley, 1854), p. 1.

2 John Eagles, 'A Few Passages Regarding Omens, Dreams, etc.', *Blackwood's Edinburgh Magazine* 48 (1840), 194–204; p. 200.

3 *Footsteps of Spirits: A Collection of Upwards of Seventy Well-Authenticated Stories of Dreams, Impressions, Sounds and Appearances* (London: Burns and Lambert, 1859), pp. 5–6.

4 For a discussion of the continuing influence in the nineteenth century of eighteenth-century scholastic theology, especially in relation to the 'evidences' of miracles, see Joseph L. Altholz, 'The Mind of Victorian Orthodoxy: Anglican Responses to *Essays and Reviews*, 1860–1864' in *Religion in Victorian Britain, Volume Four: Interpretations*, ed. Gerald Parsons (Manchester University Press / Open University, 1988), pp. 28–40; p. 34–7.

5   Baden Powell, 'On the Study of the Evidences of Christianity' in *Essays and Reviews* (London: John W. Parker, 1860), pp. 94–144; pp. 150–1. Emphasis as in the original.

6   James M'Cosh, *The Natural in Relation to the Supernatural* (Cambridge: Macmillan, 1862), pp. 101–2.

7   Owen Chadwick, *The Victorian Church*, 2 vols. (London: A. & C. Black, 1966–70), vol. II, p. 31.

8   Walter Cassels, *Supernatural Religion: An Inquiry into the Reality of Divine Revelation*, 3 vols. (London: Green and Co., 1874), p. 1.

9   Horace Bushnell, *Nature and the Supernatural as Together Constituting the One System of God* (Edinburgh: Alexander Strahan, 1862), p. 19.

10 William Howitt, *The History of the Supernatural*, 2 vols. (London: Longman, Green, Roberts and Green, 1863), p. v.

11 Alfred Russel Wallace, *The Scientific Aspect of the Supernatural* (London: F. Farrah, 1866), pp. 4, 7.

12 John Rutherford, 'Dreams', *Cornhill Magazine* 29 (1874), 720–6; p. 726.

13 Emmanuel Swedenborg, *Spiritual Diary: A Brief Record, During Twenty Years, of his Supernatural Experience, Vol. I*, trans. J. H. Smithson (London: Newbery / The Swedenborg Society, 1846), p. xii.

14 Catherine Crowe, *The Night-Side of Nature, or Ghosts and Ghost-Seers*, 3rd edn. (London: George Routledge, 1852), p. 11.

15 Howitt, *History of the Supernatural*, p. 4.

16 *Astounding Disclosures in Connection with Spiritualism and the Spirit World! Supernatural Visits at the House of a Clergyman in Bayswater* (London: J. Onwhyn, 1864), p. 4.

17 John Jones, *The Natural and Supernatural, or Man Physical, Apparitional and Spiritual* (London: H. Bailliere, 1861), p. 7.

18 Ibid., pp. 217–8.

19 Walter Scott, *Letters on Demonology and Witchcraft Addressed to J. G. Lockhart Esq.* (London: John Murray, 1830), p. 48.

20 John H. King, *The Supernatural: Its Origin, Nature and Evolution*, 2 vols. (London: Williams and Norgate, 1892), p. 22.

21 Ibid., p. 13.

22 Crowe, *Night-Side of Nature*, p. 69.

23 Ibid., p. 8.

24 'The Literature of Dreams', *Bentley's Miscellany* 59 (1866), 267–71; p. 268.

25 Stephen Greenblatt, *Shakespearean Negotiations: The Circulation of Social Energy in Renaissance England* (Oxford: Clarendon Press, 1988), p. 1.

26 Peter Buse and Andrew Stott (eds.), *Ghosts: Deconstruction, Psychoanalysis, History* (London: Macmillan, 1999), p. 5.

27 On crypts and phantoms in psychoanalysis see Nicholas Abraham and Maria Torok, *The Wolf-Man's Magic Word: A Cryptonomy*, trans. Nicholas Rand, with an introduction by Jacques Derrida (Minneapolis: University of Minnesota Press, 1986); Nicholas Abraham and Maria Torok, *The Shell and the Kernel*, vol. I, ed. and trans. Nicholas Rand (Chicago: University of Chicago Press,

1994); Maria Torok and Nicholas Rand, *Questions for Freud: The Secret History of Psychoanalysis* (Cambridge, MA: Harvard University Press, 1997). On ghosts and history see Jacques Derrida, *Specters of Marx: the State of Debt, the Work of Mourning, and the New International*, trans. Peggy Kamuf (London and New York: Routledge, 1994); Jean Michel Rabaté, *The Ghosts of Modernity* (Gainesville: University Press of Florida, 1996).

28 Sigmund Freud, 'Mourning and Melancholia' (1917), *Standard Edition of the Complete Psychological Works of Sigmund Freud*, trans. and ed. James Strachey *et al.*, 23 vols. (London: Hogarth Press, 1957), vol. xiv, pp. 237–58.

29 Terry Castle, *The Female Thermometer: Eighteenth-Century Culture and the Invention of the Uncanny* (Oxford: Oxford University Press, 1995).

30 Derrida, *Specters of Marx*, p. 4.

31 Karl Marx, *The Eighteenth Brumaire of Louis Napoleon* (London: Lawrence & Wishart, 1954), p. 10

32 Buse and Stott, *Ghosts*, pp. 10–11.

33 Gauri Viswanathan, 'The Ordinary Business of Occultism', *Critical Inquiry* 27 (2000), 1–20.

34 Steven Connor, 'The Machine in the Ghost: Spiritualism, Technology and the "Direct Voice"' in Buse and Stott, *Ghosts*, pp. 203–25; p. 204.

35 Gillian Beer, ' "Authentic Tidings of Invisible Things": Secularizing the Invisible in Late Nineteenth-Century Britain' in *Vision in Context*, eds. Teresa Brennan and Martin Jay (New York and London: Routledge, 1996), pp. 83–98.

36 Janet Oppenheim, *The Other World: Spiritualism and Psychical Research in England, 1850–1914* (Cambridge: Cambridge University Press, 1985), Alex Owen, *The Darkened Room: Women, Power and Spiritualism in Late Victorian England* (London: Virago, 1989), and Alison Winter, *Mesmerized: Powers of Mind in Victorian Britain* (Chicago: University of Chicago Press, 1998).

PART I

Supernatural science

CHAPTER I

Spiritualism, science and the supernatural in mid-Victorian Britain

Richard Noakes

INTRODUCTION

In December 1861, a few months after he published the first instalment of his supernatural masterpiece, *A Strange Story*, the distinguished novelist Edward Bulwer Lytton told his friend John Forster that he wished 'to make philosophers inquire into [spirit manifestations] as I think Bacon, Newton, and Davy would have inquired. There must be a natural cause for them – if they are not purely imposture. Even if that natural cause be the admission of a spirit world around us, which is the extreme point. But if so, it is a most impartial revelation in Nature.'[1]

Lytton thus expressed the dilemma of many people in mid-Victorian Britain who had experienced the manifestations of Spiritualism, undoubtedly one of the most controversial aspects of Victorian culture, and one that was reaching new heights of popularity in the 1860s. His remark implicitly represents the Victorian association of Spiritualism with the supernatural, but also problematises that association by identifying the Victorian quest for order behind phenomena purporting to come from the other world – the 'naturalisation of the supernatural' as it was called by one early historian of Victorian psychical research.[2] While some firmly believed that manifestations were opposed to every known natural law and were by definition supernatural, others upheld the possibility that such manifestations might derive from 'natural causes', whether these were well-known mental mechanisms, new forces associated with the body, or intelligences from the spirit world.

Historians and literary scholars have long puzzled over the resurgence of interest in the supernatural in the Victorian period. This period has been called the 'age of science', a period of increasing belief that the cosmos was governed by immutable natural laws rather than capricious supernatural agencies or divine whim, and when supernatural beliefs were increasingly dismissed as superstition.[3] The construction of empirically grounded laws was widely regarded as one of the highest goals of scientific endeavour and those monuments of ordering physical phenomena – the laws of celestial mechanics – were upheld by Victorian scientists as the ideal to which all scientific enterprises should aspire. Moreover, since natural laws were widely regarded as authoritative accounts of the natural world, scientific practitioners, whose empirical evidence underpinned such laws, were generally seen as the supreme authorities on the natural world.

As this essay will show, Victorian investigators of Spiritualism believed that the erratic phenomena of the séance could be reduced to natural laws and that their enterprises could thereby gain scientific credibility. However, this was a difficult goal to achieve since many critics of Spiritualism questioned the very possibility of a naturalistic approach to phenomena that were ostensibly beyond nature, and actively defined the natural sciences in opposition to Spiritualism. For many Victorian scientists, Spiritualism had to be banished from the natural enquiry because it threatened the rapid progress of the sciences and the intellectual edifice on which the scientific profession based its claims for professional authority.[4] George Carey Foster, a London physics professor and evangelist for the new cultures of laboratory physics teaching, spoke for many who had devoted their lives to building the intellectual and architectural spaces of the sciences when, in 1894, he asked the psychical researcher Oliver Lodge 'is not the whole progress of physics based on the assumption that these [Spiritualistic] things do *not* happen?'.[5] In articles in mass circulation periodicals, textbooks, in public lectures and in classroom teaching, Victorian professionalisers and popularisers of science enforced the contrast between science and Spiritualism, and helped represent Spiritualism as beyond the domain of natural enquiry.

Recent scholarship has rightly argued that since the Victorian period witnessed such fierce scientific, intellectual and theological debates over the boundaries between science and Spiritualism, science and pseudo-science, we cannot take such boundaries for granted in our historical analyses.[6] These boundaries are the *explanandum* not the *explanans*. One of the most important benefits of this scholarship is that it draws attention to the complexity of the debates out of which these boundaries emerged and shows that controversies over Spiritualism were not, as traditional historiography suggests, struggles between proponents of 'science' and 'pseudo-science', but fights between individuals who disagreed on what counted as the proper scientific approach to the spirit world.

The new historiography of the occult sciences also challenges the use of natural and supernatural as unproblematic categories for analysing disputes over Spiritualism, and prompts us to understand how boundaries between natural and supernatural emerged from disputes over spirit manifestations. Recent literature on the supernatural, however, testifies to the continuing usefulness and persuasiveness of classifying Spiritualism as 'supernatural'.[7] While such a classification respects the categories used by historical characters, it is not sensitive to the provisional, contradictory or other uses to which 'supernatural' was put in Victorian Britain. Neither does it represent the complex *natural* interpretations of Spiritualistic manifestations.[8] This essay attempts to recover some of this complexity of mid-Victorian controversies over Spiritualism – the period of the most intense and revealing of all such controversies. The following section charts the problematic cultures and claims associated with Victorian Spiritualism, and examines the ways in which Spiritualists sought to achieve scientific credibility for their enquiries by promulgating the argument that manifestations would eventually be found to be results of natural laws. This was exactly the position taken by the most outspoken Victorian opponents of Spiritualism – physiologists, psychologists and medical practitioners – and my examination of their competing naturalistic explanations of Spiritualistic phenomena shows that the more intense disputes over Spiritualism sprang from only subtle differences of interpretation. I develop this approach in the third section, which uses the clashes between two of the most eminent Victorian scientific investigators of Spiritualism – William Crookes and William Benjamin Carpenter – to show that conflicts over the naturalistic provenance of manifestations were also conflicts over what constituted a proper scientific authority on Spiritualism. In these clashes, judgements on the interpretation of Spiritualistic manifestations were bound up with judgements on the appropriateness and reliability of the training, experience and expertise that informed this interpretation. Although the long-term impact of these controversies on Victorian Spiritualism, the supernatural and science falls outside the scope of this essay, I conclude by suggesting how the approaches developed here can generate new insights into old questions of the ultimate trajectory of Victorian Spiritualism.

THE CULTURAL AND THE NATURAL IN VICTORIAN SPIRITUALISM

In June 1853 the *Illustrated London News* regretted that the 'matter-of-fact people of the nineteenth century' were 'plunged all at once into the bottomless deep of Spiritualism'. It continued:

Railroads, steam, and electricity, and the indubitable wonders which they have wrought, have not proved powerful enough to supersede and destroy that strong

innate love of the supernatural which seems implanted in the human mind.
Thousands of people in Europe and America are turning tables, and obsti-
nately refusing to believe that physical and mechanical means are in any way
connected in the process. Hats, too, are turned, as well as the heads that wear
them.

Thousands of people seemed to be exploring the table-turning and Spiritualistic phenomena that had arrived in England from America and the
Continent in late 1852. In a country already weakened by recent outbreaks
of mortal diseases, the 'epidemic' of table-turning and of Spiritualism had
seized on 'not only the ignorant and the vulgar, but the educated and the
refined' like a '*grippe* or the cholera-morbus'.[9]

The *Illustrated London News* was not alone in comparing Spiritualism
to a recrudescence of the supernatural in an apparently enlightened age.
Throughout the mid- to late-Victorian period, Spiritualism was associated with a wide range of ancient and contemporary supernatural phenomena, including Christian miracles, witchcraft and sorcery, apparitions
of the living and dead, haunted houses, fairies and second sight. Neither was the *Illustrated London News* alone in likening Spiritualism to a
disease or something similarly despised, and throughout its Victorian hey-
day, Spiritualism was condemned as the work of Satan, a sordid commercial 'business', an 'epidemic delusion', a 'wretched superstition', 'filth' and
humbug.[10] The vehemence and frequency with which hostile remarks were
levelled at Spiritualism reflect its popularity in mid-Victorian Britain. By
the 1860s Spiritualism had become a conspicuous and, to many, lamentable
part of Victorian cultural life, with its mediums, specialist newspapers,
pamphlets, treatises, societies and private and public séances.[11] Its rapid
spread had manifold causes but it certainly owed much to widespread
and long-established preoccupations about the afterlife and the immortality of the soul, as well as pre-existing cultures of religious nonconformity
and mesmerism (from which Spiritualists borrowed such notions as the
magnetic fluids by which disembodied intelligence was supposedly transmitted). Its growing presence in Victorian culture also owed much to the
fact that it could serve a wide range of religious, intellectual, emotional,
and social interests. For example, spirit manifestations furnished powerful empirical proofs of Scriptural miracles for those Christians whose
faith had been undermined by Higher Biblical Criticism and startling
new biological and geological evidence for human origins, but manifestations were also used by anti-clerical plebeian Spiritualists for building democratic alternatives to Christianity, and furnished rich sources for

scientific research into abstruse physical, psychological and physiological phenomena.[12]

Most people gained their experience of Spiritualism in the domestic séance, typically in the presence of a Spiritualist medium. Those attending séances in Britain during the early 1850s could expect to experience such remarkable phenomena as clairvoyance, tables rapping out coded messages from professed spirits of the dead, and the levitation of objects by 'spirits'. By the early 1870s, however, the mediumistic repertoire had been vastly enriched with such feats as mediums who levitated around the séance, direct and mediated 'spirit' writing, and most spectacular of all, the materialisation of fully-formed spirits. The most controversial aspect of Spiritualism was undoubtedly the interpretation of such manifestations, whether the higher 'mental' or the cruder 'physical' phenomena. Most Spiritualists insisted that manifestations furnished proof of one or more of the following claims: the independence of spirit and matter, the survival and immortality of the spirit following bodily death, the eternal progress of all in the other world, and the possibility that under certain conditions spirits of the dead could manifest themselves to the living. For many enquirers, assent to these interpretations was based on an elimination of trickery, self-delusion and other 'physical' mechanisms as plausible hypotheses: although intellectually more difficult to accept, the 'Spiritual' theory was simply better at explaining the 'facts' of the séance.[13]

While many used Spiritualism to support Christianity, and to combat atheism, agnosticism, materialism and rationalism, others believed Spiritualist activities threatened cherished Protestant beliefs. They lambasted Spiritualists' abolition of the boundary between this world and the next, their rejection of eternal damnation, their exchanges with spirits who were most likely to be evil, their use of crude mediums and vulgar spirits in matters of pure faith and their subversion of scriptural and clerical authority as morally perilous and unholy.

It was the presence of notoriously tricky and avaricious mediums, the questionable reliability of witnesses and other contingencies of the séance that many enquirers into Spiritualism believed threatened the objective reality of spirit manifestations. The *Saturday Review* spoke for many when, in 1871, it criticised the way in which Spiritualistic manifestations only occurred 'in the most capricious manner' rather than appearing on demand, and, five years later, it argued that spirit manifestations could not be reduced to a 'true' 'law of nature' because they were 'never performed in a straightforward open way, like any honest experiment. They are either done in the dark, or only before known believers and confederates, or within a specially prepared place; and even when they are done in the daylight, the operator is full of tricks to distract attention, and to produce mysterious bewilderment.'[14]

For many séance-goers, the only circumstances under which manifestations appeared were those that militated against the very idea of rational scientific enquiry. Henry Dircks, an eminent civil engineer and the co-inventor of the popular theatrical illusion, 'Pepper's Ghost', neatly expressed this in 1872 in letters to *The Times* that developed a long-established distinction between the regularity, utility and sanitised wonder of enlightened scientific enquiry, with the caprice, gratuitousness and dangerous spectacle of early modern praeternatural philosophy.[15] He contrasted science, which 'always brings its miracles to the light of day', which concerns reproducible and useful 'wonders', and which relates to 'certain laws of nature', with Spiritualism, which not only 'shrouds itself in dark chambers, has its special mediums, and shuns the light', but has not led to any 'practical results', contains 'an amazing amount of childish jugglery', 'relates to the supernatural, and is opposed to every known natural law'.[16]

The views of Dircks and, as we have seen, Lytton, illustrate the centrality of questions of natural and supernatural in debates over Spiritualism. In many ways, these debates intersected with the much wider intellectual and theological controversies over the meanings of the terms 'supernatural' and 'natural law', the plausibility of biblical miracles and the bearing of the claims of 'modern science' on other Christian teachings. Nevertheless, a survey of books, pamphlets and articles on Spiritualism from the mid-Victorian period underlines the lack of consensus on the provenance of Spiritualistic manifestations, with works upholding a range of natural and supernatural explanations including evil spirits, angels, conscious acts of trickery, unconscious psychological and physiological mechanisms or hitherto unknown forces associated with the human body. A sense of the complexity of the debate is evident in an 1859 work on natural law and revelation by Baden Powell, the eminent Oxford mathematician and 'Broad Church' clergyman. Anticipating the remarks of Dircks quoted earlier, Powell insisted that: 'In so far as [spiritual phenomena] are alleged to be of a supernatural kind, not referable to some physical laws, they must be absolutely discarded from all philosophical enquiry.'[17] But having allowed for the possibility that spirits might be miraculous, Powell was confident that '"spirit-rapping", table-turning and the like' would 'be ultimately found perfectly conformable to some great determinate laws, which the science of the future will elicit'.[18]

Although Powell was hostile to Spiritualism and favoured the physiological theories of 'spirits' advanced by mid-Victorian medical practitioners, his
naturalistic interpretation of spirits closely resembles the positions adopted
by British and American Spiritualists to defend their activities from the
kinds of criticism represented by the *Saturday Review* and Henry Dircks.[19]
The views of Robert Dale Owen, Alfred Russel Wallace and William Henry
Harrison powerfully illustrate how leading Victorian Spiritualists argued
for the ultimately law-like nature of manifestations, and therefore sought
to persuade sceptical Victorian audiences that Spiritualism was a subject fit
for what Powell called 'philosophical enquiry'.

In his widely-read *Footfalls on the Boundary of Another World* (1860),
Owen, a radical American politician who had been converted to Spiritualism in the late 1850s, lamented the fact that in an age where 'modern
science' had subsumed most phenomena under general laws of the universe,
the tendency was to reject 'evidence for a modern miracle' because these
alleged occurrences violated natural laws and thus what could be taken
as possible.[20] Like many Victorian Spiritualists, Owen engaged with the
eighteenth-century philosopher David Hume's notorious argument against
miracles, which insisted that it was more likely that witnesses to such events
were mistaken than the laws based on 'firm and unutterable experience'
had been violated. Owen retorted that since 'no experience is *unalterable*'
in a 'world all over which is stamped the impress of progress', then experience and the laws built from experience were only provisional and
not reliable guides to what was naturally possible and impossible. He also
dismissed Hume's argument that miracles were 'an effect of the special intervention of God' because we could have no conception of 'His thoughts'
and what we took to be miracles might be God 'employing natural causes
and general laws to effect His object'.[21] For Owen, there was enough well-
attested evidence for hauntings, apparitions of the living and dead, and
related spontaneous spectral occurrences to suggest that they were 'ultra
mundane phenomena . . . governed by laws yet unknown or obscurely dis-
cerned' but which deserved 'thorough, searching, sedulously accurate, and
in the strictest sense of the term impartial' enquiry.[22]

Alfred Russel Wallace undoubtedly agreed. In 1866 this eminent naturalist and co-inventor of the theory of evolution by natural selection was
so impressed with his experiences in séances that he followed Owen's example of buttressing a philosophical argument for the naturalistic status of
strange spectral phenomena with the testimony of putatively trustworthy
witnesses.[23] Wallace admitted that miracles had 'no place' in 'modern science' which had engendered 'a firm conviction in the minds of most men of

education, that the universe is governed by wide and immutable laws', but emphatically warned that '*the apparent miracle may be due to some undiscovered law of nature*'.[24] Wallace went much further than Owen, however, because he held that miracles *per se* and the alleged miracles of disembodied spirits could be accommodated within the bounds of modern scientific enquiry. There was no reason, he argued, why anybody 'acquainted with the latest discoveries and the highest speculations of modern science' should deny the '*possibility*' of the existence of invisible intelligent beings capable of acting on matter. The discovery of Foraminifera, 'those structureless gelantinous organisms which exhibit so many of the higher phenomena of animal life without any of that differentiation of parts' deemed essential for life, made possible the existence of 'sentient beings unrecognisable by our senses'. Similarly, one of the 'grandest generalisations of modern science' – the attribution of 'all the most powerful and universal forces of nature' to the 'minute vibrations' of the 'almost infinitely attenuated form of matter', the 'spacefilling ether' – made possible the action of immaterial spirits on 'ponderable bodies'.[25]

Like many Spiritualists, Owen and Wallace used historical testimony of spectral phenomena and the ongoing observational evidence from contemporary séances to support the argument that there was order behind the apparent caprice of spirit manifestations. Few Spiritualists articulated this position and its implications for the progress of Spiritualism more vigorously than William Henry Harrison, a scientific journalist who in 1869 became the founder editor of one the most successful of all Victorian Spiritualist periodicals, the *Spiritualist*. His views were apparent from the opening editorial, which boasted that:

Not much observation of the phenomena of Spiritualism is necessary to learn that the manifestations are governed by physical and mental laws, though very few of these laws are at present known. Systematic, scientific research applied to Spiritualism would therefore . . . be sure to give very valuable results, by clearing away much of the mystery overhanging the borderland between this world and the next, and by strengthening the conditions which now enable spirits to communicate.[26]

Harrison believed that abolishing 'the words "miracle" and "supernatural" as applied to Spiritualistic phenomema' would help make such phenomena legitimate subjects for 'scientific research', and would also fulfil the crucial goal of preventing 'the public' from believing that Spiritualism was a baseless superstition or that 'the phenomena we know to be true are based upon the same evidence as that which . . . satisfies the Jews that Joshua made the sun stand still'.[27] Harrison and other 'naturalistic' Spiritualists also tended to use 'Spiritual' analogues to electrical and magnetic forces in explanations of how spirits manifested themselves, attempting to turn séances into scientific sites for probing connections between the known physical and the unknown 'spiritual' forces, and hoping that their new 'scientific religion' would become a branch of existing scientific disciplines including psychology, physics and physiology.[28]

However, the argument that the 'supernatural' phenomena of Spiritualism could be reduced to natural causes was shared by those popular conjurors who sought to show how mediumistic feats were 'really done' with legerdemain and concealed machinery.[29] Moreover, this interpretation was fiercely upheld by medical practitioners, physiologists, psychologists and other scientists and intellectuals who shared these conjurors' profound hostility to Spiritualism. Drawing on studies of 'altered' mental states, empirical research in human physiology and much older philosophical and psychological works, these explorers of Spiritualism also naturalised spirits, but did so by rejecting the 'spiritual theory' and promulgating arguments that well-known psychological and physiological causes were sufficient to explain what happened in the séance.[30] For physiologists and medical practitioners, 'Spiritualistic' phenomena were well known as consequences of agencies within the body. Their extensive knowledge of mental disorders, including insanity, hysteria and somnambulism, underpinned this naturalistic interpretation.

The anti-Spiritualist position was vigorously upheld in periodical articles, public lectures and textbooks by William Benjamin Carpenter, a distinguished Victorian physiologist, medical practitioner and zoologist, whose influential interpretations of Spiritualism are fairly representative of the mid-Victorian medical response to Spiritualism.[31] A staunch Unitarian, Carpenter believed that the laws of the material universe were direct expressions of God's will and that natural laws could not be broken without His will. Carpenter had strong metaphysical grounds, therefore, for doubting the plausibility of supernatural phenomena and for locating them within the known laws of the universe. Building on the researches on bodily and mental reflexes by such early Victorian physicians as Marshall Hall and Thomas Laycock, the associationist psychology of David Hartley, and his own extensive studies of mesmerism, table-turning, spirit-rapping, somnambulism and hysteria, Carpenter developed the notion that all mental activity was, in the first instance, automatic or spontaneous, and that the more developed the species, the more unconscious mental reflexes could be regulated by the will. For Carpenter, 'epidemic delusions' were propagated by individuals who, under the influence of erroneous 'dominant

ideas' from within or suggestions from without, had become the sorry victims of their automatic mental reflexes and thus experienced sensations
and motor responses that were entirely dependent on false ideas and stimuli. While maintaining that witnesses to such extraordinary and unlikely
phenomena as 'spirits' were honest in reporting what they experienced, he
disagreed on their interpretations of the phenomena. Their interpretations
could not be trusted because they usually entered séances already possessed
by the 'dominant idea' of disembodied spirits, a strong expectation that
severely weakened their ability to control unconscious mental and physical
responses with educated judgement, and thus made them highly susceptible to self-delusion, lapses of memory, hallucination, observational errors
and mediumistic jugglery. Accordingly, Carpenter argued that the 'so-called
spiritual communications come from *within*, not from *without*, the individuals who suppose themselves to be the recipients of them' and that such
communications were governed by 'laws of mental action'.[32] Like others
who participated in the lengthy mid-Victorian debates about national education, Carpenter's solution to such worrying examples of public ignorance
as Spiritualism was, unsurprisingly, proper mental training, because such
discipline would control mental reflexes and enable people to make sound
judgements about the sensory world automatically and thus avoid the mis-
takes made by séance-goers.

   This did not, however, perturb those who denied that physiologists and
medical practitioners had the requisite séance experience to make these
apparently authoritative claims, and who rejected the claim that their evidence for extraordinary manifestations could be reduced to the unconscious
actions of mind and body. For example, they denied that unconscious muscular action could explain the levitation of bodies with which séance-goers
had no contact. It was to explore the alternative laws of spirit, mind and
body suggested by their own séance experiences that Spiritualists and other
enquirers launched organisations such as the Psychological Society of Great
Britain (f. 1875) and the Society for Psychical Research (SPR, f. 1882).

SENSE OR SENSES? CONTESTING THE NATURAL AND THE
AUTHORITATIVE IN VICTORIAN SPIRITUALISM

In 1877 Carpenter concluded a public lecture on Spiritualism by warning that when assessing the extraordinary phenomena of the séance, 'we
should trust rather to the evidence of our *sense* rather than to that of our
senses'. Carpenter thus reiterated his belief that common sense, achieved
through proper mental education, was the ultimate court of appeal for

sensory experience, which was 'liable to many fallacies' resulting from the unconscious operations of the mind. It was for this reason that we earned 'the right to reject the testimony of the most truthful and honest witnesses' regarding phenomena that violated common sense and the 'Laws of Nature'.[33] Carpenter's claim neatly illustrates the intimate connections between what was sensed regarding Spiritualism and who had the sense to judge manifestations. Victorian disputes over the interpretation of Spiritualistic manifestations were therefore also disputes over authority. Thus, the conflicts that we have described between Spiritualists and medical practitioners stemmed not simply from differing 'naturalistic' interpretations of spirits, but from rival notions of what constituted the mental training, experience and 'scientific' expertise needed to make such interpretations authoritative.

This section shows how this approach can illuminate the controversies surrounding the researches of one of the most celebrated of all Victorian investigators of the 'supernatural', William Crookes.[34] Throughout the 1870s Crookes's researches sparked heated exchanges in a wide range of public and private forums, notably with Carpenter. We might see the conflict between Crookes and Carpenter as a straightforward contest between on the one hand, the pseudo-scientific, the Spiritualistic and the supernatural, and on the other hand, the scientific, the psychological and natural. However, there was agreement as well as disagreement between Crookes and Carpenter. Both promoted non-Spiritual theories of manifestations and both sought control of the séance, but their different notions of the natural causes of manifestations and of authority sparked bitter and prolonged exchanges.

By 1870, the year that he first publicly announced his intention to conduct a scientific investigation of Spiritualism, Crookes had established himself as a leading analytical chemist and respected editor of several specialist scientific periodicals. He was also known as the discoverer of the element thallium, an achievement based on his skill in the new technique of spectrum analysis. As editor of the *Quarterly Journal of Science* (*QJS*), Crookes encouraged contributions that discussed the startling new frontiers of science and emphasised the crucial role that scientific practitioners could play in the solution of such social problems as food adulteration, water pollution and disease. In 1870 Crookes used his periodical to confront another subject that was a social problem containing potentially rich sources for extending the authority of science – Spiritualism. Crookes appears to have begun investigating in 1867, and while this move may have been prompted by a family bereavement, it probably owed more to the positive séance experiences of close scientific colleagues, and the example set by Michael Faraday, Robert Hare and other scientific investigators of Spiritualism, who had made Spiritualism a legitimate scene of scientific enquiry. Moreover, Crookes saw the séance as a potential site for solving problems of the natural order. 'New Forces must be found', he explained in 1871, 'or mankind must remain sadly ignorant of the mysteries of nature. We are unacquainted with a sufficient number of forces to do the work of the universe.'[35] Crookes had evidently had enough séance experiences to convince him of the existence of phenomena that 'cannot be explained by any present law at present known'. Accordingly, in his first *QJS* article on Spiritualism, he insisted that a proper scientific investigation of the séance would establish 'a class of facts ... upon which reliance can be placed' and would 'drive the worthless residuum hence into the unknown limbo of magic and necromancy'.[36] Crookes was satisfied that the 'pseudo-scientific Spiritualist', with his sloppy séance protocols and vague physical theories of manifestations, could not undertake 'investigations which so completely baffle the ordinary observer'; rather, this task was for the 'thorough scientific man' who was trained in 'care and accuracy' and skilled in using the sensitive instruments needed to produce, under test conditions and independently of spiritual or any other theory, decisive evidence of the physical manifestations of the séance.[37]

By the time *QJS* readers digested this pronouncement on the proper authorities on Spiritualism, Crookes was already trying to implement his ideas in an extensive series of séances with the celebrated medium Daniel Dunglas Home. Over the next few months, Crookes became increasingly impressed by the medium's apparent ability to levitate objects and relay spirit communications, and his willingness to submit to close scientific investigation and insistence on holding séances in the light. For Crookes, a medium of this power and apparent probity was exactly the resource he needed for his investigations, and in the summer of 1871 he constructed several mechanical instruments for registering the power that seemed to emanate from Home's body, and then used them in test séances conducted with the assistance of the astronomer William Huggins and other scientific colleagues. Satisfied that Home had not secretly manipulated the apparatus or performed any other trickery, Crookes was confident that his apparatus had registered the existence of a 'new force, in some unknown manner connected with the human organisation', a capricious 'Psychic Force' which produced kinetic and audible effects beyond the body of the medium.[38]

Although Crookes failed to convince highly sceptical Royal Society referees of the merits of his research, his decision to publish reports on the experiments in the *QJS* won him a much larger audience than he would have gained through Royal Society publications. Indeed, according to one report, Crookes's reports 'set all London on fire, and the Spiritualists rabid with excitement'.[39] The response was certainly mixed. Several commentators accused Crookes of giving scientific respectability to a disreputable subject, of being taken in by mediumistic jugglery and of making fatal experimental blunders, while others were startled by the research and saw it as a sign for a decisive investigation of Spiritualism.[40] Spiritualists were also divided. Many congratulated Crookes for providing weighty confirmation of their fireside séance experiences, but others argued that his research showed that scientific men had nothing to show Spiritualists that they did not already know through their own experience. None was more critical than James Burns, the leading plebeian Spiritualist, journalist and publisher, who denied that Crookes had explained 'the nature of the power which produces the phenomena' and earlier challenged the very basis of the chemist's claims to authority in the séance. 'Could all the paraphernalia of Mr. Crookes's workshop', he asked, 'reveal to him the presence of a spirit?', and proceeded to explain that the individuals best able to discern the 'laws and conditions for the regulation of the phenomena' and the ultimate psychological cause of spirits were not the victims of 'a "long line of learning"' but those who possessed 'senses and forms of consciousness' adapted to the psychological 'plane'. It was these individuals who were building the 'science of Spiritualism'. Like many Spiritualists, Burns agreed that physical scientists could indeed illuminate the 'material phenomena developed by spirit power', but their mental training made them inferior to Spiritualists in discerning the psychological laws of the séance.[41]

While Crookes appears to have ignored these attacks on the authority of physical scientists on Spiritualism, he certainly did not dismiss the hostile responses from fellow scientists. Penetrating criticism from the physicist George Gabriel Stokes, for example, prompted him to attempt to display psychic forces independently of mediums and therefore the disreputable milieu of Spiritualism, and for this he turned to highly sensitive vacuum apparatus he was developing to explore an apparently anomalous force associated with radiation. However, no criticism hurt Crookes more than that of William Benjamin Carpenter, who published a scathing article in the *Quarterly Review* in late 1871 which angrily reiterated the psychophysiological theories of spirits he had been promulgating for over twenty years, and castigated scientific witnesses to 'powers unknown to men of science' as unprofessional, self-deluded and poorly educated converts to Spiritualism. 'Such scientific amateurs labour', he argued, 'under a grave disadvantage, in the want of that broad basis of *general* scientific culture, which alone can keep them from the narrowing and perverting influence of a limited *specialism*.' Crookes's want of the disciplining effects of a broad scientific education was apparent from the fact that he had seemingly entered his investigations already prejudiced in favour of the objective reality of Spiritualistic phenomena and was not 'acquainted with what had been previously ascertained in regard to the real nature of kindred [Spiritualistic] phenomena'. Carpenter was clearly annoyed that Crookes had not deferred to the authority of those with greater experience of psychological disorders (notably himself and the physician Thomas Laycock) because this 'specialist of specialists' would have trusted medical common sense rather than his own senses, guarded himself against self-deception and other sources of error and recognised that psychic force was nothing more than known mechanical forces cunningly exerted by Home out of sight of the experimenters. The case of Crookes dramatically illustrated how 'a man may have acquired a high reputation as an investigator in one department of science, and yet be utterly untrustworthy in regard to another'.[42] Thus Carpenter, like his Spiritualist enemies, denied that expertise in the physical laboratory meant expertise in the séance, but unlike the Spiritualists, believed that the only forces suggested by Crookes's investigations were those psychological forces which clouded Crookes's judgement.

Predictably, Crookes was furious and presented his first retort in *Psychic Force and Modern Spiritualism* (1871), an explosive defence of his scientific credibility and a denial of Carpenter's claim that he was a Spiritualistic convert. Although Crookes was clearly dissatisfied with Carpenter's explanations of Spiritualism and irritated with Carpenter's apparently delusive attachment to his pet theories, he was struck by the similarity between himself and Carpenter. He emphasised that both he and Carpenter believed in 'a *new force*', although Carpenter was apparently resisting attempts to displace the forces associated with 'unconscious cerebration' and the 'ideomotor principle' with psychic force – a force that, in the opinion of Crookes and his allies, was better than rival psychological theories at explaining the types of Spiritualistic phenomena they had encountered.[43] But what infuriated Crookes was Carpenter's general critique of his experimental abilities and particular dismissal of specialist technical expertise as a qualification for authority on Spiritualism. Crookes retorted that since the production of 'broad, tangible, and easily demonstrable facts' about Home's alleged power turned on the 'question of apparatus' used to register such powers, then it was precisely one 'who is trustworthy in an enquiry requiring technical knowledge' who could best undertake this task.[44] Accordingly, Crookes was baffled by the implication that the technical knowledge that had earlier given scientists confidence in his claims about the capricious physical phenomena of spectral lines also weakened their trust in his claims about the no more capricious physical manifestations of psychic force.[45] Like Carpenter, Crookes was at this time participating in the larger debates about scientific education in British schools and universities, and as editor of scientific periodicals he regularly championed the virtues of a specialist rather than general scientific training. While Carpenter believed that a 'broad basis of *general* scientific education' furnished Britons with the soundest mental discipline and the best weapons against popular fads, Crookes retorted that the very specialist technical skills that apparently threatened his authority on Spiritualism were 'just those of the highest value in this country. What has chiefly placed England in the industrial position she now holds but technical science and special researches?'[46]

This was by no means the end of the controversy. Between 1872 and 1877 Crookes and Carpenter published a stream of articles in specialist and generalist periodicals in which their rival 'natural' solutions to the problems of Spiritualistic phenomena were bound up with their competing claims to authority in the séance. Thus, in 1876, Carpenter criticised Crookes in a way that asserted the plausibility of his psycho-physiological theory of alleged manifestations and again implicitly represented Carpenter and his medical allies as the authorities on the thorny subject. Like most other witnesses to the 'supernatural', Crookes had undoubtedly been 'honest' in reporting manifestations, but his reportage was still unreliable because he had been influenced by a 'strong "prepossession" to believe in the creations of [his] own visual imagination'.[47] Although Carpenter identified Crookes as one of the many deluded witnesses to the 'supernatural', his main problem was Crookes's attempts to smuggle apparently bogus new *natural* forces into elite scientific forums, forces which threatened to displace his own. Thus, in articles and correspondence in *Nineteenth Century* and *Nature*, Carpenter compared Crookes's research on a new radiation force to his work on psychic force. In his opinion, both showed Crookes to have been the sorry victim of the automatic actions of his mind – engendered by a delusion about new forces – although the subsequent history of Crookes's radiation experiments showed the chemist to have 'evinced the spirit of the true philosopher' and eventually corrected his erroneous inferences in line with common-sense kinetic theories of gases.[48]

In the context of such damaging criticism, it was crucial for Crookes to defend his reliability as an experimenter and to distance himself from dangerous associations with supernaturalism and Spiritualism. Thus, in 1874 he represented himself to *QJS* readers as a scientific 'traveller' in the land of the 'Phenomena called Spiritual', a traveller who had 'endeavoured to trace the operation of natural laws and forces where others have seen only the agency of supernatural beings' and upheld his conviction that mediums and indeed, everybody at séances, possessed 'a force, power, influence, virtue or gift' which 'intelligent beings' use to 'produce the phenomena observed'. This was distinct from the supernatural – because the force proceeded somehow from 'nerve organisation' – and Spiritualism: while advocates of psychic force held that there was 'as yet insufficient proof' that the force was directed by spiritual agents rather than the 'Intelligence of the Medium', the Spiritualists believed in such agents without proof.[49] But like Carpenter's theory, Crookes's naturalistic interpretation of Spiritualistic manifestations continued to depend on a particular idea of the mental education and skills that would qualify somebody as an authority on Spiritualism. Thus, in 1877 Carpenter insisted that 'a knowledge of the physiology and pathology of the Human Mind, of its extraordinary tendency to self-deception in regard to matters in which its feelings are interested, of its liability to place undue confidence in persons having an interest in deceiving, and of the modes in which fallacies are best to be detected and frauds exposed' enabled him to reliably discriminate the 'genuine from the false' in Spiritualism. In the same year, Crookes, basking in the warm scientific reception accorded to his researches on a new radiation force, maintained that the 'man of disciplined mind and finished manipulative skill' was best able to investigate 'unanticipated phenomena' that appeared to defy common sense, but which formed the basis of 'new elements, new laws, possibly even of new forces'.[50] The implication was that those skilled in manipulating instruments could be trusted to produce evidence for new forces – psychic, radiative or otherwise – and thus extend the boundaries of science.

Although Crookes and Carpenter never resolved their differences, they did not engage in any direct public fights after 1878, a development that owes much to the fact that by this time, Crookes was devoting most of his research to radiation and vacuum phenomena rather than Spiritualism, although his dwindling explorations of Spiritualism owed more to a want of time and reliable mediums than a lack of interest in Spiritualism *per se*. His first publication on Spiritualism, in fact, appeared five years after Carpenter's death in the SPR *Proceedings* for 1889–90, and consisted of his notes on the Home séances of the early 1870s.[51] In many ways, the 'psychic force' interpretation that Crookes maintained for these investigations fitted well with the theories developed by the intellectuals and scientists who dominated the SPR, of which Crookes was a loyal member and president. Keen to maintain a respectable scientific front, these practitioners worked hard to rid their enterprises of the intellectually and theologically controversial associations with the supernatural and Spiritualism. Accordingly, they promulgated such terms as 'supernormal' and 'supersensory' as more accurate and safer ways of interpreting the telepathic, Spiritualistic and other strange psychological phenomena on which they worked, a development informed by their belief that, in the words of its leading researcher, 'by far the larger proportion' of Spiritualistic phenomena 'are due to the action of the still embodied spirit of the agent of the percipient himself'.[52] This collapse of spirits into the body did not, of course, please Spiritualists, who upheld the abundant evidence for spiritual intelligences beyond those of séance-goers and mediums, and either fiercely criticised or resigned their membership of the organisation they hoped would have provided them with crucial support.[53] However, like other controversies and 'opposing' positions in Victorian Spiritualism, the differences were not simple matters of natural and supernatural, but of competing and, in many cases, irreconcilable versions of what could be taken to be natural.

CONCLUSION

This essay has demonstrated the complexity of Victorian controversies over Spiritualism and the need to be more sensitive to the terms in which these controversies were conducted. It is tempting to reduce these controversies to simple matters of 'science versus Spiritualism', 'science versus pseudo-science', 'natural versus supernatural', 'law versus caprice', not least because many participants in these controversies used these kinds of binary oppositions.

Closer analysis of several Spiritualistic controversies, however, suggests that matters were not so straightforward. What was at stake were rival notions of the scientific, the natural and the lawful, with participants agreeing implicitly that spirits were natural and lawful, and that their own approaches were the most scientific, but fiercely disagreeing over what exactly counted as natural and lawful, and who counted as scientific. Far from providing straightforward resolutions to mid-Victorian problems of spiritual manifestations, these terms were as much the subject of dispute as the reality of manifestations themselves. Although this essay has, for reasons of space, not explored the impact of these negotiations on the long-term trajectory of Victorian Spiritualism and on its relationships with the sciences and the supernatural, it has suggested that one of the most fruitful ways of addressing such important questions will be through a deeper understanding of the ways in which Victorians distinguished, related and negotiated such terms as natural, supernatural, law and authority. Systematic studies of the changing Victorian uses of this potent language are long overdue and will greatly advance historical debates on the cultures and natures of Victorian Spiritualism and the Victorian supernatural.

I would like to thank Louise Henson, Geoffrey Cantor and the editors for their help in the preparation of this essay. Permission to quote from manuscript material has been granted by University College London Library.

1 Edward Bulwer Lytton to John Forster, 3 December 1861, cited in Earl of Lytton (Victor Alexander George Robert Lytton), *The Life of Edward Bulwer Lytton, First Lord Lytton*, 2 vols. (London: Macmillan and Co., 1913), vol. II, p. 47.
2 Frank Podmore, *The Naturalisation of the Supernatural* (New York and London: G. P. Putnam's Sons, 1908).
3 David M. Knight, *The Age of Science* (Oxford: Blackwell, 1986).
4 Frank M. Turner, *Contesting Cultural Authority: Essays in Victorian Intellectual Life* (Cambridge: Cambridge University Press, 1993), pp. 131–228.
5 George Carey Foster to Oliver Lodge, 25 October 1894, Oliver Lodge Papers, University College, London, MSS. Add 89/33. Foster's emphasis.
6 Roger Cooter, *The Cultural Meaning of Popular Science: Phrenology and the Organisation of Consent in Nineteenth-Century Britain* (Cambridge: Cambridge University Press, 1984); Logie Barrow, *Independent Spirits: Spiritualism and the English Plebeians, 1850–1910* (London: Routledge and Kegan Paul, 1986); Alison Winter, *Mesmerized: Powers of Mind in Victorian Britain* (Chicago: University of Chicago Press, 1998); Richard J. Noakes, 'Telegraphy is an Occult Art: Cromwell Fleetwood Varley and the Diffusion of Electricity to the Other World', *British Journal for the History of Science* 32 (1999), 421–59. For examples of revisionist historical and sociological approaches to other 'pseudo-sciences' see H. M. Collins and T. J. Pinch, *Frames of Meaning: The Social Construction of Extraordinary Science* (London: Routledge and Kegan Paul, 1982). Examples of traditional historiography include Frank Podmore, *Modern Spiritualism: A History and a Criticism*, 2 vols., (London: Methuen and Co., 1902); Trevor H. Hall, *The Spiritualists. The Story of Florence Cook and William Crookes* (London: Gerald Duckworth and Co., 1962); Janet Oppenheim, *The Other World: Spiritualism and Psychical Research in England, 1850–1914* (Cambridge: Cambridge University Press, 1985); Gordon Stein, *The Sorcerer of Kings: the Case of Daniel Dunglas Home and William Crookes* (New York: Prometheus Books, 1993).
7 One recent example is D. J. Enright (ed.), *The Oxford Book of the Supernatural* (Oxford: Oxford University Press, 1994).

8   For a contemporary discussion of the diverse uses of 'supernatural' see Duke
     of Argyll (George Douglas Campbell), *The Reign of Law*, 19th edn (London:
     John Murray, 1890), pp. 1–54.

9   Anon., 'The Mystery of the Tables', *Illustrated London News*, 18 June 1853,
     481–2; p. 481.

10   N. S. Godfrey, *Table-Moving Tested, and Proved to be the Result of Satanic
     Agency* (London: Sealeys, 1853); Charles Dickens, 'The Spirit Business', *House-
     hold Words* 7 (1853), 217–20; Leslie Stephen, 'The Scepticism of Believers',
     Fortnightly Review 22 (1877), 355–76; p. 355; William Benjamin Carpenter,
     'Mesmerism, Odylism, Table-Turning and Spiritualism, Considered Histor-
     ically and Scientifically', *Fraser's Magazine* 15 (1877), 135–57, 382–405; p. 136;
     William Thomson, 'Six Gateways of Knowledge [1883]' in *Popular Lectures
     and Addresses*, 3 vols., 2nd edn (London: Macmillan and Co, 1889–94), vol. I,
     pp. 253–99; p. 258; P. T. Barnum, *Humbugs of the World: An Account of the
     Humbugs, Delusions, Impositions, Deceits, and Deceivers Generally, in all Ages*
     (New York: Carleton, 1866).

11   For overviews of Victorian Spiritualism see Podmore, *Modern Spiritualism*,
     vol. II; Oppenheim, *Other World*; Brian Inglis, *Natural and Supernatural: A
     History of the Paranormal from Earliest Times to 1914* (London: Hodder and
     Stoughton, 1977), pp. 199–451.

12   Alan Gauld, *The Founders of Psychical Research* (London: Routledge and Kegan
     Paul, 1968); Oppenheim, *Other World*; Barrow, *Independent Spirits*.

13   See, for example, 'A. B.' [Augustus de Morgan], 'Preface' in 'C. D.' (Sophia
     de Morgan), *From Matter to Spirit: The Result of Ten Years' Experience in Spirit
     Manifestations* (London: Longman, Green, Longman, Roberts and Green,
     1863), p. vi.

14   Anon., 'Spiritualism', *Saturday Review*, 21 October 1871, 518–19; p. 519; Anon.,
     'The British Association and Spiritualism', *Saturday Review*, 16 September
     1876, 345–7, p. 346.

15   On this distinction see Lorraine Daston, 'Preternatural Philosophy' in *Biogra-
     phies of Scientific Objects*, ed. Lorraine Daston (Chicago: Chicago University
     Press, 2000), pp. 14–41.

16   Henry Dircks, 'Science versus Spiritualism', *The Times*, 27 December 1872,
     p. 10; Henry Dircks, 'Spiritualism and Science', *The Times*, 2 January 1873,
     p. 12.

17   Baden Powell, *The Order of Nature Considered in Reference to the Claims of
     Revelation* (London: Longman, Brown, Green, Longmans, & Roberts, 1859),
     p. 263.

18   Ibid., pp. 265, 269.

19   R. Laurence Moore, *In Search of White Crows: Spiritualism, Parapsychology,
     and American Culture* (New York: Oxford University Press, 1977), pp. 3–39.

20   Robert Dale Owen, *Footfalls on the Boundary of Another World* (London:
     Trübner and Sons, 1860), pp. 42, 43.

21   Ibid., pp. 46, 44, 50, 57.

22   Ibid., pp. xi, xii, 25.

23 For Wallace and Spiritualism see Malcom Jay Kottler, 'Alfred Russel Wallace, the Origin of Man, and Spiritualism', *Isis* 65 (1972), 145–92; Frank M. Turner, *Between Science and Religion: The Reaction to Scientific Naturalism in Victorian Britain* (New Haven: Yale University Press, 1974), pp. 68–103.

24 Alfred Russel Wallace, *The Scientific Aspect of the Supernatural* (London: F. Farrah, 1866), pp. 1–2.

25 Ibid., pp. 4–5.

26 William Henry Harrison, 'Opening Address', *Spiritualist* 1 (1869), 5.

27 William Henry Harrison, 'Miracles', *Spiritualist* 1 (1870), 117.

28 Citation from James Burns, 'The Philosophy of the Spirit Circle', *Medium and Daybreak* 1 (1870), 308. For Spiritualists' use of physical forces see, for example, Burns, 'Philosophy' and Emma Hardinge, 'Rules to be Observed for the Spirit Circle', *Human Nature* 2 (1868), 48–52. For examples of séances as laboratories for testing spiritual laws see James Burns, 'Professor Tyndall and the Spiritualists', *Human Nature* 2 (1868), 454–6 and William Henry Harrison, 'The Scientific Investigation of Spiritual Phenomena', *Spiritualist* 1 (1869), 5. For examples of Spiritualist connections between their enterprises and established scientific disciplines see Emma Hardinge Britten, 'Science and Spiritualism', *Spiritualist* 1 (1870), 124–7; William Henry Harrison, 'Spiritualism', *Spiritualist* 3 (1873), 306.

29 Edwin A. Dawes, *The Great Illusionists* (Secaucus, NJ: Chartwell Books, 1978), pp. 155–68, 184–202.

30 For examples of the medical response see Anon., 'Spiritualism Tested', *British Medical Journal*, 15 July 1871, 71–2; p. 71; Henry Maudsley, *Natural Causes and Supernatural Seemings* [1886] (London: Watts and Co., 1939). For discussion of this reaction see S. E. D. Shortt, 'Physicians and Psychics: The Anglo-American Response to Spiritualism, 1870–1890', *Journal for the History of Medicine* 39 (1984), 339–55.

31 For Carpenter see Winter, *Mesmerized*, pp. 276–305; Louise Henson, 'Charles Dickens, Elisabeth Gaskell and Victorian Science', PhD thesis, University of Sheffield (2000), pp. 46–117.

32 William Benjamin Carpenter, 'Spiritualism and its Latest Converts', *Quarterly Review* 131 (1871), 301–53; p. 308; Carpenter, 'Mesmerism', p. 506.

33 Carpenter, 'Mesmerism', p. 405.

34 Richard J. Noakes, '"Cranks and Visionaries": Science, Spiritualism, and Transgression in Victorian Britain', PhD thesis, University of Cambridge (1998), pp. 157–221.

35 William Crookes, *Psychic Force and Modern Spiritualism: A Reply to the 'Quarterly Review' and other Critics* (London: Longmans, Green, and Co., 1871), p. 5.

36 William Crookes, 'Spiritualism Viewed by the Light of Modern Science', *Quarterly Journal of Science* 7 (1870), 316–21; pp. 317, 321.

37 Ibid., pp. 318–19.

38 William Crookes, 'Experimental Investigation of a New Force', *Quarterly Journal of Science*, new series 1 (1871), 339–49; pp. 339, 347.

39 The editor of the *Birmingham Morning News* cited in Anon., 'Spiritualism and the Newspapers', *Spiritualist*, 1 (1871), 189.

40 Anon., 'Psychic Force', *Saturday Review*, 18 July 1871, 82–3; Anon., 'A Scientific Testing of Mr Home', *Spectator*, 8 July 1871, 827–8.

41 James Burns, 'About Scientific Spiritualism', *Medium and Daybreak* 1 (1870), 201–2; p. 201; James Burns, 'Spiritualism and Science', *Medium and Daybreak* 1 (1870), 108.

42 Carpenter, 'Spiritualism', pp. 327, 343, 342, 340.

43 Crookes, *Psychic Force*, p. 6.

44 Ibid., pp. 12–13.

45 William Crookes to William Huggins, 16 June 1871, cited in E. E. Fournier D'Albe, *The Life of Sir William Crookes* (London: T. Fisher Unwin, 1923), pp. 209–10.

46 Crookes, *Psychic Force*, pp. 12–13. On Carpenter's contribution to the education debates see Winter, *Mesmerized*, pp. 300–304.

47 William Benjamin Carpenter, 'On the Fallacies of Testimony in Relation to the Supernatural', *Contemporary Review* 27 (1876), 279–95; p. 285.

48 William Benjamin Carpenter, 'The Radiometer and its Lessons', *Nineteenth Century* 1 (1877), 242–56; p. 254.

49 William Crookes, 'Notes of an Enquiry into the Phenomena called Spiritual, During the Years 1870–1873', *Quarterly Journal of Science*, Second Series, 3 (1874), 77–97; pp. 77, 96, 97.

50 Carpenter, 'Mesmerism', p. 137; William Crookes, 'Another Lesson from the Radiometer', *Nineteenth Century* 1 (1877), 879–87; p. 886.

51 William Crookes, 'Notes on Séances with D. D. Home', *Proceedings of the Society for Psychical Research* 6 (1889–90), 98–127.

52 Frederick William Henry Myers, *Human Personality and its Survival of Bodily Death*, edited and abridged by S. B. and L. H. M. (London: Longmans, Green and Co., 1927), p. 7.

53 On the controversies between Spiritualists and the SPR see John Cerullo, *The Secularization of the Soul: Psychical Research in Modern Britain* (Philadelphia: Institute for the Study of Human Issues, 1982), pp. 70–84.

CHAPTER 2

Investigations and fictions: Charles Dickens and ghosts

Louise Henson

I have always had a strong interest in the subject, and never knowingly lose an opportunity of pursuing it. But I think the testimony which I cannot cross-examine sufficiently loose to justify me in requiring to see and hear the modern witnesses with my own senses, and then to be reasonably sure that they were not suffering under a disordered condition of the nerves or senses, which is known to be a common disease of many phases.

Don't suppose that I am so bold and arrogant as to settle what can and what cannot be, after death. The truth is not so at all.[1]

In his 1874 biography of Charles Dickens, John Forster recalled that Dickens 'had something of a hankering' after ghosts, and 'such was his interest generally in things supernatural that, but for the strong restraining power of his common sense, he might have fallen into the follies of Spiritualism'. Forster, however, also recognised that 'no man was readier to apply sharp tests to a ghost story or a haunted house though there was just as much tendency to believe in any such "well-authenticated" [sic] as made perfect his manner of telling one'.[2] Dickens had a central role in the development of the Victorian ghost story. His hugely successful Christmas Books of the 1840s forged the cultural association of ghosts and Christmas. These popular seasonal hauntings continued throughout the 1850s and 1860s in many of the collaborative Christmas stories carried by his weekly miscellanies *Household Words* (*HW*) and *All the Year Round* (*ATYR*). Yet as a journalist, Dickens had an important role in influencing the public mind on matters supernatural: not only did he circulate well-attested ghost stories to an eager reading public, but he also insisted on careful enquiry into ghostly phenomena, and always reacted critically to what he saw as bald credulity and superstitious belief.

Throughout his working life, Dickens participated in wide-ranging and sometimes fierce debates about the nature and authenticity of ghostly phenomena, but this aspect of his work has rarely been considered in conjunction with the ghost stories he wrote. Rather, Dickens's reputation as a major novelist has resulted in the extraction of his ghost stories from the specific historical context in which they were produced. My purpose in this essay is to return the fiction to this historical context, first by examining the scientific and medical writing about apparitions that shaped Dickens's views, and second by focusing on the debates in which he participated as a journalist. My readings of Dickens's ghost stories will draw upon this contextual framework in order to demonstrate the ways in which these tales dramatise key debates and the conflicting points of view to which they gave rise.

A PHILOSOPHY OF APPARITIONS

In 1848 Dickens reviewed Catherine Crowe's *The Night-Side of Nature; or Ghosts and Ghost-Seers* for the *Examiner.* His article offered 'a few obvious heads of objection' against the authenticity of some of the ghosts that appeared in Crowe's collection. Crowe's stated intention was to persuade readers to enquire into ghost stories and reflect upon them as important testimony for the immortality of the soul. Dickens accused her of writing with an implicit belief in all she narrated, and, in an effort to communicate her beliefs to her readers, of standing by 'her weakest ghost as manfully as her strongest'. Dickens protested against what he saw as this 'common fault of seeking to prove too much' when the independent existence of ghosts rested on:

imperfect grounds of proof [and] in vast numbers of cases [spectres] are known to be delusions superinduced by a well-understood, and by no means uncommon disease . . . in a multitude of others, they are often asserted to be seen, even on Mrs Crowe's own showing, in that imperfect state of perception, between sleeping and waking, than which there is hardly any less reliable incidental to our nature.[3]

Dickens stressed the importance of critical evaluation, responding to well-known tales of ghostly encounters that had appeared in countless popular volumes. Apparitions and spectral illusions were widely discussed in early and mid-nineteenth-century mental philosophy in relation to the involuntary functions of the mind, including dreaming, somnambulism, reverie and more serious cases of mental derangement. Dickens was well read in such material. Throughout his life he collected ghost stories as an important source of enquiry into the mysteries of the mind, and it was as contributions to human psychology that he viewed many of the sensational tales that came under his notice. The anecdotal use of ghost story to illustrate psychological theory was widely used in informal medical writing, and

Dickens participated in the exchange of such material, notably with John Elliotson, Edward Bulwer-Lytton and Wilkie Collins.

Catherine Crowe, however, was consciously writing against the 'spectral illusion theory' of apparitions which had been promulgated in two of the most influential early nineteenth-century books on apparitions and their physical causes: Samuel Hibbert's *Sketches of the Philosophy of Apparitions* (1824) and David Brewster's *Letters on Natural Magic* (1832). Hibbert argued that apparitions were 'nothing more than ideas or the recollected images of the mind, which have been rendered more vivid than actual [external] impressions' as a result of some physiological change in the body.[4] The mind, therefore, could not be seen as independent of corporeal functions. Bodily disorders caused by illness, dyspepsia, stimulants or narcotic substances produced correspondingly vivid mental effects, such as those experienced during dream states, and instances of somnambulism. *Natural Magic* endorsed Hibbert's theory of apparitions as the abnormally intense images of the 'mind's eye', but David Brewster went further to argue that

the 'mind's eye' is actually the body's eye, and . . . the retina is the common tablet on which both impressions are painted, and by means of which they receive their visual existence according to the same optical laws. Nor is this true merely in the case of spectral illusions: It holds good of all ideas recalled by the memory or created by the imagination, and may be regarded as a fundamental law in the science of pneumatology.[5]

Focusing on the physiological basis of mental functions, Hibbert's and Brewster's theories of apparitions de-privileged perception and thus problematised the externality of apparitions and the testimony of the ghost-seer.

Dickens had consulted the work of both Hibbert and Brewster in 1845 during his treatment of the nervous illness of Augusta de la Rue.[6] The symptoms of this ailment – convulsions, catalepsy and insomnia – were attended by alarming spectral illusions, and Dickens set himself the task of treating them using the mesmeric techniques introduced by his mentor, John Elliotson, who, in the late 1830s, had conducted a series of mesmeric demonstrations at University College Hospital. This technique involved inducing artificial somnambulism (the mesmeric sleep, or trance) as a means of provoking the symptoms of the patient's illness, and hence of affording relief, exploring its causes and, ultimately, effecting a cure.[7] Dickens had first witnessed Elliotson's work in 1838, when he declared himself a believer in all he had seen, and soon developed his own powers as a mesmerist. His first-hand experience of the mysterious powers of mind displayed during Mme de la Rue's illness and the mesmeric treatment he applied made a deep impression upon him and coloured his subsequent attitude to ghosts. In magnetic sleep, Mme de la Rue described spectral figures, and the presence of a man, 'whom she is afraid of, and "dare not" look at'. 'I connect it', Dickens wrote to her husband, Emile, 'with the figure whom she calls her bad spirit.'[8] After some hesitation Dickens located the origin of this phantom in some disturbance of her nervous system, 'the representative of some great nerve or set of nerves on which her disease has preyed – and begins to loose its hold now, because the disease of those nerves is itself attacked by the inexplicable agency of the magnetism'.[9]

Dickens used what he believed he had learned from his mesmeric treatment of Mme de la Rue as a case study when writing about the causes of spectral illusions, echoing the approach and the language of David Brewster. Brewster's own case study in *Natural Magic* was 'Mrs A.' (Richarda Airy, wife of George Airy, the Astronomer Royal), who, over the course of a year, had been troubled by vivid spectral illusions. However, 'both she and her husband were well aware of their nature and origin', and Mrs A. never wavered in her belief in their mental source.[10] Dickens expressed Mme de la Rue's experience in similar terms, representing her as 'a lady, perfectly acquainted with the nature and origin of the phantoms by which she was haunted', and though she was 'sometimes threatened and beaten by them: and the beating . . . left an actual soreness and local affection there . . . experience had taught her, that the approaching real effect suggested the imaginary cause; and she never became a ghost-seer from otherwise connecting the two'.[11]

The possibilities suggested by altered states of mind – magnetic sleep, conventional dream states, and hallucinatory experiences associated with apparitions – were already important narrative resources for Dickens. The therapeutic possibilities of animal magnetism are apparent in the plot structures of *A Christmas Carol* (1843) and *The Chimes* (1844). The apparitions in these stories are bound up with the identity of the protagonists, with memory playing a crucial role, supplying the 'ideas or recollected images of the mind' from which the spectres take their form. Sensations from the present are interwoven with ideas from a remembered past which temporarily become dominant, and are closely related to apprehensions about the future. A drama of the self, triggered by the psychological tensions within the individual, is played out.

The visionary sequences commence as the protagonists sit by the fire meditating upon the day's events and subsequently undergo a change of consciousness, suggestive of magnetic sleep. In *A Christmas Carol* the visionary sequence revolves around Scrooge's memories of Marley on Christmas

Eve, the anniversary of his death. The two men 'had been kindred spirits';
Marley's name still shows above the warehouse door, Scrooge still answers to
it and lives in the apartments of his deceased partner. The traces of Marley
still around him, his hallucinatory vision of a face in the door-knocker, and
the ideas and emotions triggered by the Christmas season, stimulate the
ideational content of Scrooge's visions. Similarly, the narrative structure of
The Chimes juxtaposes the actual events of a day in the life of Toby Veck with
the magical echoes of the New Year bells. Both Scrooge the miser and Veck,
representing the collective urban poor, have internalised what Dickens
regarded as Malthusian harshness, institutionalised in the 1834 Poor Law
Amendment Act. Scrooge, turning his back on Christmas charity, insists
that the poor, who would rather die than enter the workhouse, 'had better
do it, and decrease the surplus population'.[12] Veck, however, internalises
such doctrines indirectly through the intimidating rhetoric of Filer, whose
pronouncements on 'surplus population' and the relative shortage of food,
condemn him for eating his meagre fare on the theoretical assumption that
he is thus depriving others of the same. The occasion of the forthcoming
marriage of Veck's daughter, Meg, occasions a similar protest against such
blatant disregard for the social 'virtues' of economic prudence and delayed
marriage. Alderman Cute predicts disaster for the marriage: 'Perhaps your
husband will die young and leave you with a baby. Then you'll be turned
out of doors, and wander up and down the streets . . . And if you attempt,
desperately and ungratefully to drown yourself, or hang yourself, I'll have
no pity on you.'[13] The newspaper he reads that evening solidifies these associations in Veck's mind and 're-directed [his] thoughts into the channel
he had taken all day, and which the day's events had so marked out and
shaped . . . He came to an account of a woman who had laid her desperate
hands not only on her own life but also on her young child. A crime so
terrible, and so revolting to his soul, dilated with the love of Meg' (150). The
purpose of Veck's dream is to compel him to face the moral consequences of
his placid acquiescence in the pronouncements of the political economists.
In his subsequent visions, Meg acts out the predictions of Cute, but her
degradation is revealed to be, in part, a consequence of the self-negating
attitude he has accepted without question.

In this trance-like sleep the power of reason is entirely subordinated to the
flow of fantastic images associated with the ascendancy of internal ideation,
and thus neither Scrooge nor Veck is able to assert volitional control over
what he perceives. Scrooge, knowing well the tendency of the senses to
deceive, attempts to deny the presence of the ghost of Marley because 'a
little thing makes them cheats': 'You may be an undigested bit of beef, a

blot of mustard, a crumb of cheese, a fragment of an underdone potato. There's more of gravy than of grave about you, whatever you are!', he declares, citing the 'heavy supper' theory of the vivid dream (23). In the visionary dream world, however, Scrooge's efforts to divert his attention away from Marley and to resist the demands of the spirits are futile. The temporary absence of volitional control is, in fact, crucial to Scrooge's reformation, for the purpose of the visitation is to release him from his well-practised habit of miserliness. These stories suggest that individuals can wilfully imprison themselves in their mental habits. Hence the therapeutic powers of the magnetic sleep transform the attitudes of both Scrooge and Veck, endowing them with a kind of clairvoyance, so that they may see the moral consequences of the attitudes to which they adhere, and thus empowering them to overturn their habitual modes of thinking. While Scrooge is challenged to avoid the fate of Marley and to break the habits of the miser, the self-assertion that Toby Veck cannot realise in his conscious waking hours is assumed in his dream by the goblin voices of the bells, which teach him that a greater crime lies in an unquestioning acceptance of the complacent claims of the political economists.

The change back to full consciousness brings with it the capacity to act with a reformed will. Scrooge's return to consciousness is proportional to the diminishing power of the Ghost of Christmas Yet-to-Come. Grabbing and retaining the spectral hand of the resisting ghost and then, 'holding up his hands in a last prayer to have his fate reversed, he saw an alteration in the Phantom's hood and dress. It shrunk, collapsed, and dwindled down into a bedpost' (90). Likewise, Toby Veck's sudden ability to intervene in his dream and prevent his daughter and her child from plunging into the river correlates with the emergence of his reformed conscious will. With this reawakening of will both Veck and Scrooge learn that the future is truly redeemable. 'Men's courses will foreshadow certain ends', Scrooge warns, 'to which if persevered in, they must lead . . . but if the courses be departed from, the ends will change' (89).

Dickens endowed the apparition with psychological depth in these early Christmas books, and the unconscious mind has a moral power that is unusual in his ghost stories, where it is often a potential source of danger. Nevertheless, Dickens consistently created dramatic effect in his ghost stories by exploiting the accepted idea that volitional control over the mind must necessarily cease in certain states of consciousness, thus subordinating rational understanding to the automatic ideational faculty, and problematising the objective status of the apparition. The 'strange influence' of sleep problematises the authenticity of a nocturnal apparition in Dickens's story of the Bride's Chamber from *Lazy Tour of Two Idle Apprentices* (1857). Francis Goodchild (Dickens) and Thomas Idle (Wilkie Collins) arrive at an inn with a reputation for being 'spiritually troubled'. During the night Goodchild learns the story of the Hanged Man's Bride from the spectral figure of the Hanged Man. The spectre claims to be in purgatory, haunted by images of his misdeeds, and knowing that 'this punishment would never cease, until I could make its nature, and my story, known to two living men together'.[14] Ghostly tradition is set against the fallibility of human judgement as the problematic nature of the evidence to support this kind of ghost story is dramatised in the spectre's predicament. The absence of two conscious witnesses who can corroborate events is thus the curse of the apparition, condemned always to relate its narrative to a solitary listener.

'THERE'S NO GHOST IN THAT BUT SOMETHING FULL AS STRANGE'

When a certain man is coming to see you, unexpectedly; and without his own knowledge, sends some invisible messenger, to put the idea of him into your head all day, what do you call that? When you walk along a crowded street... and think that a passing stranger is like your friend Henrich, and then that another stranger's like your friend Henrich, and so begin to have a strange foreknowledge that presently you'll meet your friend Henrich – which you do – what do you call *that*?

When the old Marchesa starts up from the card-table, white through her rouge, and cries, 'My sister in Spain is dead! I felt her cold touch on my back!' – and when that sister *is* dead at that moment – what do you call that?[15]

Dickens and Crowe shared an enthusiastic interest in animal magnetism, but they drew contrasting inferences about the mental states that the practice allowed them to witness. Unlike Crowe, Dickens's interest in mesmerism was largely therapeutic, and decidedly non-spiritual, and he shared John Elliotson's phrenological interest in the material configurations of the body and mind. Elliotson's therapeutic aims, however, were rapidly eclipsed by the more sensational aspects of mesmeric phenomena, particularly the manifestation of clairvoyant or previsionary powers in the subject, which were to lead to his professional discrediting and eventually his resignation from University College. Nevertheless, both men persisted in the belief that the mysterious agent of animal magnetism was a physical one, and that the extraordinary mental powers of the mesmeric subject were physiological in their nature. Dickens himself is reported to have experienced several incidents of intuitive precognition. Mamie Dickens claimed that her father experienced the peculiar premonitory feeling that he would meet a certain friend in the street, and that such premonitions were usually fulfilled. In 1863 Dickens wrote to John Forster about a dream he had had of a lady in a red shawl who announced herself as Miss Napier. The following evening he gave a public reading and recounted how, the reading over, there 'came into my retiring-room, Mary Boyle and her brother, and *the* Lady in the red shawl whom they present as "Miss Napier"!'[16]

For Dickens, animal magnetism afforded a crucial means of investigating clairvoyant powers and sympathetic bonds between individuals. Elliotson described the clairvoyant trance as a manifestation of the 'highly magnetised' state, whereby the subject, whose sensory faculties were intensified to an extraordinary degree, might perceive beyond physical barriers, predict future events and sense otherwise imponderable forces or emanations. Insisting on the physical nature of premonition, or psychic sympathy, mesmerists understood the mind to be operating *mediately* in such cases. Chauncy Hare Townshend speculated on the analogous functions of the 'pervading media' in nature – electricity, heat and light – and the mind's 'peculiar atmosphere, or ocean of sensibility'. Mesmerism was the agency by which nervous power and the surrounding media were brought together, thus enabling one individual to influence another 'from a distance'.[17]

During his treatment of Mme de la Rue, Dickens claimed to have experienced sympathetic impressions and was himself affected from afar by Augusta's disturbed mind. He explained to Emile how he sensed her distress in uneasy moments of his own and imputed this to the magnetism between them, 'a part of such a strange and mysterious whole'.[18] In a reply to Emile's report of strange voices that had been heard in his wife's sick room, Dickens attributed the phenomenon to the same cause, though it was often mistaken for the otherworldly. The agency of animal magnetism, he wrote 'is a philosophical explanation of many Ghost Stories. Though it is hardly less chilling than a ghost story itself. There is no reasonable doubt that the woman received the impression magnetically from Madame de la Rue.'[19]

Dickens turned his attention to sympathetic mental phenomena in 'To Be Read at Dusk', published in *Heath's Keepsake* in 1852. Like many ghost stories of this period it comprised a number of anecdotes about reputedly authentic experiences: a man sees the phantom of his dying brother just prior to that brother's death, and a woman senses the cold touch of her dying sister at the moment of her sister's death. Elizabeth Gaskell complained that Dickens had stolen one of these anecdotes – the 'story of the English bride' – from her. It tells of a woman haunted by dreams of an unknown man, subsequently revealed be the Signore Dellombra, who arrives at her home sometime later. Dickens explained his purpose in collecting this story for his own use in a placatory letter to Gaskell:

It came into my mind (you remember that it struck me very much when you told it) as a very remarkable instance of a class of mental phenomena at which I have glanced in the little sketch – certainly the best known, the best certified, and the most singular class out of many. It also led up, by natural degrees, to another story . . . which I told in the same place, and which I believe to be, in the slightest incident, perfectly true. I told it some time ago, to Elliotson, who printed it in a note to his Physiology.

Ghost stories illustrating particular states of mind and processes of the imagi-nation, are common property, I always think – except in the manner of relating them.[20]

'To Be Read at Dusk' is more than a narrative illustrative of remarkable mental phenomena, however: it engages with contemporary anxieties about the effect of superstitious belief on mental health. In his handling of the story of the English bride Dickens also drew on his treatment of Augusta de la Rue and her temporary subjection to the phantom of her imagination.[21] In the mental physiology of the mid-nineteenth-century spectral illusions were viewed, in the words of the pre-eminent physician Henry Holland, as a link 'in the chain betwixt sound reason and madness', and medical studies of the apparition commonly promoted practices and methods of policing the deranged mind and of cultivating accurate judgement.[22] Such was Dickens's therapeutic aim in his treatment of Augusta, and he insisted that the patient maintain rational control over the mind, even as the body was threatened by destabilising pathological influences. In his letters to Emile during his treatment of Augusta, Dickens warned of the consequences if the spectre ever gained ascendancy over her imagination. Wary of the 'extent to which her thoughts are directed to, and clustered round', the figure 'so closely connected with the secret distresses of her very soul', Dickens believed that the phantom threatened to bind her to her disease and 'must have linked her in the course of time to Madness'.[23] Hence during the mesmeric treatment he was resolved on 'the beating down of this phantom', directing the magnetic fluid by the superior power of his will.

In Dickens's rendition of the story of the English Bride haunted by the face of Signore Dellombra, however, the bride's inability to subordinate her superstitious terror to her rational will causes her to yield to powers of a more sinister nature. The husband of the English Bride similarly urges his wife to subordinate her terror of Dellombra, arguing that to 'encourage such fancies was to invite melancholy, if not madness . . . That if she once resisted her strange weakness, so successfully as to receive Signor Dellombra as an English lady would receive any other guest, it was forever conquered.' The rapport between Dellombra and his wife, however, is directed and controlled by the will of Dellombra, who takes advantage of the latter's subjection to her superstitious fears. Indeed, she would look at Dellombra 'with a terrified and fascinated glance, as if his presence had some evil influence or power upon her' (313). She is last observed crouching submissively in a carriage with Dellombra and the two are seen no more.

Stories of precognitive visitations by the dying, or the dead, had been discussed by Catherine Crowe as strong evidence for the existence of ghosts. 'To Be Read at Dusk' was a defiant riposte to those like Crowe who claimed that even spectral visitations of the living were spiritual entities. 'There's no ghost in that, but something full as strange', one of Dickens's narrators claims about the story of the English bride, insisting rather that the story was exemplary of an important class of phenomena, yet to be explained.

Dickens's passion for collecting and classifying ghost stories was given greater focus after 1850 when he launched *HW*. The staff journalists echoed Dickens's opinions on ghostly matters. There was always a place for the well-authenticated ghost story, but Dickens's opinions about such things as mesmeric clairvoyance were apparent in the writings of others, particularly Henry Morley and W. H. Wills, and were reflected in articles which discussed a range of sympathetic mental phenomena and warned against uncritically attributing such phenomena to the manifestation of ghosts.

In 'New Discoveries in Ghosts', for example, Henry Morley discussed hypothetical links between apparitions, clairvoyance and sensitivity to surrounding atmospheric forces, focusing particularly on the researches of the industrial chemist Karl von Reichenbach, who claimed to have identified a new imponderable force – named *odyle* in English translation – to which certain individuals displayed a sensitive reaction. Morley wrote:

There can be no doubt that in our minds or bodies, there are powers latent, or nearly latent, in the ordinary healthy man, which, in some peculiar constitutions, or under the influence of certain agents, or certain classes of disease, become active and develope [*sic*] themselves in an extraordinary way. It is not very uncommon to find people who have acquired intuitive perception of each others' current thoughts, beyond what can be ascribed to the community of interests, or comprehension of character.[24]

Dickens's attempt to normalise the extraordinary powers of the mind continued in *ATYR* with a new theory about ghostly presentiment which was attributed to physiological impressions on the brain. The

'thought-impressing' hypothesis substituted the agency of the supernatural with a theory of 'moral electricity', similar in its conception to the
mesmeric rapport between individuals, for its basic premise was that 'man
has on man an influence, emanating from mind, and from peculiar states
of cerebral excitement; an influence which may, occasionally, touch the
springs of consciousness within another's brain'.[25] This form of psychic
sympathy was shown to be thoroughly common and mundane, so much so
that the home was identified as the most likely place for its manifestation:

> Persons who live together, acquire mysterious likenesses, not only of voice, but of
> face. The resemblance of married people to each other (which began by unlikeness)
> is proverbial. A sympathetic atmosphere envelopes families, and amongst every
> domestic circle, if the attention be once drawn to the subject, a great deal of human
> influence, and transmission of silent thought, will be everywhere perceived. (348)

The domestication of psychic sympathy was an important aspect of the
attempt to normalise the phenomenon, but it also gained plausibility in
the context of the fast-developing communications industry. Thus thought-
impressing was conceived as an 'electric impulse' registering the mental
action of one individual on the sensory nerves of another, and indeed,
metaphors associating the physiological processes of the body with those of
technological activity abounded in the decades that saw the development
of telegraphy. The notion of the 'telegraphic motions' of the human brain
was a familiar concept in the mental philosophy of the 1850s.[26]

Technological developments, however, lent plausibility to both spiritual
and non-spiritual interpretations of clairvoyant and sympathetic phenomena, and the advent of modern American Spiritualism exacerbated the differences already existing between mesmerists. In late 1852 *HW* became one
of the first periodicals to report on the activities of the American medium,
Maria B. Hayden, newly arrived in London in the company of the electro-
biologist, G. W. Stone. Dickens sent Morley and Wills to investigate the
'Spiritual Manifestations' announced by Stone in *The Times*. Stone's theory
of mediumship, that 'there are some people whose nervous systems appear
to act – as conductors, as magnets' for spiritual communications, was conceptually identical to the mesmerist's terrestrial cosmology.[27] Nevertheless,
Morley and Wills's report was damning: not only were the spirits wrong
in their responses, but Hayden had apparently made use of the inaccurate
information that they had fed her. Dickens suggested a title for the ensuing
article – 'The Ghost of the Cock Lane Ghost'. The allusion was to the
similar case of a knocking spirit which gripped the capital in 1762, drawing
crowds from across the social hierarchy, and stimulating investigation and

debate for and against the plausibility of communicating spirits, before being officially exposed as imposture (though in the popular imagination it remained an inconclusive case). *HW* endorsed the official view of the Cock Lane Ghost and drew parallels between this case and early American Spiritualism, suggesting that there were similar private interests fuelling these latter displays. Thus it was noted that the 'Fox family, by whom this ghostly rapping was revived in America ... were so successful in their venture – retiring soon upon a little independence – that the spirit trade, as carried on by them, became at once an established business'.[28] The profit-seeking motives of 'a fraud, which trades upon our solemn love towards the dead', the way in which Christian teaching was being used to support its claims, and a disregard for the rules of evidence, were particular points of objection which also appeared in Dickens's critique, 'The Spirit Business' (1853), and he continued to raise protest in *ATYR* throughout the 1860s.

HAUNTED HOUSES AND HAUNTED MEN

In 1859 the former *HW* contributor, William Howitt, on a crusade to publicise 'truths' about spiritual laws, complained to Dickens about the thought-impressing article in *ATYR*, which, in denying that a supernatural agency was necessarily involved in premonitions, also cast doubt on the authenticity of spiritual communications between the living and the dead. In his response to Howitt, Dickens tactfully claimed that he was 'perfectly unprejudiced and impressible on the subject. I do not in the least pretend that such things are not.' Nevertheless, he warned Howitt that 'I positively object, on most matters, to be thought for ... I have not yet met with any Ghost Story that has proved to me, or that had not the noticeable peculiarity in it – that the alteration of some slight circumstance would bring it into the range of common probabilities.'[29] Dickens was determined to investigate and judge independently; he offered to visit any suitably haunted house suggested by Howitt, and with Wills, Wilkie Collins and John Hollingshead accordingly set off on an unsuccessful attempt to locate and investigate a house at Cheshunt.[30]

Dickens based the collaborative *ATYR* Christmas number for 1859, the *Haunted House*, on the incident, and it was to involve *ATYR* in an on-going dispute with Howitt and his allies at the newly-founded Christian *Spiritual Magazine* throughout the 1860s. A house with a reputation for being haunted is occupied as a challenge by the narrator for the purpose of investigating the source of the ghostly phenomena. In sketches which detailed his personal objections to the kinds of ghostly incidents endorsed by Howitt, Dickens mobilised arguments that were now well known in medical aetiology, including Michael Faraday's assessment of table-turning as the effect of a quasi-muscular action in the participants. In a direct parody of the séance, the investigations of Dickens's narrator are impeded by the 'moral infection' which spreads among his servants, who unconsciously animate the house with sinister noises and alarms in the same way that Faraday claimed that table-turners unconsciously manoeuvred the table. Thus the servants are 'afraid of the house; and believed in its being haunted; yet . . . would play false on the haunting side' by unconsciously inventing alarms. This 'preposterous state of mind', Dickens observed, is known to 'every intelligent man who has had a fair medical, legal, or other watchful experience', and 'is one of the first elements, above all others rationally to be suspected in, and strictly looked for, and separated from, any question of this kind'. Neither is Dickens's rationally minded narrator fortified against cognitive deception brought about by expectant attention:

Noises? With that contagion downstairs, I myself have sat in the dismal parlour listening, until I have heard so many and such strange noises, that they would have chilled my blood if I had not warmed it by dashing out to make discoveries. Try this in bed, in the dead of the night; try this at your own comfortable fireside, in the life of the night. You can fill any house with noises, if you will, until you have a noise for every nerve in your nervous system.[31]

In the *Haunted House* Dickens threw down a challenge to Howitt by undercutting the independent status of the mind. His second sketch, 'The Ghost in Master B.'s Room', reinforced this point by focusing on the recollected image theory of spectral illusion. Dickens's narrator learns about the source and the nature of apparitions in the semi-conscious state between waking and sleep, when the spectres of the mind intrude upon the sensory images of the present. These associations are called forth by the suggestive atmosphere of the early morning:

The tranquility of the hour is the tranquility of Death. The colour and the chill have the same association . . . I once saw the apparition of my father, at this hour . . . He was alive and well, and nothing ever came of it, but I saw him in the daylight, sitting with his back towards me . . . Amazed to see him there, I sat up and watched him . . . I spoke to him more than once. As he did not move then, I became alarmed and laid my hand upon his shoulder, as I thought . . . there was no such thing . . . I find the early morning to be my ghostly time. Any house would be more or less haunted, to me, in the early morning. (2–3)

All the ghosts in Dickens's haunted house are unambiguously traced to a mental origin. 'The Ghost in Master B.'s Room' draws on the spectral illusion theory, a favourite motif of the Dickensian ghost story. 'The Mortals in the House', however, combines the traditional haunted house story with more recent theories about expectant attention, where the mind provokes a physiological response and the individual's own unconscious agency is taken for that of a supernatural power.

Dickens's last ghost story for *ATYR*, 'No. 1 Branch Line: The Signalman' (1866), similarly blends several perspectives on ghost-seeing – theories of spectral illusion, clairvoyance and psychic sympathy, and notions of suggestion and expectation. A signalman working on a particularly dismal line is haunted by ghostly visitations portending accidents on the railway, visions that find a sinister correspondence in the tragedies that follow. In his ensuing despair, he relates his story to the narrator, whom he meets two days before being killed himself, unable, it seems, to distinguish between the apparitional figures and the actual engine that eventually cuts him down. Dickens's sensitive exploration of the psychology of ghost-seeing, and his startling juxtaposition of the signs and signals of spectral communicants with those of an advanced technology, disorientate the interpretative strategy of the narrator, which oscillates between an understanding of these apparitions as cognitive delusion on the part of the signalman, and an acceptance of real supernatural intervention. This ambiguity helps to maintain the complexity of the narrative, as the narrator cannot quite allow himself to believe the signalman, nor to dismiss his story as that of a madman. The confusion that the text evokes reflects that experienced by many contemporaries who attempted to define the boundary between madness and sanity in questions of the uncanny and the marvellous.

Dickens presents the railway line as an apposite and sinister space for the modern urban ghost story. The solitary, dark and dismal surroundings of the embankment and the forbidding black tunnel are associated with death and otherworldliness. These associations evoke irrational, animistic sensations in the narrator, and although he acts as a mouthpiece for scientific rationalism, and lists well-documented examples of individuals released from superstitious terrors of their own making, he cannot quite liberate himself from the influence of a seemingly primeval physiological stimulus that accompanies the signalman's disclosure of the fulfilment of these premonitory warnings. He is thus forced to admit, a 'disagreeable shudder crept over me, but I did my best against it':

Resisting the slow touch of a frozen finger tracing out my spine I showed him how that this figure must be a deception of his sense of sight; and how that figures, originating in disease of the delicate nerves that minister to the functions of the eye, were known to have often troubled patients, some of whom had become conscious of the nature of their affliction, and had even proved it by experiments upon themselves.[32]

The signalman's own mental preoccupations form the substance of the fears that haunt him. Dickens's exploitation of the magical immediacy of telegraphy to frame these ghostly portents on the railway draws on contemporary attitudes towards the technology. In Britain the telegraph was an integral part of the expanding railways, and the ring of the electric bell had particular associations for the popular mind. Frederick Knight Hunt observed that: 'The greater part of the dispatches sent by this wonderful invention in England relate, we believe, to occasions of disaster and surprise.'[33] In such an atmosphere of expectation, one would hardly wonder that the thoughts of the signalman are dominated by his fears about safety on the line. Indeed, his visitations represent a strange mockery of his own industrial function, the spectral figures that haunt him embodying, in their posture, the very qualities required by his occupation: vigilance and responsibility. In the figure of the signalman, Dickens parallels the signalling functions of the mind with the signalling activity of the railway, and implies that it is the signalman's inability to distinguish between these mental and technological signals that leads to disaster. While equally subject to similar kinds of morbid and uncanny impressions and fully prepared to admit to them, the narrator, on the other hand, is able to subordinate his primary, and initially fantastic, sensations to a secondary rational response to the 'possible'. The contrast between his impressions and those of the signalman lies in the thoughts that follow. When he returns to the line on the day of the signalman's death, the narrator sees a figure gesticulating in exactly the same manner as the signalman's phantom:

I cannot describe the thrill that seized upon me when, close at the mouth of the tunnel, I saw the appearance of a man with his left sleeve across his eyes, passionately waving his right arm. The nameless horror that oppressed me, passed in a moment, for in a moment I saw that this appearance of a man was a man indeed. (25)

The signalman's predicament is inextricably linked to the conditions in which he works. In this solitary post, contact with the outside world takes place via a technological medium which substitutes mediated, spatially distant communication for the immediacy of human presence. His occupation, moreover, demands a disproportionate amount of mental to physical endeavour, his sole responsibility consisting of exactness and watchfulness, unrelieved by any social interaction:

Manual labour he had next to none. To change that signal, to trim those lights, and to turn this iron handle now and then, was all he had to do under that head.

Regarding those many long and lonely hours of which I seemed to make so much, he could only say that the routine of his life had shaped itself into that form and he had grown used to it. He had taught himself a language down there – if only to know it by sight, and to have formed his own crude ideas of its pronunciation, could be called learning it. He had also worked at fractions and decimals, and tried a little algebra; but he was . . . a poor hand at figures. (21)

The disengaged signifiers which preoccupy the signalman, the language he has taught himself to recognise but cannot speak, and his lack of dexterity with algebraic symbols are peculiarly suggestive of his tortuous predicament. He remains without an authoritative referent by which to assess events, for his alarm about these disturbing visual and auditory visitations will find no affirmation with the railway authorities, and thus no correspondence with 'reality'.

The narrative of 'The Signalman' does not refute the veracity of the protagonist's precognitive visitations. Rather, it highlights the controversy surrounding the clairvoyant in the rationalised, modern, industrial world, where prediction was increasingly viewed as a scientific discipline. Moreover, the 'normative' influence of the mental physiology of Henry Holland and William Benjamin Carpenter further marginalised clairvoyance. Their mental philosophy recognised little distinction between the chronic pathological behaviour of the mentally deranged and those incidents of heightened intuition reconcilable with the magnetic temperament. This is a view which, in spite of himself, Dickens's narrator endorses. The signalman must adhere to the signals of technology, rather than his own telegraphic intuition, and thus he is condemned to the 'mental torture of a conscientious man, oppressed beyond endurance by an unintelligible responsibility involving life.' (24)

ATYR carried many more ghost stories and articles about ghosts than *HW* had done and Dickens was clearly responding to the climate of supernaturalism that had been shaped by the growth of Spiritualism. The ghost story featured as both a popular form of entertainment and as a subject of philosophical debate and scientific investigation in accordance with the miscellany's endeavour to provide both instruction and entertainment by blending sensation with improving reading matter. Nevertheless, as an editor, Dickens prided himself on carrying quality ghost stories and indeed some of the best-known practitioners in the form – Wilkie Collins, Edward Bulwer-Lytton and Sheridan Le Fanu – came under his editorial direction. Dickens applied high standards to all the tales that were offered to him, and insisted that contributors should consider difficult matters of evidence, authority and belief. In 1867 he rejected a series of reputedly authentic ghost stories offered by Frances Elliot for publication in *ATYR*. He recognised among them 'an old one, perfectly well known *as* a story. *You* cannot tell it on the first hand testimony of an eye-witness', he told Elliot. In rejecting her stories, Dickens explained that were he to print them with her claims to authenticity, 'I should be deservedly pounced upon. If I were to put them in *without* your claim, I should be merely republishing a stereotyped set of tales.'[34]

Dickens also printed well-authenticated ghost stories without seeking to impose an explanation. In 1861 he twice printed the sensational ghostly encounter of the portrait painter, Thomas Heaphy. The first was a retelling of Heaphy's experience, but after hearing Heaphy's own account of events, Dickens was sufficiently astounded to purchase the first-hand account for *ATYR* and his short introduction to Heaphy's narrative offered 'no theory of our own towards the explanation of any part of this remarkable narrative'.[35] Dickens's willingness to circulate unexplained ghostly encounters was seized upon by the *Spiritual Magazine* as a means of attacking his integrity, and he was accused of secretly endorsing Spiritualism.[36] Modern scholars have also perceived apparent inconsistencies in the way that *ATYR* strongly endorsed scientific explanations for ghosts, at the same time as retelling the most sensational ghost stories.[37] Dickens, it must always be acknowledged, was ever ready to exploit the popular appeal of the ghost story. Yet, quite apart from this, the combination of rationalism and anecdote to be found in *ATYR* was a convention which appeared not only in credulous treatises in favour of ghosts, but also in the medical and scientific writings of such sceptics as Samuel Hibbert. The accumulation of ghost stories, however sensational, was as important to many contemporaries as the theories that were circulated to explain them. Dickens's own ghost story, 'To Be Taken with a Grain of Salt' takes up this point, and attributes the mystery shrouding 'psychological experience[s]' 'of a strange sort' to individuals' hesitancy in recounting them:

Almost all men are afraid that what they could relate in such wise would find no parallel or response in a listener's internal life, and might be suspected or laughed at . . . The consequence is, that the general stock of experience in this regard appears exceptional, and really is so, in respect of being miserably imperfect.[38]

The narrator of 'To Be Taken with a Grain of Salt' documents his peculiar 'psychological experience' without setting up, 'opposing, or supporting, any theory whatever'; it is the accumulation of material that is necessary if such phenomena are to be assessed and eventually understood. Indeed, this approach would be institutionalised at the Society for Psychical Research in 1882, after Dickens's death.

Dickens's journalism and fiction reveal how broadly the subject of ghosts was defined in the early Victorian period. In *HW* and *ATYR* under misleading titles referring to 'ghosts' there are to be found articles that promote naturalistic concepts of mind, and explanations of the nature of optical delusions and the aetiological causes of apparitions, as well as articles that treat clairvoyance and sympathetic phenomena within a world-view inseparable from the growth of communication technologies. Dickens's position in the ghost controversy can thus be identified as a naturalistic one, although the explanations he endorsed relied on occult as well as known physical forces. Dickens's writings, those of his associates and his adversaries, moreover, reveal how complex ideas and debates about the nature and origins of ghosts were before 1860, a richness somewhat masked by this essay's concentration on the largely sceptical views of Dickens. Yet scholars interested in the Victorian preoccupation with ghosts and spirits and with the increasingly scientific understanding of the supernatural in general have not explored the early Victorian period in the same depth as the later decades, when the full impact of Spiritualism had been felt. Still less have the influential texts, theories and beliefs inherited and developed by the early Victorians received the detailed consideration they merit. The pre-1850 corpus of literature about apparitions, and the spiritual and non-spiritual uses of mesmerism are important contexts for the early Victorian ghost story. By indicating the terms upon which the cultures of supernatural belief and non-belief were taking shape before 1850, these contexts can offer new insights into the work of such figures as Dickens, for whom authentic ghost stories and Spiritualism were very different phenomena.

NOTES

1 Dickens to William Howitt, 6 September 1859, *The Letters of Charles Dickens*, ed. Kathleen Tillotson *et al.*, 11 vols. (Oxford: Clarendon, 1965–99), vol. IX, pp. 116–17.
2 John Forster, *The Life of Charles Dickens*, 3 vols. (London: Chapman & Hall, 1874), vol. III, p. 483.
3 *Examiner*, 26 Feb 1848, reprinted in Phillip Collins, 'Dickens on Ghosts: An Uncollected Article', *Dickensian* 59 (1963), 5–14; pp. 8–9.
4 Samuel Hibbert, *Sketches of the Philosophy of Apparitions; or, an Attempt to Trace Such Illusions to their Physical Causes* (London: Whittaker, 1824), p. iii.
5 David Brewster, *Letters on Natural Magic, Addressed to Sir Walter Scott* (London: John Murray, 1832), p. 49.

6 See Dickens to Emile de la Rue, 28 July 1845 in Dickens, *Letters*, vol. iv, pp. 337–9.
7 See Fred Kaplan, *Dickens and Mesmerism: The Hidden Springs of Fiction* (Princeton: Princeton University Press, 1975), pp. 74–105.
8 Dickens to Emile de la Rue, 15 January 1845 in Dickens, *Letters*, vol. iv, pp. 247–9.
9 Dickens to Emile de la Rue, 27 January 1845 in Dickens, *Letters*, vol. iv, pp. 254–5.
10 Brewster, *Natural Magic*, p. 47.
11 Collins, 'Dickens on Ghosts', p. 11.
12 *A Christmas Carol* in *The Christmas Books, Centenary Edition of the Works of Charles Dickens*, 36 vols. (London: Chapman and Hall, 1910), p. 16.
13 *The Chimes*, in Dickens, *The Christmas Books*, p. 127.
14 *The Lazy Tour of Two Idle Apprentices*, Chapter the Fourth, *Household Words* 16 (1857), 385–93; p. 392.
15 'To Be Read at Dusk', *Reprinted Pieces*, ed. Andrew Lang (London: Chapman & Hall, 1903) pp. 303–18; pp. 306–7.
16 Mamie Dickens, *My Father as I Recall Him* (1897) quoted in Kaplan, *Dickens and Mesmerism*, p. 108; Dickens to John Forster, 30 May 1863 in Dickens, *Letters*, vol. x, p. 256.
17 Chauncy Hare Townshend, *Mesmerism Proved True and the Quarterly Reviewer Reviewed* (London: Thomas Bosworth, 1854), p. 163.
18 Dickens to Emile de la Rue, 10 February 1845 in Dickens, *Letters*, vol. iv, p. 264.
19 Ibid.
20 Dickens to Elizabeth Gaskell, 25 November 1851 in Dickens, *Letters*, vol. vi, p. 546.
21 See Ruth Glancy, 'To Be Read at Dusk', *Dickensian*, 83 (1987), 40–7.
22 Henry Holland, *Chapters on Mental Physiology* (London: Longman, Orme, Brown, Green and Longman, 1852), pp. 144–5.
23 Dickens to Emile de la Rue, 25 January 1845, 27 January 1845 in Dickens, *Letters*, vol. iv, pp. 249–50, 252–3.
24 Henry Morley, 'New Discoveries in Ghosts', *Household Words* 4 (1852), 403–6; p. 404.
25 'A Physician's Ghosts', *All the Year Round* 1 (1859), 346–50; p. 348.
26 Ibid.; 'A Physician's Dreams', *All the Year Round* 2 (1859), 109–13; pp. 135–40.
27 Henry Morley and W. H. Wills, 'The Ghost of the Cock Lane Ghost', *Household Words* 6 (1853), 217–23; p. 220.
28 Ibid.
29 Dickens to William Howitt, 6 September 1859 in Dickens, *Letters*, vol. ix, pp. 116–17.
30 See Harry Stone, 'The Unknown Dickens', *Dickens Studies Annual* 1 (1971), 1–22.
31 Charles Dickens, *The Haunted House, All the Year Round* Extra Christmas Number, 1 (1859), 1–48; p. 5.

32 Charles Dickens, 'No. 1 Branch Line: The Signal-man', *Mugby Junction, All the Year Round* Extra Christmas Number 16 (1866), 20–5; p. 23.
33 Frederick Knight Hunt, 'Wings of Fire', *Houshold Words* 2 (1850), 241–5; p. 245.
34 Dickens to Frances Elliot, 12 September 1867 in Dickens, *Letters*, vol. ix, p. 425.
35 Thomas Heaphy, 'Mr H.'s Own Narrative', *All The Year Round* 6 (1861), 36–43.
36 See *Spiritual Magazine* 2 (1861), pp. 543–4, and 6 (1867), p. 98.
37 See particularly Elaine Ostry, '"Social Wonders": Fancy, Science, and Technology in Dickens's Periodicals', *Victorian Periodicals Review* 34 (2001), 54–78; p. 66.
38 Charles Dickens, 'To Be Taken with a Grain of Salt', *Dr Marigold's Prescriptions, All The Year Round* Extra Christmas Number, 14 (1865), 33–8; p. 35.

PART II

Invisible women

CHAPTER 3

Spectral politics: the Victorian ghost story and the domestic servant

Eve M. Lynch

Mrs Rouncewell . . . considers that a family of such antiquity and importance has a right to a ghost. She regards a ghost as one of the privileges of the upper classes; a genteel distinction to which the common people have no claim.[1]

The Victorian ghost story thrived during an age devoted to literary realism and rational control of unwieldy forces. Ghost stories offered evidence that the home was no haven from powerful and exacting social pressures. Differentiating the arenas of public and private life, writers exposed new boundaries in the ghostly residue of buried secrets traipsing their private status out into public performance. Exposures of the hidden shames of domestic life found popularity in a constellation of magazines and fiction collections that circulated through all classes and household members. It is not surprising, then, to find that these stories often stress the conjunction of external, and by extension public, class status and internal, private matters. For this reason ghost stories, like Victorian homes, were populated by that ubiquitous sign of public and private transition, the domestic servant.

By the mid-century, Victorian ghost stories frequently turned their horror on the perceived proximity of servants to supernatural phenomena, arcane folk beliefs, intuitive and irrational knowledge and the uncanny. Those nursemaids, cooks and scullery-maids who haunted the subterranean regions of the house were a ready body of characters who could drag any ghost out of hiding and *know* the import of its visit. Long before a ghost could show its spectral form to the master and mistress of the household, every maidservant and butler had bumped into the visitor somewhere on the back stairwell. And like the apparition appearing out of nowhere, the silent housemaid appeared from out of nowhere at the pull of the cord, responding to some as yet unspoken desire of the mistress or command of the master. Like the ghost, the servant was *in* the home but not *of* it, occupying a position tied to the workings of the house itself. Like the spectral spirit,

67

servants were outsiders in the home secretly looking in on the forbidden world of respectability, as A. S. Byatt reminds us:

There are people in a house, you know, who know everything that goes on – the invisible people, and now and then *the house* simply decides that something must happen . . . Yes. There are people in the houses, between the visible inhabitants and the invisible, largely invisible to *both*, who can know a very great deal, or nothing, as they choose.[2]

Like this supernatural influence of the house itself quietly imposing its own order on the will of the domestic inhabitants, the domestic servant suggested a silent estate of discontent and dis-ease cohabiting the same physical space as the family, but imagined by that family as immaterial and invisible. The cook and the maid seemed to go with the house – and sometimes did, being 'inherited' by succeeding families – furnishing the home with a ghostly agency that moved the tables and chairs, emptied the grates and chamber pots, and disappeared around corners and through passages to the 'other side' of the green baize door.

In an industrial age determined to rationalise, categorise and control the inexplicable and foreign, servants, with their rural origins and lack of education, appeared as unstable outsiders persisting in outmoded belief systems stamped as superstitious. Yet ghost stories themselves were enormously popular among all classes of readers, with copies floating back and forth between the kitchen and the drawing room. Christmas editions of magazines from the 1850s through the end of the century carried the obligatory and much-anticipated yuletide ghost story to chill the soul on an evening around the fire. Early leaders in publishing the genre were Dickens' *Household Words*, begun in 1850, and its successor *All the Year Round*. *The Cornhill Magazine*, *St James's Magazine*, *Belgravia*, *Temple Bar*, *Saturday Review*, *Tinsley's*, *Argosy* and *St Paul's* all contributed their share to a readership addicted to the thrill of momentarily losing rational control over the ordered Victorian world.

This essay examines the relationship between this popular literary genre and representations of domestic servants. Writers of ghost stories often depict an alliance between the supernatural and the household servant as a means to break into the ideological boundaries separating private life from overt social critique. By drawing a continuum between the inexplicable agency of the supernatural and the rational, domestic social structure, writers of the ghost story could construct an apparatus for examining a spectrum of social anxieties of the day. While critical attention to the Victorian ghost story has addressed their overt psychological, sensational and aesthetic content, I aim here to recast critical examination into the class content of this genre.[3]

Ghost stories most frequently take place within the bounded space of the home, perhaps because the most ardent producers of these tales throughout the Victorian era were women. Writers such as J. S. Le Fanu, Charles Dickens, Wilkie Collins and Arthur Conan Doyle have been famous in the twentieth century, but it was writers such as Amelia Edwards, Mary Elizabeth Braddon, Catherine Crowe, Rhoda Broughton, Charlotte Riddell, Mrs Henry Wood, Margaret Oliphant, Vernon Lee, Rosa Mulholland and Edith Nest who filled the volumes of *Belgravia* and *Cornhill Magazine* to popularise spectral tradition. Jessica Salmonson has estimated that as much as 70 per cent of the supernatural fiction in Victorian periodicals was the work of women.[4] From within the domestic world women writers paired up spectacular spirits from the underworld with the very material bodies from below stairs to expose the secrets of the guilty house. For this reason, ghost stories often bring to light a hidden social dilemma that 'airs' itself in the public arena of its readership.

The spirit that airs the private failings of the home can be traced to a popular reference to the demon Asmodeus, whose roof-raising activities were first written by Alain-Réné Le Sage in 1707 in his *Le Diable Boiteux*. This tale, echoed in numerous Victorian fictive references, features a limping demon, Asmodeus, who haunts the rooftops of Madrid, lifting off the tops of houses to expose the hidden crimes carried on beneath. For the Victorian writer, this omniscient voyeur offered a cogent symbol for laying open the impacted problem secreted away in the private sphere. Dickens, in *Dombey and Son*, calls on this figure to bring the private torments of Victorian life to the surface:

Oh for a good spirit who would take the house-tops off, with a more potent and benignant hand than the lame demon in the tale, and show a Christian people what dark shapes issue from amidst their homes, to swell the retinue of the Destroying Angel as he moves forth among them! For only one night's view of the pale phantoms rising from the scenes of our too-long neglect . . . ![5]

But if a spirit was tantalisingly suitable for mediating quietly between private mysteries and public histories, the servants in the household were a very real hazard to family secrets. Servant gossip always threatened to pull the tops off houses, a problem of control the English sought to resolve in their architecture: unlike continental apartment-buildings, where servants from multiple households were quartered together at the top of the building, exchanging gossip freely, English terraced housing was designed to house servants under separate attics so that the master and mistress could regulate the amount of time their employees visited with domestics from other households.[6] It was one thing to air a 'genteel' family ghost, as Mrs Rouncewell, the Chesney Wold housekeeper in *Bleak House*, tells us, and quite another to air the family laundry.

If servants could leak secrets out of the house, they were also conduits from the regions beyond the home, bringing in with them the alien culture, ancient rural beliefs, folklore, superstitions and oral traditions that underpin ghost stories. Children looked to the nursemaid and the parlourmaid for the panorama of social values lying beyond the middle-class home. In the servant, the magical and the material met, making the nursemaid a phenomenal resource for children's imaginations. It is not surprising that the rise of the ghost story takes place so prominently in an era when servants inhabit a spacious role in rearing children. In his 'Nurse's Stories', Dickens complains of his own nurse's malignant influence, especially in the

quantity of places and people – utterly impossible places and people, but none the less alarmingly real – that I found I had been introduced to by my nurse before I was six years old, and used to be forced to go back to at night without at all wanting to go. If we all knew our own minds...I suspect we should find our nurses responsible for most of the dark corners we are forced to go back to, against our wills.[7]

The constellation of anxieties inherent in ghost stories is extensive: fear of deranged spatial and psychological boundaries, feelings of desertion and isolation, ancestral longings and guilt, ambivalence about domestic privacy, fear of domestic imprisonment, and madness are but a few of the anxieties that surface repeatedly in stories from the mid-century on. They suggest a provisional sense of the arrangement and constitution of a middle class being formed and reformed in a country under tremendous social and geographic dislocation. Alienated from the traditional regulatory terms of ancestry that shaped upper-class identity, and at the same time rejecting the rural community values and folk culture that unified the lower classes, the Victorian middle class self-consciously sought to locate an identity that could accommodate both private and social coherence under one roof. Charlotte Riddell, Rhoda Broughton and Margaret Oliphant wrote numerous ghost stories delineating a middle class moving its way through a domestic world haunted by reminders of the social and psychological regions beyond their control.

The spectral memory of long-dead relations and former owners that haunt the passages and corridors of the house in these stories geared up to meet the older, communal web of inhabitants that filled the subterranean regions below. For the middle class living in close nuclear families, the maid-of-all-work and the housekeeper or cook most fully embodied both the outsider breaking into the home and the domestic life cut loose from blood relations: servants only rarely returned to their families, living instead on the periphery of domestic affiliation. These uncanny inhabitants, silent and 'invisible' themselves in the home, became magnets for fictive apparitions that oversee and provoke themes of social mobility and dislocation, orphaned and deserted children, emigration and immigration and disinherited outcasts of all sorts. One of the most prolific of ghost writers, Mary Elizabeth Braddon, author of *Lady Audley's Secret* and a host of novels and short stories, returned frequently to this constellation of spectres to explicate the social problems she saw underlying English life and home. A careful examination of her ghost stories reveals the interrelationships among household alliances, domestic servants, spectral visitors and the Victorian social critic.

MARY ELIZABETH BRADDON AND THE SPIRIT(S) OF SOCIAL REFORM

In Braddon's 1864 novel, *The Doctor's Wife*, her character Sigismund Smith, a writer of serial penny fiction, ruminates on the restrictive boundaries of producing for a sensation-hungry weekly audience when he yearns to write 'a great novel'. Hemmed in by the voracious demands of the plot-driven tale of crime and woe, Sigismund chafes at the necessity of maintaining temporal and factual realism in his narrative, scoffing: 'If you tie me down to facts... I can't write at all.'[8] This succinct protest serves as a reigning principle for his literary creator, Braddon herself, whose talent for writing sensational, outlandish fiction kept Victorian audiences enraptured while it made her rich. Yet the crime-filled penny dreadfuls and novels she serialised in low-brow magazines posed a problem for Braddon because they confirmed her writings as plot-driven page-turners, tied to the 'facts' of highly paced, intricate schemes and allowing little room for developing overt critical commentary. Like her mouthpiece Sigismund, Braddon agitated to experiment with fiction that considered more pressing social issues, particularly in the problems she saw arising out of Victorian reform policies that ignored the private domestic trials of women and the poor. Braddon repeatedly returned in her fiction to exposing the *laissez-faire* individualism and complacency that allowed the wealthy and the middle classes to desert the poor and dependent women in the prosperous mid-century.

Braddon experimented in 1866 with writing a social novel not tied to mystery and murder sensation in *The Lady's Mile*. This novel examined life beyond the conventional social boundaries of the Hyde Park riding circuit, noting, 'but on the highway of life the boundary-line is not so clearly defined. There are women who lose themselves in some unknown region beyond the Lady's Mile, and whom we never hear of more.'[9] Braddon's interest in women who 'lose themselves in some unknown region beyond' drew her past the idle women in *The Lady's Mile* and into a broad acquaintance with the political, social and economic issues directing the lives of Victorian women of all classes.

Braddon's use of the 'unknown region' metaphor borrowed from a widely recognised image explaining economic and social divisions in England as a business of national boundaries. Gertrude Himmelfarb has noted that Victorian authors frequently testified to a chasm supposedly separating the 'two nations' of England, the 'low' and the 'high', and located the 'other' nation in a 'foreign' or 'unknown' country: 'With predictable and monotonous regularity every parliamentary report, social novel, and journalistic exposé announced itself, and was hailed by reviewers, as an excursion into "distant lands", "dark and unknown regions".'[10] For Braddon, that 'unknown region beyond' increasingly came to serve as a metaphor for an 'impenetrable' English domestic space that lurked side-by-side with respectable society but was silently isolated by convention, shame and secrecy, covering up the despair of social ills haunting Victorian life. English domesticity is, Braddon proposes, dangerously 'alien' to itself.

Robert L. Wolff has argued that *The Lady's Mile* was an early, singular experiment for Braddon in serious social commentary, with Braddon returning to sensational murder plots in the face of her own social ostracism for her unorthodox liaison with publisher John Maxwell.[11] Wolff asserts that Braddon set aside her desire to protest social conventionalities when savage personal criticism was levelled at her own life with Maxwell, returning instead to writing the popular fiction of graphic and incidental sensation until the mid-seventies, when she once again sounded an insistent radical note. I argue, however, that Braddon did not abandon her radical social criticism during this period, as can be seen in numerous short stories that turn their interest on the plight of characters caught in the alienation of social and economic, rather than criminal, desperation. If her novels returned to the lurid and improbable tales of murder, her social writing transmuted into a newly popularised form that could carry the weight of her critical examination while appearing to deliver the quick thrills of popular sensation that brought her audiences and income. Throughout the sixties, and particularly after she took over the editing and writing of *Belgravia* magazine in 1866, Braddon was able to indulge her desire for exploring the undercurrents of social problems within a genre ideally suited to adapting a double effect, the uncanny ghost story. The enormous popularity of supernatural tales, especially the Christmas ghost stories, provided Braddon with a venue for exploiting the sentimental genre of the social/psychological tale while maintaining her audience's desire for ghastly effect. This vehicle allowed Braddon to deflect the sensational aura of murder, criminal scheming, insanity and violence into an arena of obscure supernatural agency, one not bound by the facts of everyday life and journalistic sensation, thus retaining the intrigue and suspense of a good murder story while paradoxically suppressing the expected emphasis on crime and detection. Discovery and exposure continued to drive the plot towards a satisfaction of psychological tension, but the effect was enhanced by suspending and subverting the sensation over the course of the story, rather than producing a series of dramatic, revelatory climaxes. In Braddon's ghost stories, as is typical of the genre, the final revelation leads the reader deeper into the murky territory of reflection, rather than detection.

With her audience satisfied that the chill would still arrive in the *dénouement*, Braddon could indulge her exploration of the unmarked 'boundary-line' dividing the public world of social conventions from the 'unknown region beyond' that lay hidden in private frustration as a reminder of English social and psychological dislocation. Those murky regions were the ambiguous and fluctuating outlines of inequities Braddon saw persisting in the affluent decades of high Victorianism in spite of political reform, economic expansion and philanthropic volunteerism. Braddon's ghostly tales repeatedly expose social inequalities from within the apparent comfort of home and hearth, suggesting that the parameters of the unknown regions shadowing Victorian life are more familiarly and cannily drawn than the spatial metaphor implies: in the ghost story, the 'other side' typically conjoins the mysterious and the material, the visible and the invisible, in the same enclosed, domestic arena. To this end, Braddon's tales are filled with characters culled from the lower orders, especially servants from the regions 'below stairs' whose social position in the house was analogous to the spectral apparition that haunted it.

The class and spiritual discontinuity represented in the household relationships gave Braddon a domestic population through which she could survey the disturbing landscape of English social reform. Freed from the 'facts' of realism, crime and detection, Braddon could conjure the spirits of social crime that continued to haunt women and the poor, dispossessed

of equal standing and a voice in the affairs of the nation that affected
their lives. In effect Braddon became a *ghost writer* of their complaints to
the nation. Supernatural stories turning on apparitions, mesmerism, fantastical occurrences and inexplicable omens – the stock in trade of tales
of domestic 'possession' – were readily paired with the dilemmas of those
dispossessed members of the household lacking property, education, social
standing and independence. It is a mark of her commitment to social critique that Braddon's ghostly tales often refuse to resolve themselves in easy
spectral explanation; in the end, Braddon frequently remains ambiguous
about whether the fantastical element that *seems* to haunt each story is adequate to account for the devastation that ensues – the 'ghost' appears to
have a shadow behind it, haunting the conclusion with nagging persistence.
Braddon suggests that more worldly and human forces, such as poverty,
greed, pride and complacency, are what follow the characters around and
re-form their fates.

   That Braddon turned to this genre in the years surrounding the second
Reform Bill of 1867 speaks to the ways in which a spirit of national social
reform, one that could give voice to the outer regions of the politically
disenfranchised, enacts a 'spirit' of literary reformulation that voices her
social conscience. It is not surprising that the decades in which this ghostly
genre exploded in popularity also saw an overhaul of social reform leading
to parliamentary acts on education, married women's property, custody of
infants, matrimonial causes, university admission for women, medical education and franchise rights for women at local government levels. A host of
legislative statutes responded to insistent voices that haunted England over
national education, the rights of married women, the rights of mothers,
and, on various levels, the franchisement of a broader, more democratic
spectrum of the country. The Reform Bill of 1867 became a national cen-
trepiece for generating support for social improvement and political action,
philanthropic and educative projects. In taking up the ghost story genre in
the 1860s and 1870s, Braddon found a home for her criticism that could
coexist with – and even enhance – the sensational plot. The ghosts that
haunt her stories from this period serve for Braddon as emblems of what
Victorian society is unwilling to 'see' in its social condition: *laissez-faire*
liberalism in home policy divides the Victorian social realm into isolated
'worlds' of rich and poor, dependent and independent, public and private,
visible and invisible. The supernatural spirits in her ghost stories remind us
of what is being suppressed socially or repressed psychologically in Victorian
society. Schelling's definition of *das Unheimlich* as the 'name for everything
that *ought* to have remained . . . hidden and secret and has become visible'

identifies the process through which societal problems continued to surface: social reform in the first half of the century that *ought* to have resolved England's problems had merely suppressed them, Braddon warns, and like the spectral hauntings of the house, the problems arise with untimely and forbidding insistence.[12]

Braddon's ghost stories from the 1860s delineate the anxiety of dispossession that permeated the estate of dependent women and domestic workers. The theme of the women detached from communal help, dependent and helpless to direct their own fate, is most fully developed in 'Ralph the Bailiff', a novelette that ran serially in *St James's Magazine* in 1861 and formed the lead story in Braddon's first collection of short stories, published in 1867. In this tale, the woman must face the demon that haunts her because of earlier hidden crimes of her husband. Her isolation in the home becomes a form of terror that magnifies her desperation, threatening to drive her to madness. The husband, a weak-willed Lincolnshire farmer who had secretly poisoned his elder brother to inherit the family property, Grey Farm, falls prey to his ubiquitous servant, Ralph, the bailiff, who blackmails his master for his crime. The bailiff shadows his employer's every move, eavesdropping on his conversations, taking on the office of butler to control the dining room, taking over the accounting books for the farm to control the money, and insinuating himself into every decision made until the master falls 'under the thrall of his inseparable retainer'.[13] When the farmer marries a young orphan, Jenny Trevor, a rector's ward, she becomes haunted by hallucinations in the dead of the night and uncanny, hissing whispers of her husband's guilt. Extending the realm of his power, the bailiff overwhelms the young wife with his sinister demeanour and his insolent rejection of her authority as mistress. Under the pressure of this influence and lacking trust in her husband, Jenny sickens in feverish despair and determines to run away from home. Instead, she finds herself imprisoned on the lonely farm by the bailiff and descends into madness.

Alarmed by a dream one night in which she imagines herself holding a wailing infant who is strangling her and dragging her down, the young wife awakens to hear the low wail of a baby in the house, recalling to her mind the ghost stories attached to Grey Farm. Following the wail of the child through the house, Jenny eavesdrops through a keyhole to hear her husband's conversation with the bailiff and Martha, Ralph's sister and Grey Farm's former housekeeper, and learns the source of the servant's power: he has blackmailed his master with the knowledge of the old murder. But even more destructive to Jenny's security is the bailiff's revelation of his master's secret earlier marriage to his servant Martha, who has borne him a son. For their continued silence, Ralph demands full entitlement to the farm as well as the dowry that Jenny Trevor had brought into her marriage. Devastated by this betrayal that leaves her status as wife null, her home lost, and her dowry confiscated, Jenny flees the farm and is taken back into her old home at the Rector's, where she soon learns of her husband's suicide on the night of her escape. Grey Farm, now in Ralph's possession with the rest of the estate, is sold by the bailiff, who emigrates to Australia to set up his own farm, complete with servants, his sister and his former master's infant son.

This story turns on reversals of authority and possession between husband and wife and between master and servant. In fact, Braddon interweaves the theme of 'possession' – both in its spectral and material senses – between the seemingly supernatural, metaphysical authority characters hold over each other, and the legally sanctioned authority they hold over the physical and economic properties of the estate. Jenny becomes 'possessed' by hallucinations and the supernatural 'hissing whispers' reminding her of her husband's guilt (23). But it is her possession by him *as her husband* that most confounds her:

'Why had she married Dudley Carleon?' She sometimes asked herself this question, as if she had suddenly awoke from a long sleep to find herself in a strange country. She did not love him, she did not even admire him, but she had allowed him to gain so strong an influence over her, that it was only now and then she remembered this. (23)

In the somnolent 'strange country' of her marriage, that 'unknown region beyond' that she belatedly awakens to, the wife is mesmerised by the 'influence' of her pernicious husband, an influence that borders on the demonic. His psychological hold over her, however, is made more concrete in the bailiff's control over her movements, confining her to the home and, finally, to her room, until she feels herself under an 'unseen influence' that is 'sapping' her very life (31). The marital 'strange country' she inhabits is cut off from communal security by the bailiff, who becomes an 'impassable barrier between the mistress of Grey Farm and the world without' (38). Jenny becomes the material sign of dispossession trapped inside the house.

Complicating this theme of demonic domestic possession is a reversal of power in the relationship between master and servant that deranges the barriers separating the classes and defining the family: the farmer's secret marriage to the housekeeper and the existence of her son as legitimate heir to his father's property adumbrates the division between these two parallel domestic worlds, 'upstairs' and 'downstairs'. The house itself becomes the defining boundary line between two worlds driven apart but cohabiting the same space. The revelation that Martha, the 'invisible' house-keeper – and not Jenny – is actually the legally sanctioned wife, transposes the mistress–servant relationship: significantly, it is Jenny who is 'crouching at the threshold of the door', spying through the keyhole to observe her fall from authority, while the housekeeper sits inside by the fireplace with the master, holding his infant son (37). This reversal of domestic portraits mirrored through the keyhole reveals the maternal economy of the woman's place at the hearth: aggravated by her ghostly dream of the infant strangling her that brought her to the point of surreptitiously watching through doors, Jenny is confronted in the fireside scene by her own childlessness and loss of marital authority. With her dowry left in her husband's hands, Jenny sees her assets slipping out of his control, to be passed on to the housekeeper's son if the bailiff does not appropriate them sooner. Dispossessed of her hus-band and familial position, Jenny is finally deprived of the only property she has brought into her marriage, rendering her the 'alien' in the home, mate-rially, legally and socially emptied of meaning. She has become the ghostly wife, unseen, unheard, looking in on the 'real' family that inhabits the house.

Braddon's tale of possession and dispossession offers little sympathy to the lower orders, who are here portrayed as sinister, malevolent demons corrupting the household and destroying her economic position. That Braddon allows the bailiff to escape with his master's property to Australia underscores her portrait of him as criminal and social outcast siphoning off resources from both family and nation. At the same time, however, Braddon clearly shows the husband's weakness as haunting Jenny's mar-riage and devastating the family: he, after all, has killed his own brother to take possession of the farm and then abrogated the power of head of house-hold, thereby threatening not just his own position, but his wife's as well. For Jenny, who already suspects her husband's crime of murder, the social crime of secretly marrying his housekeeper and bigamously remarrying to obscure the status of mistress and wife has more devastating consequences. With both the physically intrusive bailiff and the secretly invasive house-keeper reformulating the terms of familial structure, the foundations of lineage and inheritance are distorted, corrupting the children of marriage into terrifying incubi that strangle the legal rights of the woman. Braddon directs her sympathies into the plight of the woman with no marital prop-erty rights and no familial control, dependent on her husband and a fragile legal footing that can shift in the dead of the night to leave her destitute and stripped of all domestic posture. In the insanity that descends on the mistress locked in domestic impotence Braddon suggests that the secret crime of marriage is the madness of possession that conjures the wife into an unknown region bound inside the house, isolated from community, robbing her of the protection of society and dispossessing her of property, authority and her own mind.

If 'Ralph the Bailiff' plays judiciously with the blurred lines of demonic possession and haunted domesticity, Braddon's spectral tales in the decade of the 1860s give way gradually to more vividly constructed apparitions while at the same time sharpening the focus of her social criticism that lies in wait behind those shadows. Her concern that the wealthy ranks of society were deserting their responsibility to the poor and dependents became more deeply entrenched and caustic as she explored the ephemeral shades of the world beyond social recognition in two ghost stories of the 1870s: 'At Chrighton Abbey' (1871), and 'The Shadow in the Corner' (1879). 'At Chrighton Abbey' links the theme of charity for the poor to the fragile, shadowy position of the governess who is only charitably placed in the home. Braddon criticises systems of private philanthropy that are dependent on the integrity of the landed rich: she shows a spirit of voluntary responsibility for the poor carried on by the disinherited governess and servants while a rising mood of arrogance, indifference and economic isolationism haunts the rich.

'At Chrighton Abbey' is narrated by Sarah Chrighton, a dispossessed governess and distant relative of the Chrighton family who has been sent out to service in far off Vienna and St Petersburg. Like the the servants in Chrighton Abbey who are privy to the ghosts of the family secrets, Sarah, returning for a holiday, can 'see' the doom about to descend on the Chrighton line as they position themselves with indifference towards the poor inhabiting a separate 'nation' on the skirts of the ruling class. As a mediator between seemingly superstitious servants, the impoverished community and family tragedy, Sarah operates as a ghostly, familiar figure who signals what is 'hidden' and difficult in Victorian idealism.[14]

Braddon begins this story by extending her earlier theme of dispossession, updated here in the governess who has lost her home and must earn her living abroad. Like her brother in the Indian Civil Service, Sarah has lost both hearth and native country, returning as a visitor from her expatriation in the foreign regions beyond English society. Sarah lives like a ghostly reminder of the plight of single women who have no house to hold them, forced into wandering the globe in search of a home. Braddon directly critiques the Victorian practice of promoting the emigration of governesses to reduce the ranks of single women in England. From the middle

of the century, benevolent organisations such as the National Benevolent
Emigration Society, the Society for the Employment of Women and the
Female Middle-Class Emigration Society regularly sent women out to
the colonies to improve employment and marriage prospects.[15] These
projects receive Braddon's implicit censure for securing the 'respectable' and
'invisible' employment of women selectively culled from the ranks of an
impoverished and disinherited middle class.

Crossing and recrossing the British border, negotiating between visibility
and invisibility, Sarah Chrighton inhabits a ghostly realm of English consciousness. Patrick Brantlinger has argued that this policy of emigration has
'complex, unconscious interconnections' with British imperialist ideology
and the rage for occultism that thrived in the latter part of the Victorian
era: conquering the borderland between the 'foreign' realms of territory
and death posited a way of controlling frontiers as English anxiety about
empire became more shrill.[16] Certainly Sarah's exile out to the eastern edges
of European culture signals an English desire to harbour its 'excess' popula-
tions in an invisible, alien world produced by commerce and international
influence. But Sarah's dislocation is not only physical and commercial; it is
also social, for she has lost her standing in the English home and now must
'haunt' an unbounded world of social and political dissociation. Braddon
suggests, through this ghostly reminder, that England cannot afford to
isolate itself from national and domestic obligations, even if they have
been removed to international realms. Joining the recurrent debate about
'two nations' isolated from each other and reduced to an impersonal cash
nexus, Braddon comes down clearly on the Tory side of maintaining class
connections through human relations and social involvement between the
classes. She sees the active and humanised involvement of patronage as part
of a long-standing and mutually constitutive social exchange that would
be broken down by institutional, detached modes of public charity that
absolve the wealthy of personally engaging their poorer neighbours. Sarah's
ability to cross over crucial social boundaries allows her to 'see' the fate of
the wealthy English family fatally isolating itself from its dependent neighbours and the poor. Braddon's depiction of the governess's view into the
bleak, ghost-ridden future of the ruling classes suggests that it is only by
crossing over the borders of class and national ideologies that the shadowy
body of humanity below can be 'seen'.

Braddon again returns to the conjunction between the ghostly apparatus lurking behind and within the domestic arena and the class distinctions
isolating ways of seeing and forms of knowledge in her 1879 story, 'The
Shadow in the Corner'. In this tale, she critiques a system that reserves

educational resources to the wealthy and middle class while ignoring those who must earn their own living in miserable domestic labour. Michael Bascom, a retired university professor of natural science who lives for his quiet and lonely research labours, occupies the old house at Wildheath Grange with his two elderly servants, Daniel Skegg and his wife. Skegg hires Maria, a 'waif and stray', the recently orphaned daughter of a small tradesman, to help his wife out as a maid-of-all-work.[17] When Maria turns out to be a pleasant, intelligent young woman, the master takes an interest in the 'pretty thing' dusting and straightening his books (4). But after her first night in the house, Maria begins to sicken and grow pale and attributes the problem to a nightmarish shadow of a hanged man that arises in the pre-dawn hours on the wall of her lonely attic room, awakening her early each day and disappearing at broad daylight. The master determines to expose Maria's fears as irrational by sleeping in the room himself. When he is awakened by the shadow that appears in the corner, he too feels weighted down by an 'agonising memory of a life wasted; the stings of humiliation and disgrace, shame, ruin' (9). In the full morning light, however, he despises himself for succumbing to the strange sensation, and when Skegg suspects that his master has also seen the phantom, Bascom boasts of an uninterrupted, restful night's sleep and retreats to his solitary studies in proud embarrassment, loath to let his servant think that he is also superstitious. Maria, informed by the jealous servant that her master denies seeing the apparition and thinks her a fool, returns to her garret room and in the early morning hangs herself in the corner.

In this tale Braddon criticises the way education continues, in spite of national reforms, to be the narrow reserve of the urban and the wealthy, isolating classes and endangering poor young women. Further, she suggests that the scientific rationality that underlies educative ideology is an unfeeling, cold basis for categorising and controlling knowledge, and that in the end this rationality is just as open to prejudice and self-serving application as the superstitious belief systems it replaces. The airy elitism of Bascom's 'fanatic' love of scientific research is shown to be wholly inadequate when the scientist faces the inexplicable shadow in the corner: he ultimately denies his own eyes and experience in the attic in order to uphold his authority over his servants and maintain a strict division of knowledge and rank between classes. At the same time Braddon suggests that the obtuse ignorance of the selfish old servants abuses the plight of rural girls who have few opportunities to get out from under the drudgery of serving other people.

Maria's education and work life are paired in this story with her master's to suggest the 'heavy burden of care' that weighs her down and contrasts her 'wasted' life toiling in Wildheath Grange with the comfortable ease of her employer. The 'stings of humiliation and disgrace, shame, [and] ruin' that worry Bascom in his night in the garret room seem self-pitying echoes of the real humiliation and ruin a life of drudgery causes Maria (9). The deathly shadow that forms on the wall in the early pre-dawn recalls the dreary hours of the Victorian maid-of-all-work. Like a spectral shadow of her real-life counterpart, Maria is also up early cleaning in Bascom's study and then 'disappearing' in broad daylight like a ghost: 'Whatever work she did there was done early in the morning, before the scholar's breakfast' (4). As the Victorian maidservant, Maria labours out of sight, a spectral agency moving the tables and chairs, tidying the books and emptying the grates, and disappearing to the 'other side' of the house, behind the walls, for most of the day. Braddon asks us to compare the days of these two workers, the scholar and the drudge, to see the common waste that confronts each: Maria's dusting of the volumes of books in Bascom's library is immediately mirrored in Bascom's 'dry-as-dust career' as a natural scientist (3–4). But it is Maria who is finally worked into the deadly corner; Bascom, fleeing from the 'melancholy fate' that meets his maid, ends his days at Oxford, 'where he found the society of congenial minds, and the books he loved' (11). Braddon suggests that the consequences of a wasted life take their toll more brutally on the poor working girl whose 'corner' is not a cloistered shelter of intellectual retreat, but a numbing boredom and exhaustion caused by tedious days that begin at unholy and unhealthy hours.

Maria's modest education is shown to be the crux of the problems she faces making a living. She had been educated by her father, who 'spared no expense' in giving her 'as good an education as a tradesman's daughter need wish for' (4). Yet both Bascom and the servant Skegg agree that her education is an impediment to her domestic work: Skegg growls that Maria's father was a 'fool' to educate her 'above her station' and Bascom concedes that this makes a 'bad bargain' for Skegg and his wife: 'You don't want a young lady to clean kettles and pans', Bascom tells his servant (3). Education, it seems is fine for the master, but neither man wants the char to entertain such airy pursuits. Writing at the end of the first decade of compulsory education, Braddon sharply exposes the lingering effects of a national ambivalence about educating young girls whose prospects remain tied to domestic labour. In rural England, Braddon suggests, little has changed since passage of the Education Act of 1870. The fate of serving girls remained dismally unchanged since the prior decade when, as one commentator had noted, rural complaints about the 'weakness' of girls in domestic service was directly attributed to their education:

Farmers' wives complain that girls of the present day are weaker than they used to be twenty or thirty years ago. They attribute this weakness, whether rightly or wrongly, to the effects of 'schooling'; and in some parts of the country a pound a year extra wages is given to a girl who cannot read, as that is a security that her constitution has not been injured by too much study. It must be allowed, that five hours a day of sedentary work, even in a well-ventilated school room, is a bad preparation for a life of incessant activity.[18]

Without a purpose for her education, Maria's careful preparation can only end in the futile desperation of such 'incessant activity'. But if Maria's background is perceived as over-educating her for work, her belief in the ghost is also seen by the men as ruinous, an annoying sign of under-education and rural ignorance: Bascom admonishes her to get 'these silly notions' out of her head or she 'will never do for the work-a-day world' (5). For rural women, the 'work-a-day world', for all its alienation, wants neither superstition nor education: her body is all that is required of her – her mind is best left empty. Reduced to a corporal mechanism, emptied of human agency and motivation, the working woman becomes a mere automaton, hollow and vague like the shadow in the corner.

Yet if Maria is caught in an untenable position between her mind and her body, her education and her labours, Braddon suggests that Bascom's own education has failed to prepare him for the world he inhabits as well. A professor at the university for ten years before retiring to his aloof studies at Wildheath Grange, Bascom is absorbed in work that seems as barren as Maria's. If her lot employs her body and wastes her mind, he is unable to return from the intellectual desert he inhabits to fully comprehend the living body next to him. Confused by the 'fair' and 'delicate' girl with 'translucent skin' and 'soft and pleasing accents issu[ing] from those rose-tinted lips', he cannot respond humanely and retreats to his 'considerations about dry bones', wondering about her as 'a creature of species hitherto unknown to him' (4). His training and disposition as a 'stern materialist' living among his books restrict his view so that Maria is to him a 'fellow-creature' to be dissected, studied and finally 'conquered':

For him the universe, with all its inhabitants, was a great machine, governed by inexorable laws. To such a man the idea of a ghost was simply absurd – as absurd – as the assertion that two and two make five, or that a circle can be formed of a straight line. Yet he had a kind of dilettante interest in the idea of a mind which could believe in ghosts. The subject offered an amusing psychological study. This poor little pale girl, now, had evidently got some supernatural terror into her head, which could only be conquered by rational treatment. (7)

Braddon shows little tolerance for the fixed laws and 'rational treatment' that categorise and conquer with indifference, ignoring the corporal and emotional qualities of human experience. She portrays such rationality as a cooler but equally brusque version of the 'perpetual warfare with spiders and beetles' that Mrs Skegg carries out in the solitude of the kitchen she 'rules over' (3). The lowly species of creatures that enter each of these private, enclosed empires – both Mrs Skeggs's and Bascom's – meet equally indifferent and arbitrary authority that witlessly destroys them.

Braddon shows in Maria's plight the futility of educating young women if they are to remain locked into drudge work surrounded by both high and low ignorance. Without gainful employment that considered them as more than mere vacant bodies to be exhausted in despairing conditions, orphaned girls and dependent women – regardless of education – would not find a way out of the corner in which they were trapped. The jealous servant Skegg ironically cuts to Braddon's point when he complains, 'Education might be hanged for him, if this was all it led to' (8). Clearly for Maria, whose life is wasted in dreary, menial work, education *is hanged* in the lonely garret corner of the scholar's home.

Braddon's ghost stories served during this period to provide her with a successful outlet for directing her growing discontent with social conditions in England. By 1882 and publication of her Christmas story, 'Flower and Weed', in *Mistletoe Bough*, Braddon was producing writing that, as Wolff notes, 'barely conceals its bitter social commentary on the behaviour of the upper classes'.[19] Her writing career increasingly continued to explicate the need for well-planned reform of philanthropic, educational and economic conditions. If the earlier years of her career had been haunted by her own precarious social position that left her open to attack, she quite made up for it in her later career, when she no longer feared recrimination could spoil her success. But her commitment to re-forming the outlines of those 'unknown regions beyond' the visible realm of respectable Victorian society had remained a constant, provocative motivation for her commentary. For Braddon, as for many more writers trafficking in the murky, ephemeral outlines of the Victorian ghost story, these tales served as a fantastic arena where the writer could cut herself loose from the 'facts', as Sigismund Smith had remonstrated, to write the truth of the stories that haunted the imagination. The supernatural tale became, then, a vehicle for translating what was truly scary in private and public life, what was always lurking in the shadows in the corners, what could not be hidden in the domestic comfort of the hearth.

The Victorian ghost story widely continued to refract the spirit of social reformation that shaped a modern England out of the traces of ancient relationships and the porous framework of a 'private' domestic arena. For Mary Elizabeth Braddon – and scores of other writers looking out to the world from the uncanny centre of the home – the alliances of the working household produced a full and marvellous body of textual material stepping silently into the parlour, crossing over the threshold dividing social realms of the home, and flitting across the view from the writer's desk to filter that local spectacle out to the world beyond the Victorian fireside.

NOTES

1 Charles Dickens, *Bleak House* (1854) (New York: W. W. Norton, 1977), p. 83.
2 A. S. Byatt, 'Morpho Eugenia' in *Angels and Insects* (New York: Vintage, 1994), p. 177.
3 For studies of the critical context of the ghost story, see P. Messent (ed.), *The Literature of the Occult: A Collection of Critical Essays* (Englewood Cliffs, NJ: Prentice Hall, 1981); J. Sullivan, *Elegant Nightmares: The British Ghost Story from Le Fanu to Blackwood* (Athens, GA: Ohio University Press, 1978); Virginia Dickerson, *Victorian Ghosts in the Noontide: Women Writers and the Supernatural* (Columbia and London: University of Missouri Press, 1996); Martin Tropp, *Images of Fear: How Horror Stories Helped Shape Modern Culture, 1818–1918* (Jefferson, NC and London: McFarland, 1990); Julia Briggs, *Night Visitors: The Rise and Fall of the Ghost Story* (London: Faber, 1977); T. Heller, *The Delights of Terror: An Aesthetics of the Tale of Terror* (Urbana: University of Illinois Press, 1987); Jenny Uglow, 'Introduction', *Victorian Ghost Stories by Eminent Women Writers*, ed. Richard Dalby (New York: Carroll and Graf, 1988); P. Penzoldt, *The Supernatural in Fiction* (New York: Humanities Press, 1965); Tsvetzan Todorov, *The Fantastic: A Structural Approach to a Literary Genre*, trans. R. Howard (Cleveland, OH: Case Western Reserve University Press, 1973); W. P. Day, *In the Circles of Fear and Desire: A Study of Gothic Fantasy* (Chicago: University of Chicago Press, 1985); M. Aguirre, *The Closed Space: Horror Literature and Western Symbolism* (Manchester and New York: Manchester University Press, 1990); John Grixti, *Terrors of Uncertainty: The Cultural Contexts of Horror Fiction* (London and New York: Routledge, 1989); and Mario Praz, *The Romantic Agony*, trans. A. Davidson, 2nd edn (London and New York: Oxford University Press, 1970).
4 J. A. Salmonson (ed.), *What Did Miss Darrington See?* (New York: Feminist Press, 1988), p. x.

5   Charles Dickens, *Dombey and Son* (1848) (London: Mandarin, 1991), p. 696. Dickens did not, however, endorse the public scrutiny of the private home without some ambivalence. In *American Notes* he criticises the New York press for 'dealing in round abuse and blackguard names; pulling off the roofs of private houses as the Halting Devil did in Spain'. Charles Dickens, *American Notes* (1842) (Oxford University Press, 1957), p. 88.

6   Donald J. Olsen, 'Victorian London: Specialisation, Segregation and Privacy', *Victorian Studies* 17 (1974), 265–78; p. 271.

7   Charles Dickens, 'Nurse's Stories', *The Uncommercial Traveller and Reprinted Pieces* (Oxford: Oxford University Press, 1958), p. 150.

8   Mary Elizabeth Braddon, *The Doctor's Wife* (London: J. Maxwell and Co., 1864), p. 99.

9   Mary Elizabeth Braddon, *The Lady's Mile* (London: Ward, Lock and Tyler, 1866), pp. 13–14.

10 Gertrude Himmelfarb, *The Idea of Poverty: England in the Early Industrial Age* (New York: Vintage, 1985), p. 404.

11 Robert L. Wolff, *Sensational Victorian: The Life and Fiction of Mary Elizabeth Braddon* (New York: Garland, 1979), p. 288. Recent analysis of Braddon's work has attempted to move beyond the autobiographical study into a critical context beyond the 'sensationalism' of her writings. See especially Marlene Tromp, Pamela K. Gilbert and A. Haynie (eds.), *Beyond Sensation: Mary Elizabeth Braddon in Context* (New York: State University of New York Press, 2000) and J. Carnell, *The Literary Lives of Mary Elizabeth Braddon* (Hastings: Sensation Press, 2000). For further studies including discussion of Braddon's works, see Patrick Brantlinger, 'What is Sensational about the Sensation Novel?', *Nineteenth-Century Fiction* 37 (1982), 1–28; Solveig C. Robinson, 'Editing *Belgravia*: M. E. Braddon's Defense of "Light Literature"', *Victorian Periodicals Review* 28 (1995), 109–22; Winifred Hughes, *The Maniac in the Cellar: Sensation Novels of the 1860s* (Princeton: Princeton University Press, 1980); Mary Elizabeth Braddon, *The Fatal Marriage and Other Stories*, ed. Chris Willis (Hastings: Sensation Press, 2000); and Richard Dalby (ed.), *The Cold Embrace and Other Ghost Stories* (Ashcroft, BC: Ash-Tree Press, 2000), which collect several of Braddon's short stories long out of print.

12 Cited in Sigmund Freud, 'The Uncanny' (1919), *Penguin Freud Library* vol. XIV: *Art and Literature*, ed. Albert Dickerson (London: Penguin, 1985), p. 345.

13 Mary Elizabeth Braddon, *Ralph the Bailiff and Other Stories* (London: Ward, Lock and Tyler, 1867), p. 15. Further references are included in the text.

14 Mary Elizabeth Braddon, 'At Chrighton Abbey' in *Victorian Ghost Stories: An Oxford Anthology*, eds. Michael Cox and R. A. Gilbert (Oxford: Oxford University Press, 1991), p. 163.

15 M. J. Peterson, 'The Victorian Governess: Status Incongruence in Family and Society' in *Suffer and Be Still: Women in the Victorian Age*, ed. Martha Vicinus (Bloomington: Indiana University Press, 1972), pp. 3–19; pp. 16–17.

16   Patrick Brantlinger, *Rule of Darkness: British Literature and Imperialism, 1830–1914* (Ithaca: Cornell University Press, 1988), p. 249.

17   Mary Elizabeth Braddon, 'The Shadow in the Corner', *All the Year Round*, New Series 23 (1879), Extra Summer Number, 1–11; p. 3. Further references are included in the text.

18   'On the Scarcity of Good Maidservants', *The Englishwoman's Review: A Journal of Woman's Work* 1 (1866), 12–26; p. 18.

19   Wolff, *Sensational Victorian*, p. 288.

CHAPTER 4

George Eliot's prophecies: coercive second sight and everyday thought reading

Pamela Thurschwell

In 1886, exactly ten years after George Eliot's final novel *Daniel Deronda* was published, another novel appeared with a sympathetic approach to the plight of Jews and a beautiful Jewish heroine named Mira. Set in Poland, Stuart Cumberland's shilling shocker *The Rabbi's Spell: A Russo-Jewish Romance* begins with the murder of Aaron Rosinsky, a Jewish moneylender. The evil Count Soltikoff, who has borrowed money from Rosinsky, is obviously responsible, but manages to pin the blame on Geza Polinsky, the lover of Rosinsky's daughter, Mira. Geza was meeting with a fugitive nihilist friend at the time of the murder. He refuses to betray his friend to claim him as an alibi and is therefore thrown in jail. At Geza's trial the nihilist friend arrives to vindicate Geza, but only manages to get both of them jailed for nihilism. In the meantime the Chief Rabbi is working like a detective on the case, as well as rallying the community. He carves a mysterious curse in Hebrew onto the tree under which Mira's father was murdered. Eventually Geza's innocence of both nihilism and the murder is proved; an attack on the Jews provoked by the Count's stirring up of anti-Semitic feeling is partially prevented; and the Count, under the influence of the Rabbi's spell, hangs himself on the same spot where the murder was committed. The curse in Hebrew that the Rabbi wrote turns out to read, 'He who hath done this bloody thing shall on this very spot render up his own life.'[1] Just as *Daniel Deronda* ends with Deronda and Mirah on the verge of making the long-awaited journey to Palestine, *The Rabbi's Spell* ends with Geza, Mira and the Chief Rabbi on a boat to Canada, having escaped the pre-pogrom anti-Semitism of Russia and Poland, gazing upon 'the land of liberty and hope in the purple distance'.[2]

Besides Judaism, one theme that connects *The Rabbi's Spell* to *Daniel Deronda* is a concern with the effects of second sight and thought transference. Just as *Daniel Deronda* contains, as I will argue, two very different prophetic figures in Mordecai and Gwendolen, *The Rabbi's Spell* also boasts two seers, one of whom is Jewish and deeply religious. The Rabbi is a powerful mystic figure for the Jewish community: 'He was their Delphic Oracle.'[3] Count Soltikoff fears the Chief Rabbi's supernatural powers, pointing out that he has a piercing mesmeric eye and that he 'is said to foretell the future'.[4] The other thought-reader in the book is the Czar's friend and confidant Prince Bela Krinitza: 'The prince had the character of being a seer, one who read men's hearts like an open book, and who could even forecast the future, having, it was said, acquired this faculty as much on the ground of his Tartar descent as from long residence in the East.' Prophecy is thereby defined in the novel as both learned and racially inherited. The Prince claims to have 'a deep psychological interest in crime'; he can mesmerise people, 'and when thought-reading came into vogue he speedily proved himself an adept in the art of divining the thoughts of others'.[5] On Mira's pleading, he travels to the prison where her lover is about to be executed for nihilism, to try to divine the truth of the charges, finally convincing the Czar that the charge should be dropped after 'reading' Geza and discerning that he is neither nihilist nor murderer.

The concerns of *The Rabbi's Spell* were timely because thought-reading did come into vogue during the 1880s, largely due to the popularity of the book's author. Stuart Cumberland made a career for himself as a thought-reader. His fame peaked in the 1880s with demonstrations of his prowess on subjects as various and well-known as W. T. Stead, Oscar Wilde, Grant Allen, Rudyard Kipling, Arthur Conan Doyle, Marie Corelli, Henry Labouchère and numerous crowned heads and political leaders from a long list of countries, culminating in a session at the House of Commons in which he 'read' the prime minister, William Gladstone.[6] Cumberland's significance lies both in the now-forgotten popular and scientific interest in thought reading and the difficulty of classifying what precisely it was he did. As Roger Luckhurst describes it, Cumberland's typical performance was 'something between an experimental demonstration, an entertainment, and a séance'.[7] Descriptions of his act makes it sound similar to a party game: a blindfolded Cumberland would find a hidden object that a person had picked out to concentrate on, or he would announce the numbers on a banknote that someone in the room had memorised for that purpose. Another, more dramatic, demonstration was the murder game, in which Cumberland would ask someone in the room to imagine murdering someone else in the room and the way they intended to do it. Cumberland would then read his subject's thoughts, identify the victim and act out the crime.

Luckhurst has discussed how performances such as Cumberland's contributed to ongoing debates about the nature of the psyche and to the developing field of psychology. The character of his performances opened up questions about the relationship between physiology and the supernatural. Cumberland himself always insisted that his readings were materialist and anti-Spiritualist: he read people's minds by reading their minute muscular movements, he claimed. Yet he performed for audiences and offered himself up for experimental surveillance by scientists as if there was something mysterious to reveal, something beyond the conjuring tricks he was sometimes accused of purveying.

He himself professed to believe in no psychic force. His performances could only be done by holding the hand of the person whose thoughts he read (although he did sometimes vary this by tying himself to his subject with a wire or a silk handkerchief).[8] This physical contact, so crucial to Cumberland's art, brought him into dispute with the Society for Psychical Research, who were looking for proof of telepathy as a dematerialised force. In his numerous books and articles on the subject, Cumberland argued that they would search in vain: 'It is not given to any thought-reader to read the thoughts of another save on the principle of physical interpretation, despite the assertions of the Psychical Society to the contrary.'[9] Cumberland was unusual in making no distinction between the likelihood of telepathic thought transference and communication with the dead, maintaining that both were impossible. He initially made his reputation through debunking Spiritualist mediums, and always insisted that his practices bore no relation to those of the Spiritualists. His readings were based on physical indications, not supernatural divination: 'The mind of man can be read, but not on the basis of what is termed telepathy . . . The mind is encased in matter and readable only by and through that matter.'[10]

Cumberland's career and novel are interestingly in tension, then. In his statements about his own work, he insists that thought-reading is a proper, methodical, material practice. But in *The Rabbi's Spell*, and the other sensational novels he writes, Cumberland relies on the spectacular effects of the supernatural forces of prophecy and clairvoyance. I use his work here to introduce some questions I will explore more fully in Eliot's work: questions about the agency of the subject who has second sight. Second sight and clairvoyance function in Eliot's work as on the one hand prophetic, elevated, nation- and vocation-forming, and on the other hand uncontrollable and unwanted, or banal and mundane, as in *The Lifted Veil*, a matter of an onslaught of unprocessable material information. The vision of the prophet is both reduced and raised by comparing it with the vision of the scientist, who looks closely and discerns much more than the eye could normally see (or in *The Lifted Veil*, than the ear could normally hear).

Cumberland's self-presentation, his novels and his non-fictional writings negotiate, in a different register, some of the same concerns about the agency of the seer as *Daniel Deronda*. Cumberland's unusual career path indicates one surprising use of clairvoyant powers in the 1870s and 80s, even when those powers are defined by their owner as well within the realm of scientific explanation (and well within his own control).

Eliot's favoured term for prediction in *Daniel Deronda* is 'second sight', although references to prophets and prophecy also abound. Prophecy has an ancient history, but 'second sight' is a more recent term. According to Martin Martin, writing in 1703, second sight is a prophetic phenomenon peculiar to the inhabitants of the Scottish Isles. Martin describes it as 'the singular faculty of seeing an otherwise invisible object'.[11] Samuel Johnson expands on that definition in his *A Journey to the Western Islands of Scotland* of 1775: 'The receptive faculty, for power it cannot be called, is neither voluntary nor constant. The appearances have no dependence upon choice: they cannot be summoned, detained, or recalled. The impression is sudden and the effect often painful.'[12] Second sight is therefore involuntary (a 'receptive faculty' rather than an active 'power') and disquieting; it is by no means desired by those upon whom it prevails. It is a vision of something far distant in space or time, or both. A. J. L. Busst has traced the ways in which, by the second half of the nineteenth century, the term 'second sight' becomes removed from its imagined origins in the Highlands and diffuses as a more general characteristic of human nature, an outbreak of the supernatural that could potentially appear in anyone.[13] By the time Eliot employs it in *Daniel Deronda* it has migrated from the mysterious Scot to the mysterious Jew, but also to the very English consciousness of that 'frail' and superstitious 'vessel', Gwendolen.

This essay explores some competing versions of the permeable, impressionable subject of second sight who experiences the world as dangerously or pleasurably encroaching – whose own mind is breached by the contents of other minds or by knowledge of the future. Can one take control of second sight or does it always take control of you? Stuart Cumberland makes a career of appearing clairvoyant and telepathic, but he insists that he is not subject to second sight. Instead of being a passive recipient of vision, he is an active reader. What he does resembles the developing hermeneutic method of reading the detail, a power that will come to be exploited and described by such diverse fictional and non-fictional practitioners as Sherlock Holmes, T. H. Huxley and Sigmund Freud.[14] Second sight, on the other hand, appears as gift or curse, not as method to employ or goal to achieve. And yet the dynamics of second sight in the book are by no means as cut and dried as that definition implies. By looking at the portrayal of second sight in *Daniel Deronda* (1876) we can trace some of the ways in which anxieties about political and psychological agency in the late nineteenth century are traversed by the supernatural. And by thinking about different kinds of voluntary and involuntary prophetic vision – both that of Eliot's omniscient narrative voice and that of Mordecai and Gwendolen – we can begin to understand how these differences help determine the narrative shape of *Daniel Deronda*.

In his book *Telepathy and Literature*, Nicholas Royle has catalogued *Daniel Deronda*'s relentless incursions from the 'other world' of the Victorian supernatural. The novel 'is pervaded by ghosts and "spirits", by forecasting, foresight and "second sight", by strange intuitions, fantastical coincidences, instances of apparent telepathy or omniscience'.[15] For a book justly celebrated for its psychological realism, this insight suggests a paradox, one that extends more broadly to all of Eliot's work and becomes even more apparent with the onset of psychoanalytic theories of the mind and modernist renderings of the subject: that is, that attempting to represent the workings of the human mind realistically, through all its sudden turns, unwanted memories and unconscious desires, inevitably brings one into the metaphorical and literal spaces of the supernatural. Terry Castle has pointed to this phenomenon as a legacy of the Gothic novel. Around the end of the eighteenth century, Castle claims, the mind became a potentially supernatural site.[16] Castle's analysis suggests one interesting way of viewing the incursion of the supernatural into the nineteenth-century realistic novel (as well as the place of the supernatural in the development of modern psychology). Gothic elements not only invade the mind when, for instance, characters are 'haunted' by memories or obsessive thoughts, but these Gothic elements also structure the narrative world of Eliot's fictions. Telepathy, as Nicholas Royle has suggested, is an unavoidable convention of the modern psychological novel.

This becomes clear when we examine the nature of Eliot's omniscient narration. As many critics have noted, Eliot's strong narrative voice is not as consistent as it might initially appear: her narration slips between the perspective of the removed, all-knowing sage and an identification with the position of the uninformed reader or character eagerly awaiting what might happen next. One of Eliot's central concerns is how – or if – we can possibly interpret correctly those who make up our social world. For Eliot, a just interpretation of someone always requires an act of sympathetic understanding.[17] She often focuses on the difficulty of predicting the inner motivations of a person from their outer bearing, as in *Adam*

Bede, where her narrator discourses at length on the dangers of reading too much moral good into Hetty's perfect eyelashes, which are simply an accident of inheritance rather than a secure indication of the soul within.[18] Her focus on misreadings and failures of understanding, such as those between Lydgate and Rosamond in *Middlemarch*, serves to highlight the fact that the nineteenth-century omniscient narrator has a seemingly uncanny knowledge of the minds and motivations of her characters. Eliot's narrative method relies on dissecting her characters' interiority: it is an unrealistic incursion into their otherwise private thoughts. As Richard Menke puts it, speaking of Eliot's most obviously supernatural tale, *The Lifted Veil* (1859), 'Not only clairvoyance, but also science, raises the veil of individual subjectivity in *The Lifted Veil* . . . As they do so they simultaneously highlight and defamiliarise a convention so basic that it is difficult to fully recognise it as such: that realist fiction may, without forgoing its realism, pretend to give us access to something we never encounter in real life – the unspoken thoughts of others.'[19]

Eliot's final novel revisits many of the questions raised by *The Lifted Veil*. In *Daniel Deronda* second sight is integral to what motivates both Mordecai and Gwendolen, and to the way they influence the highly susceptible Deronda. Mordecai and Gwendolen seek to pull Deronda in different directions partly in reaction to their very different prophetic visions, as well as their yearning spiritual and erotic desires for him.[20] Deronda, constantly attempting to fulfil these needs, is beset by a vision of his own inevitable failure: 'It was as if he had a vision of himself besought with outstretched arms and cries, while he was caught by waves and compelled to mount the vessel bound for a far off coast.'[21] Prefiguring Grandcourt's death by drowning, as well as his own final journey to the East, this imagery also indicates the massive pull of the demands of others that the susceptible, sympathetic Deronda experiences. He begins the book as an intensely permeable subject, wanting to be all things to all people, but he eventually realises that this permeability has its limits; choices have to be made. Mordecai and his Jewish ancestry get under his skin (and into his mind) where Gwendolen and the English aristocracy cannot.

Second sight helps set this narrative trajectory. Gwendolen and Mordecai predict their two plot lines, and Deronda initially tries to satisfy both before realising he must relinquish his place in one. Chapter 38 of *Daniel Deronda* opens with the following assertion:

'Second-sight' is a flag over disputed ground. But it is a matter of knowledge that there are persons whose yearnings, conceptions – nay, travelled conclusions – continually take the form of images which have a foreshadowing power: the deed they would do starts up before them in complete shape, making a coercive type; the event they hunger for or dread rises into vision with a seed-like growth, feeding itself fast on unnumbered impressions. (453)

The rhetoric of the passage works to establish second sight as a given, a 'matter of knowledge' (whose knowledge, we might want to ask?); events follow the desire for them (or the fear of them) naturally, through 'a seed-like growth'.[22] But, importantly, the vision of second sight is also a 'coercive type', two significant words to which I will return. The 'ground' of the reality of the supernatural is being debated vigorously at this time by investigators who will go on to become psychical researchers. But in yet another sense the metaphor also reminds us that planting a flag takes unmarked ground and makes it into a nation – that materially elusive psychic construction that relies more on common linguistic and cultural bonds between people than on the land beneath their feet. For Jews such as Mordecai, the nation is an imaginary one: a mixture of prophetic desire for a united future and nostalgia for a lost past.[23]

In this paragraph about second sight we can see Eliot's ideal model of Mordecai's prophetic gifts taking shape. Mordecai is an active seer; his visions may rise of their own accord but he will also make them grow: 'Mordecai's mind wrought so constantly in images, that his coherent trains of thought often resembled the significant dreams attributed to sleepers by waking persons in their most inventive moments; nay, they often resembled genuine dreams in their way of breaking off the passage from the known to the unknown' (455). The work of Mordecai's conscious mind resembles a dream-world; he conjures up prophetic truth through imaging, and his power lies in controlling those visions. If dreams are one connecting point between the known and the unknown, Mordecai's dreams need to be made solid and significant by a sympathetic narrator, as well as by his own interventions, in order for the unknown to become conceivable. The book naturalises prophetic vision by ratifying Mordecai's hallucinatory desires. Deronda really is a dream come true, and Mordecai has worked hard for his vision.

Eliot attempts to make the passage from the unknown to the known palatable by picturing Mordecai's visions as similar to that of an experimental scientist: 'Mordecai lifted his cap and waved it – feeling in that moment that his inward prophecy was fulfilled. Obstacles, incongruities, all melted into the sense of completion with which his soul was flooded by this outward satisfaction of his longing. His exultation was not widely different from that of the experimenter, bending over the first stirrings of change that correspond to what in the fervour of concentrated previ-sion his thought had foreshadowed' (473–4). His prevision is justified and supported by the experimental framework that similarly foreshadows and predicts. Deronda himself seems almost to become a product of Mordecai's scientifically-sanctioned forecasting imagination: an experiment in creating a Jew that necessitates his discovery of Jewish ancestry. As Cynthia Chase has pointed out, conversion is not imagined as a possibility in the world of the book: 'To be a Jew (and this is emphasised by the narrator, who never suggests that Deronda might simply "embrace" the Jewish "faith") is to have been born a Jew, not merely to take up the spiritual and cultural tradition of Judaism.'[24]

Mordecai's second sight is motivated by his 'yearning for transmission' of Judaism, both as biological and cultural inheritance (454). He needs someone who will carry on his work and transmit his writings to a wider public, who will be his 'executive', active self after his death. Before the ar-rival of Deronda, Mordecai teaches Hebrew to young Jacob Cohen, whose obvious deficiencies as a pupil he overlooks because 'The boy moved him with that idealising affection which merges the qualities of the individ-ual child in the glory of childhood and the possibilities of a long future' (457). Mordecai, on the verge of death himself, disregards Jacob's indi-vidual foibles to see him as representing life and youth, the possibility of transmission into the future. Eliot's repeated use of the word 'type' in relation to Jacob and Deronda foreshadows the 'coercive type' of second sight.[25] Hans Meyrick describes Jacob as 'that remarkable type of young Israel' (620). Typing suggests racialising and stereotyping Jews, but from Mordecai's perspective it is also key for propelling Judaism into the fu-ture. It is this sense of Jacob embodying potential transmission that draws Mordecai into metaphorically 'typing' his knowledge onto him, making Jacob his medium of transmission of himself, in lieu of a better one. The passage that ends with Mordecai seeing in Jacob 'the possibilities for a long future' continues with 'and this feeling had drawn him on, at first without premeditation, and afterwards with conscious purpose, to a sort of outpour-ing in the ear of the boy' (457). Mordecai pours himself and his thoughts into Jacob, who reluctantly learns to repeat them: '"The boy will get them engraved within him," thought Mordecai; "It is a way of printing"' (458). Printing or engraving onto people is an evocative image of the kind of rad-ical transmission, involving both Jewish blood and Jewish scripture, that Eliot's work requires. When Deronda does come along to satisfy Mordecai's intense predictive longing, he can only be the proper, prophesied vessel if he is Jewish. But he is also clearly the type Mordecai has been searching for.

Before Deronda's arrival on the scene, Mordecai has searched for his 'type' of Jewish successor in the superior physical specimens of the art museums, as well as in dreams: 'Sensitive to physical characteristics, he had, both abroad and in England, looked at pictures as well as men, and in a vacant hour he had sometimes lingered in the National Gallery in search of paintings which might feed his hopefulness with grave and noble types of the human form, such as might well belong to men of his own race' (454). In his first encounter with Deronda in the bookshop, Mordecai 'saw a face and frame which seemed to him to realise the long-conceived type' (460). The 'type' of the friend which he has imagined is indeed the 'coercive type' of the event that second sight predicts. Art seems to verify the possibility of the erotically charged object of political and social desire, the sympathetic, Jewish Englishman that Mordecai forecasts and that the narrative produces. When Mordecai spots Deronda from his look-out on Blackfriars Bridge, he has long imagined exactly that scene, with himself as viewer. He has repeatedly pictured this unknown figure advancing towards him:

It began to advance, and a face became discernible; the words youth, beauty, refine-ment, Jewish birth, noble gravity, turned into hardly individual but typical form and colour: gathered from his memory of faces seen among the Jews of Holland and Bohemia, and from the paintings which revived that memory. Reverently let it be said of this mature spiritual need that it was akin to the boy's and girl's picturing of the future beloved; but the stirrings of such young desire are feeble compared with the passionate current of an ideal life straining to embody itself, made intense by resistance to imminent dissolution. (456)

This passionate imaging is compared to an Eve of St Agnes scenario in which a youth pictures his or her own future love in a dream which turns into reality. But Mordecai's love is also bound up with his intense battle against his coming disappearance into death. The ideal life he yearns to both embrace and set on its course is an erotic image, but also a narrative one. Unlike the hero of *The Lifted Veil*, who longs for death, Mordecai seeks an extension of his own life through conjuring up a vessel of transmission who will continue the narrative, taking it from the personal to the grandly historical.

Mordecai is, then, an active seer, using second sight to ward off his own dissolution. He coerces others, particularly Deronda, by imposing his vision of the future upon them. However, the novel appears to ask how we could structure lives or novels without coercion. Mordecai's annexing of Deronda cannot be condemned as entirely coercive, because Deronda is searching for a past, a future and a cause; he wants to be annexed.[26] His early inability to commit to a career is bound up in his desire for that overwhelming vocational call that must be answered. The sensible Sir Hugo sees this explicitly in terms of Deronda's desire for revealed prophetic truth. Trying to convince Deronda to go into politics, he says to him, 'The business of the country must be done – her Majesty's Government carried on, as the old Duke said. And it never could be, my boy, if everybody looked at politics as if they were prophecy, and demanded an inspired vocation' (367).

But in this book of course politics *are* prophecy when it comes to Judaism. Deronda finds his inspired vocation when he is 'strangely wrought upon' by Mordecai (475). He lets Mordecai's dreams infect his own. When Deronda goes to Genoa to meet his mother and discover his origins, he thinks about the exiled Spanish Jews who landed briefly in Genoa in the fifteenth century, and he finds his own desires entangled with his historical imagination:

Inevitably dreamy constructions of a possible ancestry for himself would weave themselves with historic memories which had begun to have a new interest for him on his discovery of Mirah, and now, under the influence of Mordecai, had become irresistibly dominant. He would have sealed his mind against such constructions if it had been possible, and he had never yet fully admitted to himself that he wished the facts to verify Mordecai's conviction: he inwardly repeated that he had no choice in the matter, and that wishing was folly. (598)

Deronda's mind has been irresistibly invaded by Mordecai's plans for him – sealing himself against them is no longer an option. A passage like this one indicates the way in which the individual's erotic desires become interwoven with the desire for a history; prophecy makes that interweaving more plausible. Deronda's 'dreamy constructions' of the Spanish diaspora pull him almost literally into the ancestry he desires.

Initially, Deronda is seen as too permeable and malleable, open to too many stories, too many demands. When Deronda finds Mirah by the river his thought processes are almost self-annihilating in his openness to outside influence:

He was forgetting everything else in a half-speculative, half-involuntary identification of himself with the objects he was looking at, thinking how far it might be possible habitually to shift his centre till his own personality would be no less outside him than the landscape – when the sense of something moving on the bank opposite him where it was bordered by a line of willow-bushes, made him turn his glance thitherward. (181)

Deronda's desire to shift his centre, to find his own personality outside himself, seems to result in an actual occurrence – something moves on the bank. Mirah, as she turns out to be, is here portrayed as a projection of Deronda's need to find a cause or motivating force outside himself, just as Deronda's identity is shown as a projection of Mordecai's. Deronda's desire, before the finding of his own past and identity, is for the evacuation of desire, a self lost in the landscape, or in that sea of outstretched needy hands begging him to save them from drowning. The novel portrays the movement from Deronda's half-speculative, half-involuntary identifications with others to his adoption of Mordecai's prophecies for him as his own. In becoming an active agent, in taking up his birthright and fulfilling Mordecai's desires for him, Deronda chooses his vision of the future. The question of coercion becomes, like the possibility of conversion, beside the point.

Yet the question of coercion must be significant to a novel that begins with it in its first paragraph:

Was she beautiful or not beautiful? And what was the secret of form or expression which gave the dynamic quality to her glance? Was the good or the evil genius dominant in those beams? Probably the evil; else why was the effect of unrest rather than of disturbed charm? Why was the wish to look again felt as coercion and not as a longing in which the whole being consents? (5)

Establishing the difference between a longing in which the whole being consents and that which is experienced as coercion is a difficult task. Would not that type of overwhelming longing simply be the most successful coercion of all: Mordecai's power, rather than Gwendolen's? The book suggests that that first mesmeric, dynamic glance between Gwendolen and Deronda coerces him into redeeming her necklace and entangling himself with her life. But Gwendolen is also coerced by her own terrifying prevision of (and desire for) her husband's death. By contrast, Mordecai's enveloping second-sight is coercive for the whole novel, lending it, and Deronda, a plot line and teleology as well as origin – the dream of a Jewish birth and a Jewish nation. That 'flag over disputed ground' comes to signify national as well as individual desires. Prophecy moves from the realm of the individual to the political.

Mordecai and Gwendolen, then, are the two figures in the novel most strongly associated with second sight. However, Mordecai's prophetic statements are supported by a series of comparisons to scientific and artistic accomplishment, while Gwendolen's susceptibility to portents is portrayed as atavistic and superstitious.[27] Early in the book Gwendolen's young half-sister Isabel opens a hinged panel in their new home to disclose 'the picture

of an upturned dead face, from which an obscure figure seemed to be fleeing with outstretched arms' (24). According to Isabel, the panel indicates
Gwendolen's fate, rather than that of any of the other people present.
She predicts ominously, 'You will never stay in this room by yourself,
Gwendolen' (24). Later, when Gwendolen is performing for company the
part of Hermione in a tableau from *The Winter's Tale*, the panel flies open,
revealing its morbid scene:

> Everyone was startled, but all eyes in the act of turning towards the opened panel
> were recalled by a piercing cry from Gwendolen, who stood without change of
> attitude, but with a change of expression that was terrifying in its terror. She looked
> like a statue into which a soul of Fear had entered: her pallid lips were parted; her
> eyes, usually narrowed under their long lashes, were dilated and fixed. (56)

Later, the panel and the tableau scene will haunt Gwendolen as a foreshadowing of her own helpless relation to her despised husband's death by
drowning. The image of Gwendolen as a statue 'into which the soul of Fear'
has entered is appropriate to the book's dynamics of agency and paralysis
around foresight. Gwendolen, playing Hermione, plays a heroine silenced,
made into a statue, by her husband's cruelty. She is about to awaken, to re-
assert herself into the play. Gwendolen similarly wants the tableau to allow
for a little movement on her part, a little action: 'Gwendolen urged that
instead of the mere tableau there should be just enough acting of the scene
to introduce the striking up of the music as a signal for her to step down
and advance' (55). When Gwendolen freezes at the sight of the unwanted
portent, she becomes subject to a pre-determined future, incapable of participating in the action she desires to control. She freezes similarly at the
actual moment of Grandcourt's death. Her relationship to the prophetic is
that of a rabbit caught in the headlights, a paralysed, pessimistic relation.

James Caron has divided what he calls the novel's 'rhetoric of magic'
into two categories: the passive, 'a superstitious dread in which events seem
to occur outside one's ken and therefore have a threatening kind of magic
about them', and the active, 'the sorcery of the conscious imaginative will
in which events are seen as a dialectic of planning and circumstance and
the sense of magic comes from circumstances conforming to the plan'.[28]
Gwendolen and Mordecai are the exemplars of these two positions of superstitious dread and imaginative will. The heightened fear Gwendolen
feels at the sight of the panel with the *tableau vivant* of the dead face and
fleeing figure prefigures her paralysis at the moment of Grandcourt's death
by drowning; conversely Mordecai's yearning desire for the founding of
a Jewish homeland inspires his prophetic certainty that Deronda is the

(Jewish) man for the job: his desire appears to make Deronda's discovery of his Jewish ancestry necessary and inevitable.[29] Both Mordecai's and Gwendolen's wishes can be seen to make things happen in the world of the narrative, but their status as active (prophetic) and passive (hysterical) helps determine the way they are valued.

Caron's emphasis on the 'rhetoric' of magic indicates that the book's use of magic masks other, non-supernatural ideas, a series of questions about the nature of agency, motivation and fate. *Daniel Deronda* is undoubtedly driven by these questions, but there is also, as I have suggested by tracing a line from *Deronda* through to the concerns of the novelist and performer, Stuart Cumberland, a way in which the naturalisation of magic is itself a subject for debate, outside the bounds of rhetoric. The novel presents a world which is mired in crises of motivation. Many of its characters are threatened by a dangerous lack of direction: Grandcourt and Gwendolen's aristocratic malaise leaves them drifting, bored, even violent; Deronda's diffuse sympathy threatens him with ineffectuality and feminisation. Mordecai's prophetic visions seem to be the only effective solution to these crises of motivation. The right sort of 'magical future vision' endows a person with something towards which to strive. The much-maligned 'Jewish' half of the novel provides a blueprint for action, leaving the English aristocrats, particularly the widowed Gwendolen, struggling for some sort of meaning or motivation. Deronda's parting words to her amount to telling her to 'get a life'. After Deronda leaves her for Palestine, Gwendolen is reduced to insisting upon her own will to existence: '"I am going to live", said Gwendolen, bursting out hysterically' (777). Gwendolen's 'hysterical' insistence upon life undermines her desire to do as Deronda tells her. As Mary Jacobus points out about the *The Lifted Veil*, the disease of hysteria belongs to a paralysed time-frame – the subject of hysteria is caught up in the repetition of the past.[30] How can we believe Gwendolen at the end of the book, when it is not at all clear what the content of her life might be?

Gwendolen's second sight is against her from the start. Interestingly, her first instance of second sight is in relation to Deronda's redemption of her necklace: 'Something – she never quite knew what – revealed to her before she opened the packet that it contained the necklace she had just parted with' (17). When the accompanying note refers to a 'stranger who has found Miss Harleth's necklace', 'she at once believed in the first image of "the stranger" that presented itself to her mind. It was Deronda' (17–18).[31] Later her extreme reaction to the panel is in keeping with her liability to 'fits of spiritual dread . . . Solitude in any wide scene impressed her with an undefined feeling of immeasurable existence aloof from her, in the midst of which she was helplessly incapable of asserting herself' (59). Here, prophetic dread functions similarly to the sublime – a terrifying but potentially empowering recognition of vastness that can be harnessed to the artist's purposes, if one actively uses it rather than feeling overwhelmed in the face of it. But Gwendolen can find no active place for herself in her superstitious version of second sight; she cannot put her fear to good use. In fact Deronda's priest-like offers of assistance urge her in the other direction, towards passivity. He advises her to harness her dread and remorse, in the face of her humiliating marriage, to keep her from desperate action. He describes it as another version of second sight: 'Take your fear as a safeguard. It is like quickness of hearing. It may make consequences passionately present to you. Try to take hold of your sensibility, and use it as if it were a faculty like vision' (436).

A psychoanalytic-inflected reading of second sight in the novel points towards a disturbing difference between Mordecai's and Gwendolen's visions – the active and the paralysing. In *Daniel Deronda*, prophecy works splendidly for men, but disastrously for women. The successful male prophet's patriarchal prerogative allows him to recruit Deronda to his beloved political project: the future founding (or re-founding) of the state of Israel. Deronda rescues the Jewish son and brings him back to the fold, so that he can bear more Jewish sons. On the other hand, Gwendolen, the female seer, is a hysteric who foresees only death, bears no children, predicts the murder of the patriarch, and wishes to return to an untroubled presymbolic, pre-Oedipal maternal attachment – stasis or repetition, rather than the vaguely defined, but presumably forward-looking 'life' Deronda urges her towards.[32] Early in the book, after rejecting Rex's marriage proposal, Gwendolen finds herself overwhelmed by a sense of despair: '"Oh mamma, what can become of my life? There is nothing worth living for!"' (77). If life for Gwendolen, and for the other thwarted ambitious women in the book (Mrs Glasher, the Princess), is defined by marriage and propagation, she rejects it and retreats, saying to her mother, '"I can't bear anyone to be very near me but you"' (77).

The chastening of Gwendolen comes, in a sense, because her vision of the future is bleakly bound by the impossible relations between the sexes. The last section of the book is labelled 'Fruit and Seed'; Gwendolen, like the Princess Halm-Eberstein (who does not wish to be a 'makeshift link' in a chain of paternal Judaic transmission), is the enemy of fruitful transmission. Fearful of further injuring Lydia Glasher and her displaced son, Gwendolen dreads offspring even more than she dreads physical contact with Grandcourt. She is repeatedly criticised throughout the book for not seeing beyond her own small and personal perspective, for not imagining that Deronda may have ties other than to her. Of course, Mordecai's vision in this instance is similarly limited. He sees Deronda as unfettered by other ties; it is only Mirah who anxiously worries about the claim of the 'Vandyke duchess' on him. But it is Gwendolen who is punished for an egotism that makes her visions terrifying rather than productive. The moment when Deronda tells her of his plans to go to the East and devote himself to the Jews is experienced by her as an annihilating confrontation with the sublime of history, or others' experiences:

The thought that he might come back after going to the East, sank before the bewildering vision of these wide-spreading purposes in which she felt herself reduced to a mere speck... There comes a terrible moment to many souls when the great movements of the world, the larger destinies of mankind, which have lain aloof in newspapers and other neglected reading, enter like an earthquake into their own lives – when the slow urgency of growing generations turns into the tread of an invading army or the dire clash of civil war, and grey fathers know nothing to seek for but the corpses of their blooming sons, and girls forget all vanity to make lint and bandages which may serve for the shattered limbs of their betrothed husbands. Then it is as if the Invisible Power that has been the object of lip-worship and lip-resignation became visible according to the imagery of the Hebrew poet, making the flames his chariot, and riding on the wings of the wind, till the mountains smoke and the plains shudder under the rolling fiery visitation. (774)

The imagery of this passage shows the necessity for a kind of world-historical sympathetic permeability that Gwendolen lacks, or that only comes to her in terrified and uncontrollable moments of divination. If the experiences of others enter gently and constantly, as they do for Deronda, in half-speculative, half-involuntary identifications, then they will not enter like an earthquake and destroy the self. But perhaps what we have been defining here as Gwendolen's paralysed, hysterical second sight just foresees a different kind of future: a future, or lack of one, for women. This is not so much a lack of politics as a different kind of politics. Meeting Grandcourt's mistress, Mrs Glasher, for the first and only time, she experiences another moment of second sight: 'Gwendolen, watching Mrs Glasher's face while she spoke, felt a sort of terror: it was as if some ghastly vision had come to her in a dream and said, "I am a woman's life"' (145). The Princess Halm-Eberstein fulfils a similarly feminist prophetic function in the book, and is similarly silenced and killed off so that Mordecai's version of second sight, which is linked to that of the patriarchal desire for transmission of Deronda's grandfather, can prevail.

In her apparently realist novel Eliot uses the occult thematically and as narrative catalyst to enable and disable individual, national and cultural transmission. In the process, the telepathic and prophetic yearning of a man, Mordecai, for another man becomes the motor for a successful religious, national and cultural 'transference of self' – the replenishment and renewal of the Jews. Finally, *Daniel Deronda* tells a story of two kinds of prophetic transmission which cannot be easily separated but which seem unable to coexist; that of the fearful English woman and the powerful Jewish mystic; the powerless Cassandra and the spiritually, if not physically, vigorous prophet. The efficacy of second sight is related to its active and passive forms, as well as its productive and non-reproductive possibilities: the novel uses it for men and for women to extend some possible plots and cut off others. Helped by various kinds of metaphorically naturalised but still mysterious thought-transmission, including prophetic forecasting, *Daniel Deronda*'s eponymous hero learns how to be a permeable (but not too permeable) subject, and about which coercions to welcome and which to avoid.

NOTES

1   Stuart Cumberland, *The Rabbi's Spell: A Russo-Jewish Romance* (London and New York: Frederick Warne and Co., 1886), p. 183.
2   Ibid.
3   Ibid., p. 32.
4   Ibid., p. 49.
5   Ibid., pp. 120, 118.
6   Cumberland told his stories many times in memoirs, including *A Thought-Reader's Thoughts: Being the Impressions and Confessions of Stuart Cumberland* (London: Sampson, Row, Marston, Searle and Rivington, 1888) and *That Other World: Personal Experiences of Mystics and their Mysticism* (London: Grant Richards Ltd, 1918). The only recent writing on Cumberland is Roger Luckhurst's brilliant article on him and the American performer Washington Irving Bishop, 'Passages in the Invention of the Psyche: Mind-Reading in London, 1881–4' in *Encounters: Transactions between Science and Culture in the Nineteenth Century*, eds. Josephine McDonagh and Roger Luckhurst (Manchester: Manchester University Press, 2002), pp. 117–50. I discovered Luckhurst's work on Cumberland in the midst of my own and it has been invaluable to me.
7   Luckhurst, 'Passages in the Invention of the Psyche', p. 117.
8   Stuart Cumberland, 'Pin-Finding and Thought-Reading at Charing Cross', *Pall Mall Gazette* 39 (1884), 10. Also in Cumberland, *A Thought-Reader's Thoughts*, p. 29.

9   Cumberland, *A Thought-Reader's Thoughts*, p. 316. Cumberland and ri-
    val thought-reader Bishop were denounced by William Barrett in *Journal
    of the Society for Psychical Research* as 'pseudo' thought-readers. Whereas
    Cumberland insisted that physical contact was necessary, Barrett and the
    SPR were only interested in dematerialised thought transmission. They also
    questioned the spectacular, public nature of Cumberland's exhibitions, en-
    dorsing the laboratory conditions of the Society's experiments as more sci-
    entific. William Barrett, 'Pseudo Thought-Reading', *Journal of the Society for
    Psychical Research* 1 (1884), 10. See Luckhurst, 'Passages in the Invention of
    the Psyche'.
10 Cumberland, *That Other World*, p. 172.
11 Martin Martin, *A Description of the Western Islands CIRCA 1695, Including a
    Voyage to St Kilda by the Same Author and a Description of the Western Islands
    of Scotland by Sir Donald Munro*, ed. Donald J. Macleod (Stirling: Aeneas
    Mackay, 1934), p. 321.
12 Samuel Johnson, *A Journey to the Western Isles of Scotland*, ed. Mary Lascelles
    (1775; New Haven: Yale University Press, 1971), p. 89. Cited in Catherine
    Wynne, 'Mesmeric Exoticism, Idolatrous Beliefs, and Bloody Rituals:
    Mesmerism, Catholicism and Second Sight in Bram Stoker's Fiction',
    Victorian Review 26 (2000), 43–63; p. 58.
13 A. J. L. Busst, 'Scottish Second Sight: The Rise and Fall of a European Myth',
    European Romantic Review 5 (1995), 149–77.
14 See Carlo Ginzburg, 'Morelli, Freud, Sherlock Holmes: Clues and Scientific
    Method', in *The Sign of Three: Dupin, Holmes, Pierce*, eds. Umberto Eco
    and Thomas Sebeok (Bloomington: Indiana University Press, 1983) pp. 81–
    118. See also T. H. Huxley's article, 'On the Method of Zadig: Retrospective
    Prophecy as a Function of Science' (1880) in *Collected Essays*, vol. IV (London:
    Macmillan and Co., 1893), pp. 1–23.
15 Nicholas Royle, *Telepathy and Literature* (Oxford: Basil Blackwell, 1990),
    p. 92.
16 Terry Castle, *The Female Thermometer: Eighteenth-Century Culture and the
    Invention of the Uncanny* (Oxford: Oxford University Press, 1995).
17 An understanding of the nature of sympathy in Eliot is key to understanding
    her uses of thought transference and second sight. Royle discusses this, but a
    particularly nuanced discussion of sympathy in *Daniel Deronda* can be found
    in David Marshall, *The Figure of Theater* (New York: Columbia University
    Press, 1986).
18 George Eliot, *Adam Bede* (1859), ed. Leonee Ormond (London: Everyman's
    Library, 1992), pp. 171–3. Eliot's interest in reading character dovetails with her
    interest in physiognomy and phrenology. See also B. M. Gray, 'Pseudoscience
    and George Eliot's 'The Lifted Veil'', *Nineteenth-Century Fiction* 36 (1992),
    407–23 and 'Afterword' in George Eliot, *The Lifted Veil* (1859), ed. Beryl Gray
    (London: Virago, 1985), pp. 69–91.
19 Richard Menke, 'Fiction as Vivisection: G. H. Lewes and George Eliot', *ELH*
    67 (2000), 617–53; p. 630. Menke's argument about the close connections

between current debates on vivisection and the realist novel's dissection of consciousness has been exceedingly helpful to my formulations here. The problem of how you actually retrieve the content of others' minds, however, is not exhausted by the experimental psychology (Gwendolen as experimental subject/frog) that he explores, since it measures only reactions to stimuli, not the workings of the inner mind. The late-nineteenth-century fascination with telepathy can be seen as intersecting with the more radical desires of Eliot's fiction to uncover the workings of consciousness in all its ambivalence and confusion. For more on telepathy at the end of the nineteenth century, see Pamela Thurschwell, *Literature, Technology and Magical Thinking 1880–1920* (Cambridge: Cambridge University Press, 2001).

20   For a fascinating recent exploration of the homoerotic nature of Mordecai's relationship to Deronda, see Jacob Press, 'Same-Sex Unions in Modern Europe: *Daniel Deronda, Altneuland*, and the Homoerotics of Jewish Nationalism', in *Novel-Gazing: Queer Readings in Fiction*, ed. Eve Kosofsky Sedgwick (Durham, NC: Duke University Press, 1997), pp. 249–68. I would also like to take this moment to register my indebtedness to the work and teaching of Anita Sokolsky, whose unpublished PhD thesis, 'A Dark Inscription: Questions of Representation in *Daniel Deronda*' (Cornell University, 1983), has greatly influenced my own thinking about *Deronda*.

21   George Eliot, *Daniel Deronda*, (1878), ed. John Rignall (London: Dent Everyman, 1999), p. 544. Further references are included in the text. His vision does eventually come true, in the sense that he does leave Gwendolen, with metaphorically outstretched arms, behind, as he mounts the vessel bound for Palestine. Throughout the book Deronda is represented as saving people from drowning, whether it is literally, as with Mirah, or figuratively, as with Gwendolen and Hans Meyrick.

22   And 'seed' is one of Eliot's favourite words – see Neil Hertz, 'George Eliot's Pulse', *Differences* 6 (1994), 28–45.

23   Benedict Anderson, *Imagined Communities: Reflections on the Origin and Spread of Nationalism* (London: Verso, 1983).

24   Cynthia Chase, 'The Decomposition of the Elephants', in *Decomposing Figures* (Baltimore: Johns Hopkins University Press, 1986), pp. 157–74; pp. 168–9.

25   There may also be at play here the sense of Christian typology in which events in the Old Testament were seen as foreshadowing those in the New. For Mordecai, contemplating the uninspiring Jacob, as for readers of the Old Testament in a Christian context, the greater story is still to come.

26   Press makes similar points about the erotics of the Mordecai–Deronda relationship: 'Mordecai wants to – spiritually – penetrate a young man. He is looking for nothing except an aesthetically appropriate receptacle into which to release himself. Deronda longs to be dominated; Mordecai is looking for someone to dominate. It is a match made in heaven.' Press, 'Same-Sex Unions in Modern Europe', p. 309.

27   As Royle points out, many minor characters display second sight as well: Anna Gascoigne's 'fears gifted her with second-sight' (62), when she tells

Rex not to let Gwendolen ride to hounds; Lush 'had a second-sight' for the evil consequences of the marriage between Gwendolen and Grandcourt (309).

28 James Caron, 'The Rhetoric of Magic in *Daniel Deronda*', *Studies in the Novel* 15 (1983), 1–9; p. 6.

29 See Chase, *Decomposing Figures*, pp. 157–74, for a deconstructive reading of Deronda's ancestry.

30 Mary Jacobus, 'Hysterics Suffer Mainly from Reminiscences' in *Reading Woman: Essays in Feminist Criticism* (London: Methuen, 1986), pp. 249–74; p. 271.

31 This moment of foresight previews the novel's rich thematic connections between the redemption (and theft) of women and their jewellery. See Catherine Gallagher, 'George Eliot and *Daniel Deronda*: The Prostitute and the Jewish Question' in *Sex, Politics and Science in the Nineteenth-Century Novel*, ed. Ruth Bernard Yeazell, *Selected Papers from the English Institute*, new series, 10 (1983–4), pp. 39–62.

32 For an interesting feminist–psychoanalytic reading, which stresses Gwendolen's return to her mother at the end of the book, see Mary Wilson Carpenter, '"A bit of her flesh": Circumcision and "The Signification of the Phallus" in *Daniel Deronda*', *Genders* 1 (1989), 1–23.

PART III

Raising the Dead

CHAPTER 5

Browning, the dramatic monologue and the resuscitation of the dead

Adam Roberts

'Your ghost will walk . . .'
('De Gustibus' (1855), 1)[1]

I

This paper proposes to read Browning's dramatic monologues as aesthetic attempts to call forth particular dead individuals and hear what they have to say to us. It figures 'the dramatic monologue' as a form of verbal resuscitation of the dead, a quasi-Spiritualist voicing of dead men and women. It is perhaps odd to position Browning in this way, given that he has traditionally been seen as implacably hostile to the developing discourses of nineteenth-century Spiritualism, in sharp contradistinction to his wife Elizabeth Barrett, who was energetically enthusiastic about séances, table-rapping, hauntings and other aspects of the Victorian supernatural. Browning, according to this traditional interpretative narrative, was materialist in contrast to his wife's Spiritualist leanings, conventionally religious where she was interested in the unconventional.

Despite this, when Browning wrote his masterpiece, *The Ring and the Book* (1868–9), he included at the centre of its first book a powerful characterisation of himself as a poetic Resurrectionist. This passage explicitly identifies Browning's epic project, and by extension the form of the dramatic monologue itself, as a 'resuscitation of the dead', in which Browning connects spiritually (by sending forth 'half his soul') with long-dead individuals, and allows them to speak through his poetry. In this way, 'something dead may get to live again' and the poet 'makes new beginning, starts the dead alive' (*The Ring and the Book*, 'The Ring and the Book', 722, 726).

Set alongside Browning's great epic, though, is another of his most famous poems from the same period. 'Mr Sludge, the "Medium"' (1864) remains the most famous Victorian attack on mediumship as quackery. Indeed the remarkable vitriol Browning injects into his portrait of Sludge, based on the medium Daniel Dunglas Home, suggests a powerful personal animadversion to the very notion of the communication with the dead. What makes it all the more striking is the realisation of just how thoroughly Browning's poetry is haunted by ghosts, how comprehensively it comprises the poet using his powers medium-like to give voice to dead men and women.

II

My starting point for discussion is the mid-period complexity of *The Ring and the Book*, Browning's most celebrated and most extended exercise in necromancing poetics. It is in the first book of this epic that Browning introduces himself as a character in his own creation, and tells us the story of how he encountered the raw material for his fact-based poem, the 'Old Yellow Book', bought from a stall in a Florence market. The narrator then turns to the question of the legitimacy of introducing the poet's fictionalising imagination into this tale of 'pure crude fact', defending himself with the Coleridgean observation that the poet's imagination creates as a smaller version of the Divine act of creation: that after the basic truth of 'In the beginning God made heaven and earth', the poet

> Repeats God's process in man's due degree,
> Attaining man's proportionate result, –
> Creates, no, but resuscitates, perhaps.
> ('Ring and the Book', 702, 710–12)

It is this 'resuscitation' of dead speakers that is the core of Browning's conception of his own work. He goes on to elaborate it in fifty striking lines, before drawing a line under such aesthetic theorising with a brisk 'Enough of me! / The Book!' ('Ring and the Book', 765–6). There are a number of fascinating features of this passage. One is the way it places the whole of *The Ring and the Book* under the tutelage, almost, of a mysterious figure identified only as 'the Mage':

> Why did the mage say, – feeling as we are wont
> For truth, and stopping midway short of truth,
> And resting on a lie, – 'I raise a ghost'?
> 'Because,' he taught adepts, 'man makes not man.
> Yet by a special gift, an art of arts,
> More insight and more outsight and much more
> Will to use both of these than boast my mates,
> I can detach from me, commission forth,
> Half of my soul; which in its pilgrimage

> O'er old unwandered waste ways of the world,
> May chance upon some fragment of a whole,
> Rage of flesh, scrap of bone in dim disuse,
> Smoking flax that fed fire once: prompt therein
> I enter, spark-like, put old powers to play,
> Push lines out to the limit, lead forth last
> (By a moonrise through a ruin of a crypt)
> What shall be mistily seen, murmuringly heard,
> Mistakenly felt: then write my name with Faust's!'
> Oh, Faust, why Faust? was not Elisha once? –
> Who bade them lay his staff on a corpse-face.
>   ('Ring and the Book', 735–61)

I have argued elsewhere that the 'Mage' is based upon the Renaissance alchemist and magician, Cornelius Agrippa.[2] If Browning is one of the 'adepts' taught by this mysterious figure, then the art learnt has unavoidable occult overtones. Of course, 'nothing which had never life / Shall get life from him, be, not having been', but nonetheless, 'something dead may get to live again' if only a suitable person can send out half their soul and occupy the corpse ('Ring and the Book', 720–1, 722). We might want to read the parenthetical line 750 '(By a moonrise through a ruin of a crypt)' as an indication that the author of 'Mr Sludge' has not surrendered himself entirely to occult or Spiritualist enthusiasms – it does, after all, suggest a certain ironic detachment, an acknowledgement of the egregious Gothicism of the whole thing. But at the same time this quasi-Spiritualist 'mimic creation' is a 'glory' ('Ring and the Book', 732–3). The Mage, too, has similarities with the sorts of powers claimed by Spiritualists from Browning's day.[3] 'The life in me abolished the death of things', Browning-as-narrator declares, as a Sludge or a Mesmer might. More than this, Browning calls his 'mimic creation' 'galvanism for life', which itself suggests a different sort of occult spectre, a notion of the speakers of his dramatic monologues as Frankenstein's monsters, corpses reanimated by electricity ('Ring and the Book', 520, 733).

But from Cornelius Agrippa and Faust, Browning moves on to a more religious paradigm for bringing the dead back to life. He introduces the story of Elisha from 2 Kings 4:29–34 – quoting it word for word, largely, fitting the King James Bible's phrases directly into pentameters. In other words, Browning carefully balances an occult version of resurrecting the dead with a pious, religious one. Indeed, both these contexts are in dialogue with one another throughout his writing career as tropes for the poetic art, conflicting versions of 'starting the dead alive'. This poses the question of 'poetry' in a particular way: is the poet an occult necromancer, or is he a divinely inspired prophet? In both cases there is an unsettling, uncanny element.

This figuring of poetry as resurrecting the dead filters into the subject of Browning's poetry as well as questions of poetic strategy. In *The Ring and the Book*, as in his career as a whole, Browning focuses his necromancer poetics by returning again and again to figures that straddle life and death. By the end of *The Ring and the Book* three of its ten speakers are dead. In particular, Pompilia acts as the most transitional of these speakers, by virtue of delivering her monologue on her death-bed and actually dying during the course of it. She is also transitional in being both, in a sense, the most material figure in the poem – her body, as the site of alleged sexual transgression and actual violence, is somehow ever before us – as well as the most spectral. Seventy lines from the end she declares: 'Ah! Friends, I thank and bless you every one! / No more now: I withdraw from earth and man', and after another verse-paragraph of ambiguous live–dead speaking, her soul literally ascends before our eyes:

> Through such souls alone
> God stopping shows sufficient of His light
> For us i' the dark to rise by. And I rise.
> ('Pompilia', 1768–9, 1843–5)

This uncanny, indeed ghostly, image exists in a network of representations of Pompilia throughout *The Ring and the Book* as a haunting spirit. She is repeatedly described in ghostly terms, 'tall, pale, sad and strange', a resident of 'the long white lazar house' ('The Other Half-Rome', 35). Guido feels he has killed her, having stabbed her repeatedly, but still she returns to condemn him. He asks

> Whom find I?
> Here, still to fight with, but my pale frail wife?
> – Riddled with wounds
> . . .
> She too must shimmer through the gloom o' the grave,
> Come and confront me.
> ('Guido', 1674–80)

Guido's second monologue is haunted with this speaking ghost ('there she stands, there she is alive and pale!' ('Guido', 963)), appropriately enough since her testimony condemns him effectively from beyond the grave. But Pompilia's dead–alive ghostly status in particular throws significance upon the poetics Browning is employing.

Ghosts are present all the way through *The Ring and the Book*. For Guido's meandering lawyer Archangelis it is Guido's murdered honour (slain by Pompilia's adultery) that haunts the case:

> *Quod dominus Guido* that our noble Count
> *Occidit*, did the killing in dispute
> *Ut ejus honor tumulatus*, that
> The honour of him buried fathom-deep
> In infamy, *in infamia*, might arise,
> *Resurgeret*, as ghosts break sepulchre!
> ('Dominus Hyacinthus de Archangelis', 1634–9)

Interleaving Latin and English, as Browning does throughout this monologue, also points up the situation: this dead language and this living one tangled together, blurring the border of death and life. But few of the other speakers see Guido's honour as something possessing the potency to haunt the text in this manner. For the Pope it is 'truth' that haunts the trial (and therefore the poem), despite the best efforts of Guido and his team to murder it. He concludes his monologue with a memory of a lightning strike he witnessed once in the middle of 'a night so dark':

> There lay the city thick and plain with spires
> And, like a ghost disshrouded, white the sea.
> So may the truth be flashed out by one blow.
> ('The Pope', 2118–26)

Throughout *The Ring and the Book* there is this sense of text haunted by a ghost, a spirit, that communicates and speaks. For some of the speakers – the Pope, say – this spirit is the Holy Spirit, and this truth 'like a ghost disshrouded' is also absolutely implicated with speech: 'He, the Truth, is, too, / The Word' ('The Pope', 375–6). For 'Browning', the speaker of the first book, the spirit is more specifically that of his dead wife, Elizabeth Barrett. The ghostly presence of Browning's Muse, the 'Lyric Love' invoked at the start of the poem, informs the portrait of Pompilia, as well as the poem's discourses of truth and of the resurrection of the dead. Ultimately, it is the dead Elizabeth Barrett who most thoroughly haunts *The Ring and the Book*; she who has 'taken sanctuary within the holier blue' and who there sings 'a kindred soul out to his face' ('Ring and the Book', 1391–5).

In other words, *The Ring and the Book* is a poem explicitly figured as a séance, a ghostly haunting, its ten speakers called back from the dead by Browning's occult power to tell their tales. As such it is a poem about the passage from life to death (and back), and about the borderline state

ambiguous between death in life and life in death. It is a text haunted by
the brutality of the point of death, the ontological wrenching figured as
physical pain. It is haunted by spectres: of Pompilia, of Elizabeth Barrett,
of 'honour' and 'truth'. It is Browning's masterwork because it embraces
these themes so expertly: the dead returning to life, life haunted by death.
These same themes characterise Browning's poetry throughout his career.

III

Death has traditionally been seen in criticism as the ultimate point of
resistance to discourse. According to Garrett Stewart,

> death necessitates a mastery of 'the Impossible' by style. When the linguistic forms
> *death, dead* and *die* are extrapolated from their own referential vacuum into any-
> thing like a subjective episode of narrated dying, language unfolds a definitive
> instance of pure story, unapproachable by report . . . As narrative event, death is
> the ultimate form of closure plotted within the closure of form.[4]

Stewart's concern is with death-bed scenes in the novel rather than
Browning, but his observation pinpoints two key features of this poetics of the resuscitated dead. The first is that death obviates the third-person
report: once we speak of somebody else dying there comes a point beyond
which there is no more we can report. Only a resuscitated first-person narrative, only the testimony of a spirit called back by a Sludge-like Spiritualist
allows us imaginative access to this state. The second is that giving voice to
the dead radically problematises closure: it unpicks the closure of form by
reversing a form of closure.

So many of Browning's poems are positioned on this troubled boundary that it might almost be identified as the key defining feature of his
verse. He writes a great many death-bed poems: 'The Bishop Orders his
Tomb', 'Prospice', 'Confessions', 'Holy Cross Day', 'A Death in the Desert',
'Doctor –' and many others. More than this, in some of his most famous poems the speaker actually dies in the process of voicing his or her monologue
(as with 'Pompilia'). In others a speaker describes the process of actually
dying. His first collection of dramatic monologues, *Dramatic Lyrics* (1842),
is full of poems that give voice to the dead. This is to say more than the fact
that Browning's poems of necessity give voice to historical speakers, like the
fifteenth-century Duke of Ferrara in 'My Last Duchess' or the English Civil
warrior of the 'Cavalier Tunes'. It is to observe the way these poems (taking
as they do the dead speaker's speeches) are so frequently plotted against
content that expresses the passing from life to death and back again; poems
that deliberately straddle the death–life border. 'My Last Duchess', for

instance, is poem that obliquely records a death. This speaker, resurrected from the fifteenth century to tell his story, has murdered his wife and replaced her with a portrait. In other words, this speaker considers himself to have resurrected his dead wife in a superior form, a form of undying beauty over which he has complete control. The phrase he repeats about her, 'as if she were alive', 'as if alive', reinforces the simulacrum of life in an individual killed and resurrected as art ('My Last Duchess', 2, 49). The poem becomes a critique of the limitations of the resurrectionist aesthetic.

'Incident of the French Camp' is another poem that straddles the border between speaking in life and speaking in death. A young boy in Napoleon's army comes to the Emperor to tell him that they have successfully captured the city of Ratisbon. Napoleon observes:

> 'You're wounded!' 'Nay,' the soldier's pride
> Touched to the quick, he said:
> 'I'm killed Sire!' And his chief beside
> Smiling the boy fell dead.
> ('Incident of the French Camp', 37–40)

The boy insists that he is dead: he speaks as a dead man, and reinforces his status as dead by collapsing in the poem's final line. The pun on 'quick', in its archaic meaning of 'life', underscores this strange dead–alive status: being told that he is alive 'touches the soldier to the quick', to his life, which prompts the declaration of his death, his speaking out of death. It is not surprising that this curious anecdote – a true one – stuck in Browning's mind as a subject for a poem. It crystallises the trope of dead-man-as-speaker via a figure who, through extraordinary circumstances (in this case, his extraordinary courage and strength), speaks out of death. The early monologue, 'Porphyria's Lover', is also about the dead subject resurrected, this time as a controlled 'object' by the paranoid male subject. Here, a male narrator strangles his lover, only to bring her back to life with a kiss.

The religious language of resuscitation (the narrator of 'Porphyria's Lover' boasts that 'yet God has not said a word!') is present in Browning's work in both Christian and pagan versions. 'Artemis Prologizes' is presented as the prologue to an unwritten Greek play, the subject of which would be the resurrection from death of Hippolytus, killed at the end of Euripides' *Hippolytos*. But what is interesting here is the way this resurrection of the dead is figured in detailed and even grotesquely realised physical terms. In the poem, Asclepios reverses the violent death of the young man:

> [he] has soothed
> With lavers the torn brow and murdered cheeks,

Composed the hair and brought its gloss again,
And called the red bloom to the pale skin back,
And laid the strips and jagged ends of flesh
Even once more, and slacked the sinew's knot
Of every tortured limb.

('Artemis Prologizes', 105–11)

This is death figured as a violent dissociation of the material being, and resurrection figured accordingly as a reversal of this example of the 'ends of flesh'. Here Browning insists on this resuscitation metaphor for the dramatic monologue as *more* than just a vocal, disembodied thing: the way it becomes fully material, fully physical. Browning's 'classical–pagan' poetry uses the same idea of the resurrection of the body and voice after death, with the same emphasis on a violent materiality, as his 'Christian' monologues.

This insistence on the material reality of the resurrected speaker finds ironic self-commentary in a central poem from Browning's next collection of dramatic monologues, *Dramatic Romances and Lyrics* (1845), 'The Bishop Orders His Tomb at Saint Praxed's Church'. The speaker here has been resurrected by Browning from a sixteenth-century Italian context ('Rome 15–' says the subtitle), and speaks – again – on his death-bed. The sensuality, which has made him a bad bishop (his licentiousness and cupidity, and so on) shapes his sense of what his existence will be after his death to the point where he imagines himself alive again on the far side of his own death, observing the goings-on in the chapel around him:

And then how shall I lie through centuries,
And hear the blessed mutter of the mass,
And see God made and eaten all day long,
And feel the steady candle flame, and taste
Good strong thick stupefying incense-smoke!

('The Bishop Orders His Tomb at Saint Praxed's Church', 80–5)

This hearing, feeling, seeing, tasting dead man is doing everything but speaking, which in its own way points up the extent to which the whole poem can be figured as the speech of a dead man. Isobel Armstrong points out that the Bishop 'can only think of his magnificent tomb from the perspective of someone lying on it, just as he is lying on his death-bed. The irony is that from this position looking outward into the church one could see precisely what a spectator in front of it could not see – but one would have to be dead.' Armstrong thinks the poem embodies 'the violent power of the gaze, a greedy appropriation of the aesthetic and the sexual, and a complete failure to imagine or comprehend death', but this little vision of the dead started alive is the most muffled portion of this vibrant, sensual poem.[5] In the Bishop's version of being dead–alive, speech is reduced to a mutter, light to a candle flame, consciousness is 'stupefied'.

One notable aspect of the poem is the way the Bishop's profane attachment to pagan iconography (his desire, for instance, to have 'Pans and Nymphs' in bas-relief around his tomb) conflates pagan and Christian, just as the speaker of the first book of *The Ring and the Book* folds together an occult version of resurrection from the dead with a Christian-religious one. This tension between understanding the resurrection of the dead in purely religious terms, and seeing it as something occult, something un- or pre-Christian, is right at the heart of Browning's necromantic poetics.

'An Epistle of Karshish' provides another spin on the same topic. Here the speaker – an Arab physician resuscitated by Browning from the first-century AD – has actually spoken with Lazarus after he was raised from the dead by Christ. Karshish insists on a material explanation, that Lazarus suffered an epileptic attack and was cured by a 'learned leech', but his account of the case is shot through with the uncanny sense of something greater. The earthquake that marked the crucifixion he thinks of as 'prefiguring . . . the loss/To occult learning, of our lord the sage' ('An Epistle of Karshish': 253–4). Lazarus, he concludes dismissively, was 'stark mad' ('Karshish': 264); but nonetheless he ends his poem with the ghostly meeting of Arab and Jew, Karshish and Lazarus, in an appropriately gothic setting.

> I met him thus:
> I crossed a ridge of short sharp broken hills
> Like an old lion's cheek teeth. Out there came
> A moon made like a face with certain spots
> Multiform, manifold and menacing:
> Then a wind rose behind me. So we met
> In this old sleepy town at unaware,
> The man and I.
> ('Karshish', 2907)

The uncanny tone of this exactly captures the occult implications of the divine resurrection. The alliterative linking of 'multiform, manifold and menacing' foreshadows the trinitarianism of the coming Christianity, but it is weighted towards the final term. There *is* something unnerving about the idea of coming to meet a dead man. In fact, Browning's description here has the closest resemblance to the nightmare landscape of 'Childe Roland to the Dark Tower Came', another of the *Men and Women* poems. Loy Martin has pointed out how the extended simile near the beginning of 'Childe Roland' about the man on his death-bed encapsulates the tenor of the whole. Like moments in any one of the dozens of Browning's death-bed poems, this grim little simile precisely articulates the wavering life–death ambiguity that so fascinates Browning.

> As when a sick man very near to death
> > Seems dead indeed, and feels begin and end
> > The tears and takes the farewell of each friend,
> And hears one bid the other go, draw breath
> Freelier outside, ('since all is o'er,' he saith,
> > 'And the blow fallen no grieving can amend;')
> While some discuss if near the other graves
> > Be room enough for this, and when a day
> > Suits best for carrying the corpse away
> With care about the banners, scarves and staves:
> And still the man hears all, and only craves
> > He may not shame such tender love and stay.
> > ('Childe Roland to the Dark Tower Came', 25–36)

Martin notes that 'critics have ignored this remarkable passage almost unanimously', and goes on to argue that the simile here presents in miniature the larger pattern of the poem as a whole: 'Both the poem as a whole and the dying man simile concern the separation of an individual from his intimate associates through death.'[6] Reading 'Childe Roland' as being the speech of a dead man, a vision of a hellish afterlife, is plausible enough, but the power of the simile comes from its ambiguity. The mourners consider the man dead and are planning his funeral; he still hears them but says nothing, feeling only shame that he has not actually departed. It is moot as to whether he is alive or not. He is almost a reluctant ghost, haunting a scene he would rather abandon. It is hard to see what holds him to the scene, in fact, unless it is – in textual terms – the intertextuality by which Donne's 'Valediction: Forbidding Mourning' is inverted. Browning plays with Donne's well-known lines:

> As virtuous men pass mildly away,
> > And whisper to their souls to go,
> Whilst some of their sad friends do say
> > The breath goes now, and some say, no:[7]

Browning's simile becomes, as does the whole of 'Childe Roland', a valediction *insisting upon* mourning – insisting upon, in other words, the continued acknowledgement of death, the continuing presence of death in life. That is what Browning's fifty resuscitated speakers in *Men and Women* are doing: marking the site of mourning, the eruption of death into the realm of life.

This issue of mourning is an important context for Browning's necromancing poetics. As I have been arguing, Browning's fascination with resurrecting the dead is apparent from early in his career. But 1864 is a crucial point in the development of the aesthetic, a focusing point, because this is the date of Elizabeth Barrett's death. From marking an abstract ontological anxiety, the bringing back of the dead becomes an acutely personal issue. It becomes, in other words, a form of mourning itself.

Browning's mourning of Elizabeth Barrett was sometimes extravagant. He became one of the age's most celebrated widowers, and his attachment to his dead wife 'beyond the grave' interrupted his chances of ever marrying again (something evidenced, for instance, in his abortive marriage proposal to Lady Ashburton, and the anger and pain that followed). This death is present in numerous ways in Browning's post-1864 poetry. *Balaustion's Adventure* (1870), for instance, includes a complete translation of Euripides' *Alkestis* – a play, of course, about the bringing back to life of a much-loved wife. Narrated by a fictional, classical version of Elizabeth herself (Balaustion), Admetus' loss of his wife and the intervention of Herakles, who brings her back from the underworld, the poem is thoroughly haunted by Browning's loss, and haunted too by Elizabeth Barrett, to whom it makes a number of deictic references. *The Ring and the Book* was haunted by Elizabeth too, among its many hauntings. And there is no space here to speak of the many poems from Browning's later period in which dead women haunt the living, or otherwise speak from beyond the grave ('The Householder', the epilogue to *Fifine at the Fair*, 1872; *Red Cotton Night-Cap Country* and *The Inn Album* both from 1874, 'Numpholeptos' from 1876, the return to the story of Alkestis in the prologue to *Parleyings* 1889, and many other examples). The specific death of Elizabeth Barrett introduces considerations of mourning into Browning's resurrectionist poetics: the resurrections become versions of one wished-for coming-back-to-life, that of the mourned love-object.

IV

Alongside the considerations of mourning in Browning's poetry is the issue of *the gift*, which connects the act of mourning and the poetics of resurrecting the dead. In particular, there is one famous act of poetic 'giving' at the core of Browning's output. *Men and Women*, as we have seen, contains fifty men and women, largely resurrected from death to speak, and many of these poems are about death, dying or returning from death. This death–life collection concludes with a performative piece of poetic giving,

'One Word More', a coda poem addressed to Elizabeth Barrett, in which all fifty poems are given by Browning to his wife.

Browning subtly understood the ways in which 'gifts' are complicit with the discourses of death. His repeated fascination with the bringing together of the finite and the infinite, which many critics have explored in his work, finds a particular expression in the imbalance between the 'life' and 'death' halves of the gift equation. He himself saw his poetics as exploring the disjunction between the equation of 'the finite' and 'the infinite', for instance the disjunction between 'mortal, human, finite' and 'divine, eternal, infinite' that necessarily occurs when man meets God, or experiences one of the aspects of God, such as love.[8] To quote Herbert Tucker: 'By putting the infinite within the finite through the use of a style that acknowledges its own insufficiency, Browning styles himself a romantic poet in full pursuit of the sublime.' That this Romantic sublime should also express a Romantic–Gothic supernaturalism is not surprising. According to Tucker, Browning's poetry 'intensifies at moments when the negotiation of a frontier marks out a new beginning'.[9] Bringing the dead back to life is one key form of this sublime new beginning, this linking of finite and infinite. This bridging of the gap between finite and infinite is where Browning himself situates his poetry, and he is repeatedly interested in the infinite gift, the gifts from the eternal to the transient. After Elizabeth Barrett's death, this becomes Browning's fascination with (to cite Derrida's phrase) a religiously figured 'gift of death'.

This is evident in the first collection of dramatic monologues published after her death, *Dramatis Personae*. The two longest dramatic monologues in this relatively brief collection – the longest by a long way – are both about the resurrection of the dead: 'Mr Sludge, the "Medium"' and 'A Death in the Desert'. These two poems balance one another: 'Mr Sludge' on the one hand mocks false resurrection of the dead wholly from within the perspective of the contemporary – that is to say, living – world; 'A Death in the Desert' provides the corrective, a religious, Christian perspective on the literal resurrection of the dead body of Christ, articulated through the dying perspective of St John. It should not surprise us that it is the contemporary figure (the one who has not required resuscitation by Browning's poetics) – Sludge, the 'Medium' – who is used to critique the pretensions of fraudulent, imitation resurrection of the dead. 'A Death in the Desert', on the other hand, 'starts the dead alive' by resurrecting a series of narrators, nested within one another, all testifying to the possibilities of resuscitating the dead from a Christian perspective. This last poem in particular is explicit about the 'gift of death', which links this religious discourse with Browning's intimate, gift connection with the dead Elizabeth. St John, on

his death-bed, talks about the transcendent qualities that 'God could give, /
And did give', insisting that 'this is death and the sole death, / When a man's
loss comes to him from his gain' ('A Death in the Desert', 482–92). This is
what Derrida talks of:

The gift made by God as he holds me in his gaze and in his hand while remaining
inaccessible to me, the terrible dissymmetry of the *mysterium tremendum* only
allows me to respond and only rouses me to the responsibility it gives me by
making a gift of death, giving the secret of death, a new experience of death.[10]

Derrida's suggestion that 'Christian themes can be seen to revolve around
the *gift* as gift of death, the fathomless gift of a type of death: infinite
love' illuminates Browning's return in many of his later poems to Jewish
or Christian religious themes.[11] For Browning, giving is wholly implicated
with this religious sense. 'One Word More' begins briefly with Raphael's
love sonnets, but moves quickly and emphatically to the religious, to the
fact that 'Heaven's gift takes earth's abatement!' ('One Word More', 73).
Moses on the mountaintop ('the Sinai forehead's cloven brilliance') was the
conduit for God's gifts, and was ready to give his own life ('ready in the
desert to deliver . . . life') to the women he loved ('One Word More', 97,
106–8). Browning characterises himself as Moses-like, comparatively poor
in comparison with the impossible infinitude of the divine gift, but willing
to give what he can:

> This of verse alone, one life allows me;
> Verse and nothing else have I to give you.
> Other heights in other lives, God willing:
> All the gifts from all the heights, your own, Love!
> ('One Word More', 113–16)

His gift is death in two senses: firstly, the gift of his own death, metaphorically; his willingness figuratively to lay down his life. This is the gift of death
as self-sacrifice that invests *Alkestis* – in which Alkestis gives her life that
her husband Admetos might live – with such potency in Browning's later
imagination, and this explains why he returns to the myth in *Balaustion's
Adventure* and *Parleyings with Certain People*. Derrida's 'gift of death' is this
as well: 'It is indeed dying *for the other* in the sense of dying *in place of* the
other . . . only a mortal can give.'[12] But in a second, almost facetious sense,
Browning 'gives death' in passing on the resuscitated dead that constitute
his monologues. He has gathered the dead men and women, 'Lippo,
Roland or Andrea', 'Karshish, Cleon, Norbert and the fifty', and then he
has 'enter[ed] each and all . . . [Spoken] from every mouth, – the speech, a
poem' ('One Word More', 129–38). It is this necromantic act, repeated over
and over in the collection, that constitutes his gift to Elizabeth Barrett.

It would be interesting to explore the way Browning deals with gifts in his verse in a more general manner; but what would surely emerge from such a study would be the scrupulousness with which he treated the business of giving, of how acutely aware he was of the claims of obligation it involves us in. He gives his wife poems in 1855 to return a precious gift of hers (she had given him the love poetry of the *Sonnets from the Portuguese* in 1849). Gift is matched to gift. Only after Elizabeth's death does it become impossible to make a (mortal, finite) return to the infinite gift of death. By contrast, the Duke in 'My Last Duchess' murders his wife because of her inability to respond to, or even comprehend, the inequality in giving. She 'gave' her joy to all around her ('her looks went everywhere'), whereas she did not respond appropriately to his gift to her, 'she ranked / My gift of a nine-hundred-year's-old name / With anybody's gift' ('My Last Duchess', 24, 32–4). This inequality can only be resolved, from the Duke's point of view, via the death of the Duchess herself.

The connection of the notion of the gift with death has found its fullest exploration in Jean Baudrillard's analysis of the gift-economy, *Symbolic Exchange and Death* (1976). 'Death', Baudrillard argues, 'is neither resolution nor involution, but a reversal and a symbolic challenge.' Freud's 'death drive' does not apprehend the situation. 'What Freud missed', Baudrillard thinks (and what, we might add, Browning fully understands) was 'the curvature of life in death, he missed its vertigo and its excess, its reversal of the entire economy of life.'[13] Baudrillard is particularly interested in the ways some gifts – the gift of life, for instance, or the gift of labour that the capitalist bestows upon the worker – are so great that they cannot be returned, that no possible return-gift can undo the obligation of the recipient. In Mike Gane's words, 'the capitalist presents the gift of work to the proletarian. Because the proletarian cannot return this gift and cannot cancel it he cannot cancel the power of the capitalist.'[14] But Baudrillard's analysis has more than a merely Marxist point to it. This unavoidable power of obligation within the logic of the gift-economy connects in direct ways with the trope of 'giving' speech to the dead that characterises, or even defines, Browning's dramatic monologues. Take for example the status of the slave. According to Baudrillard the power of the requirements of symbolic exchange in the gift-economy are made manifest in the very etymology of the word 'slave':

All this becomes clear in the genealogy of the slave. First, the prisoner of war is purely and simply put to death (one does him honour in this way). Then he is *'spared'* [*epargné*] and *conserved* [*conservé*] (= *servus*), under the category of spoils of war and a prestige good: he becomes a slave and passes into sumptuary domesticity. It is only later that he passes into servile labour. However, he is no longer a 'labourer', since labour only appears in the phase of the serf or the *emancipated* slave, finally relieved of the mortgage of being put to death. Why is he freed? Precisely in order to work. Labour therefore everywhere draws its inspiration from deferred death. It comes from deferred death . . . By removing death, the master removes the slave from the circulation of symbolic goods. This is the violence the master does to the slave, condemning him to labour power.[15]

Slavery, of course, was a live issue throughout the nineteenth century, and one in which Robert Browning and Elizabeth Barrett were very engaged. We might focus the interrelations of death and the gift in Browning's art by asking one particular question: why, in all of his hundreds of dramatic monologues, does he never write a poem in which a *slave* is the speaker? What gives this question bite is the fact that one of Elizabeth Barrett's most famous short poems does precisely this: 'The Runaway Slave at Pilgrim Point' (1848). Indeed, the abolitionist movement in Britain in the nine-teenth century was organised around the image of a slave given voice, such that (on medals and in prints) a black man in manacles is made to ask the question: 'Am I not a man and a brother?' Barrett and her fellow abo-litionists had no problem making this supplementary 'gift' to 'the slave', giving him or her a voice, certain words. By refusing to do this Browning was refusing to implicate 'the slave' in this crushing economy of symbolic exchange. At some level he appreciated how close the relations are between giving (for instance giving words to) and death itself. To put it another way, he understood what many twentieth-century critics of the white abolition-ist movement have tended to say. It is more than patronising, more than condescending to make this gift, to speak on behalf of the slave: 'making' the slave say 'am I not a man and a brother' is oppressive in the same way (although clearly not in the same degree) as enslavement itself.

The nearest Browning comes to a slavish dramatic monologue is the implied narrative by Cleon's slave. Cleon begins his monologue by thanking Protus for his gifts ('gift after gift; they block my court . . . and one white she-slave from the group dispersed / Of black and white slaves'), and then imagines forcing words into the mouth of the one slave woman:

> Making this slave narrate thy fortunes, speak
> Thy great words, and describe thy royal face –
> Wishing thee wholly where Zeus lives the most,
> Within the eventual element of calm.
> ('Cleon', 8–12, 39–42)

Cleon does not actually wish Protus dead, of course; he is fancifully imag-ining an immortality for the tyrant. But the ambiguity in the lines at least suggests a form of death, and in turn the unpleasantness of the slave's condition is emphasised by the fact that she has no control over her words.

V

This constellation of the resuscitation of the dead – of, in other words, ghosts, spectres and animated corpses – with the work of mourning (for Elizabeth Barrett) and the economy of giving (of debt) recalls Derrida's *Specters of Marx* (1994), a famous analysis of 'haunting' in nineteenth-century (and other) texts. Derrida looks at the presence of spectres in Shakespeare's *Hamlet*, and at Marx's *Capital* and *Communist Manifesto* in the light of Marx's statement that 'a spectre is haunting Europe . . . the spectre of Communism'. He elusively characterises this 'ghost' or 'spectre' as a version of the Hegelian *Geist*, as the forms of Hegelianism that still haunt Marx's materialist philosophy:

The production of the ghost, the constitution of the *ghost* effect is not simply a spiritualisation or even an autonomisation of spirit, idea, or thought as happens *par excellence* in Hegelian idealism. No, once this autonomisation is effected, with the corresponding expropriation or alienation, and only then, the ghostly moment *comes upon* it, adds to it a supplementary dimension, one more simulacrum, alienation or expropriation. Namely, a body! In the flesh! For there is no ghost, there is never any becoming-specter of the spirit without at least an appearance of flesh.[16]

Browning's own spectre-poetics is implicated in 'the flesh' in precisely this manner: partly via his sense of 'galvanism for life', the walking-and-talking corpses that are so prevalent in his poetry, but more crucially in the very materialism of the dramatic monologue form itself. A speaker implies a speaking body, and many of Browning's dead–alive speakers make specific reference to their bodies, from the Bishop at Saint Praxed's sensualism to Mr Sludge's gasps of pain as his interlocutor grasps him by the throat ('Aie – aie – aie! / Please, sir! Your thumbs are through my windpipe sir! / Ch-ch!', 'Mr Sludge, the "Medium"', 16–18). More than this, every dramatic monologue records an actual instance of speech, and therefore the physical act of speaking; every such poem interpellates a speaker in a particular circumstance. If read aloud, according to the Victorian custom, the dramatic monologue repeats and enacts this production of locution. The dramatic monologue is a materialist form. It is also implicated in what Derrida calls 'the three things' that would 'decompose in analysis this single *thing*, spirit or specter', 'the *three things of the thing*':

1. First of all mourning . . . [which] consists always in attempting to ontologise remains, to make them present . . . by *localising* the dead . . . 2. Next, one cannot speak of generations of skulls or spirits except on condition of *language* – and the voice . . . 3. Finally the thing *works*, whether it transforms or transforms itself, poses or decomposes itself: the spirit, the 'spirit of the spirit' is *work*.[17]

Derrida's punning new discipline, 'hauntology', his spectre-ontology, is also the governing discourse for Browning's dramatic monologues, his compositional work, his giving voice to the dead, his acts of mourning the materiality of the dead.

Browning was a working poet. Daniel Karlin has convincingly demonstrated the extent to which Browning saw his vocation in 'economic as well as aesthetic' terms, saw himself as a 'worker': 'The sense of a duty laid on him by God is strong in Browning, but so is the sense of being a workman who fulfils his side of the bargain by honest endeavour. "I write from a thorough conviction that it is the duty of me."'[18] Where Derrida talks about the work that 'poses or decomposes', it calls to mind Browning's *Dramatis Personae*, the collection of poems most immediately complicit with Browning's mourning for his dead wife. The epilogue to that volume explores different attitudes to religion, and concludes:

> That one Face, far from vanish, rather grows,
> Or decomposes but to recompose,
> Becomes my universe that feels and knows.
> ('Epilogue', 99–101)

Of course, this use of 'composition' puns on the material work of composing poetry, of giving voice to the dead speakers. But the face, which is in one sense Christ's, is also the apparition of Elizabeth Barrett, the 'composing' manifestation of spirit and muse that hovers over the whole collection, as over *The Ring and the Book*. Browning works, mourns and above all speaks, gives voice to. His poetic 'hauntology' is about the way the dead speak to us, and the way that by speaking to us they are in fact demonstrating how alive they remain. There is a spectre haunting Browning's poetry, the spectre of the dead voice.

So many dead people in Browning's poetry; so close a proximity of life and death, to the point almost of a continual exchange between the two states: this elaborates and explains both subject and form in Browning's work. His necromancing, resurrectionist poetics mark him out from the mainstream of Victorian poetics. Tennyson, by contrast, writes no poems about the resuscitation of the dead: he has no death-bed monologues. His key figures either cannot die, like King Arthur in the *Idylls of the King*, or have moved from this world in a way that denies the possibility of return, like Arthur Hallam. *In Memoriam* is about the ways Hallam does not haunt the present, the ways in which Tennyson's narrator has to come to terms with his absence. Tennyson's wizard-figure for the poet (Merlin) is a bard, where Browning's (Cornelius Agrippa) is a necromancer: the bard conjures spells, but the necromancer brings actual, material dead people back to life. This is presumably why so many of Tennyson's dramatic monologue speakers are contemporaries, where so many of Browning's – the overwhelming majority – are long-dead historical figures. Matthew Arnold is another contrary figure: his invocation of the dead, as in 'The Scholar Gipsy', is designed to mark out how far the modern world has fallen away from the idyllic past. In other words, his Scholar Gipsy disappears into an unrecoverable past before our eyes as we read the poem. Only Browning explores the presence of the dead to the living, and the way mourning an individual or a past time is an ontological activity focused on the material particulars. His haunted poetry works at giving voice to the dead by way of situating the dead as always already with us, as simultaneously sinister and uncanny (occult) and as promises of divine resurrection (Christian). This is why so many of his poems concern dying people, or dead people, death and the processes of death.

Writing to Isabella Blagden on the third anniversary of Elizabeth Barrett's death, Browning talked about the way his dead wife continued to communicate with him, but made a point of distancing himself from 'Sludge'-like excesses. 'The difference between me and the stupid people who have "communications"', he said, 'is probably nothing more than that I don't confound the results of natural working of what is in my mind, with vulgar external appearances.'[19] But, of course, by the work of writing Browning shifts the location of the dead from purely and simply 'in my mind' to a textual position that is still 'in the mind' (an act of imagination) and also out of the mind, on the page, in the minds of others. It is as Derrida says, the 'spirit that one would oppose to its letter', this 'ghost' haunting its written or spoken letter: 'It is neither in the head nor outside the head.'[20] (And this is also one of the themes of *The Ring and the Book*: 'The letter kills, the spirit keeps alive', 'Guido', 1529.) But Browning, in this letter to Isabella Blagden, voices obliquely the *labour* of this resurrection of a voice from the grave, what he calls 'the natural working of what is in my mind'. This is the 'natural' work, the mourning, the gift, of Browning as resurrectionist.

NOTES

1   Robert Browning's poetry and letters are quoted from: *The Ring and the Book*, ed. Richard D. Altick (Harmondsworth: Penguin, 1971); *The Ring and the Book, Books I–IV*, vol. VII of *The Complete Works of Robert Browning*, ed. Roma King (Athens, GA: Ohio University Press, 1985); *The Oxford Authors: Robert Browning*, ed. Adam Roberts, introd. Daniel Karlin (Oxford: Oxford University Press, 1997).

2   For the identification of the Mage as Agrippa, see Adam Roberts, 'The Ring
    and the Book: the Mage, the Alchemist, and the Poet', *Victorian Poetry* 36
    (1998), 37–46; p. 38.
3   In fact Roma King misidentifies the 'Mage' as Franz Mesmer in *The Ring and
    the Book*, p. 279.
4   Garrett Stewart, *Death Sentences: Styles of Dying in British Fiction* (Cambridge,
    MA: Harvard University Press, 1984), pp. 5–6.
5   Isobel Armstrong, *Victorian Poetry: Poetry, Poetics and Politics* (London:
    Routledge, 1993), p. 287.
6   Loy Martin, *Browning's Dramatic Monologues and the Post-Romantic Subject*
    (Baltimore and London: Johns Hopkins University Press, 1985), p. 187.
7   John Donne, *Selected Poetry*, ed. John Carey (Oxford: Oxford University Press
    World's Classics, 1996), p. 112f.
8   This is a repeated theme in Browning, 'all poetry', as he told Ruskin, 'being
    a putting of the infinite into the finite' (Robert Browning to Ruskin,
    10 December 1855), Browning, *The Oxford Authors*, pp. 691–3; p. 692. See for
    instance the close of 'Two in the Campagna', 'Infinite passion, and the pain /
    Of finite hearts that yearn' (59–60). Critics have worn this particular pathway
    of inquiry smooth over the years: see in particular Herbert Tucker,
    Browning's Beginnings: the Art of Disclosure (Minneapolis: University of
    Minnesota Press, 1980), William Raymond, *The Infinite Moment* (Toronto:
    University of Toronto Press, 1950); Warwick Slinn, *The Discourse of the Self
    in Victorian Poetry* (London: Macmillan, 1991).
9   Tucker, *Browning's Beginnings*, p. 15.
10 Jacques Derrida, *The Gift of Death*, trans. David Wills (Chicago: University
    of Chicago Press, 1995), p. 33.
11 Ibid., p. 49.
12 Ibid., p. 43.
13 Jean Baudrillard, *Symbolic Exchange and Death* (1976), introd. Mike Gane,
    trans. Iain Hamilton Grant (London: Sage Publications, 1993), p. 156.
14 Ibid., p. xii.
15 Ibid., pp. 39–40.
16 Derrida, *Specters of Marx*, p. 126.
17 Ibid., p. 9.
18 Daniel Karlin, 'Introduction', in Browning, *The Oxford Authors*, p. xv. The
    quotation is Robert Browning to Elizabeth Barrett Browning, 11 February
    1845.
19 Robert Browning to Isabella Blagden, 19 December 1864, cited in Browning,
    The Oxford Authors, p. 702.
20 Derrida, *Specters of Marx*, pp. 171–2.

CHAPTER 6

Baron Corvo and the key to the underworld

Colin Cruise

In His Own Image (1901) by Frederick Rolfe (1860–1913) is a collection of thirty short stories of Italian life, sometimes light-hearted, sometimes deliberately obscurantist, which in part satirise the Italian church and its clerics, but which also suggest their author's own dissident sexual feelings encoded in dense literary and cultural references.[1] The stories are narrated by an Italian peasant boy, Toto, to his English 'master', 'Baron Corvo', (Rolfe himself, using one of his pseudonyms), a painter, photographer and writer who is living in the hills above Rome. Neither their circumstances nor their relationship are explained or elaborated upon. In the words of A. J. A. Symons, the stories are 'retellings of the legends of Catholic saints in the manner of Greek mythology, with quaint attributions of human characteristics and motives to the saints in their heavenly functions, reminding the reader irresistibly of the Gods of Olympus'.[2]

Toto is a peasant and is nearly completely illiterate, but several wider cultural ambiguities are played out in the stories he narrates. One is the implication that they are reminiscences of an oral folk tradition and that these are not, strictly, Toto's stories but versions of the stories of his ancestors. He is, in effect, simply the repository for the stories and the medium through which they are recounted. Indeed, as I will demonstrate in this essay, the idea of mediumship, in both exact and extended meanings, is extremely important for the operation of Rolfe's larger intention for *In his Own Image*. The presentation of Toto as Italian and illiterate is counterbalanced by the demonstration of his abilities as a storyteller rooted in an oral, folkloric tradition, and his 'knowledge' of crystal-gazing, trance states and Spiritualism which gives him, ultimately, experience of the 'other world'. The story that this essay focuses upon, 'About these Tales, the Key and Purgatory', concerns a séance, presented through a dense web of quotations and allusions to Dante's *Inferno*. The story centres on Toto's account of a mediumistic trance. Toto tells Rolfe about his ability to 'see' and 'hear' – about his clairvoyance and clairaudience: '"I can see what I want to see in other things; not quite so well as in the crystal ball [belonging to Baron Corvo] but well enough; and these I use when I am in strange places."[3] In the action that follows Toto 'dies', descends into the underworld and returns having narrated his experiences from a trance state to his master. Although this is the only séance in Rolfe's works we can relate it to his other interests, not only in magic and the supernatural, but also in deep meditative states of prayer in communing with God through meditation. The very singularity of the séance may be due to the author's recognition that Catholicism – the religion to which he was converted from Anglicanism in 1885 – did not 'need' the Spiritualist impulse which was having such an impact on contemporary Anglican and non-conformist churches. Through its emphasis on the ritual of the consecration, Catholicism was already implicated in magical and occultist practices.

Toto's voice is conveyed parodically in an elaborate but broken English full of neologisms and quaintnesses; at the same time, however, Rolfe plays archly with the status of the stories as both authentically oral and dense with literary allusions. We know that there was a Toto (Rolfe recorded his existence in letters and photographed him), and storytelling may have been part of his personality. But although Rolfe presents the stories carefully as Toto would have told them, with asides from their 'editor' giving details of their telling and describing landscape settings, the stories also reveal an uncharacteristically fey Rolfe, enjoying the ambiguities of his Italian scenario and using his innocent narrator to expound his own idiosyncratic opinions and foibles.

Rolfe's vision of Italy in *In His Own Image* is similar to ideas about Ireland to be found in works by W. B. Yeats and others from the 1890s. The Irish were perceived by some English and Anglo-Irish observers to be steeped in a semi-pagan tradition, only a little touched by the modern world of science, materialism and capitalism. The 'old religion' was thought not to have been entirely replaced by a highly organised, dogmatic Catholicism which should have overtaken it; instead there flourished a traditional, orally-transmitted belief in the closeness of the spirit world to everyday existence. The Italians were similarly seen in ambiguous, contradictory ways which impinged upon other elements of their persons and lives: beautiful but corrupt, lazy but artistic and resourceful, naively superstitious but intellectually sophisticated, debased but noble. While Italy might elevate – even ennoble – it was also a dangerous, destabilising place, its religion and its politics representing both conservative, anti-progressive forces (Catholicism) and the revolutionary spirit of the *Risorgimento*.[5] This double-edged perception gave the nation a vast symbolic importance despite its impoverished international political and economic position.

Italy had been the centre of a vast empire now lost; it had renewed itself several times and was now a vast cabinet of curiosities, ripe for casual looting by wealthy tourists looking for art. The 'idea of Italy' acted as both the opposite to a progressive Britain, throwing into relief the power of its empire and its industry, and as a warning of the possibility of indolence, degeneration, loss of empire and decay of British culture. The political, religious and cultural differences between England and Italy inflect popular English descriptions of Italy and Italians, and in particular the complex parallels between Italy's past and England's present power manifest themselves in descriptions of social relations between the English tourist and the Italian people, especially the peasant. For some, the peasant became a metaphor for the differences of Italian culture – certainly for its picturesque beauty, but also for the pervasive power of Catholicism which, while adding to the picturesqueness of the daily scene, was perceived as being an agency of control and degradation. The popularity of paintings representing informal worship at wayside shrines, for example, is accounted for by the wavering fascination and repulsion of Italian Catholicism for the English Protestant viewer. Such paintings might be said to represent an essential Italian-ness for some travellers. These paintings render picturesquely such cultural constructions as closeness to nature and a primitive religious instinct.[6]

For Rolfe it is the classical elements of Italian culture – the survival of the Graeco-Roman ideal and its uneasy coexistence with modern Catholicism – that fascinate and offer multiple opportunities for fantasy. The persistence of tradition, a factor which Yeats detected in Irish culture, is strongly present in Rolfe's fascination with Italy. The incorporation of the pagan gods into a popular, contemporary Catholicism demonstrably appeals to Rolfe. Italy became a rich source for his imagination, and most of his published works refer to or concern themselves with aspects of Italian culture and history. The figure of Toto allows Rolfe to synthesise some of the disparate or seemingly contradictory elements of Italy, particularly those which illustrate the instability of discourses of the primitive and the sophisticated. However, in the Toto stories, Rolfe's Italy is a kind of heaven with 'Baron Corvo' (English, yet supposedly ennobled by Italy) as God and Toto as an entertaining angel.

Frederick Rolfe's career as an artist and writer was like that of a contemporary medium – the adopted identity and false names ('Baron Corvo', for example), the pretence to obscure knowledge (as a translator and historian), and the constant threat of exposure and penury (the journalistic attack on 'Corvo' as an impostor in the Aberdeen *Daily Free Press*, for example) – all are shared with the pretenders to the 'keys' and 'paths' of Spiritualist knowledge.[7] It is possible to see Rolfe as part of that Spiritualist or occultist culture of late nineteenth-century Britain rather than the Catholic culture which he attempted to embrace. Indeed, through him and other Spiritualist-inclined figures, it is possible to identify links between two camps which otherwise seem polarised – Catholic converts and Spiritualists. In Britain both types of conversion were seen as moves from the centre to the margins. Both were reactions to the perceived extreme materialism of the period as well as to the austerity of non-conformism and of 'pre-ritualised' Anglicanism. Some converts to Catholicism were famous for their alternative, experimental belief-systems – Daniel Dunglas Home, the most famous male medium of his day, and Anna Kingsford, inventor of *The Perfect Way*, both of whom I discuss further in this chapter, were among the most unorthodox converts to Catholicism. But Rolfe himself made several attempts at establishing some reputation in the alternative and not very respectable worlds of Spiritualism and magic. He came into contact with W. T. Stead, the editor of *Review of Reviews* and *Borderland*, himself a convert to Spiritualism, who acted as a benefactor for a short time in 1890. Rolfe's connection with Harry Pirie-Gordon, with whom he attempted to set up an organisation called the Order of Sanctissima Sophia, gave rise to the adoption of titles, robes and rituals which gave it a resemblance to Macgregor Mathers's Order of the Golden Dawn or Helena Blavatsky's Theosophical Society. His conversion to Catholicism was surprising only in that, having expressed unorthodox beliefs for many years, he continued to seek ordination to the priesthood even after his expulsion from the Scots College, Rome. His expulsion only served to heighten similarities to Home, who had been expelled from Rome by the papal police following accusations that he was a sorcerer.[8]

One can see evidence for Rolfe's interest in the esoteric in his work in illustration and photography as well as in his writings. In his cover for *Hadrian the Seventh* (1904) (Fig. 1), for example, he depicted his hero celebrating Mass watched by his familiar – a particularly graphically conceived cat – and surrounded by arcane symbols. The novel, which is a highly original conflation of the ecclesiastical and magical, signals several of the author's ambitions, commercial as well as artistic and religious – not the least being his desire for ecclesiastical power. With its similarity to the title page of Macgregor Mathers's *The Book of Sacred Magic* (1897) (Fig. 2), one might be forgiven for thinking that Rolfe's cover indicated a novel which was entirely about Spiritualist, magical or Theosophist practices.[9] It

Figure 1   Frederick Rolfe, cover design for *Hadrian the Seventh*.

Figure 2 Moina Mathers, title page design for Macgregor Mathers, *The Book of Sacred Magic*.

Figure 3   Frederick Rolfe, *Nude Photographic Study.*

concerns, however, a struggling novelist: an unsuccessful Catholic writer
who has been refused Holy Orders. Out of the blue he is approached
to be the new Pope, is ordained, crowned Pope, installed in the Vatican,
reforms the Catholic Church, engages in deeply unorthodox practices and
reveals strange, un-Catholic thought processes. Finally, he is assassinated.
The novel received praise from many Catholics, among them the influential
convert and priest Robert Hugh Benson, himself interested in magic and
the supernatural; the two planned collaborative religious and historical
works. *Hadrian the Seventh* combined pretences to the highbrow and the
learned (even didactic), with elements of the arcane, comparable to the
exotic Spiritualist works of popular writers like Marie Corelli. As such,
the novel and its cover might be seen as a perfect solution to Rolfe's desire
to write a bestselling novel in an age of sensational bestsellers.

Rolfe's attempts to find fame had included experiments in photography
and painting as well as in literature. His photographs of the male nude,
taken in his early visits to Italy, depict naked youths, languid, beautiful
and indolent, who act as a metaphor for the beauty and inactivity of the
country itself. This iconographic metaphor also reveals a continuity with
earlier Classical cultures, both Roman and Greek, a complex of the histories
of sexuality and sculpture, tastes in behaviour, morals and art which were
being rewritten and reconsidered at the turn of the nineteenth century.
Rolfe's photograph of an adolescent boy lying prone and stretched (Fig. 3),
which was published in the *Studio*, encodes this vision of Italy as a pagan,
immoral delight which has a double-edged message – our delight in the
beauty of the figure, his delight in being alive.[10] This delight is central to the
production and understanding (if not the enjoyment) of *In His Own Image*
and it is in many ways a literary extension of the vogue in the visual arts
for depictions of beautiful young Italian men like those who feature in the
work of artists like Simeon Solomon, William Blake Richmond, Frederic
Leighton and Walter Crane, all of whom favoured Italian male models.[11]
We might see Rolfe, like his contemporary Baron von Gloeden, as using

the image of a languid, naked male muse in much the same way as artists like Leighton, Moore and Sandys had used female models. These female 'Olympian' figures, asleep in the heat of an ancient afternoon, dozing at the heart of the Royal Academy, are not quite in a trance, but their blanking out of their surroundings, their closed eyes and slumped figures suggest a communion with a private world of their own or with an interior part of themselves. Further, in depictions of priestesses or sorceresses – like Circe, for example – this staring oblivion heralds the possession of a kind of knowledge, a powerful, if suspect, alternative to the over-rationalised and masculinised culture of modernity. In this dreaminess or staring the representation of these female figures contrasts sharply with the ways in which the male figure is represented conventionally – active, alert, awake, at work.

Rolfe's imagining of the nude male is not confined, of course, to the visual arts. At several points in *In His Own Image* he introduces Toto and his male friends in languorous, seductive tableaux. A description of Toto's friend Desiderio illustrates how ambiguous passive male voluptuousness is, and how it too can suggest an underlying and understated psychic power. This is Toto's 'editor', 'Baron Corvo', narrating:

It was in the Bosco dell' Ombra, near by Monte Nicola; and I was painting Desiderio in the character of Love the Dreamer. For this purpose I had acquired him, seeing him to be a veritable reincarnation of the Sun of Kythereia, with his yellow hair, and yellow eyes, and his white smooth skin, glossy from head to foot with the finest yellow silken down, which made him shine as though he were chiselled in pale gold. He never wished to speak; he fed as delicately as a little bird; was always drowsy and generally asleep; lived his own happy little life; and at fourteen, showed a slim round shape like David of Donatello, crowned with short and wavering curls.[12]

While this might be read as simply an erotic tableau, it also stimulates a reading of the male figure as a link between the past and present – as a kind of 'eternal' masculinity with several images of the past intermingled in and suggested by the vivid yet passive presence of the male body. In the sleepy atmosphere there is a suggestion of ambiguity: does Desiderio represent a lack of communication or a communication with something 'unseen', something which tradition brings to him without effort on his part?

At the start of the story which contains the séances, we are alerted to a similarly feminised voluptuousness, this time in Toto himself:

Lying on his back, on the wooded slopes of Monte Saraceno, Toto lavished the long rose-brown sinuosities of youth: the right leg here, stretched out in a straight line with his body; the left there, flexed at the knee, leaning away in strenuous abandonment. His arm framed the density of his hair; his head and throat full back and upward to the sky.[13]

In the story that follows Toto reveals that, if this oblivion is not in itself a kind of passive gathering of knowledge, it masks that potential in and for the young male. (Indeed, we must ask, how much of the almost endless siesta of the boys' lives is itself a kind of séance?) He reveals that he has been taught by a country priest, Frat Innocente-of-the-Nine-Quires (i.e. the Nine Choirs of Angels), how to meditate, communicate through trance and hear spirit voices through nature: 'I must go away in loneliness, and think, and listen to the wind, or to the sea, or to the voices of the flowers, or to the whispers of the earth. This I have done, and I do: therefore I know many things of which no man has told to me.'[14]

Toto's explanation suggests the mental preparation of a medium. Yet as a young man, he would have been almost unique in Spiritualist circles, which were, by the 1880s, dominated by female mediums. Indeed, a division of labour seems to have developed at that later stage of the Spiritualist movement: women were the mediums whose messages were recorded or whose veracity was tested by male researchers and observers. Fictional medium-performers, like Du Maurier's *Trilby* or Verena Terrant, from Henry James's *The Bostonians*, had their real-life counterparts in personalities like Cora L. V. Tappan-Richmond. This American 'inspirational speaker', the model for Verena Terrant, began her enormously successful tours in the 1870s, impressing her audiences as much by her beauty as by her psychic powers.[15] Male mediums of the same period are rare, and after the retirement in 1870 of Daniel Dunglas Home, even rarer. During the entire latter half of the century, young male mediums are conspicuous by their absence. The male showman mediums of the 1860s and 70s were supplanted by female mediums whose work could rarely be confused with the conjuring tricks of male colleagues, but which consisted frequently of trance communications. Rolfe would have been aware of several of these famous, even infamous women – like Madame Blavatsky and Annie Besant. But at least two of these female mediums, Anna Kingsford and Eusapia Palladino, who came from different sectors of psychical performance, have some more direct bearing on Rolfe's choices in life and work.

Although Kingsford wrote novels at the earliest part of her career, her fame rested on a series of books on Spiritualism, vegetarianism and anti-vivisectionism. She was known as a seer and a prophet, and Blavatsky, her great rival, called her, with some irony, 'the mystic of the century', as

well as 'the divine Anna'.[16] She converted to Catholicism and became devoted to the Virgin Mary, and this became central to her beliefs.[17] Her last
work, *Clothed with the Sun* (1889), published posthumously, was a series
of 'illuminations' with a cover showing the Virgin standing in the sun, an
apocalyptic vision of the eternal feminine. She qualified as a doctor and
practised medicine in London, while still making public appearances and
writing works on Spiritualism. Her trance writings and her attempt to synthesise various esoteric traditions with Christianity led her to set up her own
semi-religious society, a rival to Blavatsky's Theosophical Society. The aim
of her book, *The Perfect Way: or the Finding of Christ* (1888, co-authored with
Edward Maitland), was to demonstrate that Christianity was 'a symbolic
synthesis of the fundamental truths contained in all religions', an enterprise
strikingly similar to Blavatsky's *The Secret Doctrine* (1888), which had the
subtitle 'The Synthesis of Science, Religion and Philosophy'.[18] Kingsford
was the closest of her contemporaries to Rolfe's interests, both in exploring the possibilities of a new, synthesised Catholicism and in 'alternative'
practices (he, too, was a vegetarian), although Rolfe's unorthodoxies finally
expressed themselves in a somewhat overstated orthodox interpretation of
the Catholic tradition.

The case of Eusapia Palladino may have helped provide a focus for Rolfe's
identification of spiritual powers in the Italian peasantry.[19] Palladino was
the most famous European medium of her generation. She rose to fame
following a series of sensational séances in the 1880s. An illiterate Neapolitan
peasant, she astonished witnesses with the production of various spirit
bodies, rappings and elevations. Only after Rolfe's death was she finally
exposed as a fraud, and although the evidence otherwise had never been very
secure, the will to believe in her overwhelmed scepticism. Kingsford and
Palladino represent opposite ends of the public discourse of Spiritualism.
Despite their different social class and nationality, they might be seen to
have been united in their Catholicism, their performative Spiritual powers
and their femininity.

Kingsford's identification of her spirit guide as a figure who looked like
Dante provides another parallel with Rolfe's Toto stories. The idea of Dante
as a hero of Spiritualism, as opposed to literature, is itself part of the tenor
of late nineteenth-century British cultural life, beginning with Rossetti's
perception of Dante as a ghostly figure.[20] In his early Pre-Raphaelite drawing 'The First Anniversary of the Death of Beatrice' (1849; Birmingham
Museum and Art Gallery), he depicted Dante as an automatic draughts-
man producing art in a kind of trance. Dante looks up, confused, while
his friends variously stare at him, whisper about his confusion or examine

the drawing. The angel and Dante were depicted by Rossetti in several ambitious paintings, notably in the several versions of *Dante's Dream at the Time of the Death of Beatrice* (1856 and 1871) and *Beata Beatrice* (1864, 1871, 1872).[21] Rossetti identifies Dante with a new occultism, a forerunner of the automatic, dream-inspired, late Romantic poet-medium that Rossetti himself would become. The artist changed both the visual representation of Dante and the audience for his work: he associated his hero with the tenebrous and the mystical, rather than the other qualities for which Dante had been known in contemporary literary and cultural scholarship. Significantly, Rossetti moves away from the landscapes of Heaven, Hell and Purgatory to the inner person, the soul – often feminised, as in the early story 'Hand and Soul' (1848). Rossetti's Dantesque paintings act as a bridge between a 'high culture' of poetry and painting, with their references to the religious art of the past, and contemporary, populist religious activities like séances and planchette sessions.

In many ways, the re-evaluation of Rossetti's paintings in the 1870s and 80s depends as much upon a culture sensitive to occultism and Spiritualism as to the popularity of Dante. So when the psychical researcher F. W. H. Myers wrote about the visual arts, it was upon Rossetti that his investigative mind rested. In his final years Rossetti's reputation was based on his representations of women, and for Myers, it was in conveying the mediumistic qualities of women that the painter was at his most powerful. In 'Rossetti and the Religion of Beauty' (1883) Myers invoked Dante to place Rossetti in a tradition of the spiritual in art, poetry and the occult:

Rossetti is but a Dante still in the *selva oscura*; he has not sounded hell so profoundly, nor mounted into heaven so high. He is not a prophet but an artist; yet an artist who, both by the very intensity of his artistic vision, and by some inborn bent towards symbol and mysticism, stands on the side of those who see in material things a spiritual significance, and utters words of universal meaning from the fulness [*sic*] of his own heart.[22]

For Rossetti and for some of his critics, the mediumistic extends and consolidates the more familiar features of the repertoire of femininity – woman as nature, woman as soul, woman as eternal. Significantly, however, as we have seen, for Rolfe, the medium is young, male, illiterate and foreign: qualities which 'other' him and 'feminise' him. Yet, as we will see, Rolfe invokes Dante in promulgating an occult connection with the underworld in which the feminine is supplanted by the masculine, and 'nature' by 'culture' (here, by poetry and poetic tradition).

Rolfe teases his readers with some Dante connections within the Toto stories. Toto's brother is called Guido, perhaps as a reference to Dante's friend, the poet Guido Cavalcanti.[23] And we are informed that at some earlier but unspecified time in their acquaintance, Toto had introduced his girlfriend, Beatrice, to Baron Corvo. Rolfe's difficulty in writing about femininity, or even in including female characters at all, is here exemplified in his attitude to this boyish Beatrice. In a later story we are informed, almost casually, that Toto's Beatrice has died, thus allowing the little all-male community to remain intact, unthreatened and unchallenged. But her death allows the development of the séance sequence in 'About These Tales, the Key and Purgatory', where Toto confesses that he had formerly used Beatrice as a sort of medium for access to the spirit world: 'Not now – Sir, my throat aches when I think – Excuse me – *Requiescat in Pace*.'[24] The larger implication of these parallels between Dante and Toto is that in Toto, Rolfe has found a source of European storytelling, of poetry and romance. In this instance Toto is Dante, just as elsewhere he is Ovid. In 'About These Tales, the Key and Purgatory', the author both reveals and conceals his sources, playing a game with the reader. Rolfe's own pederastic tone is taken over by a disingenuous Toto. Arguably Toto's innocence intensifies the voyeuristic pleasure contained in the narrative. When speaking of his friend Desiderio, Toto describes his eyes:

Eyes are very good; and the flavian eyes of Desiderio suit me better than all other eyes, better even than the pure eyes of that dove, my brother Guido. That is why I make the creature ride astride my knees, when I recite histories in these forests. I wrap him in my arms, and hold him still, and I look into his eyes. And what I see there, is told by my lips. O, eyes of a glorified cat! O lovely eyes! Eyes clear as the golden wine of Nido di Corvo![25]

Here the tone is Rolfe's own (rather than Toto's) and the use of the word 'flavian' (also used frequently in the later novel *Don Renato* and meaning 'golden yellow') and the unresisted self-reference 'Nido di Corvo' are quite obviously his, too. There is also the densely-worded symbolic world which is at the heart of most of Rolfe's writing, especially in the novels *Don Renato* and *The Desire and Pursuit of the Whole*, a language full of personal significance for the author: 'The flavian eyes of Desiderio suit me better than all other eyes.' The desirability of Desiderio is here underlined, but the name is given another inflection. Desiderio: the desired one; Desiderio: the slothful. Rolfe unites two Latin words: the verb *desidero* – to desire, to long for, to yearn for – and the adjective *desidiosus* – slothful, idle, lazy. Elsewhere Toto addresses Desiderio as 'Monster of Sloth'.[26]

As Toto speaks to his master, his young friend lies asleep in the shade. Toto needs to use him in the séance, and Desiderio is dragged out of a siesta. He 'had a little lazy smile playing on his half-open rosy lips . . . He appeared to be aware of drowsy pleasures in store.'[27] This is the suggestive pederastic tone; the youth becomes the living embodiment of the voluptuous Hellenistic sculpture of the Barberini Faun, a symbol of male sexual availability. As Martha Vicinus points out in her essay 'The Adolescent Boy: Fin-de-Siècle Femme Fatale?', 'the boy was as troubling for the turn-of-the-century artist as the better-known predatory woman.'[28] Desiderio is a good example of the troubling adolescent male. Certainly, in Rolfe's *In His Own Image*, he becomes a substitute for the feminine, displacing fatal women, new women, bluestockings and domestic angels.

Toto's description of his mediumistic powers is given verbally to 'Baron Corvo', and then demonstrated in a bizarre manner; he tells him:

Frat' Innocente-of-the-Nine-Quires has told me many tales . . . he taught me to watch the world with diligent eyes, but especially the people who are on it . . . He said that I should learn wisdom by observing people without their skins . . . at times I must go away in the loneliness, and think, and listen to the wind, or the sea, or to the voices of the trees and flowers, or to the whispers of the earth.[29]

Then he informs his master:

You have called me improvisatore . . . and you are wrong. It is simply the histories which I have from Frat' Innocente-of-the-Nine-Quires given in his proper words; or in my own words, descriptions of what I know, having seen, having heard . . . I am not Domeniddio, who can create things from nothing. I must have grapes and clean feet, before I can make wine.[30]

So much for the externals of Toto's 'knowledge' of how to tell a story, of how to watch with 'diligent eyes'. But Toto explains how he renews his knowledge too. There follow perhaps the most extraordinary pages in Rolfe's extraordinary writings where the novelist reveals himself and his inspiration, while explaining the inspiration of his Italian peasant boy. First, Toto dives alone into 'whatever water may be near':

While I am down there, my eyes pierce the shadows of the depths, and I see; there are voices, and I hear them sing . . . Afterward, I gain the bank, and I spread myself in the sun like one crucified, until my face is dry; and I stare into the sun, or the moon, or a star which I shall choose . . . Then I nail myself face downward, stretching hands and feet far and wide; and I breathe the breath of the earth. All the time I keep my eyelids open to the full and fixed and steadfast; till I see new things, as well as things that I have seen before. And so I learn.[31]

We should note the near-sacrilegious 'like one crucified' and 'I nail myself face downward', Christ-like identifications like those which Rolfe makes from time to time for himself. The theme of bathing (or diving), too, is a recurrent one for Rolfe. Usually he is the spectator of these youthful sports. In the story 'About Some Friends', the theme is used in a more conventional way and represents the renewal of baptism. Here, the immersion is part of a process of personal, spiritual renewal as the preliminary for an even more extraordinary process.

Then begins a sequence of disjointed sentences which last some thirteen pages of text, the record of Toto's séance, his journey to Hell. If the reader is not already alerted by the idea of a journey to Hell itself, Rolfe slyly scatters references to Dante's *Divine Comedy*. In the following quotation, for example, Toto is rambling in his self-imposed trance.

'Poor souls, in the dark silence and the ice-cold water.
'I shall come her. Oh yes!
'Yes, ready.
'A grey ladder.
'Light fixed to my head. Hands free.
'I follow you.'[32]

In its main details this is a transcription of lines from the *Inferno*, even to '*Più lunga scala convien che si saglia*'.[33] As he leaves Hell Toto sees 'glimmering sparks' which might be taken to represent the stars seen by Dante on his return to the earth.[34]

Toto is led into the depths of the earth by the Grey Angel, the Angel of Death, referred to as such in the story 'About the Four Things Necessary'. Here, in this story, the reference may be to Virgil, who conducts Dante into both Purgatory and Hell. Toto is anxious to avoid what he describes as 'the Brown Kingdom'. The underworld he enters, however, is noticeably brown. Rolfe uses the colour sixteen times to describe the descent: 'brown cave', 'brown darkness', 'brown rocks streaked with veins all white, or patched with lumps of glittering grey', 'little brown hole', 'brown nothingness', solid wall of brown'. 'Is that brown bottomless abyss a lake?' seems to be Rolfe's reconstruction of Dante's boiling lake of pitch in Hell. The image of a bridge above the lake strengthens the similarities between the two descriptions.[35] The reader is tempted to see the 'Brown Kingdom' as a synonym for anal intercourse, an expression, perhaps, of Rolfe's sexual fears or desires. But is this image of sexual intimacy meant to suggest an actual act done to Toto when he is in a trance, or one done to Desiderio, his 'muse'? Or is it a more general invitation into the spiritual through the sexual? It is unlikely that Rolfe would have wanted any definitive answer to these rhetorical questions. The story needs both close reading and differing interpretations by several readerships; it needs to remain suggestive to several potential audiences. Perhaps one of the ironies of the sexualised contact that permits the medium to go into a trance – Toto's intimacy with Desiderio – is in its very dissidence as an act of same-sex desire. It can be read as a comment upon Dante's expression of concern for the Florentine sodomites he meet in Cantos xv and xvi of the *Inferno*.

The extraordinary landscape of the underworld – brown walls, grey ladders, 'streaks glittering grey' – is an evocation of Dante's eighth circle of Hell.

> Luogo è in inferno detto Malebolge
> Tutto di pietra di color ferrigno,
> Come la cerchia che dintorno il volge.[36]
>
> There is a place within the depths of hell
> Call'd Malebolge, all of rock dark-stain'd
> With hue ferriginous, e'en as the steep
> That round it circling winds.

Malebolge (the evil pouch) is the colour of iron or iron-rust (*ferrigno*), which may have suggested to Rolfe this brown-ness. But in the immediacy of Toto's telling he re-enacts Dante's poem. It is not only – as it was in the 'Epick of Sangiorgio' – a borrowing of 'the measure of the *Commedia* of Dante', but of the episodes of the *Inferno* reflected upon, commented upon, distorted, even.[37]

Toto is involved in two phenomena of Spiritualism: trance-speaking and description of the spirit world or of the after-life. The one-sided, reported commentary (without the angel's replies or contributions) means that the reader must supply the missing side of the conversation and interpolate it. This leads to further ambiguities, the ambiguities and confusions of similar scattered gnomic words of the medium's meaning. Meanwhile Rolfe, as the recorder of the activity, can afford the kind of benign dispassionateness adopted in reports by writers like Frank Podmore, F. W. H. Myers and Edmund Gurney for the Society for Psychical Research.

Several questions arise from a reading of 'About These Tales, the Key and Purgatory'. Is Toto meant to be a reincarnation of Dante, a possibility only revealed during the séance? Or has he been taken over temporarily, during the séance, by the spirit of the dead poet? Is Toto revealing a previously hidden memory of a former existence? Or is his utterance simply a confused reminiscence of an episode in the *Divine Comedy*? Is he voicing a hitherto unknown folkloric tale which predates Dante's poem (a version of Proserpine's story, perhaps), known by Dante but hitherto undetected by literary historians? Or is he expressing some shared cultural memory in a kind of precognition of Jung's concept of a 'collective memory'? All of these possibilities are linked and not mutually exclusive. Certainly the implication of the discovery of a hitherto 'lost' source has been a characteristic of the historical novel since Romanticism, and was a device later used by Rolfe himself in *Don Renato*, while the idea of a hidden memory and the possibility of several personal identities had already been aired by various writers. William James, for example, reflecting in 1897 upon current psychical research, observed:

I have myself, as American agent for the census, collected hundreds of cases of hallucination in healthy persons. The result is to make me feel that we all have potentially a 'subliminal self', which may make at any time irruption into our ordinary lives. At its lowest, it is only the depository of our forgotten memories; at its highest, we do not know what it is at all.[38]

James agrees, more or less, with what he has observed of the work of F. W. H. Myers, which he describes as 'learned and ingenious'.[39] He quotes Myers:

Each of us has in reality an abiding psychical entity far more extensive than he knows, – an individuality which can never express itself through any corporeal manifestation. The self manifests itself through the organism, but there is always some part of the self unmanifested, and always, as it seems, some power of organic expression in abeyance or reserve.[40]

In creating Toto – or recreating him – I want to suggest that two processes have taken place for Rolfe. Firstly, he sees the beauty of the boy and is inspired by it. Secondly, he endows the boy's beauty with a cultural, rather than with an erotic or purely personal significance. Like Toto gazing into Desiderio's eyes, Rolfe gazes into his favourite boy's eyes and sees his story or, perhaps, history. The two creative processes are linked. Yet the specifically Italian context is important and the vast history of literature that is revealed in this dual process is both Italian and Catholic. In the two processes Rolfe translates the contemporary, celebrated Spiritualist mediums, most often women, from the parlour or the consulting rooms or the concert hall into a young male in a natural setting – an Italian woodland. Toto is able to tap a putative masculine intuition which brings him in touch with poetry, sex and the underworld at the same time. It is significant that Toto, as a male medium, travels downwards to Hell rather than upwards to Heaven, the usual direction for nineteenth-century Spiritualist mediums.

Yet in the other stories in *In His Own Image*, Rolfe constructs an image of a paradise on earth, a kind of Heaven illuminated by male beauty but ultimately controlled by a faith in God and a fear of punishment. Rolfe's glimpse of Hell through Toto's eyes – for all its Spiritualistic unorthodoxy – is a reminder that the medieval construction of Hell has a purpose in the modern world. On the other hand, Rolfe's vision of an all-male terrestrial paradise leading eventually to a heavenly paradise follows much of the thinking mooted by Kains Jackson in his polemic, 'The New Chivalry', which appeared in the *Artist* in 1894:

The New Chivalry . . . will not ask that very plain question of the Marriage Service, 'Will it lead to the procreation of children?' It will rest content with beauty – God's outward clue to the inward Paradise.[41]

Male–male relationships in all their variety – social, sexual, moral, theological – were to take on a millenarian, revolutionary note: they would *change* things. Whether we see this early gay rights movement as ultimately misogynistic, or whether we see it, like the feminisms of the latter part of the nineteenth century, as the beginnings of a much-needed, fundamental recognition of change in gender relations, is a debate which will not be settled easily (and not in this essay). But its revolutionary nature was at odds with its inherent conservative elements: the intensification of a status quo which accepted the oppression of women and of the feminine. It supplanted the traditional, institutionalised inequalities of marriage for those of relationships between young working-class men and rich or aristocratic men, albeit in the guise of some 'educational' relationship.

In Rolfe's *In His Own Image* the boy is the symbol of a coming change in gender and sexual relations. Toto, a male medium, a boy, contacts both the other world and the poetic springs of European culture. Like the psychic investigator, Rolfe is in awe of the medium who speaks to him in trance. Yet in writing up the account he manipulates and recasts the medium. Rolfe can interpret Toto's communications and reveal their significance, an act which is beyond the poor boy himself.

NOTES

My thanks go to Peter Francis, Patsy Williams and Ruth Clayton at St Deiniol's Library, Flintshire; to Nicola Bown and Liz Prettejohn, both of whom read an earlier draft of the chapter and made helpful suggestions; to Ruth Brown, Albert Boyer and Jane Bennett at Staffordshire University; to the School of Art and Design at Staffordshire University for research funding. Some of the research underlying this chapter was done many years ago at the University of Keele under the supervision of Professor Andor Gomme, now retired, whose patience and encouragement was important to the development of my interest in interdisciplinary research.

1　The stories were first published in the *Yellow Book* as 'Stories Toto Told Me' in 1895–6, were expanded into a pamphlet in 1898 and finally published in book form by John Lane in 1901, including some material that had appeared in *The Butterfly* in 1900. Bibliographic information on Rolfe's publications (1860–1913) has been taken from Cecil Woolf, *A Bibliography of Frederick Rolfe, Baron Corvo* (London: Rupert Hart Davis, 1972).

2　A. J. A. Symons, *Essays and Biographies* (London: Cassell, 1969), p. 10.

3　Baron Corvo (Frederick Rolfe), *In His Own Image* (London: John Lane, 1901), p. 213. Toto's speech quoted here is one of two in which he relates his particular talent for crystal-gazing. In the other (213), he lists a number of the ways in which reflective surfaces might be used to see into the future. The list is close to that produced by Andrew Lang in his essay 'Crystal Visions, Savage and Civilised' to indicate the range of methods and materials used for 'scrying'; this essay appears as Chapter 5 of his *The Making of Religion* (London: Longman's, Green, 1898). Lang expanded on these ideas on several occasions, notably in his article 'Crystal-gazing' for the eleventh edition of the *Encyclopaedia Britannica* (1910–11).

4　A suspicion of the magical element of Catholic ritual had been a part of the Protestant anti-Catholic polemic since the Reformation. Keith Thomas, in *Religion and the Decline of Magic: Studies in Popular Beliefs in Sixteenth- and Seventeenth-Century England* (Harmondsworth: Penguin, 1973), p. 60, summarises this Protestant argument with a question: 'What was transubstantiation but a curious piece of legerdemain?' By 1918 J. Arthur Hill could write that there should be a change in the attitude of the Catholic church towards Spiritualism, which was perceived as particularly violent in expression. He quoted F. W. H. Myers to support his position: that Spiritualists 'are proving the preamble of all religions – the existence of a spiritual world'. Arthur Hill, *Spiritualism: Its History, Phenomena and Doctrine* (London: Cassell, 1918). Earlier in the century and at the height of the Spiritualist 'craze' in England, the *Spiritual Magazine* was particularly exercised by the continual disavowal of Spiritualism by Catholic clerics. In 1863 leading articles in the March and July issues had pointed out the inherent Spiritualistic nature of the practices of two leading Catholic historical figures: the Curé d'Ars and Ignatius Loyola. In 1866 an article condemned what it saw as the confusion of the Catholic position in 'The Catholics and Spiritualism', *Spiritualist Magazine*, New Series, 1 (1866), 12–16. Generally, however, the complicated relationship between Spiritualism and the established Christian denominations was due to two conflicting tendencies within Spiritualism itself: some adherents being anti-Christian, some more broadly anti-materialist. For an exhaustive account of Spiritualism in relation to organised religion and social class see Logic Barrow, *Independent Spirits: Spiritualism and the English Plebeians, 1850–1910* (London: Routledge and Kegan Paul, 1986). For a broader discussion of the issue of religion and

Spiritualism, see Janet Oppenheim, *The Other World: Spiritualism and Psychical Research in England 1850–1914* (Cambridge: Cambridge University Press, 1985), especially pp. 59–103.

5 For a survey of British interest in Italian society in the nineteenth century, see Maura O'Connor, *The Romance of Italy and the English Political Imagination* (London: Macmillan, 1998), especially Chapter 2.

6 For examples of wayside shrine and *ex voto* subjects see Phillip Hook and Mark Poltimore, *Popular Nineteenth-Century Painting: A Dictionary of European Genre Painters* (Woodbridge, Suffolk: Antique Collectors' Club, 1986). For an earlier generation such scenes had a different meaning; see, for example C. P. Brand, *Italy and the English Romantics* (Cambridge: Cambridge University Press, 1957): 'The superstition of the uneducated Italian, the severity of the convents, the relics of paganism in the Catholic ritual, these and a dozen objections caused the average English man to turn from a Catholic Italy with disgust' (219). For a discussion of English attitudes to Italian and French Catholic practices in the nineteenth century, see Sheridan Gilley, 'Supernaturalised Culture: Catholic Attitudes and Latin Lands 1840–60' in *The Materials, Sources and Methods of Ecclesiastical History*, ed. Derek Baker (Oxford: Blackwell, 1975), pp. 309–23.

7 See A. J. A. Symons, *The Quest for Corvo* (London: Cassell, 1934); Donald Weeks, *Corvo* (London: Michael Joseph, 1971); Miriam Benkowitz, *Frederick Rolfe: Baron Corvo* (New York: Putnam, 1977). For an account of the Aberdeen exposure of 'Baron Corvo' see Weeks, *Corvo*, p. 152.

8 I am not aware that the strong similarities between Rolfe and Home have been explored before. Ruth Brandon suggests that there was a covered-up homosexual scandal involving Home which might be a further ground for comparing the two men. See Ruth Brandon, *The Spiritualists* (New York: Alfred Knopf, 1983). Home's expulsion from Rome for 'sorcery' is commented upon frequently in the London-based publication the *Spiritual Magazine* throughout 1864. The magazine was particularly supportive of Home and reported his exploits with a somewhat partisan enthusiasm.

9 The title page of *The Book of Sacred Magic of Abra-Melin the Mage* (London: J. M. Watkins, 1897) was designed by Mathers's wife Moina Mathers (née Moina Bergson).

10 'The Nude in Photography: With Some Studies Taken in the Open Air', *Studio* I (1893), 105–6. The published photograph is referred to in the story under consideration here. Toto offers a picturesque description of the processes of photography: 'You pinch the ball of a box: you pour venom from blue bottles over glass in the dark; you make little me come there, leaping or wrestling with that beast Otone, or lying at my ease taking my siesta, just as I live.' Corvo, *In His Own Image*, p. 211.

11 One should note the Pre-Raphaelite nature of Rolfe's 'Love, the Dreamer', with its similarities to Edward Burne-Jones's various series of paintings on the theme of love and, more particularly, Simeon Solomon's allegories which

personify love as an adolescent youth wearing a dreamy, introspective or sorrowful look, for example, *One Dreaming by the Sea* (1871; University of Wales, Aberystwyth School of Art Gallery).

12   Corvo, *In His Own Image*, p. 323.

13   Ibid., p. 207.

14   Ibid., p. 208.

15   For an account of Richmond's career, see Alex Owen, *The Darkened Room: Women, Power and Spiritualism in Late Victorian England* (London: Virago, 1989), pp. 210–11.

16   See the references to Kingsford in A. Trevor Barker (ed.), *The Letters of Helena Blavatsky to A. P. Sinnott* (Pasadena, CA: Theosophical University Press, 1973).

17   See the entry for Kingsford (1846–88) in the *Dictionary of National Biography*, ed. Leslie Stephen (London: Smith, Elder, 1892).

18   Anna Kingsford, quoted from the publisher's advertisement contained at the back of *Clothed with the Sun* (London: Redway, 1889). Macgregor Mathers dedicated *The Kabbalah Unveiled* (1887) to Kingsford and Maitland, 'the authors of *The Perfect Way*'. In her introduction to a new edition of the work (London: Routledge and Kegan Paul, 1926), Moina Macgregor Mathers explained that Mathers was more drawn to Kingsford's 'ideals of esoteric Christianity and the advancement of woman. Moreover he was profoundly interested in her campaign against vivisection, in which he vigorously aided her', p. xiii.

19   For a recent view of Palladino see Oppenheim, *The Other World*, pp. 149–52. For contrasting contemporary evaluations of her career, see Frank Podmore, *The Newer Spiritualism* (London: T. Fisher Unwin, 1910) and Cesare Lombroso, *After Death: What?* (London and Manchester: Sherratt and Hughes, 1910).

20   For a contemporary discussion of Rossetti's early perception of Dante, see 'Some Reminiscences of Christina Rossetti' by William Sharp in *Papers Critical and Reminiscent* (London: Heinemann, 1912), p. 80. For a recent discussion of the importance of Dante for Rossetti, see Alison Milbank, *Dante and the Victorians* (Manchester: Manchester University Press, 1998). A story that Dante had appeared after his death as an apparition to help uncover the missing cantos of the *Divina Commedia* had been given new currency by William Michael Rossetti in the *Athenaeum* in March 1861 and had also been the subject of a letter to the *Spiritual Magazine* in that year.

21   My chronology of these works is taken from Virigina Surtees, *Dante Gabriel Rossetti 1828–1882: The Paintings and Drawings: A Catalogue Raisonné* (London: Oxford University Press, 1971).

22   F. W. H. Myers, 'Rossetti and the Religion of Beauty', *Essays Modern* (London: Macmillan, 1897), pp. 312–34; pp. 321–2.

23   Toto refers to 'the pure eyes of that dove, my brother Guido' in Corvo, *In His Own Image*, p. 213. Guido Cavalcanti had become familiar to Victorian readers frollowing the publication of Rossetti's *Dante and his Circle: With*

the Italian Poets Preceeding Him (1100–1200–1300) (London: Ellis and White, 1874), which was a reworking of his earlier volume, *The Early Italian Poets* (1861).

24 Corvo, *In His Own Image*, p. 213.
25 Ibid.
26 Ibid., p. 227.
27 Ibid., pp. 214–5.
28 Martha Vicinus, 'The Adolescent Boy: Fin-de-Siècle Femme Fatale?', in *Victorian Sexual Dissidence*, ed. Richard Dellamora (Chicago and London: University of Chicago Press, 1999), pp. 83–108; p. 83.
29 Corvo, *In His Own Image*, pp. 207–8.
30 Ibid., p. 208.
31 Ibid., pp. 209, 210.
32 Ibid., p. 212.
33 Dante, *Inferno*, Canto xxiv. 55.
34 Corvo, *In His Own Image*, p. 212. Dante, *Inferno*, Canto xxxiv. 29, '*E quindi uscimmo a riveder le stelle*' ('Thus issuing we again beheld the stars'). Translations are taken from Dante Alighieri, *The Vision; or Hell, Purgatory and Paradise*, trans. Revd Henry Francis Cary (London: Henry G. Bohn, 1860), the standard nineteenth-century translation.
35 Cary's translation runs '*Così, di ponte in ponte, altro parlando . . . Tal, non per foco, ma per divina arte / Bollia lagguiso una pegola spessa / Che inviscava la ripa da ogni parte.*' ('Thus we from bridge to bridge, with other talk . . . So, not by force of fire but art divine / Boil'd here a glutinous thick mass, that round / Limed all the shore beneath.')
36 Ibid., Canto xviii: 1–3.
37 Cecil Woolf (ed.), *Without Prejudice: One Hundred Letters from Frederick Rolfe 'Baron Corvo' to John Lane* (London: Allen Lane, 1963), Letter 21, 24 June 1898. Presumably in response to a question from John Lane, Rolfe replies: 'Toto's "San Giorgio" *was* a long poem, which he had learnt somewhere' (p. 39, Rolfe's emphasis). For Toto's version of the 'long poem', see Corvo, 'Being an Epick of Sangiorgio, Protector of the Kingdom', *In His Own Image*, pp. 35–65.
38 William James, 'What Psychical Research has Accomplished' in *The Will to Believe: and Other Essays in Popular Philosophy* (New York, London and Bombay, Longman's, Green and Co., 1897), pp. 299–327; p. 321.
39 Ibid., p. 315.
40 Cited in ibid., p. 316.
41 Cited in Timothy d'Arch Smith, *Love in Earnest* (London: Routledge and Kegan Paul, 1970), p. 87.

PART IV

Envisioning the Unseen

CHAPTER 7

What is the stuff that dreams are made of?

Nicola Bown

In John Anster Fitzgerald's painting *The Stuff That Dreams Are Made Of* (1858, Fig. 4) a girl lies sleeping, surrounded by her dreams. She is fully clothed still, too tired to undress after the evening, perhaps; too tired to take the wreath of roses out of her hair. The moon, shining through a Gothic embrasure, outlines the spectral forms of dream-figures which hover over her while, surrounded by a nimbus of smoke or mist, her image stands under the mistletoe with a handsome young man. In the folds of her brocade skirt and round the sumptuous bed are a number of sinister goblin-like figures clashing cymbals and banging drums. One even stands on her pillow, hanging over her apparently oblivious head. From her flushed cheeks we infer that her dreams are stirring, whether they are delightful or disturbing or both at once.

This picture is almost the only nineteenth-century instance of this sub-ject: there are a handful of Renaissance and Baroque paintings of dreams, two famous images by Fuseli and Goya, and that is nearly all, until in the early twentieth century the influence of psychoanalysis prompted the interest of Surrealists in dream-images.[1] What gave Fitzgerald the idea of picturing dreaming like this? Fitzgerald's dream picture seems at first sight to be a made-over version of Fuseli's enormously influential painting, but a closer look shows that this is not the case. All pictures of dreamers and dreams have something to say about the stuff that dreams are made of, because the pictorial devices artists have used to give visual form to images seen only with the inward eye also signify a theory of the origin and mean-ings of dreams. Do dreams come from outside the dreamer by supernatural means, as messages and portents? Or are they simply meaningless pictures in the mind, and the result of overeating and indigestion? In Fitzgerald's picture dreams are neither one thing nor the other: they are both physical and supernatural, material and spiritual. In the nineteenth century the stuff that dreams are made of was the subject of intense debate and speculation,

Figure 4   John Anster Fitzgerald, *The Stuff That Dreams Are Made Of.*

and at its centre was the supernatural. The dream-images that populate Fitzgerald's painting give a visual form to that debate.

In Enlightenment thought the sceptical enquiry into the nature of dreams was an important part of wider philosophical and medical investigations into the nature of mind and of 'fundamental life processes including sleeping, waking, digestion and disease'.[2] Dreams were discussed by thinkers such as Hobbes, Locke, Dugald Stewart and David Hartley, who treated them either as distorted recollections of the day's events or as mental images produced by physical causes such as heat, cold, sounds or disease. The prevailing rationalism of the educated classes evidenced in such accounts of dreams influenced artists' representation of dreams and dreamers. One of the most famous images of a dream is Henry Fuseli's *The Nightmare* (1781, Fig. 5), which shows a sleeping woman with a demon crouched upon her chest, and a mysterious horse's head appearing from behind a curtain. Rather than representing the dream as a symbolic image to be deciphered, as earlier artists had done, Fuseli, as Nicolas Powell has shown, depicts instead the sensation, the physical experience of a nightmare.[3] The 'demon'

Figure 5   Henry Fuseli, *The Nightmare.*

sitting on the woman's chest is a visual representation of the crushing weight on the chest routinely associated with nightmare, and termed 'incubus'. Rather than having a supernatural connotation, 'incubus' meant the mental phenomenon in which sensations produced within the sleeper's body (such as the effects of too much blood in the brain) were referred outwards by the sleeping brain to an imaginary cause. A vivid account of the sensation is given in John Bond's *An Essay on the Incubus, or Nightmare* (1753): 'The nightmare generally seizes people sleeping on their backs, and often begins with frightful dreams, which are soon succeeded by a difficult respiration, a violent oppression of the breast, and a total privation of voluntary motion. In this agony they sigh, groan, utter indistinct sounds, and remain in the jaws of death, till, by the utmost efforts of nature, or some external assistance, they escape out of that dreadful torpid state.'⁴ The horse's head emerging from the curtain, with its white-blind eyes, is identified by Powell as a visual pun combining references to legends of the *mara*, a spirit from northern mythology, and the *Morre* or *Smarre*, Italian names for vampire- and incubus-like creatures, with the 'mare' in 'nightmare' (thought by Samuel Johnson to originate in the *mara*).[5] The mirror on the dressing table beside the bed refers to the metaphor of the mind as a looking-glass reflecting the external world, used by Locke in arguing against the notion that dreams are the thoughts of the soul: 'And the soul, in such a state of thinking, does very little if at all, excel that of a looking-glass, which constantly receives a variety of images, or *ideas*, but retains none: they disappear and vanish and there remain no foot-steps of them; the looking-glass is never the better of such *ideas*, nor the soul for such Thoughts.'[6] The iconography of Fuseli's painting brings together references to theories of the physical origins of dreaming and to the comparative study of language and mythology. Both of these were part of the wider Enlightenment campaign against superstition and supernaturalism: therefore, what appears initially to be a study in the supernatural turns out to be the expression of rationalist and sceptical Enlightenment thinking. And by disposing his symbols of the physiological phenomena of dreams around the dreamer's sleeping body and framing the composition in suggestive dark spaces and folds of drapery, Fuseli turns the picture space into an externalised representation of the interior of the sleeper's mind. For the first time, the picture space symbolises the consciousness of the dreaming subject, turned, as it were, inside out.

This innovation is repeated in Goya's famous *El sueño de la razón produce monstruos*, no. 43 of *Los Caprichos* (1796–8, Fig. 6). In this print the figure, often thought to be based on Goya's friend Jovellanos, sleeps at his desk, his head resting on his papers. Around his head and body, and then streaming away into the darkness surrounding him, are the 'monsters': bats and owls, creatures of the night, and a lynx, a wild, untameable creature.[7] The shadowy darkness that fills the frame again suggests that the picture space represents the dreamer's consciousness, furnished, while he is asleep, with monstrous dreams. The relation between the dreamer's sleeping and waking worlds, and thus the origin of his dreams, is also signified pictorially. A diagonal sweep leads up from the papers, through the dreamer's head and the owl hovering directly above it, upwards and outwards to the obscure, sinister shapes of his dreams. Directly below his head, on the side of his desk, is the caption, normally translated as 'the sleep of reason produces monsters'. Yet as well as 'sleep', *sueño* also means 'dream', which would render the caption 'the dream of reason produces monsters', and in fact this title fits better with Enlightenment theories of the origins and processes of dreaming than the usual translation.[8] The print is often seen as an allegory of the social effects of reason's sleep, but it also embodies the idea that in sleep, the normal mental processes of memory and association of ideas and

Figure 6   Francisco de Goya, *El sueño de la razón produce monstruos.*

images carries on, although untempered by reason and judgement. The irrationality of dreams was a central tenet of philosophical investigations of dreaming; Locke, for instance, opined: 'It is true, we sometimes have instances of perception whilst we are *asleep*, and retain the memory of those *thoughts*; but how extravagant and incoherent for the most part they are, how little conformable to the perfection and order of a rational being, those who are acquainted with dreams need not be told.'[9] Monsters are the dream of reason, because dreams are made out of the jumbled and nonsensical combinations of ideas, images and memories ordered in the waking mind by reason according to the law of association. Thus, the writing in which the dreamer has been engaged and the monsters in the darkness of his sleeping brain are equally creations of his reasoning mind: separated by his head, on one side the waking exercise of intellect and rationality, on the other side the fantastic creatures of dream.[10]

Fuseli and Goya transformed the pictorial conventions for portraying dreams from a division of the picture space into distinct areas occupied by the human sleeper and the divine dream to the use of the picture space to represent the dreamer's mind, and this change in pictorial conventions apparently mirrors an advance from the belief in divine, prophetic dreams to sceptical, Enlightenment enquiry into their nature.[11] Yet belief in the supernatural provenance of dreams persisted, both in popular and educated circles: Romantic poetry, prose and visual art repeatedly strives to represent the existence of another realm beyond the everyday, to which one might gain access through poetic intuition, sympathetic communion with the external world, religious experience or dreams.[12] Shelley's famous lines from 'Mont Blanc', 'Some say that gleams from a remoter world/Visit the soul in sleep', are one instance of a widespread interest in dreams as a conduit to a transcendent reality.[13] In William Blake's watercolour, *The Youthful Poet's Dream* (1816–20, New York: Pierpoint Morgan Library), the poet is asleep, the pen in his hand transcribing his dream into a manuscript book. The dream itself is contained within a sphere, a device Blake borrowed from Raphael's *Joseph's Two Dreams Interpreted* (1517, Vatican: Loggia), and the sphere is held on either side by an angel. Both the angels and the separation of the dream from the earthly world of the poet signify clearly that his poetic inspiration is heavenly. Blake's return to the pictorial conventions of the Renaissance is perfectly consonant with his belief, voiced throughout his writings, in the supernatural origin of dreams.

No less does *The Stuff That Dreams Are Made Of* confound the idea that there is a neat historical progression from the belief in the supernatural origin of dreams to the scientific attempt to understand them. Whilst its

Figure 7   Frontispiece, 'Dreamer's Wonderful Visions', from *The Dreamer's Sure Guide, or Interpretation of Dreams Faithfully Revealed*.

setting in the sleeper's bedroom suggests that it depicts the intimate and private world of the dreamer's consciousness rather than the public stage upon which biblical and mythological personages dream their dreams, implying that the dreams which hang in the air are psychological phenomena, it is also filled with supernatural and prophetic or divinatory elements. Although it is probable that Fitzgerald knew Fuseli's and Goya's pictures, *The Stuff That Dreams Are Made Of* closely resembles neither of them.[14] The girl stretches out in sleep, but her body is not contorted, like that of Fuseli's nightmare-racked dreamer, and though her dreams hang in the air, they do not stream away into darkness, but partake of the brilliantly-coloured scene; the dreams fill the picture space rather than clustering around her head.

There is, however, a close visual resemblance between *The Stuff That Dreams Are Made Of* and the picture that forms the frontispiece to one of the many cheap dream books available in the period, *The Dreamer's Sure Guide, or Interpretation of Dreams Faithfully Revealed* (1830, Fig. 7). The frontispiece, entitled 'Dreamer's Wonderful Visions', is a large, hand-coloured engraving showing a dreaming girl stretched out fully clothed.

By her side, the dreamer's 'sure guide' points to the dream-visions that hang in the air around her. Above the couch is a series of scenes that form a narrative: courtship, marriage and children. Surrounding the bed, and swathed in dark clouds, are a number of symbolic dreams whose meaning may be found in the lexicon: a ghost, a skeleton, a lion and a serpent, fire, a coffin, keys and jewellery, playing cards, a comet and a mirror. The dreams are evidently symbolic images that can be interpreted to divine the future. The clouds which swathe the dream-symbols might be taken as a symbol of their supernatural provenance, yet the darkness of the picture space here also suggests the recesses of the dreamer's mind, just as it does for Fuseli and Goya. This picture is an image of the inside of the dreamer's mind, but it shows the mind as permeable to the outside, for at its centre stands the strange figure of the 'sure guide', pointing out and explaining the dreamer's dreams.

The figure of the sleeping girl acts as a representative of the dream book's reader, for most were aimed at women, concentrating on subjects such as childbirth, marriage and courtship. Maureen Perkins comments that most middle-class 'contemporaries regarded fortune-telling as something resorted to by the lower orders', and the low price and cheap paper and printing of such books suggests that they were mainly bought by poorer women.[15] However, middle-class women were not immune to the prophetic power of dreams. If the frontispiece to *The Countess of Blessington's True Interpreter of Dreams, Visions and Omens of the Wedding Day* (1861) is to be believed, then oneiromancy, crystal-ball-gazing and fortune-telling with playing cards were all practised in drawing rooms and parlours, and this is borne out by an article in *The Englishwoman's Domestic Magazine* from 1867, entitled 'Divination for the Drawing Room'.[16] The bedroom in *The Stuff That Dreams Are Made Of* is luxurious, and the girl's clothes are obviously expensive: she is no credulous servant, but a wealthy young lady. The striking resemblance between the frontispiece to *The Dreamer's Sure Guide* and Fitzgerald's painting suggests that he may have drawn upon it as a source for his picture; it also suggests that interest and belief in the supernatural and prophetic power of dreams was not limited to the uneducated who were the main readers of dream books, but that it was widespread in the middle class. Fitzgerald produced at least two versions of this subject, and this testifies to the interest it held for his middle-class patrons.[17]

There are other possible sources for Fitzgerald's treatment of dreams and dreamers. His interest in the subject might also have been stimulated by the exhibition in 1848 and 1856 of illustrations to Keats's 'The Eve of St Agnes' by William Holman Hunt and Arthur Hughes. Many of Richard Doyle's illustrations for *Punch* feature grotesque figures and imp-like creatures with enlarged heads and elongated limbs floating in space, and he produced an illustration for Dickens's *The Chimes* (1844) showing a dreaming figure surrounded by dreams; in his illustrations to Dickens's *Barnaby Rudge* (1841) Hablot K. Browne ('Phiz') also used this motif.[18] There was, then, an existing repertoire of images that Fitzgerald may well have used in developing his pictures; however, he looked beyond his sources to produce a rich and complex image which brings together many visual ideas about dreams. It combines vignettes that seem to represent omens or wishes, figures banging drums and blowing trumpets or sitting on the dreamer's shoulder, cloudy nimbuses from which the dreams emerge and strangely spectral translucent figures which hang in the air. If previous dream pictures embodied ideas about the origin and nature of dreams from philosophical and medical writings, so too did Fitzgerald's. The presence of these elements in his picture is a pictorial representation of the numerous and sometimes contradictory ideas about dreams circulating in the thirty years or so before Fitzgerald made it: even the tag that forms his title occurs frequently in contemporary writings on dreams.[19] Mixing elements from Fuseli's and Goya's Enlightenment images, popular prints, book and periodical illustration, he found a way to give a compelling visual form to a question that preoccupied his contemporaries: what is the stuff that dreams are made of?[20]

Although speculation about the nature of dreams had formed a current in Enlightenment thinking about the nature of the human mind, this developed in the course of the nineteenth century into an explosion of interest in the nature of dreams, and it became an important issue in debates over the nature of consciousness and the relationship between the mind and the external world. At the centre of these debates was the problem of whether dreams and, by extension, the human mind are supernatural or material. Did dreams originate in the soul, and was consciousness spiritual, or were the workings of the mind physical and dreams merely a normal, if strange, form of mental functioning? Did dreams come from outside the dreamer, or were they all in his or her own mind? Because the boundaries between the supernatural and the material were both contested and obscure, the debate was not simply a question of whether dreams had a supernatural origin or not. On the contrary, theorists repeatedly discussed the origin of dreams in order to elucidate the relationship between mind, body, soul and spirit, and between our human consciousness and whatever supernatural forces or beings might surround us.

Those who wrote on dreams did so from widely differing perspectives, reflecting that fact that the developing science of psychology lay on the borders between philosophy, physiology and medicine, as Jenny Bourne Taylor has shown.[21] Frequently drawing on the theories of Stewart and Hartley, and emphasising such empirical observations of dreams and dreamers as they were able to make, physicians and physiologists were keen to understand dreaming as part of the physiological functioning of the brain. Others wrote from a theological perspective, promoting the physiological and empirical understanding of dreaming in order to combat the superstition of the uneducated and the influence of Swedenborg, who had claimed in his spiritual diaries (published in an English translation in 1846) to have conversed with angels and other supernatural beings in his dreams.[22] These writers, whatever their differences, saw dreams as physiological rather than supernatural phenomena: indeed, they were all concerned to refute the belief that dreams were meaningful and that they might contain supernatural messages, arguing instead that dreams were entirely a mental phenomenon. On the other side of the debate were a loose collection of 'supernaturalists' ranging from Spiritualist writers fully committed to the idea that dreams are supernatural messages with prophetic powers, through the authors of dream lexicons and guides to divination by dreams who may equally have been 'true believers' or cynics, to those who, despite their general scepticism and condemnation of superstition, admitted to a lingering fascination with the idea that dreams might be supernatural.[23]

At the beginning of the chapter on dreams from *The Philosophy of Sleep* (1830), Robert Macnish gives a robust statement of his theory of dreams:

Dreaming, then, takes place when the repose is broken; and consists of a series of thoughts or feelings called into existence by certain powers of mind, while the other mental powers which control these thoughts or feelings, is inactive. This theory is the only one capable of affording a satisfactory explanation of dreams.[24]

This is a bold statement of one of the major theories of dreaming: that sleep does not prevent perception, and that dreams are caused by sense-impressions reaching the mind from the external world during sleep. Macnish, for example, gives a number of instances of dreams resulting from a confused perception of a sense-impression: lying in a smoky room, one might dream of the sack of Rome, whilst the rain on the window pane causes one to dream of floods and cataracts. A more complex rendering of this idea is given by G. H. Lewes in *The Physiology of Common Life* (1859). Lewes states that in dreams, 'The train of thought may be, and must be, determined by any sensation felt during sleep', but argues these sensations can come both from the external world and from inside the sleeper's body, through what he terms the 'systemic senses'; these sensations stimulate the brain and produce the typically vivid absurdities of the dream:

If we reflect that the nervous centres must be incessantly called into activity, either through the imperfectly closed channels of the Five Senses, or through the Systemic Senses, and that these centres, once excited, must necessarily play on each other – and if we reflect farther, that the sensational and ideational activities thus stimulated operate under very different conditions, and in very different conjunctions, during sleep, we shall be at no loss to understand both the incoherence and coherence of dreams – the perfect congruity of certain trains of thought amid the most absurd incongruities.[25]

Another theory stressed the way that dreams appeared to be made out of the stores of memory already in the mind, and that the events and persons featuring in a dream had often been encountered in waking life in the day or two previously. In *Sleep and Dreams* (1851), John Addington Symonds comments that 'everyone, no matter how little accustomed to the analysis of his thoughts and feelings, must have noticed that a large proportion of the materials of dreams are derived from past experience; that they are products of a kind of memory', combined under the 'law of association or suggestion' in sometimes illogical or absurd ways.[26] Another suggested that under certain conditions dreams, especially nightmares or incubus, might be caused by too much blood in the brain or the effects of indigestion: many writers, for example, retailed the probably apocryphal story that Fuseli ate raw meat before bed in order to induce wild and fantastic dreams.

The point that dreams have physical causes and that the mechanism of dream-formation is also physical was a crucial one, with both physiological and theological implications, for it implied that the mind and brain were identical and that the mind was wholly material. In his *Essay on Superstition, Being an Inquiry into the Effects of Physical Influence on the Mind* (1830), W. Newnham asserted that dreaming is 'a condition of the *material brain*, not of the *immaterial principle*'.[27] The affirmation of the identity of brain and mind, and the assertion that only the brain is involved in the dream were intended to counter the belief that dreams are messages from the immaterial spirit which travels outside the body, meeting with other spirits in supernatural communication. Walter Dendy in *On the Phenomena of Dreams* (1832), for example, poured scorn on Swedenborg's claims to have experienced conversation with angels in his sleep, and on those 'Pseudo-psychologists' who believe that 'a dream may be the flight of a soul on a visit to other regions and its observations of their systems from actual survey'.[28]

Though dismissing this notion as impossible, however, those arguing for the physical nature of mind repeatedly returned to the relation between the interior spaces of the mind and the outside world and to the permeability of the sleeper's consciousness. In stating that the '*perfect integrity* of the brain is necessary to the manifestation of thought', Newnham implies that, because reason and judgement cannot operate while one is asleep, the brain must of necessity lose its integrity, its wholeness, while dreaming.[29] Discussing the common phenomenon of mistaking the spectral images of dream for reality – projecting them outside ourselves, as Lewes says – Henry Holland, in *Chapters on Mental Physiology* (1852) speculates that this 'appears to make a breach for a time in the identity of the rational being', because we lose the distinction between what is inside the mind and what is outside it.[30] Or as an article on 'Dreams' published in *Tinsley's Magazine* in 1863 put it: 'In reverie we know our thoughts for what they are; in the dream we take them to be things.'[31] Dreaming breaches the integrity of the mind, and thus the physical boundaries of the sleeper, because it is impossible to distinguish what is inside from what is outside. Dream images which are, in reality, inside the dreamer's own mind, appear to be outside it; spectral illusions seem to have the same material reality as the physical causes which produced them.[32] Dreams, then, were a problem for those who wished to argue for the material nature of mind and the identity of mind and brain, because in the consciousness of the dreamer the distinction between the self and the external world, crucial to the operation of reason and judgement, breaks down and is lost.[33]

The idea that the integrity of the self dissolves when we are asleep also occurs in the writings of Spiritualists, non-materialist mesmerists and others who believed in the possibility of supernatural dreams; they, however, saw this more positively. For the Spiritualist Revd Thomas Millington, only 'ridiculous or frightful' dreams could have physical causes, but dreams in which the imagination is at play are the work of a spirit body that exactly corresponds to the corporeal body but is partly separable from it:

It may be, then, that during sleep, the mind in its partial abstraction from the body learns from a higher, or at least a more independent order of spirits, those future events which it could not otherwise foresee; or by some latent faculty in itself, pierces the veil of futurity and discerns the appointed order of things to come.[34]

The spirit, which is immortal and therefore supernatural, is the source of all true dreams, and these are messages from a 'more glorious scene' in which it holds converse with other spirits.[35] A materialist version of the idea that the spirit leaves the body in sleep and brings back dreams is explored in John

Sheppard's *On Dreams, in Their Mental and Moral Aspects* (1847). Sheppard argues that the vehicle of consciousness may be minute particles, rather than the 'congeries of animal substance' the body and brain are made out of. Since the microscope has now opened to view organisms many times more minute than previously supposed possible, it is not at all unlikely, he argues, that the spirit is composed of such material:

If this is to assist us to conceive of the spirit's retaining an inexpressibly subtile organism when it lays down this exterior frame, by which it may still have and express thought and emotion, till it 'superindue' that form which shall be 'spiritual' and immortal, – the microscopic facts have for us a deeper interest as illustrations of this probability, than as mere facts.[36]

Though Sheppard dismisses those 'pseudo-psychologists' who infer from dreams an argument for the existence of a spirit independent of the body, he does believe that dreams offer evidence for the existence of the soul, and that they can bring supernatural messages. His conception of a spirit that is an 'inexpressibly subtile organism', different but not separable from the body (and perhaps visible using the microscope), suggests that in dreams the spirit passes outside the physical laws that govern the 'animal substance' of the body and mind.

In her widely-read *The Night-Side of Nature* (1848), Catherine Crowe suggests that in dreams the spirit acts both internally in the mind and as a messenger from outside. She states that dreaming 'arises from the secret activity of the spirit in the sensuous organs of the brain', implying that the spirit and brain are not only conceptually but functionally and physiologically separate.[37] Furthermore, the spirit or soul 'is designed as the mirror of a superior spiritual order', to which it belongs even when attached to the corporeal body, and in dreams it receives 'a foretaste of its future condition'.[38] Some of the most sceptical and materialist writers echoed this idea, even though they rejected the notion of dreams as supernatural messages. Walter Dendy, for instance, believed that the rapid succession of ideas in the dream is evidence of the 'divine nature of mind, – a remote resemblance' of God's infinitude, and Lewes compared this phenomenon to cloud shadows racing over a cornfield, implying through his simile that dreams are the image of something above and outside ourselves, even though he believed that they came from inside the dreamer's mind.[39]

The nature and causes of dreams was an important subject because it increasingly became central to speculations about the nature of the human mind; dreams were involved in the supernatural because the question of whether the human mind was itself part of the supernatural through

its resemblance to God's mind was central to nineteenth-century theological and scientific debates.[40] While a thoroughgoing materialism was
the characteristic attitude of the 'clever lawyer and physician in full practice', the educated classes who saw themselves as exponents of the most
progressive and scientific ideas, it was not only the 'ignorant and the half-
educated' who professed themselves 'susceptible of impressions for which
their reason cannot always account' and who admitted the 'inexplicable
and supernatural'.[41] Even those who set out to combat superstition found
themselves drawn to ideas of the supernatural when describing the effects of
their dreams. Charles Ollier, author of *Fallacy of Ghosts, Dreams and Omens*
(1848), admits that his own dreams 'have more than once appeared like a
magic mirror in which things to come, or facts which had happened at a
distance, were clearly portrayed'; though Ollier insists that all such dreams
are merely coincidental, his choice of metaphor shows how strongly the idea
of the dream as a supernatural message persisted.[42] The writer of an article
in *Once a Week* from 1862 describes the consciousness of falling asleep thus:
'The dream god has his hand on you, though he has not yet led you away.'[43]
And at the end of an essay devoted to exploding the belief in dreams as
supernatural, John Addington Symonds gives way to a lyrical evocation of
those ancient times when dreams did truly come from the gods:

And though ourselves set free from superstition, let us, when viewing dreams
in reference to the human species, consider how they have been associated in
men's minds with oracles, and revelations, and warnings; that they have seemed to
bridge over the mysterious chasm which divides us from the invisible world and
its shadowy inhabitants.

Modern scientific knowledge may have liberated humanity from superstition, but it has denuded the world of romance. The modern dreamer, who
knows his dreams for jumbled-up memories, has lost a haunting mystery,
compared with the 'dreams of men who had walked by moonlight, under
the shadows of the tombs of departed kings'.[44] It is not surprising, then,
that in the face of such thoroughgoing materialist theories of mind as those
put forward by writers aiming to formulate a scientific psychology, there
should be a yearning towards the supernatural, and towards the idea that
in the human mind is a spark of the divine, 'a certain delicate machinery planted in the human brain by the Divine hand', which enables us to
perceive and respond to the invisible and immaterial world around us.[45]
From the 1830s onwards, writers from Robert Macnish and W. Newnham
through to Henry Holland and G. H. Lewes sought to combat popular,
'superstitious' beliefs about the supernatural origin of dreams and to replace

them with an empirically-based materialist theory of mind, but they had to contend with a widespread desire – to which they, too, were sometimes prey – to preserve the possibility of dreams, and the mind, as supernatural. An article in the *Eclectic Review* from 1865 eloquently sums up the refusal of many to give up the supernatural theory of dreaming:

But, indeed, dreams, if not of supernatural origin, completely confuse and perplex all ideas which found them on mere naturalism. It is in the kingdom of dreams that the two worlds of the natural and the supernatural seem to be so united that it is impossible, with any degree of accuracy, to define in what part of the mysterious and spectral isthmus the domain of the natural terminates, and the region of the supernatural begins.[46]

In contrast to those who attempted a categorical division of the natural and supernatural, relegating the supernatural to the period of miracles recorded in the scriptures, many still thought of the supernatural as 'a region with laws of its own, beyond the code of our navigation, the limitations of our quadrant, and the application of our signals' into which anyone might enter in their dreams.[47]

It is this mass of competing and contradictory theories of dreams to which John Anster Fitzgerald gives a visual form in *The Stuff That Dreams Are Made Of*, as a detailed look at the picture shows. At the bottom of the picture, along the edge of the bed and standing on the bedside chair, is a row of goblin-like creatures. Apart from the one at the end, who is drinking a cup of tea, all are playing musical instruments: cymbals, cello, harp, trumpet and a drum. Are they playing a musical accompaniment to the dream, or are they providing the musical stimulus that prompts the formation of the dream in the girl's mind? This is a difficult question to decide, because it involves deciding on the nature of the creatures themselves. If they are playing an accompaniment to the dream, they are part of it, but what if they are not in the dream but part of the external world? Their solidity differentiates them from the spectral outlines of the other dream-goblins that surround the girl, implying perhaps that they are real. However, the suggestion that their music somehow stimulates the dream, the pictorial logic of which is strengthened by their position underneath the dreams and with the dreaming girl between them, so that the music, as it were, passes through her to become the dreams, is reminiscent of the physiological theories of dreams caused by the perception of an external stimulus. Yet the creatures are clearly supernatural beings, whether in the dream or out of it. Like the fairies in Fitzgerald's pictures such as *Cock Robin Defending his Nest* (private collection), they seem to be modelled on the therioanthropic monsters and demons of Hieronymus Bosch and Pieter Brueghel, and recall John Addington Symonds's remark that while dreaming, 'the mind may be recreated by visions of fairy scenes and unearthly forms, such as the waking eye never beheld; or it may be haunted by combinations of forms more hideous than were ever conceived even by an artist of the hag-ridden Middle Ages'.[48] Dreams resemble the supernatural world, even if they are not part of it; yet the presence of these figures serves as a reminder of how difficult it is for the dreamer to know what is dream and what is reality, especially when both seem equally supernatural.

Above the bed, surrounded in a hazy nimbus, are the figures of the dreamer, recognisable by her wreath and jacket, with a young man, who in one version wears seventeenth-century dress, and in the other oriental costume, standing under a mistletoe wreath. Various interpretations can be made of this group. Perhaps the dreaming girl has been at a Christmas fancy-dress party with the young man and the dream is a memory; or perhaps the dream is a wishful vision like that described by Robert Macnish: 'The young maiden stretched upon the couch of sleep, may have her spirit filled with the image of her lover, while her whole being swims in the ecstacies of impassioned, yet virtuous attachment.'[49] Or perhaps it is a prophetic dream of events to come, like the scenes in the frontispiece to *The Dreamer's Sure Guide*. The presence in one of the versions of the picture of several smaller scenes with the girl in them, arranged very like those in that picture, strengthens this impression.[50] The presence of the cloudy nimbus suggests yet another possibility: that the dreaming girl's spirit has left her body to commune in the spirit world with that of her lover, past, present or future, and the cloudy nimbus separates the material from the spirit world in much the same way that clouds separate Earth from Heaven in Renaissance painting. Surrounding the two figures are more 'demons', though whether their presence is malign or benevolent is hard to determine.

Lastly, the rest of the room, and, indeed the rest of the picture space, is filled with spectral outline figures, some of which are monstrous and some almost angelic. There is a similar ambiguity about the nature of these figures. On the one hand, they seem to be clustered around the girl's head, even standing on her pillow, so seeming to be creatures of her sleeping imagination. Yet they are also grouped in front of the window, for it is the moonlight shining in through the window that picks out their spectral forms, suggesting perhaps that they have come from outside the room. The transparency of their outlined bodies implies both that they are the flimsy and insubstantial creatures of dream, nothing more than images in the dreaming girl's mind, and that they are they are the forms of spiritual bodies, clustering round and conversing with the girl's own spirit. Yet the technique Fitzgerald has used to depict them, a white outline against a darker background, suggests also that they have a physical reality. In a compelling visual comparison, Ursula Seibold-Bultmann has argued that these figures resemble the illustrations of 'animalcules' under the microscope.[51] In works such as J. G. Wood's *Common Objects of the Microscope* (1862), the illustrations use just this technique of white outline against a black background, mimicking the effect of translucent creatures seen through the bright light of the microscope. As Seibold-Bultmann shows, the craze for microscopy was accompanied by popular parodies such as *Spooner's Transformations: the Microscope*, which shows an old woman looking horrified as she sees magnified by the microscope horrid monsters with grotesque forms and faces, and these are not dissimilar to Fitzgerald's dream creatures.[52] The connection between Fitzgerald's dreams and microscopic animalcules recalls Sheppard's speculation that the matter of consciousness too might one day be visible through the microscope; it suggests that the dreams are material, just as much as the bedroom furniture. The nature of these figures cannot be resolved because all the possibilities are equally likely: they are creatures of the imagination inside the dreaming girl's head, and they are supernatural beings, and they are creatures of living matter just as much as she is. Just as even those writers who aimed definitively to place the understanding of dreams on a scientific footing were compelled to use the language of the supernatural to describe the experience of dreaming, so Fitzgerald uses the visual vocabulary of scientific illustration to represent the spectral forms of dreams which might be either material or supernatural or both.

The Stuff That Dreams Are Made Of, then, meditates on a deep uncertainty among Fitzgerald's contemporaries about the nature of dreams. His various ways of visualising dreams correspond both to the efforts his contemporaries made to understand them and to the limits of their understanding. He put into the same frame pictorial conventions which were underpinned by quite different ideas about the origins of dreams, and in his representations of what dreams look like he brought together references to both science and the supernatural. Reflecting on the debate, the *Eclectic Review* temporised: 'If we could but with any degree of distinctness find out what ideas are, we suppose the whole mystery could be solved at once; for dreams and ideas are of the same stuff, and, as we have hinted, are not so much pictures of the mind and forms of mental action, as mind itself.'[53] The word 'stuff' leans towards the material, and seems to pull the picture towards the physiological and scientific understanding of dreams; yet if the stuff of mind was indeed the same as the stuff of dreams, neither science, nor Spiritualism, nor any other contemporary discourse was able fully to understand what that stuff was. As the *Eclectic Review*'s writer hints, the stuff of dreams could be conceived as supernatural just as much as material, or it could be thought of as something which partook of both, a region between the physiological and the spiritual, the material and the immaterial. That is the region Fitzgerald's pictures visualise: a region where dreams are true and meaningless, physical and supernatural, where dreams can be seen through the microscope and with the immaterial eyes of the spirit, and where they come from beyond and inside the dreamer's mind.

NOTES

1 Fitzgerald had previously exhibited *The Artist's Dream* (1857), in which an artist has fallen asleep in his studio. This picture raises many of the same questions about the representation of dreaming as *The Stuff That Dreams Are Made Of.* Examples of earlier dream subjects include: Raphael's *The Dream of Jacob* and *Joseph's Two Dreams Interpreted* (1517, Vatican: Loggia); *Jacob's Dream* by Ludovico Caracci (1605–8, Bologna: Pinoteca) and Ferdinand Bol (1642, Dresden: Gemaldegalerie); Giulio Romano's *Hecuba's Dream* (1538–9, Mantua: Palazzo Ducale).

2 Jennifer Ford, 'Samuel Taylor Coleridge and the Pains of Sleep', *History Workshop Journal* 48 (1999), 170–86; p. 172.

3 See Alice Browne, 'Dreams and Picture-writing: Some Examples of this Comparison from the Sixteenth to the Eighteenth Century', *Journal of the Warburg and Courtauld Institutes* 44 (1981), 90–100, for a discussion of the notion of the dream as a hieroglyph in relation to theories of dreaming.

4 Cited in Nicolas Powell, *Fuseli: The Nightmare* (London: Allen Lane, 1973), p. 50.

5 Ibid., pp. 49, 55–6.

6 John Locke, *Essay Concerning Human Understanding* (1690), ed. John Yolton (London: Dent Everyman, 1993), p. 52.

7 The lynx is interpreted rather differently by Ronald Paulson, who sees the lynx as symbolising the clear sight of *Fantasia. Representations of Revolution (1789–1920)* (New Haven and London: Yale University Press, 1983), p. 121.

8 Paul Ilie points out that *sueño* can mean both 'sleep' and 'dream': 'by blurring the distinction between *sleep* and *dream*, [this word] obliges the reader (if not the viewer) to hesitate before alternative associations. Either Goya depicts the *dream* of reason, thus conferring upon reason the active power of producing monsters, or else he depicts the *sleep* of reason, thus exonerating reason from responsibility for what happens during its activity.' Paul Ilie, 'Goya's Teratology and the Critique of Reason', *Eighteenth-Century Studies* 18 (1984–5), 35–56; p. 44.

9   Locke, *Essay Concerning Human Understanding*, p. 53. See also Jennifer Ford, *Coleridge on Dreaming: Romanticism, Dreams and the Medical Imagination* (Cambridge: Cambridge University Press, 1998), pp. 16–17, for a discussion of Stewart's and Hartley's accounts of dreams.

10 Janis Tomlinson points out that *monstruos* was defined in the 1786 dictionary of Terreros y Pando as 'all which goes against the common natural order'. *Graphic Evolutions: the Prints of Francisco Goya* (New York: Columbia University Press, 1989), p. 15.

11 The separation of the earthly dreamer and the heavenly dreamer is an established convention of Renaissance pictures of dreams, for example Raphael's *The Dream of Jacob*. Another convention, used by Giulio Romano in *Hecuba's Dream*, is to signify the divine nature of the dream through a touch on the dreamer's forehead by the divinity or his/her messenger.

12 Terry Castle has made a strong argument that the supernatural became internalised in this period. See Terry Castle, *The Female Thermometer: Eighteenth-Century Culture and the Invention of the Uncanny* (Oxford: Oxford University Press, 1995), pp. 168–75. See Ford, *Coleridge on Dreaming*, for an account of the wide interest in dreams amongst Romantic writers.

13 Percy Bysshe Shelley, *Complete Poetical Works*, ed. Thomas Hutchinson (Oxford: Oxford University Press, 1971), p. 533.

14 *The Artist's Dream*, though superficially like *The Sleep of Reason*, has a similar range of strategies for representing dreaming.

15 Maureen Perkins, 'The Meaning of Dream Books', *History Workshop Journal* 48 (1999), 102–13; p. 109.

16 *The Countess of Blessington's True Interpreter of Dreams, Visions and Omens of the Wedding Day* (London: H. Elliott, 1861) 'Divination for the Drawing Room', *Englishwoman's Domestic Magazine*, New Series, 3 (1867), 141–3, 204–5.

17 See *Victorian Fairy Painting*, exhibition catalogue (London: Royal Academy of Arts, 1997), pp. 115–17.

18 Charles Dickens, *Barnaby Rudge* (1841), ed. Donald Hawes (London: Dent Everyman, 1996), p. 61; Rodney Engen, *Richard Doyle* (Stroud: Catalpa Press, 1983), p. 49 and *passim*.

19 William Shakespeare, *The Tempest*, 4.1. 151–3: 'We are such stuff / As dreams are made on, and our little life / Is rounded with a sleep.'

20 Charlotte Gere and Jeremy Maas have hypothesised that this group of pictures shows evidence of Fitzgerald having had an addiction to laudanum. They argue that the presence of a 'demonic' figure holding a tray with glasses, bottles at the bedside and the Turkish-style jacket the girl wears all hint at opium as the cause of the vivid dreams that hang in the air. Indeed it is true that nineteenth-century dream theorists were interested in the effects of opium, and often quoted at length from De Quincey's *Confessions of an English Opium Eater* (1825). But they generally thought that opium merely intensified dreams rather than causing them. It is not certain how far this interpretation can be substantiated from evidence internal to the pictures. Short,

Turkish-style jackets were fashionable throughout the 1850s, and wearing them did not necessarily imply a partiality for opium, as shown by Sir W. C. Ross's portrait of the ten-year-old Victoria, Princess Royal in Turkish costume (1850, Royal Collection). I am grateful to Malcom Shifrin for drawing my attention to this picture. See also Pamela Byrde, *Nineteenth-Century Fashion* (London: Batsford, 1992). It is clear from the illustrations to this book that the women in Fitzgerald's work are dressed in ordinary, fashionable clothes for the late 1850s. In any case, to see them as merely representing the effects of opium reduces the iconographic and pictorial complexity of Fitzgerald's dream pictures to a single explanation, and ties them to a narrowly autobiographical meaning. Jeremy Maas, 'Victorian Fairy Painting' and Charlotte Gere, 'In Fairyland' (*Victorian Fairy Painting*, pp. 10–21, 62–72), see pp. 19, 68–9.

21 Jenny Bourne Taylor, 'Obscure Recesses: Locating the Victorian Unconscious' in *Writing and Victorianism*, eds. Alice Jenkin and Juliet John (London: Longmans, 1998), pp. 137–79; especially pp. 137–58.

22 See Rhodri Hayward, 'Policing Dreams: History and the Moral Uses of the Unconscious', *History Workshop Journal* 49 (2000), 142–60; Emmanuel Swedenborg, *Spiritual Diary: A Brief Record, During Twenty Years, of his Supernatural Experience*, vol. 1, trans. J. H. Smithson (London: Newbery/The Swedenborg Society, 1846).

23 On the heterogenous character of nineteenth-century psychology, see Rick Rylance, *Victorian Psychology and British Culture 1850–1880* (Oxford: Oxford University Press, 2000), p. 22; Catherine A. Bernard, 'Dickens and Victorian Dream Theory' in *Victorian Science and Victorian Values: Literary Perspectives*, eds. James Paradis and Thomas Postletwait (New York: Annals of the New York Academy of Sciences vol. CCCLX, 1981), pp. 197–216; Hayward, in 'Policing Dreams', gives a brilliant account of the competing political interests which shaped psychological theories of dreams.

24 Robert Macnish, *The Philosophy of Sleep* (Glasgow: W. R. M'Phun, 1830), p. 51.

25 G. H. Lewes, *The Physiology of Common Life*, 2 vols. (Edinburgh: Blackwood, 1859), vol. II, p. 370.

26 John Addington Symonds, *Sleep and Dreams: Two Lectures* (London: John Murray, 1851), pp. 47–8. This is the father of John Addington Symonds, the critic.

27 W. Newnham, *Essay on Superstition, Being an Inquiry into the Effects of Physical Influence on the Mind* (London: Hatchard and Son, 1830), p. 158. Emphasis in the original. The book originated as a series of essays in the *Christian Observer*.

28 Walter C. Dendy, *On the Phenomena of Dreams and Other Transient Illusions* (London: Whittaker, Treacher and Co., 1832), p. 27.

29 Newnham, *Essay on Superstition*, p. 170.

30 Holland, *Chapters on Mental Physiology*, p. 121; Lewes, *Physiology of Common Life*, p. 367.

31 'F.I.S.', 'Dreams', *Tinsley's Magazine* 2 (1868), 268–83; p. 281.

32   For a discussion of spectral illusions and hallucinations seen while awake rather than asleep, and their place in late nineteenth-century theories of perception, see Kate Flint, *The Victorians and the Visual Imagination* (Cambridge: Cambridge University Press, 2000), pp. 258–84; Sally Shuttleworth, *Charlotte Brontë and Victorian Psychology* (Cambridge: Cambridge University Press, 1996), pp. 240–2.

33   Walter Dendy asserts that: 'The mind, when excited during [sleep], may possess the power of exercising the faculties of perception, association, memory or imagination, individually or collectively, but the influence of *judgement* over the ideas thus excited being lost, imperfect conclusions are formed: in this want of integrity consists the most common species of transient illusion, Dreaming.' Dendy, *On the Phenomena of Dreams*, p. 19.

34   Revd Thomas Millington, *A Lecture on Dreams, Mesmerism, Clairvoyance & c.* (London: H. Bailliere, 1852), pp. 26, 32.

35   Ibid., p. 31.

36   John Sheppard, *On Dreams, in Their Mental and Moral Aspects* (London: Jackson and Walford, 1847), pp. 45–6, 47.

37   Catherine Crowe, *The Night-Side of Nature, or Ghosts and Ghost-Seers* (1848), 3rd edn. (London: George Routledge, 1852), p. 30. Catherine Bernard discusses Dickens' reaction to this book in 'Dickens and Victorian Dream Theory', pp. 198–202. A review in *Blackwood's Edinburgh Magazine* subjected it to withering scorn: 'To revert to that love of the marvellous – which we have noticed appearing among us in certain purlieus of the region of science – we do not know that we could find a more flagrant instance of it than Mrs Crowe affords in her *Night-Side of Nature*.' 'The Night-Side of Nature', *Blackwood's Edinburgh Magazine* 66 (1850), 265–70; p. 269. I owe this reference to Tamara Ketabgian.

38   Crowe, *Night-Side of Nature*, p. 47.

39   Dendy, *On the Phenomena of Dreams*, p. 39; Lewes, *Physiology of Common Life*, p. 370.

40   As the implications of Darwin's theory of natural selection became clear, these issues became more urgent, because Darwin's work implied that the human mind had evolved from the animal brain, and that consciousness and memory are material and inherited in origin. See Sally Shuttleworth, 'The Malady of Thought: Embodied Memory in Victorian Psychology and the Novel', *Memory and Memorials 1789–1914: Literary and Cultural Perspectives*, eds. Matthew Campbell, Jacqueline M. Labbe and Sally Shuttleworth (London: Routledge, 2000), pp. 46–59, and Jenny Bourne Taylor and Sally Shuttleworth (eds.), *Embodied Selves: An Anthology of Nineteenth-Century Psychological Writings* (Oxford: Clarendon, 1998), especially pp. 67–72. Nevertheless, these issues were important even before the publication of *Origin of Species* in 1859.

41   *Footsteps of Spirits: A Collection of Upwards of Seventy Well-Authenticated Stories of Dreams, Impressions, Sounds and Appearances* (London: Burns and Lambert, 1859), p. 3.

42   Charles Ollier, *Fallacy of Ghosts, Dreams and Omens* (London: Charles Ollier, 1848), p. 49.

43   'Dreams', *Once a Week* 7 (1862), 543–5; p. 544.

44   Symonds, *Sleep and Dreams*, pp. 87–8.

45   Joseph Hatton, 'On Some Notable Dreams', *Argosy* 5 (1867–8), 462–6; p. 462.

46   'Such Stuff as Dreams are Made of', *Eclectic Review*, New Series, 9 (1865), 516–30; p. 525.

47   Ibid.

48   Symonds, *Sleep and Dreams*, p. 52. Brueghel and Bosch were often considered as 'medieval' artists in the nineteenth century. For a discussion of the resemblances between Bosch and Fitzgerald, see Nicola Bown, *Fairies in Nineteenth-Century Art and Literature* (Cambridge: Cambridge University Press, 2001), pp. 109–40.

49   Macnish, *Philosophy of Sleep*, p. 78.

50   Private collection. Reproduced in *Victorian Fairy Painting*, p. 116.

51   Ursula Seibold-Bultmann, 'Monster Soup: the Microscope and Victorian Fantasy', *Interdisciplinary Science Reviews* 25 (2000), 211–19.

52   This picture is illustrated in Ibid., p. 212.

53   'Such Stuff as Dreams are Made of', p. 526.

CHAPTER 8

Holman Hunt, William Dyce and the image of Christ

Michaela Giebelhausen

The year 1860 saw three seemingly unrelated events: the publication of *Essays and Reviews*, a highly controversial volume of biblical criticism that sparked a heated and protracted debate; William Holman Hunt's first one-picture exhibition of *The Finding of the Saviour in the Temple*, which finally established him as a force in the English art world; and the inclusion of William Dyce's small painting of Christ in a Scottish Highland landscape, enigmatically entitled *The Man of Sorrows*, at the Royal Academy annual exhibition. Although very different in scale and importance these events shared a concern with the interpretation of biblical narrative and the recon-figuration of the image of Christ. Although apparently coincidental, each of these events can be seen as grappling with questions about the super-natural aspects of Christianity which troubled faith in the mid-nineteenth century. In their very different ways they responded to the ways contem-porary biblical scholarship had called the basic premises of Scripture into question. Robin Gilmour has characterised the mid-Victorian period as an existential moment for the Christian faith: 'if Christianity was to have a future it had to be able to look history and science in the eye'.[1] The authors of *Essays and Reviews* unflinchingly faced the challenge of confronting the different types of knowledge that history and science brought to bear on the understanding of the Bible. In this essay I map the main arguments put forward in *Essays and Reviews* and consider some of the key critical responses the volume received to create a context for the analysis of the two images of Christ which Hunt and Dyce presented to the London public during 1860.

Despite its unassuming title, *Essays and Reviews* proved to be an explo-sively controversial volume. Its publication not only provoked a pamphlet war, but also resulted in a church trial for heresy and an acquittal by the Privy Council. In short, it has been considered 'the greatest religious cri-sis of the Victorian age'.[2] The main causes for concern were the identity of the authors and the concerted statement which the volume seemed to make. Six of the seven contributors were men of the Church of England and some were influential educators, among them Frederick Temple, the rector of Rugby School, and two Oxford professors: Baden Powell, Savilian Professor of Geometry, and Benjamin Jowett, Regius Professor of Greek. Despite the disclaimer in the preface the collection came to be regarded as an important manifesto for the Broad Church movement.[3] The contributions reflected some of the current positions in biblical criticism. The authors applied the methodologies of scientific, linguistic and historical investigation to the sacred text, focusing on contentious issues such as the historicity of the Bible, the influence of geology on the interpretation of Genesis, and the exact nature of the supernatural in the biblical narrative. While all of the opinions had been expressed before in some form or other, never before had such views been put forward in one volume mostly written by important members of the established Church who were also influential educators.

Frederick Temple's essay on 'The Education of the World' set the tone for the entire collection. He argued for a progressive sense of history that depended on a gradual accumulation of knowledge throughout the ages. Consequently, he viewed the Bible as a historical document:

It is a history; even the doctrinal parts of it are cast in a historical form, and are best studied by considering them as records of the time at which they were written, and as conveying to us the highest and greatest religious life of that time. Hence we use the Bible – some consciously, some unconsciously – not to override, but to evoke the voice of conscience.[4]

Understanding the Bible as a historical document not only allowed for its idiosyncrasies and flaws but also released Temple from the intellectual contortions of so many contemporary interpreters who attempted to reconcile the biblical narrative with current scientific knowledge. However, Temple created a different double-bind. On the one hand he claimed that the Bible was a historical document and on the other he granted it the power 'to evoke the voice of conscience'. So the Bible was historicised yet not entirely stripped of its special status – an ambivalent stance, adopted by all the Essayists, that was to attract strong criticism from both radical and conservative quarters, because it glossed over the question of the supernatural in the Scriptures and their claim to be divine revelations. Temple applied the same progressive sense of history to revelation, arguing that Christ revealed himself to humankind at precisely the right moment in time:

Had His revelation been delayed till now, assuredly it would have been hard for us to recognise His Divinity; for the faculty of Faith has turned inwards, and cannot now accept any outer manifestations of the truth of God.[5]

Temple admitted to a certain jadedness of the present age that would prohibit the recognition of Jesus Christ: 'We have lost that freshness of faith', he wrote, 'which would be the first to say to a poor carpenter – Thou art the Christ, the Son of the living God.'[6] Yet he claimed that the loss of this immediate form of faith was more than compensated for by a 'greater cultivation of our religious understanding' and urged the valiant pursuit of knowledge for a deeper comprehension of the Bible.[7]

He is guilty of high treason against the faith who fears the result of any investigation, whether philosophical, or scientific, or historical. And therefore nothing should be more welcome than the extension of knowledge of any and every kind.[8]

Temple's call for a rigorous investigation of the biblical narrative was taken up by his fellow Essayists. In his contribution 'On the Mosaic Cosmogony', C. W. Goodwin severely criticised several of the reconciliatory models that attempted to square the biblical account of creation with the current state of geological knowledge. Although the arguments he put forward were well rehearsed and far from radical by 1860 – in the opinion of a twentieth-century commentator 'he wasted his efforts in tilting at windmills' and Stanley considered the whole debate 'as practically defunct'[9] – his tone was uncommonly harsh and direct:

Believing, as we do, that if the value of the Bible as a book of religious instruction is to be maintained it must be not by striving to prove it scientifically exact, at the expense of every sound principle of interpretation, and in defiance of common sense, but by frank recognition of the erroneous views of nature which it contains.[10]

Goodwin may have delighted a little too much in the quixotic and facile task of tearing apart the reconciliatory models developed by such prominent authors as William Buckland and Hugh Miller; however, his direct approach declared the geological debate dead once and for all. In the concluding remarks of his essay, Goodwin offered a reconciliation of sorts that relied on the concept of progressive knowledge proposed by Frederick Temple. He conceded that the author of Genesis did not know as much about geology as the average Victorian and hence got some of the facts wrong.[11] However, he maintained that this lack of knowledge did not undermine the value of the Bible as a historical record or as a vehicle of divine revelation.

The fallibility of the human agency involved in the production of the biblical narrative was further explored in Baden Powell's essay 'On the Study of the Evidences of Christianity'. He focused on the role of the witness when considering the biblical account as reliable evidence: 'When a reference is made to matters of *external fact* . . .', he wrote, 'it is obvious that reason and intellect can alone be the proper judges of the evidence of such facts.'[12] He argued that the eye-witness account was inherently unreliable, especially when called upon to recall exceptional events. He attempted to explain the miraculous occurrences in the Bible as 'a strong confirmation of . . . belief'; a necessary mode of narration at a given historical moment that held little value in the modern age where 'miracles are not to be expected, and consequently alleged marvels are commonly discredited'.[13] Baden Powell thus successfully destabilised the role of the witness and historicised the function of miracles as a preliminary move to rid the biblical account of all supernatural occurrences. He argued that in the present age the true believer no longer depended on external signs: his, too, was an internal revelation in harmony with the workings of reason and intellect.

Benjamin Jowett's essay 'On the Interpretation of Scripture' was in many ways the most radical contribution to the volume, in which 'the great sea-change of nineteenth-century theology, the passage from a sacred hermeneutic to a secular one, occurred'.[14] Jowett called into question most forms of interpretation because of their lack of rigorous methodology: 'The book in which we believe all religious truth to be contained, is the most uncertain of all books, because interpreted by arbitrary and uncertain methods.'[15] Consequently he argued that the main aim in interpreting the Bible should be to recover the original meaning – 'the meaning, that is, of the words as they first struck on the ears or flashed before the eyes of those who heard and read them' – rather than just to add another interpretation to the myriad already in existence.[16] For Jowett, the task of the interpreter resembled that of the historian or archaeologist. He endeavoured to strip back the accumulated layers of dogmatic and traditional interpretations to reveal the original meaning of the text by placing it in its historical context. This process also required the interpreter to make allowances for cultural differences: 'it is a book written in the East, which is in some degree liable to be misunderstood, because it speaks the language and has the feeling of Eastern lands'.[17] Jowett's central argument was contained in the following lines:

Interpret the Scripture like any other book. There are many respects in which Scripture is unlike any other book; these will appear in the results of such an interpretation. The first step is to know the meaning, and this can only be done in the same careful and impartial way that we ascertain the meaning of Sophocles or of Plato . . . No other science of Hermeneutics is possible but an inductive one, that is to say, one based on the language and thoughts and narrations of the sacred writers.[18]

As befitted the Regius Professor of Greek, Jowett put forward a means of interpretation developed in the reading of Classical texts. Overall, the Essayists were more comfortable dealing with the textual, factual and historical aspects of the Bible than with the divine, revelatory or supernatural elements. Although they repeatedly conceded that the Bible was a special book, Jowett was not alone in finding it difficult to define exactly what that special nature was. The Essayists were primarily concerned with the 'outward body or form' of Scripture which they scrutinised rigorously.[19] So rigorously, in fact, that Charles Kingsley, the writer and novelist, wrote to Arthur Penrhyn Stanley, a prominent figure in the Broad Church movement who was sympathetic to the stance that the Essayists had adopted:

Doubts, denials, destructions – we have faced them till we are tired of them. But we have faced them in silence, hoping to find a positive solution. Here comes a book which states all the old doubts and difficulties, and gives us nothing instead. Here are men still pulling down . . . and building up *nothing* instead.[20]

While Kingsley's private comment was echoed in most reviews, for some critics the Essayists had simply not gone far enough in demolishing the system of Christian belief.[21] In the *Westminster Review* Frederic Harrison, who was to become one of England's leading positivist thinkers and followers of Auguste Comte, put forward a radical attack on the Essayists. He regarded their attempts to dispose of the divine aspects of the Bible while continuing to uphold it as *the* guide to individual conscience as highly incongruous, and criticised the authors for lacking the courage of their unspoken convictions:

Let them be assured that there exists no middle course, that there is no inspiration more than natural, yet not supernatural; no theory of history agreeable to science, though not scientific; no theology which can abandon its doctrines and retain authority. The position of Scripture either rests on external authority, or is a thorough perversion of a sound estimate of literature. The Bible can hold its place either by a divine sanction or by glaring injustice to the other writings of mankind.[22]

For Harrison the authors had shied away from the inevitable conclusion of their investigation. This radicalisation of the debate cast the threat of atheism found looming between the lines of every essay into sharp relief. The Bishop of Oxford, Samuel Wilberforce, who had recently been involved in a widely publicised debate over the theories presented in Darwin's *Origin of Species* (1859), again rose to the challenge of defending the beliefs of the established Church. In his review in the *Quarterly Review* of January 1861 – both a criticism of *Essays and Reviews* and a reply to Harrison's incitement to atheism – Wilberforce took the Essayists to task for their insistence that the Bible was to be read just like any other book. He further criticised the substitution of external for internal revelation. Placing the Bible in a historical context and investigating its textual production with the methods of literary criticism, Wilberforce maintained, reduced the divine aspects of the Bible to a residuum which was 'embedded in the crust of earlier legends, oral traditions, poetical licenses, and endless parables', from which it had to be freed through the 'verifying faculty' of the individual.[23] He further warned that 'to have the dividing line between the operation of the Divine and the Human in the inspired Word marked sharply out so as to meet all objections and answer all questions' would inevitably lead to atheism.[24] Just like the radical Harrison, he fully realised the precarious balance that the Essayists had attempted to strike when characterising the volume as 'the hopeless attempt at preserving Christianity without Christ, without the Holy Ghost, without a Bible, and without a Church'.[25] However, while accounting for the limits of human knowledge, he argued for an understanding of revelation which depended on the combination of its human and divine elements.[26] Wilberforce concluded with a call for a humble faith:

to teach us that we are surrounded by mysteries of God's presence and working, which reveal themselves sufficiently to satisfy a humble faith of their undoubted reality; but which are impenetrable barriers against that proud curiosity which evermore leads men on to seek to be as gods, knowing good and evil.[27]

Nowhere, of course, is the problem of the supernatural and the paradox of the dividing line between the divine and the human more apparent than in the figure of Christ. But *Essays and Reviews* was strangely reticent on that subject and none of the authors explicitly dealt with the implications of their ideas for the figure of Christ. The omission was noticed by contemporaries: Wilberforce had called their position a 'Christianity without Christ'. In his monograph on *Essays and Reviews*, Ieuan Ellis has suggested that 'the seven shared all the motivations of the nineteenth-century quest for the historical Jesus'.[28] However, the figure of Christ remained the crucial lacuna at the centre of the collection. It is of course both tantalising and useless to speculate what kind of image the Essayists would have sketched of Jesus. The fact that they did not is suggestive of their collective unease over defining the line between the natural and the supernatural aspects of Scripture. This omission is perhaps partly due to the haphazard way in which the volume was put together, but also reflects Kingsley's view that the contributors 'are men still pulling down . . . and building up *nothing* instead'. Joseph Altholz has characterised their project 'as a negative theology, seeking to destroy false ideas and attitudes; only in hints and implications can its positive elements be found'.[29] Firmly anchored in the thorough and often relentless practices of textual analysis, their 'negative theology' nevertheless constituted an extremely important intervention in current theological debates that could afford not to develop its positive elements beyond the stage of 'hints and implications'. But for painters seeking visually to represent Christ no such prevarication was possible; the representional strategies they chose inevitably implied a theological choice and thus positioned their pictures within the debate. In the rest of this essay I consider the strategies adopted by two painters with differing theological allegiances in attempting to resolve the problems posed by the divinity of Christ through the medium of realist pictorial representation.

*

In the spring of 1860 William Holman Hunt's *The Finding of the Saviour in the Temple* (Fig. 8), begun in 1854 during his first visit to the Middle East, was finally exhibited at the German Gallery on Bond Street. After six toilsome and financially difficult years during which he had been working on the painting, the one-picture show represented a decisive turning point in Hunt's career. The art dealer Ernest Gambart had paid Hunt the unprecedented amount of 5,500 guineas for the painting and the copyright: the highest price paid for a contemporary work of art in Britain to that date.[30] The painting's public success established Hunt as the century's 'Painter of the Christ'.[31] In his autobiography published in 1905, Hunt talked about his engagement with biblical narrative and deplored – just as Jowett had done in his essay 'On the Interpretation of Scripture' – the fact 'that much of the teaching of Christ's life is lost by history being overlaid with sacerdotal gloss'. He shared with the Essayists a desire to strip back the layers and conventions of traditional interpretations, and aimed 'to make the story live as history'.[32] William Vaughan has succinctly identified the dilemma of Hunt's artistic project as the problem of how 'to reconstruct the historical Christ in a way that asserted rather than damaged his divine stature'.[33] This was particularly pronounced in Hunt's first fully historicised and orientalised

Figure 8   William Holman Hunt, *The Finding of the Saviour in the Temple.*

representation of a scriptural subject that hinges on the spiritual awakening of Christ; a moment characterised by his dual nature as both human and divine. *The Finding of the Saviour in the Temple* was based on a passage from the Gospel of Saint Luke (2.47–9). Hunt's interpretation of the scene was highly unusual and untraditional in that he chose to illustrate the moment when Christ realises his divine mission. The boy rejects his mother's fretting embrace, and to his parents' admonition that they have been looking for him all over the city for the past three days, he replies: 'How is it that ye sought me? wist ye not that I must be about my Father's business?' (Luke 2.49).

Hunt deployed a painstakingly detailed mode of representation, the methods of historical research and the support of several explanatory texts penned by the former Pre-Raphaelite Brother F. G. Stephens, which ranged from lengthy reviews to a descriptive pamphlet. He not only strove to recreate the setting, circumstances and customs of the period, but also accepted and visualised Jowett's assertion that the Bible 'is a book written in the East'.[34] Hunt's endeavour to authenticate the scene as history inevitably seemed to privilege Christ's human nature – as Stephens pointed out 'the painter could not . . . but show Him as a *man*' – while his divine awakening is expressed through his posture and gaze.[35] The awkward, halo-like glow of his hair is an uneasy compromise which draws on an iconography traditionally used to realise the supernatural aspect of Christ, while naturalising it as the effects of back-lighting in the interest of presenting Christ as human. Although at the centre of a group of people and embraced by his mother, Jesus is remote and contained. Girding his loins and ready for action, Jesus is about to take a step out of the picture's historically defined space. Both the direction and the uncertain focus of Christ's gaze suggest a realm of the divine beyond representability in the historical–realist terms established by the setting and costumes. Since the divine is simultaneously located beyond the frame and inside the self, the picture's meticulously researched and represented material world can only imply Christ's divinity as real and contained in a specific historical moment. It seems to echo Temple's assertion that 'the faculty of Faith has turned inwards, and cannot now accept any outer manifestations of the truth of God'.[36]

As Stephens pointed out, Hunt's methodology replicated that of the ethnographer, historian and archaeologist: a feature shared with the Essayists, who firmly believed in 'the extension of knowledge of any and every kind' when it came to the investigation of Scripture.[37] Hunt contributed to this process by relying on up-to-date information rather than on traditional representational formulae. The apparent precision of the research is conveyed in the work's meticulous execution and corroborated by the accompanying written accounts. In fact, the manner of the execution reminded Edmund Gosse of natural specimens rather than of a work of art. In his reminiscences, *Father and Son*, he recalled going to see *The Finding of the Saviour in the Temple*:

> The exact, minute and hard execution of Mr Hunt was in sympathy with the methods we ourselves were in the habit of using when we painted butterflies and seaweeds, placing perfectly pure pigments side by side, without any nonsense about chiaroscuro. This large, bright, comprehensive picture made a very deep impression upon me, not exactly as a work of art, but as a brilliant natural specimen.[38]

By staging the scriptural account with the pictorial means deployed in the representation of natural history, Hunt not only lent a scientific dimension to the picture but also authenticated the story *as* history. Free from what Gosse termed the nonsensical conventions of art, the picture constructed both the scene itself and its mode of representation as fact rather than fiction, offering itself up for microscopic scrutiny.

However, when closely scanned the picture reveals an intricate web of typological references which intertwine Old and New Testament events in a very traditional form of biblical exegesis that runs counter to a strictly historical reading of the text. This all-pervasive yet discreet use of typological symbolism underpins an underlying belief in the external, divine revelation of Christian belief. The doves entering the temple, the lamb taken to sacrifice, and the cornerstone being prepared in the yard all imply the wider framework of Christianity. Such typological symbols transcend the specific moment of the scene and invoke future moments in the life of Christ as well as the rituals of the Christian Church. While most reviewers shared the opinion that 'in showing us as truly as possible *the real*, we are to behold the wonder of the divine', some, however, found that the picture's vividness distracted from the 'real' meaning of the painting.[39] One reviewer pointed out that 'we are in danger of... failing to read the sublime meaning in the face of Christ, already occupied with his divine mission' because the realistic detail blocked the transmission of the revelation of Christ's divine origin.[40] Contemporary remarks such as these reflect the ambiguous nature of typological symbolism, which George Landow has summarised in the following way: 'The artistic effect of the typological image arises in the fact that it thus exists simultaneously in several locations, times, and senses. The artistic difficulty of the type arises in the same fact, for unless the work contains some sort of signal, the spectator will frequently be unable to determine whether an individual image should be read as a type.'[41]

In the *Manchester Guardian*'s somewhat breathless review, the painting's excessively polysemous nature was made abundantly clear: the critic gasped that the 'picture is replete with meaning from the foreground to the remotest distance. Indeed, it absolutely overflows with significance. There are symbols everywhere . . . Nay, the symbols have overflowed the picture, and expanded themselves all over the frame.'[42] The reviewer contended that the painting's legibility was jeopardised by this plethora of signification. Hunt sought to control the overwhelming polysemy of *The Finding of the Saviour in the Temple* with the help of a number of different texts: together with the painting's title, the verses from the Gospel of St Luke inscribed on the ivory flat of the frame enabled the viewer to identify an unusual rendering of the scene which does not rely on established pictorial formulae. A quotation from Malachi 3.1 – 'and the Lord, whom ye seek, shall suddenly come to this temple' – forms part of the actual picture. Inscribed on the temple door in both Latin and Hebrew it induced a prefigurative reading of the image and signals the complex web of typological referents. These two textual sources allowed a deciphering of both subject matter and symbolism. They offset that polysemy contemporary critics had remarked upon, and functioned as textual anchors 'intended to *fix* the floating chain of signifieds in such a way as to counter the terror of uncertain signs'.[43] While the New Testament quotation helped to identify the subject matter, the verse from Malachi provided a far less straightforward hint. Placed in a prominent position, it was simultaneously part of the symbolism of the picture, and of what Landow has called the signal to enable the decoding of the work. However, the historical veracity that the painting aspired to throughout demands that the inscription blend in, hence it is given in Latin and Hebrew. While the textual elements which remain external to the picture (the title and the New Testament quotations) help to fix its meaning, the signal deployed to unlock the picture's typological ramifications remains muted because it is submerged in the realist mode of representation. This is where the third textual tactic came into play to provide more solid anchorage.

The problem of how to unravel the visual conundrum that Hunt's painting represented is also evident in Stephens's pamphlet which accompanied the exhibition of 1860. This authenticated the process of the painting's production and cited the authority of learned scholars in regard to particular pictorial details, thus validating the work in the same way that footnotes support the writing of history. Stephens also went to some length to explain the obscure typological and symbolic meaning embedded in the picture's many details. He aimed simultaneously to confirm its historical accuracy

Figure 9   William Dyce, *The Man of Sorrows*.

and its symbolic structure. However, there is an undeniable tension between these two tasks: the demands of historical explication to validate the painting's pictorial language do not sit well with its pervasive symbolism. In a historical–realist mode of representation, what cannot be authenticated, and thus represented, is the supernatural dimension of the scene. The emphasis on realistic depiction creates an internal logic that seems to work against the successful construction of symbolic meaning.

I want to relate this problem of representation to *Essays and Reviews* because it is premised on a similar paradox. In many ways, the balance which Hunt strove to achieve between the human and the divine nature of Christ is almost as precarious and unresolved as that which the Essayists constructed in their investigation of the Bible. Their stripping back of layer after layer of traditional interpretations was seen by both radical and conservative critics as a slippery slope that would inevitably end in atheism. Hunt shared the Essayists' desire to free the biblical narrative from 'sacerdotal gloss'; he wanted to depict Christ as a tangibly historical figure located in a meticulously reconstructed setting. However, this depiction was underpinned by a complex symbolic structure incompatible with the concerns of the Essayists. Hunt strove to combine historical veracity with a desire to represent the divine aspects not only of Christ's person but of the whole system of Christian belief. Although the painting's treatment of the subject was supported by a web of typological and symbolic meaning, the realist mode of representation prioritised the human and strictly historical dimension. Hunt was a diligent reporter trained in ethnography, history and archaeology – disciplines that recover the past. His picture bore the hallmarks of an eye-witness account, but also reflected the limits of eye-witnessing because he was thus unable to represent the unseen. In an age when faith had turned inward the divinely inspired moment became difficult to represent, especially by means of a pictorial language driven by the strategies of history. Consequently, this notion of representability left very little space for the divine dimension: it became a mere gesture, epitomised by the uneasy naturalism of Christ's 'halo'.

*

William Dyce exhibited *The Man of Sorrows* (Fig. 9) at the Royal Academy in 1860. This small work shows Christ sitting in a bleak and desolate landscape, which contemporary reviewers easily recognised as the Scottish Highlands. The picture was accompanied by the following passage from 'Ash-Wednesday' – part of John Keble's popular cycle of poems, *The*

Christian Year. This text not only declared the painting's High-Church leanings, but also suggested a narrative context:

> As when upon His drooping head
> His Father's light was pour'd from Heaven
> What time, unshelter'd and unfed,
> Far in the wild His steps were driven.
>
> High thoughts were with Him in that hour,
> Untold, unspeakable on earth –

While the verses elaborated the theme of Christ in the wilderness, the painting's title, however, made such a straightforward identification of the subject matter ambiguous because it implied a deliberate reinterpretation of Christ as the Man of Sorrows. The traditional formula of the Man of Sorrows is centred on the resurrected body of Christ bearing the marks of the crucifixion, offered up for devotional meditation. It does not depict any event in the life of Christ and is detached from spatial and temporal contexts. In its aim to express a living form of belief that takes 'its character from mystical contemplation rather than from theological speculation', Christ is represented as 'dead as man and living as God'.[44]

The two textual anchors (the accompanying verse and the iconographic tradition encapsulated in the title) which pulled the picture in different directions were indicative of its complexities. Dyce deliberately carried the tension into the picture itself: he contrasted an extremely conventional representation of Christ, draped in red and blue, with a very detailed landscape setting. The combination of the historically quite unspecific image of Christ, dependent on a traditional iconography, with a Scottish Highland landscape, at the same time contemporary and timeless, defied the location of the scene in one historical moment. In his review of the Royal Academy annual exhibition for the *Athenaeum*, F. G. Stephens clearly registered the unresolved tension in the painting when he asked: 'But why – with all this literalness – not be completely loyal to the rendering of Christ himself in the land where he really lived?'[45] He implied that Dyce's attention to realistic detail was a baffling stylistic choice given that the picture in no way strove to represent a coherent moment of biblical narrative. Unsurprisingly, he suggested a resolution of the kind Hunt had proposed in *The Finding of the Saviour in the Temple.* However, Stephens either failed to realise, or simply ignored, the fact that the jarring juxtaposition between figure and landscape was intentional and essential to the meaning of the painting. The tension generated between figure and landscape, together with the use of conflicting textual anchors, heightened the picture's inherent polysemy rather than abating it. The clash between historical and time-less elements, and between realist and non-realist modes of representation, drew attention to the disjunction between the historical and mystical in the image, and made possible a process of reading originating in bafflement and wonder.

Dyce offered a complex reworking of the theme of the Man of Sorrows which strove to inspire belief in a living and explicitly divine Christ. The conflation of two distinct subjects – one devotional, the other biblical – and the deliberately incoherent notions of time and place enabled the negotiation of his divine nature. Christ's forty days in the wilderness were, of course, a time of temptation and self-questioning brought on by the public confirmation of his divinity revealed during baptism. Although Dyce's choice to render the wilderness local surprised Stephens, Marcia Pointon has argued that 'his native scenery had far more to offer an artist who valued the emotive and symbolic qualities of a landscape as a means of conveying a specific religious conviction'.[46] It undeniably gave the picture an immediate appeal due in part to the contrast between figure and landscape, and in part to the cultural significance of the Highlands explored in popular guidebooks of the period.

Popular guidebooks tended to make two recurrent points: the grandeur of nature and its geological interest. In *The Art of Deer-Stalking*, for example, William Scrope marvelled, 'Here, everything bears the original impress of nature untouched by the hand of man since its creation', and *Leslie's Tourist Guide to the Scottish Highlands* emphasised the ruggedness, solitude, gloom and sublimity of the landscape.[47] In parallel with this aestheticisation of the Highland landscape the guidebook also repeatedly mentioned geologically important features, those 'curious phenomena' that 'have been such a puzzle to geologists and other scientists'.[48] In addition to serving as a lesson in the Burkean sublime the Highlands also provided 'an intricate study' of a scientific kind.[49] This was most apparent in the work of the Scotsman Hugh Miller – 'undoubtedly the leading popular expounder of geology in the 1840s and 1850s' – whose discoveries contributed to the understanding of the Scottish landscapes, and who tried to reconcile new-found geological evidence with the Mosaic cosmogony.[50] In *Sketch-book of Popular Geology*, he asserted that 'to the geologist every rock bears its inscription engraved in ancient hieroglyphic characters, that tell of the Creator's journeyings of old, of the laws which He gave, the tabernacles which He reared'.[51] While his attempts to develop and modify the reconciliatory model were, of course, somewhat dated by 1860 – as Goodwin had pointed out so relentlessly in his contribution to *Essays and Reviews* – they nevertheless provided a texture for the reading of the Highland landscape that transcended mere geological interest.

According to Miller, 'Nature is a vast tablet, inscribed with signs' that merit detailed reading; a view shared by John Ruskin, who claimed that 'there is not a fragment of its living rock, nor a tuft of its heathery herbage, that has not adorable manifestations of God's working thereupon'.[52] Despite their differing religious convictions, Ruskin's evangelical view tallied with Wilberforce's High-Church assertion 'that we are surrounded by mysteries of God's presence and working'.[53] Ruskin repeatedly reminded his readers of the presence of God: 'There is need, bitter need, to bring back into men's minds, that to live is nothing, unless to live be to know Him by whom we live.'[54] Accordingly he maintained that the workings of God were best explored and comprehended in those solitary places that invited meditation on the divine origins of nature, which landscape painting had so far failed to capture:

Landscape art has never taught us one deep or holy lesson . . . it has never made us feel the wonder, nor the power, nor the glory of the universe; it has not prompted to devotion, nor touched with awe . . . That which ought to have been a witness to the omnipotence of God, has become an exhibition of the dexterity of man.[55]

However, the Ruskin who had made these ardent pleas for a landscape art that should attempt to capture the glory of God's workings had his religious belief shattered, for a time, by geological discoveries. His anguish about the scientific explorations that undermined biblical truths was poignantly captured in this frequently quoted passage:

You speak of the Flimsiness of your own faith. Mine, which was never strong, is being beaten into mere gold leaf, and flutters in weak rags from the letter of its old forms; but the only letters it can hold by at all are the old Evangelical formulae. If only the Geologists would let me alone, I could do very well, but these dreadful Hammers! I hear the clink of them at the end of every cadence of the Bible verses.[56]

In the juxtaposition of these two statements by Ruskin we can see exemplified the religious attitude to nature codified in natural theology (the natural world is studied to reveal the manifestation of God's glory) shifting under the pressure of doubt caused by the gradually emerging scientific knowledge of some of its most puzzling phenomena.[57]

Dyce's use of the Highland landscape, which does render every 'fragment of its living rock' and 'heathery herbage' with a Ruskinian attention to detail, remained ambiguous.[58] This was also borne out in the relationship between figure and landscape. Allen Staley has claimed that in Dyce's religious landscapes the figures seem to have accidentally strayed into pictures that would have functioned equally well as pure landscapes.[59] Although Pointon has opposed this view and persuasively argued that there is a meaningful balance between the two, Christ's position in the picture remains precarious and almost incidental.[60] Placed close to the picture's left edge and facing towards the left, he seems in danger of sliding out of the painting altogether. The multiple significations of the Highland landscape that generated ambiguous readings allowed Dyce to make a measured plea for belief in a living Christ highly appropriate for an age that – in the words of Frederick Temple – had 'lost that freshness of faith'.[61] The two textual anchors, although in themselves contradictory, spelt out Dyce's High-Church leanings and his belief in Christ 'living as God', while the ambiguous resonances of the landscape, what Pointon has called its 'emotive and symbolic qualities', left space for the suggestion of doubt.

Against this background of intentional incongruity, the detailed representation of both landscape and figure served as a means to emphasise the divine aspects of Christ. Contrary to the transparent realist strategies of orientalism and historicisation deployed by Hunt, Dyce insisted on tensions and contrasts to defy the integrating totality of a historical approach that strove for the reconstruction of a particular time and place. With its transcendence of such categories the painting made an urgent plea for the contemporary relevance of Christ's divine nature despite modern approaches to biblical studies. Dyce's image of Christ opposed the liberal forms of belief put forward by the Essayists and reflected in Hunt's painting. His *Man of Sorrows* was more in line with Wilberforce's high-Anglican criticism of *Essays and Reviews*, encapsulated in his admonition to refrain from defining the dividing line between the divine and the human aspects of Scripture but to accept both in 'humble faith'. In the face of the doubt and anxiety characteristic of the age, Dyce offered an incongruous image of Christ and invited his viewer to make a leap of faith which demanded the acceptance of Christ's divinity notwithstanding such questioning. At the same time, it resonated with those anxieties articulated through the scientific study of nature and the historical understanding of the Bible that made the problem of how to represent the supernatural so urgent in the mid-nineteenth century.

Although Hunt and Dyce made very different statements about the nature of Christ they both used a pictorial language that relied strongly on the 'real' to express their views. Gillian Beer has suggested that maybe 'we should see the Victorian insistence on the "real" as in some measure a response to the loss of a close-knit beginning and ending in the natural world'.[62] In the two paintings examined here the resolute factual reality of representation provided a means to accommodate, reflect and counter the religious uncertainties of the age.

Hunt invoked the discourse of History to present a detailed and seemingly plausible reconstruction of a specific moment. Like that of Macaulay's 'perfect historian', in Hunt's work 'the character and spirit of an age is exhibited in miniature. He relates no fact, he attributes no expression to his characters, which is not authenticated by sufficient testimony.'[63] Although appreciative of Hunt's efforts, William Dyce felt that *The Finding of the Saviour in the Temple* really was 'three pictures in one'.[64] This opinion was also reflected in some of the reviews the painting received, which commented on the proliferation of significant detail that threatened to obscure the central motive. Hunt's insistence on the 'real' is, as Beer suggests, a reaction to the loss of the scriptural stories of origins and endings in the natural world threatened by mid-nineteenth-century historical and scientific questioning. Hunt's attempt at historicising scriptural narrative should be seen as a response to the conceptual shift in the understanding of a history '[n]o longer held in by the Mosaic time order', so that, as Beer has argued, 'history became a mosaic of another sort, a piecing together of subsets into an interpretable picture'.[65] *The Finding of the Saviour in the Temple* is nothing if not a dazzling mosaic, an attempt to piece together an interpretable picture that not only reflected the recent historical approach to Scripture but which – unlike the tearing down as a form of biblical criticism practised by the Essayists – actually used it to create a seemingly smooth representation. However, the picture's proliferating meanings and ambiguities show just how precarious Hunt's attempts to use historical realism to convey the supernatural were.

By contrast, Dyce's *The Man of Sorrows* bristled with tensions. These were in part generated by the contradictory textual anchors which drew attention to a biblical as well as a devotional subject. Furthermore, the Highland landscape invoked the tensions between natural–theological and scientific–rationalist views of nature. This locally specific yet transfigured wilderness suggested multiple readings which enabled the picture's subdued and pensive mood. This is further underscored by Dyce's 'deliberate use of empty space' which helped to 'concentrate the viewer's attention on the mental condition of the protagonists'.[66] While Dyce's picture was characterised by concentration and contemplation, Hunt's demonstrated a veritable *horror vacui*, in which every inch of the canvas and even the frame was made to signify. Although Dyce employed similar stylistic means to Hunt, he used them to disrupt the historical coherence of the represented moment in order to emphasise the supernatural dimension of the subject.

Thus the picture made a strong, albeit quiet claim for a belief in the living Christ as God. Here too the fragmentation of the Mosaic cosmogony generated a mosaic of a different kind, one in which the incompatibility of the pieces, the inadequacy of historical realism to represent the mystical and supernatural, is fully apparent. Unlike the seeming transparency generated by Hunt's orientalised, historical reconstruction of Scripture, Dyce's picture invokes the leap of 'humble faith' through its refusal to efface multiplicity of signification and its invitation to the viewer to interpret its tensions.

In both private and public statements, Hunt repeatedly claimed that he had developed a new form of religious painting. While the more reserved Dyce never made such claims, his small-scale religious works of the late 1850s and early 1860s, of which *The Man of Sorrows* is one of the few that was exhibited during the artist's lifetime, represented an equally important contribution to the religious painting of the period.[67] Dyce successfully refuted Ruskin's contention that 'Landscape art has never taught us one deep or holy lesson . . . it has never made us feel the wonder, nor the power, nor the glory of the universe; it has not prompted to devotion.' Indeed, Dyce used the productive tension between the landscape and figures in his paintings to negotiate the central, pressing problem of mid-nineteenth-century religious painting: the representation of the supernatural aspect of Christ. Despite their differing theological perspectives (respectively liberal–Protestant and high-Anglican), the work of Hunt and Dyce made equally original contributions to religious painting. The typically 'Victorian insistence on the "real"', in very different ways, shaped both artists' negotiation of the supernatural in their pictures of Christ.

NOTES

1 Robin Gilmour, *The Victorian Period: The Intellectual and Cultural Context of English Literature 1830–1890* (London and New York: Longman, 1993), p. 99.
2 Ieuan Ellis, *Seven Against Christ: A Study of 'Essays and Reviews'* (Leiden: E. J. Brill, 1980), p. ix.
3 Joseph L. Altholz, *Anatomy of a Controversy: The Debate over Essays and Reviews 1860–1864* (Aldershot: Scolar Press, 1994), pp. 15, 34.
4 Frederick Temple, 'The Education of the World', in *Essays and Reviews* (London: John W. Parker and Son, 1860), pp. 1–49; p. 44.
5 Ibid., p. 24.
6 Ibid., p. 24f.
7 Ibid., p. 25.
8 Ibid., p. 47.

9   Geoffrey Cust Faber, *Jowett: A Portrait with Background* (London: Faber and
     Faber, 1957), p. 243; A. P. Stanley in his article for the *Edinburgh Review*
     (p. 475f.), quoted from Altholz, *Anatomy of a Controversy*, p. 46.
10   C. W. Goodwin, 'On the Mosaic Cosmogony', in *Essays and Reviews*, pp. 207–
     53; p. 211.
11   Ibid., p. 253.
12   Baden Powell, 'On the Study of the Evidences of Christianity', in *Essays and
     Reviews*, pp. 94–144; p. 97.
13   Ibid., pp. 108, 107.
14   James R. Moore, 'Geologists and Interpreters of Genesis in the Nineteenth
     Century', in *God and Nature: Historical Essays on the Encounter Between Chris-
     tianity and Science*, eds. David C. Lindberg and Ronald L. Numbers (Berkeley
     and London: University of California Press, 1986), pp. 322–50; p. 334.
15   Benjamin Jowett, 'On the Interpretation of Scripture' in *Essays and Reviews*,
     pp. 330–433; p. 372.
16   Ibid., p. 338.
17   Ibid., p. 367.
18   Ibid., pp. 377f.
19   Ibid., p. 389.
20   Kingsley to A. P. Stanley, 19 February 1861, in Charles Kingsley, *His Letters
     and Memories of his Life, Edited by his Wife*, 2 vols. (London: Henry S. King
     and Co., 1877), vol. II, p. 130.
21   For a detailed account of the critical reception, see Altholz, *Anatomy of a
     Controversy*, pp. 39–49.
22   Frederic Harrison, 'Art. I – Neo-Christianity – *Essays and Reviews*. Second
     Edition. London: J. W. Parker and Son. 1860', *Westminster Review*, New
     Series, 17 (1860), 293–332; p. 312.
23   Samuel Wilberforce, 'Art. VIII – *Essays and Reviews*. London. 1860', *Quarterly
     Review* 109 (1861), 248–305; p. 269.
24   Ibid., p. 304.
25   Ibid., p. 286.
26   Ibid., p. 305.
27   Ibid.
28   Ellis, *Seven Against Christ*, p. 98.
29   Altholz, *Anatomy of a Controversy*, p. 32.
30   F. G. Stephens, *William Holman Hunt and his Works: A Memoir of the Artist's
     Life, with Descriptions of his Pictures* (London: James Nisbet and Co., 1860),
     p. 79.
31   Wyke Bailyss, *Five Great Painters of the Victorian Era: Leighton, Millais, Burne-
     Jones, Watts, Holman Hunt* (London: Sampson, Low, Marston and Co., 1902),
     p. v.
32   William Holman Hunt, *Pre-Raphaelitism and the Pre-Raphaelite Brotherhood*,
     2 vols. (London: Macmillan and Co., 1905), vol. II, pp. 409, 410.
33   William Vaughan, 'Realism and Tradition in Religious Art' in *'Sind
     Briten hier?' Relations between British and Continental Art 1680–1880*,

ed. Zentralinstitut für Kunstgeschichte (Munich: Wilhelm Fink Verlag, 1981), pp. 207–23; p. 219.

34   Jowett, 'Interpretation of Scripture', p. 367.
35   Stephens, *William Holman Hunt*, p. 61.
36   Temple, 'The Education of the World', p. 24.
37   Ibid., p. 47; Stephens, *William Holman Hunt*, p. 60.
38   Edmund Gosse, *Father and Son*, 3rd edn (Harmondsworth: Penguin, 1972), p. 164.
39   Review in *Once a Week*, 14 July 1860; cited in Stephens, *William Holman Hunt*, pp. 100–4; p. 101.
40   Review in *Edinburgh News*, 23 June 1860; cited in Stephens, *William Holman Hunt*, pp. 107–10; p. 108.
41   George P. Landow, *William Holman Hunt and Typological Symbolism* (New Haven and London: Yale University Press, 1979), p. 127.
42   Review in the *Manchester Guardian*, 24 April 1860; cited in Stephens, *William Holman Hunt*, p. 115.
43   Roland Barthes, 'The Rhetoric of the Image', in *Image, Music, Text*, ed. and trans. Stephen Heath (London: Flamingo, 1984), pp. 32–51; p. 39.
44   Gertrud Schiller, *Iconography of Christian Art*, trans. Janet Seligman, 2 vols. (London: Lund Humphreys, 1972), vol. II, pp. 197f.
45   *Athenaeum* (1860), p. 653.
46   Marcia Pointon, *William Dyce 1806–1864: A Critical Biography* (Oxford: Clarendon Press, 1979), pp. 163f.
47   William Scrope, *The Art of Deer-Stalking* (1838) (London and New York: Edward Arnold, 1897), pp. 41f.; Duncan Leslie, *Leslie's Tourist Guide to the Scottish Highlands* (Perth: D. Leslie; Edinburgh and Glasgow: John Menzies and Co.; London: Simpkin, Marshall and Co., 1888), pp. 28f.
48   Leslie, *Tourist Guide*, p. 34.
49   Ibid., p. 46.
50   David R. Oldroyd, 'The Geologist from Cromarty' in *Hugh Miller and the Controversies of Victorian Science*, ed. Michael Shortland (Oxford: Clarendon Press, 1996), pp. 76–102; p. 77.
51   Hugh Miller, *Sketch-book of Popular Geology; Being a Series of Lectures Delivered Before the Philosophical Institution of Edinburgh* (Edinburgh: Thomas Constable and Co.; London: Hamilton, Adams and Co., 1859), p. 87.
52   Ibid.; John Ruskin, *Modern Painters*, vol. I in *The Works of John Ruskin*, eds. E. T. Cook and Alexander Wedderburn, 39 vols. (London: George Allen; New York: Longmans, Green & Co., 1903–1912), vol. III, p. 198.
53   Wilberforce, '*Essays and Reviews*', p. 305.
54   John Ruskin, *Modern Painters*, vol. II, in *Works of John Ruskin*, eds. Cook and Wedderburn, vol. IV, p. 32.
55   John Ruskin, 'Preface to the Second Edition', *Modern Painters*, vol. I, p. 22.
56   John Ruskin to Henry Acland, letter dated 24 May 1851, in *Works of John Ruskin*, eds. Cook and Wedderburn, vol. XXXVI, p. 115.

57 For a useful discussion, see Marcia Pointon, 'Geology and Landscape Painting in Nineteenth-Century England', in *Images of the Earth: Essays in the History of the Environmental Sciences*, eds. Ludmilla Jordanova and Roy S. Porter (Chalfont St Giles: British Society for the History of Science, 1979), pp. 84–108.

58 There is some evidence to suggest that Dyce was an acute observer of natural phenomena. See, for example, Dyce's letter to Clay, 20 October 1860, in which he gives a very detailed account of the differences between the Scottish Highlands and the landscapes of Wales (Dyce Papers, pp. 1752–5, microfiche in Hyman Keitman Research Centre, Tate Gallery, London).

59 Allen Staley, *The Pre-Raphaelite Landscape* (Oxford: Clarendon Press, 1973), p. 165.

60 Pointon, *William Dyce*, p. 164.

61 Temple, 'The Education of the World', p. 24.

62 Gillian Beer, *Arguing with the Past: Essays in Narrative Form from Woolf to Sidney* (London: Routledge, 1989), p. 16.

63 Charles Babington Macaulay, 'History. The Romance of History. England. By Henry Neele. London. 1828. (May 1828)', in *The Works of Lord Macaulay*, ed. Lady Trevelyan, 8 vols. (London: Longmans, Green and Co., 1866), vol. V, pp. 122–61; pp. 157f.

64 Cited in Hunt, *Pre-Raphaelitism*, vol. II, p. 197.

65 Beer, *Arguing with the Past*, p. 16.

66 Marcia Pointon, 'William Dyce as a Painter of Biblical Subjects', *Art Bulletin* 58 (1976), 260–8; p. 266.

67 Others in this group include: *Gethsemane* (Walker Art Gallery, Liverpool), *The Good Shepherd* (Manchester City Art Gallery) and *Christ and the Woman of Samaria* (Birmingham Museums and Art Gallery).

PART V

Imperial occult

CHAPTER 9

Knowledge, belief and the supernatural at the imperial margin

Roger Luckhurst

I

When the Society for Psychical Research was founded in 1882, it heralded a new stage in Victorian attempts to develop a science of the supernatural. Ghosts were replaced by phantasms of the living, haunted houses by phantasmogenetic centres, and superstitions regarding second sight and uncanny coincidences became evidence for the newly coined concept, telepathy. These terms aimed to re-categorise the supernatural as *supernormal* phenomena: it was merely a matter of time before they could be accepted into the framework of normal science. Tests designed to prove telepathic transfer were attended by scientists broadly interested in the human faculty (such as Francis Galton, George Romanes and James Crichton-Brown), as well as the physicists and psychologists who formed the core of the new Society, William Barrett, Oliver Lodge, Frederic Myers and Lord Rayleigh. Most histories of psychical research tend to focus on the bitter contests around the elaboration of psychical research, concepts developed by the theorists of the Society in the face of violent objections from scientific naturalists.[1] The broad membership of the Society at the *fin de siècle* is thus marginalised, even though the discourse of psychical research in crucial ways depended upon, and actively incorporated, the voices of its lay constituencies.[2] The overwhelming bulk of each issue of the *Proceedings of the Society for Psychical Research* or the 1,400 pages of their first official publication in 1886, *Phantasms of the Living*, was filled by material from letters sent to the Society by the public.

For the cultural historian, the interest in this bulk of epistolary raw material lies in exploring the kind of material correspondents chose to lodge with the Society: a quotidian archive of occult experiences. The following narratives are typical of the resources used in Frederic Myers's monumental synthesis of supernormal phenomena, 'The Subliminal Consciousness':

I was in my bedroom being undressed by my maid, Mrs Gregory, who had been with me for 41 years, and she was unfastening my bracelet when I saw, just behind her about two feet off, her exact resemblance. She was then in perfect health. I said to her, 'Why, Mrs Gregory, I see your fetch.' She smiled and said, 'Really, ma'am,' but was not in the least alarmed. On the following Sunday, she was only poorly. I went for a doctor at once, who said she was a little out of sorts. On Wednesday evening she suddenly died. It was about the same time that her double appeared to me just a week before. This was about 15 years ago.

Some years ago, I was asleep in bed here about 12 to 1 a.m., and dreamt that I was out watching in a certain place where two gates face each other, near my house; that four poachers came up to me through those gates and that I seized hold of two of them, one in each hand, and shook them and struggled with them, at the same time shouting for assistance . . . Just about that very time, and at the very place I saw in my dream, four poachers did make their appearance and stoned some of our men who were watching there.

Early in the spring of the year 1885, I was living at Colaba with my husband, a major of the Royal Artillery. Colaba is the Royal Artillery station, and is situated about two miles from Bombay. For some little time I had been studying Gregory's *Animal Magnetism*. The subject possessing a peculiar fascination for me, I had experimented occasionally, with varying success, on the different servants (Indian for the most part) of my establishment. Over one girl, a half-caste, my children's nurse, I possessed great influence, and used frequently to magnetise a tumbler of water, so that by making her look therein I might learn what my friends at a distance were doing.[3]

These three samples from over 800 cases repeat certain concerns. Class informs the content, but also constitutes the threshold for inclusion. The third letter is framed with the assurance that 'the seer, now married to an Englishman, is known to me' and is a 'trustworthy person'.[4] The regular invocation of this gentlemanly guarantee manages something of the ambivalence present in the letters. Many of these accounts render servants central to occult events in stories of the domestic uncanny. Narratives of dependence on the psychical abilities of servants exist alongside instances of clairvoyant or premonitory warnings about threats to persons and property by the nefarious lower-class. The poachers, for instance, are grouped with the theft of horses, and the mesmerised half-caste of the third sample is used to identify a thieving servant.[5] Whether supernatural capabilities rest *in* the working-class or raced body, or expose threats *from* them, these testimonies work over a general ambiguity regarding the liminality of the servant, at once inside domestic space yet outside the family.[6] Placing these familial narratives within the categories of psychical research also worked to assert its distance from Spiritualism, whose plebeian, non-hierarchical access to spirits acted, in the words of Morell Theobald, 'as a leveller of social distinctions', in his case queasily mixing family and servants in the same séance circle.[7] Stories which reached the thresholds installed by the Society, and which were re-narrated in the jargon of 'hypermnesia' or 'phantasmogenesis', helped protect correspondents from charges of (a class-inflected) superstition. But if social forms could be managed in this way, the narratives also show a marked interest in transgression. Occult relation oscillates between distance and touch, restoring and dissolving boundaries in the same moment.

There is a notable divergence in register between the letters and the psychical theories that framed them. Accounts sent to the Society often conformed to the generic conventions of folk wisdom. The narrative of the servant's fetch above anticipates that the reader knows of the folkloric belief that the double is a harbinger of death. Phantasmal visitations rehearsed the convention of ghost as witness to an untold wrong. The taxonomy of supernormal phenomena developed by Myers was meant to emphasise a new scientific organisation, but this also invited imitations. The markers of delay ('15 years ago', 'some years ago') tended to frustrate verification, but they also prompted questions of genre: were these stories waiting for the categories of psychical research to give them meaning within a structure of knowledge, or did psychical research help *constitute* their contents, which were then displaced into the haze of history? Where an accumulation of stories was read as proof of the ubiquity of such occurrences by the Society, the same reiterations suggested to sceptics that the credulous public were framing their experiences within the genre rules for ghost stories.

Rather than arguing over their evidential status, I want to argue that they constitute a set of *doxai*, a shadow-record of beliefs and semi-legitimate knowledges that circulated precisely because they dealt with material that failed to find sanction in orthodox channels of information.[8] *Doxai* might be seen among those 'subjugated knowledges' defined by Foucault as 'a whole set of knowledges that have been disqualified as inadequate to their task or insufficiently elaborated: naïve knowledges, located low down on the hierarchy, beneath the required level of cognition or scientificity'.[9] The discourse of psychical research risked 'disqualification' from what Foucault terms 'knowledges of erudition'.[10] But the cultural pervasiveness of psychical notions owed much to the provision of an institutional locus for unsanctioned narratives of occult occurrences. These tales, unverifiable, hazily located in time, rendered anonymous in the pages of the *Proceedings*, operated like rumour. Rumours work over cultural materials in 'sequences of varying narrative situations' that lend themselves to further transmission, and with a power that derives from their being always already citational: 'In the background of conversations in which this voice speaks there is a chain of anonymous speakers begun somewhere indeterminate and leading nowhere in particular. This series, this virtual network . . . gives rumours their strange authority.'[11]

But I also want to argue that these *doxai* held a different status at the edges of empire. Here, narratives concerning occult relation, uncanny methods of communication and instances of telepathic rapport abounded. 'The further one travels out from the centre towards the periphery the more uncertain is the knowledge that is to be encountered, and the more important (and unclear) is the resonance of each piece of information.'[12] Official imperialist discourse allied itself with the powers of Enlightenment, but where the writ of modernity reached the limits of Western power, leaving behind the supports of governmental, military or scientific institutions, and technologies of communication, *doxai* became a more locally responsive discourse, and the line between positive knowledge and folkloric belief became blurred. The power of scientific naturalism in London held less authority on the periphery, although agents of the empire continually transferred data from the margin to the 'centres of calculation' in London.[13] In parallel, the SPR received narratives which told of the actions of native spirits, supernatural powers of native magicians and witch-doctors, and mental sympathies that developed across racial divides. These stories alter significantly according to colonial context, and there is no single way of reading this body of texts. It could act as a passive shadowing of colonial power, mystifying its operation, but it could also disrupt the proprieties of imperialist relations.

So, for instance, in Colaba, a mesmerised native was employed as a communication device between far-flung colonists. This reflected a long-established culture of mesmerism in India, away from its marginal and abject status in England. In India, Alison Winter suggests, 'European residents invested mesmerism with a wider range of issues, relating to colonial power, cultural exchange, and the relative status of East and West.'[14] The blithe confidence of the correspondent in the rights to exercise mesmeric power over her servants merely repeated a confidence in colonial influence over a passive native population. Yet the colonial confidence in the asymmetry of power over the native could itself be regarded as uncanny. John Seeley, leading proponent of the New Imperialism, fêted those 'good number of Englishmen . . . who have exerted an almost magical ascendancy over the minds of the native races in India'.[15] This commonly used trope showed 'the penetration of magic and magical thinking into the routine of imperial rule', which, for Lewis Wurgraft, 'existed in contrapuntal relationship to the supposedly demystified doctrine of administrative order'.[16] A letter from Colaba can thus begin to unravel the ways in which occult narratives explored the complexities of distance and relation at the colonial frontier.

In what follows, I want to examine how the theorisation of telepathy and its allied phenomena by the SPR was saturated with colonial contexts. I will then focus on Andrew Lang's specific conjuncture of imperialism and psychical research. Lang was a literary critic and *belle lettriste*, who sometimes concurred with the attacks on psychical research. Addressing the readers of *Blackwood's Magazine*, the home of the Victorian ghost story, he lamented that 'the most frivolous pastimes now have a habit of degenerating into scientific exercises... Even ghost stories, the delight of Christmas Eve, have been ravaged and annexed by psychology', such that '"The oldest aunt" would forget "the saddest tale" if plied with remarks on the "dextro-cerebral hemisphere" of the brain'.[17] Yet Lang was also a founding member of the Folk-Lore Society and held an important place in anthropology, synthesising data collected in the field. When he began to assert the truth of what had been regarded as credulous reports of native capacities of clairvoyance and telepathic communication, he founded a new disciplinary knowledge which he called 'psycho-folklorism'. Lang, in other words, premised his anthropological theory on *doxai* received from the edges of empire.

II

In 'Thought-Reading', the first essay written for a wider public by the SPR in 1882, the authors deferred to an earlier conceptualisation of communication between mind and mind. James Knowles's article, 'The Hypothesis of Brain-Waves', proposed that: 'Every brain-wave is transmitted in all directions into space, and that, if anywhere it comes upon another brain under the very peculiar conditions... which make it sensitive to such a brain-wave... then and there the brain-wave will be more or less slowly interpreted into pictures or feelings.'[18] Knowles called for 'a collection of authenticated ghost stories', and offered a handful of cases.[19] In one, Count Ginnasi is said to have given a psychic reading of a cuff-link owned by Robert Browning. The object did have a violent history, Browning confirmed: it had belonged to Browning's great-uncle, murdered 'by his own slaves' on his plantation on St Kitts.[20] A second was a narrative told by Thomas Woolner, sculptor and one of the members of the Pre-Raphaelite Brotherhood, who had been stricken in Oxford Street by the thought of a friend in New Zealand, a thought which oppressed him for two hours. 'And surely,' the article continued, 'when the next mail or the next mail but one arrived, there came the horrible news that at that very day and hour (*allowance being made for longitude*) his friend had been made prisoner by the natives of New Zealand, and put to a slow death by frightful tortures.'[21]

The cases presented by Knowles implied that psychic energies reached supernormal intensity when linked to violent colonial disorder. And although 'Thought-Reading' dealt with the sedate experiments of the 'willing-game' in a respectable middle-class Liverpool home, the archive of spontaneous cases recorded the capacities of telepathic communication on an imperial measure. This was unsurprising, given that the SPR was formed during a critical passage in British imperialism, when concerted colonisation in African and Pacific spheres led to a succession of summits between the European powers, most famously the Berlin conference of 1885. Gladstone's government developed an interventionist policy, occupying Egypt in 1882, whilst campaigning for Home Rule in Ireland, a policy which split the Liberal party and fostered a radicalisation of pro-Imperialist sentiment.[22] The philosopher Henry Sidgwick, first president of the SPR, recorded the effects of these transformations on his political thinking, and correspondents to the Society inflected psychical occurrences with the contemporary political concerns.[23]

Although the SPR tried to engineer a decisive break from Spiritualism, their imbrication of occult communication and imperialism was clearly a modulation of the ways in which Spiritualism calculated the distance to Summerland. The topography of the spirit-world existed in complex relation to empire. Alex Owen has read the séance space as a phantasmatic site of mobile desire, allowing women mediums to 'perform' femininity in both conformist and transgressive ways.[24] Imperial figures traversed the séance in a similarly conflicted way. Patrick Brantlinger asserts a homology between imperialism and the occult (mutually infantile as well as expansionist), but I want to refine this suggestion.[25] Many significant mediums were controlled by Native American spirits: the famous psychical medium Mrs Piper first developed an Indian girl, Chlorine; *Medium and Daybreak* detailed how Mrs Holmes 'was soon controlled by the little Indian girl, "Rosie"', and recorded that Henry Slade had first risen to prominence at the guidance of Owosoo, a Spanish Indian.[26] The celebrated Hélène Smith called up the daughter of a fourteenth-century Arab sheikh, replete with 'a knowledge relative to the costumes and languages of the orient, the actual source of which has up to the present time not been possible to discover'.[27] Many other instances abound.

It may have been that racial difference and imperial distance were the clearest representational means of demarcating the medium and her spirit in the domestic space of the séance. The more familial and homely the circle (and its medium), the more radical the contrast indicated by racial markers in dress, voice or behaviour. Presumably, though, Spiritualist communities were attuned to the traditional *doxa* of the ghost as a kind of blockage that leaks symptoms until redressed. In this sense, directing familial contacts between the living and dead through a racial other suggested a kind of commentary on the repressed presence of empire at the heart of domesticity. There was attention to specific spheres of influence, too. Red Indian and black slave spirits had been transported from the American origins of modern Spiritualism, but the genocidal histories embodied in them spoke to a tradition of English abolitionism and aboriginal protection, dissenting projects overlapping with aspects of Spiritualist belief. Spirit controls of a more Eastern cast, meanwhile, promised ancient oriental wisdom. Forgotten 'supernatural' powers of a now degenerate Egypt or Indian subcontinent hinted at lost plenitude with a nostalgic allure which was precisely constituted by the erasures effected by Western imperialism. This was the promise offered by Theosophy, which promised the adept 'the secret knowledge of the ancient world'.[28] As Gauri Viswanathan has noted, Theosophy was a hugely successful and globally dispersed movement, generated by 'cosmopolitan emigrés travelling along the routes of empire'.[29]

Spiritualism and Theosophy were often defined as belief-systems in opposition to the orthodoxies of science, but psychical research sought as many legitimating interconnections to scientific modernity as possible. Yet one of the notable narratives repeated by correspondents to the SPR shadowed accounts of modern communication systems which supposedly spread light and stamped out native superstition. These accounts emphasised precisely the reverse: that in territories where Western communications had not reached, or were stretched to their limit, occult systems took over. In India, Lord Roberts recalled his father cancelling a party following a dream foretelling a family death. This was measured against the twelve miles per hour taken by 'the mail-carts along the Grand Trunk Road from Calcutta to Peshawar', which eventually brought confirmation of the death.[30] In Canada, the Marchioness of Dufferin, wife of the governor, confirmed the story of a drowned footman, whose servant-girl sweetheart dreamt the exact details of his death 'more than 500 miles distant in Ottawa', knowledge

received more quickly than the speed of the telegraph network.[31] Such cases
had been familiarised as 'crisis apparitions' between kith and kin, yet the
Society also took a record of those native systems which seemed to out-
pace Western devices. In the 'virgin' wilds of Uganda, for instance, Edward
Schnitzler, the explorer, accepted the intelligence of a native wizard, whose
soul travelled in an animal 550 miles distant and had 'seen' the relief steamer,
and who predicted the arrival of a messenger from Khartoum to the day.[32]
Meanwhile a colonial official on the Gold Coast informed the Society that
'the transmission of intelligence by occult means [was] treated by better
class of natives as everyday knowledge, the medicine man occasionally being asked to obtain or transmit information for various purposes'.[33] Dr Part
had witnessed a number of cases, including intelligence from a chief regarding the arrival of the Governor well ahead of the 'official wire'. Part
assured readers that these phenomena were supernormal not supernatural:
'The means by which these phenomena are obtained . . . these are secret
and their professors are members of a secret society; but I was informed
on good authority that the process gone through to obtain the power of
clairvoyance . . . is purely physical.'[34] In southern Africa, the Zulu phrase
for this clairvoyant knowledge was *isiyezi*, or 'opening the gates of distance',
which acted as 'a spiritual telegraph system', whilst W. T. Stead's *Review of
Reviews* included reports such as 'Telephone Anticipated by Wild Indians',
referring to the communication system of the Catuquinora Indians, which
used drum-skins resonating in sympathy a mile apart.[35]

Writing on Zulu clairvoyance, Andrew Lang regretted the sketchy evidence, but grasped the reason why: 'It is unusual for European travellers and
missionaries to give anecdotes which might seem to "confirm the delusions
of benighted savages".'[36] These instances were *doxai* in the sense of being
erased from official accounts which routinised them under general superstitions, leaving them to become second-hand anecdotes or unverifiable
rumours that appeared in private forms like journals or letters. Frederick
George Lee, an enthusiastic collector of oriental magic tales, broke off one
report with the comment: 'But, as the ears of Europeans would only be
shocked by assertions and statements which they would not fail of holding to be utterly fabulous and ridiculous, the subject is merely alluded
to.'[37] This statement conforms to the definition of gossip provided by Jan
Gordon: 'A discourse which enacts informational transfer while disclaiming
(or being prohibited) from any foundational responsibility or representational share in its effects.'[38] Occult *doxai* at the limits of empire share the
same structure of disavowal: they bear the marks of the pressure of Enlightenment science in their hesitations and unofficial circulation, whilst

suggesting that the supernatural was a freely used means of communication at the colonial margin. They shared, too, the citational nature of rumour: 'I have heard in India that the fakirs walk in the air', one believer in Indian magic proclaimed, 'but I have never met an eye-witness of this fact; the accounts given to me come second or third hand.'[39]

The discovery of supernormal communications in dispersed theatres of empire suggested to some accumulating evidence of pre-modern powers 'lost' to the Enlightenment, but which could be recovered with sufficient study of primitive society. It also suggests a mechanism of projection in which anxieties about the fragility of colonial rule and scanty communication could conjure occult doubles which mysteriously exceeded European systems. One founding model of hidden communication systems was the 'Hindu Secret Mail', held to have spread insurrection during the Indian Mutiny. In Charles Bray's version, written within a decade of the Mutiny:

Important news travels faster in India by Mental Telegraph than by Electric Telegraph. The results of important battles have been known days before the intelligence could arrive by the ordinary or official means. The source of these tidings cannot be traced; the natives say 'it is in the air', and there has often been a generally uneasy feeling pervading men's minds preceding ill news, when nothing definite has been known.[40]

Commentators in the 1880s still referred to the Secret Mail, remarking that it 'has puzzled Europeans for years, and during the recent Afghan troubles it eluded all efforts on the part of the British government to discover the nature of its operation'.[41] In the terms of C. A. Bayly's examination of the 'information orders' of the Indian empire, *doxai* regarding such communications emerged in the same information gaps he examines in relation to the panic around Thuggee: in 'a zone of ignorance ... away from the hubs of British power and below the level of the district office'.[42] Since, Bayly argues, 'conquerors needed to reach into and manipulate the indigenous systems of communication', the far-flung colonial official was perpetually fearful of the 'wiles of the natives'. He feared their secret letters, their drumming and 'bush telegraphy' and the nightly passage of 'seditious agents masquerading as priests and holy men'.[43] In this paranoid world, wherever there are obstacles or breakdowns in modern communication, hearsay flowers. In conjunction with challenges to imperial superiority, as with the Mutiny or Zulu defiance, the 'immense speed' of rumours and their 'power over society have a supernatural feel'.[44] Bayly encapsulates a situation at the margin, in which knowledge and belief, rationality and superstitious speculation, could intertwine: 'What emerged was a dual economy of knowledge: an "advanced" sector, which used Western forms of representation and communication subsisting within an attenuated but still massive hinterland employing older styles of information.'[45] In contrast to histories which focus on 'the official mind of imperialism', accounts lodged with the SPR give glimpses of beliefs which circulated in parallel with administrative rationality.[46]

These stories did not remain marginal in the SPR, but were integrated into psychical theories. Myers, in developing counter-arguments to the dominant conception of the personality as a 'perfect unity', suggested that the Self might be considered a 'colonial' subject.[47] He held that 'psychical unity is federative and unstable', but that the highest level of subjective integration managed 'colonial complexity' with 'centralised control'.[48] Myers's formulations were borrowed from a disciplinary knowledge which was growing in importance as the ideology of empire intensified in the late Victorian period. The conjoining of anthropology and psychical research is best examined through Andrew Lang, since it was Lang who managed to make the question of whether the data collected on primitive 'psychism' were fact or superstition, knowledge or *doxa*, an issue central to anthropological debate in the 1890s.

III

Andrew Lang had a bewildering diversity of interests. He was a professional journalist from 1875 until his death in 1912, with an extraordinarily prolific output which astonished even his contemporaries. For his obituary, the *Quarterly Review* had to employ four experts from distinct fields to assess the multiple strands of his career.[49] He was a poet, leader writer, critic, novelist, classicist, translator, Scottish historian, fairytale and myth collector, folklorist, anthropologist and psychical researcher. Individual pieces would commonly elide several of these categories, such that analysing one strand of interest tends to slide into others. Lang, for instance, has resurfaced in recent literary history principally as a critic who exerted a significant influence over popular tastes as a manuscript reader for several leading presses, and through reviews and columns such as his 'At the Sign of the Ship', which ran in *Longman's Magazine* from 1886 to 1905. An idoliser of Walter Scott, Lang was one of the engineers of the revival of the romance, hailing Robert Louis Stevenson's *Treasure Island* as a breakthrough text. He advocated the imperial adventures of Rider Haggard and Rudyard Kipling on their first appearance in the late 1880s (co-writing *The World's Desire* with Haggard in 1890). Lang regarded the romance as a virile, masculine riposte to decadent and naturalist fiction with its 'unholy knowledge of the nature of women'.[50] Against this over-refined interiority, written by the 'bald, toothless, highly "cultured"' Coming Man, Lang juxtaposed the primitive vitality of the romance, whose energies he related directly to 'the ancestral barbarism of our natures': 'Not for nothing did Nature leave us all savages under our white skins', he argued.[51] Here, Lang shifts category, deploying an anthropological language that he had learnt from Edward Tylor's *Primitive Culture* (1871), which tracked savage 'survivals', those 'processes, customs, opinions, and so forth, which have been carried on by force of habit into a new state of society'.[52] Lang further bolstered the adventure romance as the product of a tradition stretching back through the troubadour poets, Scandanavian sagas, the Homeric epic and the oral culture of 'the folk'. In 1873, when he was still at Oxford, Lang had dared to contest Professor Max Müller's philological theories of mythology as degenerations of higher and purer forms. He argued instead for a comparative evolutionary theory that valued folklore and the folk-tale as the surviving traces of 'a continual and rational progress' in human development. This argument was widely seen to have helped usher in Darwinian models to the study of folk-cultures.[53] 'The natural people, the folk, has supplied us, in its unconscious way, with the stuff of all our poetry, law, ritual', Lang later reaffirmed.[54]

'Lang was to Prof. Tylor what Huxley was to Darwin [in] that his chief and more lasting work consisted in popularising the views of his master', one commentator claimed as the general view.[55] Yet Lang's love of romance was also a love of ghost stories, of mysteries that escaped rational capture or neat theoretical systems. He was honest with general periodical readerships about the 'real attraction' of ghost stories and notions of 'telepathic hallucination': 'It is so natural to wish for a *terra incognita*, the land not yet meted out by science – the free space where Romance may still try an unimpeded flight.'[56] A Scot proudly claiming a dash of gypsy blood, Lang held to an identity associated with strong folk traditions of second sight and accesses to the supernatural. These elements of Lang's interests were in diametrical opposition to Tylorian anthropology, whose aim was, in Tylor's words, 'to expose the remains of crude old culture which have passed into harmful superstition, and to mark these out for destruction'.[57] Spiritualism had been Tylor's principal instance of a harmful survival in modern culture. As Lang tried to fuse anthropology and psychical research, rigorously defined against Spiritualism, which he regarded with 'abhorrence and contempt', he nevertheless came more and more into conflict with the demystificatory aims of late Victorian anthropology.[58]

As soon as psychical research emerged, Lang advocated the comparative anthropological study of ghost stories, proposing that 'for the better explanation of the facts, the Psychical Society might send missionaries to investigate and test the exhibitions of Australian Birraarks, and Maori Tohungas, and Eskimo Angekoks'.[59] At this stage, Lang used the comparative evolutionary method largely in accord with Tylor, confirming the view that 'Savage Spiritualism wonderfully resembles, even in minute details, that of modern mediums and séances'.[60] Even so, Lang felt that Tylor had not paid sufficient attention to 'the more or less well-authenticated cases in which savages have seen the ordinary ghost of modern society'.[61] This prompted Lang's occasional series of essays on ancient and modern ghost stories, running parallel with the SPR's growing body of material. In 1893, reviewing Myers's book, *Science and the Future Life*, Lang stated, 'I do not mind confessing that I feel myself going over to the Psychical Society', even if only as a reflection of 'an age of minds almost indecently open'.[62] Lang then collected his ghostly essays into *Cock Lane and Common-Sense* in 1894.

Cock Lane proposed to examine ghost stories from the 'anthropological aspect', synthesising data from sources gathered from around the world.[63] Lang was drawn to details which were 'universally coincident', stretching from 'Australian blacks in the Bush' to the 'London suburb'.[64] Listing 'savage "birraarks" in Australia, fakirs in India, saints in medieval Europe, a gentleman's butler in Ireland, boys in Somerset and Midlothian, a young warrior in Zululand, Miss Nancy Wesley at Epworth in 1716, and Mr Daniel Home in London in 1856–70', Lang worried about how 'to explain the uniformity of stories palpably ridiculous'.[65] Most anthropologists would have listed these instances as evidence of a false logic, unsurprisingly sustained into the present day by those that James Frazer called 'the dull, the weak, the ignorant, and the superstitious, who constitute, unfortunately, the vast majority of mankind'.[66] Lang, though, shifted emphasis, holding that 'The identity of the alleged phenomena, in all lands and all ages, does raise a presumption in favour of some kind of abnormal occurrences, or of a common species of hallucinations.'[67] The order of this hedged bet – abnormal phenomena *before* hallucination – indicated that Lang had absorbed psychical research and was using its categories to order his anthropological data.

The final chapter of *Cock Lane*, entitled 'The Ghost Theory of the Origin of Religion', served notice that Lang was in conflict not just with Tylor, but also with other anthropological theorists, such as Herbert Spencer, who speculated that the worship of dead ancestors was the origin of belief in active posthumous spirits, a position which was elaborated in the 1890s by Spencer's disciple, Grant Allen.[68] James Frazer, meanwhile, was elaborating his differentiation of magic and religion, arguing that the 'false science' of sympathetic magic was the most primitive set of beliefs, eventually overridden by more complex ideas of spirit.[69] All of these figures implicitly ordered their thinking on the Comtean trajectory away from religious and metaphysical beliefs towards the positive, demystifying knowledge of science. Lang, however, contested the view that savage 'superstitions' were based on misreadings of normal facts, arguing that a number of primitive beliefs may have been derived *correctly* from 'abnormal' instances:

Man may have faculties which savages recognise, and which physical science does not recognise. Man may be surrounded by agencies which savages exaggerate, and which science disregards altogether, and these faculties and agencies may point to an element of truth which is often cast aside as a survival of superstition.[70]

Lang's adoption of this position resulted in a rebuke from Edward Clodd, in his presidential address to the Folk-Lore Society, a body that Lang had helped to form along Tylorian principles in the 1870s. Clodd, restating the Enlightenment view that superstitions 'are the outcome of ignorance [which] can only awaken pity', analysed the SPR 'under the dry light of anthropology', and saw nothing more than 'barbaric spiritual philosophy "writ large"'.[71] Lang replied by restating the distinction between Spiritualist survivals and the genuine scientific puzzles isolated by psychical research, insisting that these investigations could prove important to the study of folklore. Psychism dealt with the individual self; folklore with 'symptoms as exhibited by the race'.[72] 'Psycho-folklorism' was a convergence of knowledges which could advance each discipline, given that 'certain obscure facts are, or may be, at the bottom of many folklore beliefs'.[73] Lang's one detailed instance came, symptomatically, from a letter from an anonymous correspondent in India, a witness to anomalous lights at dusk in a garden in Darjeeling, where the servants spoke casually of 'chota admis' (a race of 'little men'). 'Folklore classes the narrative with tales of ghostly lights and leaves it there. Psychical research tries to get more evidence about it', Lang wrote, supporting his opinion that 'we shall not understand great masses of folklore till psychical research has swept out a dozen of obscure corners in the edifice of the human faculty'.[74] Clodd's reply hinged on the distinction of knowledge and *doxa*. He repudiated psychical research as a science, because its data (collected by those 'not highly educated'), were riddled with prepossessed belief. 'The psychical researcher represents a state of feeling, the folklorist represents an order of thought', Clodd asserted.[75]

Lang's attempt to merge psychical research and anthropology culminated in *The Making of Religion*, first given in the Gifford Lectures series. The structure of the book puzzled his contemporaries. The latter half, concerning disputes over the origin of religion, constituted a critique of the theories of Edward Tylor, Lang's intellectual mentor for twenty-five years. Tylor argued, on the premise of the developmental hypothesis of the progress from simple to complex ideas, that notions of a Supreme Being could not be held by primitive peoples, who could only possess basic animistic beliefs. Lang, using fieldwork evidence from the Arunta and other tribes in Australia, drew out theistic ideas from their culture of a god who 'made' the world. This departure from Tylor was the product of the first part of the book, on psychical research. Edward Clodd, continuing to use the knowledge/*doxa* distinction, dismissed these chapters as likely to 'add only to the inane gossip of the day', before speaking much more highly of Lang's polemic against Tylor.[76] Yet the psychical material was integral to the reason for Lang's shift.

The root of Lang's objection to animistic theory, in which souls were mistaken reasonings from dreams or hallucinations, was evidence regarding distant vision (clairvoyance) and telepathy. 'The savage theory of the soul', Lang argued, 'may be based, at least in part, on experiences which cannot, at present, be made to fit into any purely materialistic system of the universe.'[77] Lang disregarded superstitions around spirits, yet claimed that savage practices of hypnotism, clairvoyance and telepathic connection were all evidence that 'savages anticipated us in the modern science of experimental psychology'.[78] Field evidence was again piled up regarding clairvoyance and telepathy as possible sources for notions of a soul. Zulus, opening the gates of distance, used the same technique as Lapps, which matched accounts of second sight in the Scottish Highlands. Lang introduced material which illustrated his own researches in crystal-gazing with Scottish women seers. The distant vistas opened by the crystal ball in Scotland included a scene grasped in India.[79] 'Anyone who can accept the assurance of my personal belief in the good faith of all concerned will see how very useful this faculty of crystal-gazing must be to the Apache, or the Australian medicine man or Polynesian priest', Lang suggested, fusing the knowledge-systems of anthropology with the appeal of the psychical researcher to 'personal belief'.[80] For Lang, this appeal was inevitable given the suppression of evidence, since 'white men . . . are afraid of seeming superstitious if they give examples, or, if they *do* give examples, are accused of having sunk to the degraded levels of Zulus or Red Indians'.[81]

After *The Making of Religion*, Lang was identified as one of the principal proponents of psychical research. He wrote introductions on the discipline and defended Myers's contributions to experimental psychology.[82] In

1911, he accepted the presidency of the Society for Psychical Research. His speech deferred to past presidents from the 'severe sciences', yet claimed his own fields of 'the historical, the folk-lorish, and the anthropological' as legitimate.[83] He upheld the rigour of the Society, remarking that he had 'lived to see many so-called scientific certainties proved to be fleeting phantasms of hypothesis'. This was the basis for his final assertion on the scientific possibility of telepathy: 'I am wholly convinced.'[84]

Lang built a career after 1900 as a Scottish historian, moving away from this phase of anthropological dispute. Yet his advocacy of psychical research indeed struck some of his fellow anthropologists as evidence of Lang having 'sunk to the degraded level of Zulus'. One suspects that it was partly Frazer's sense of affront at Lang's persistent attacks on his distinction of magic and religion that prompted him to place 'belief in the sympathetic influence exerted on each other by persons or things at a distance' as 'the essence of magic'. 'Whatever doubts science may entertain as to the possibility of action at a distance', Frazer continued acidly, 'magic has none; faith in telepathy is one of its principles.'[85] Although Frazer was putting Lang firmly in his (savage) place, notions of telepathy also became a key organising principle to order evidences of sympathetic magic in *The Golden Bough*. W. H. R. Rivers argued, more generously, that 'the great change which has taken place in recent years in the general attitude towards the subjects usually known as "psychical research" is due to Andrew Lang'.[86] This was perhaps in acknowledgement that Lang's call for trained psychologists to be integral members of anthropological expeditions had contributed to Rivers's own career as anthropological psychologist from the late 1890s.[87]

Lang's popularisation of anthropology risked over-identification with other marginal knowledges, and this was undoubtedly one of the reasons why Clodd and Frazer violently objected to Lang's elisions. When Lang stated that 'Anthropology has herself but recently emerged from that limbo of the unrecognised in which Psychical Research is pining', he revealed the weak authority of anthropology, a discipline whose 'marginality' was, in George Stocking's assessment, 'striking' even at the turn of the century, with barely a dozen men who could claim professional status.[88] Lang's amateur dabblings needed to be marked off against disciplinary expertise. His amateurism was associated with his credulous belief in witnesses from the imperial margin, and attributed to his insufficient training in the scientific methods required to sift material. Lang's location outside the boundaries of the profession explained the contamination of his anthropological evidence with superstitious *doxai*, misrecognised as ethnological knowledge.

But Lang's reassessment of evidence from the periphery, and the virulent response to it from armchair anthropologists at the imperial centre, was symptomatic of something else: a shift in the authority of the worker in the field, on the margin. For much of the nineteenth century, the person in the field was regarded as a lowly and unreliable figure, whose information had to be returned to the imperial centre and judged by experts before reaching the threshold of legitimate knowledge. Reports from missionaries were likely to be biased by prepossession, it was felt, but even professional collectors trained in scientific observation were regarded with suspicion (precisely because they were *paid* for their artefacts).[89] In the 1880s and 90s, anthropology was in the process of re-orienting its claims to be an authoritative discipline by constructing the professional fieldworker, the scientist who secured authentic knowledge by immersion in specific native cultures, and resisted the impulse to produce global, comparative theories. Branislaw Malinowski is widely regarded as consolidating the icon of the lone fieldworker in the 1920s, but in the 1890s figures like Mary Kingsley were already in the field, championing the value of local knowledge in easing problems of colonial rule, whilst being spooked by the panoply of black ghosts in West Africa.[90] The magical and the ghostly have remained central obsessions of anthropological field research to the present day, Lang's curious legacy.

The uncanniness of the field itself also prompts what James Clifford has termed 'fables of rapport', moments at which the boundaries of self and other become ecstatically or terrifyingly permeable.[91] Just as Mary Kingsley was proclaiming her expertise to 'think in black', risking all her scant authority as a woman ethnologist on her empathetic powers, so Andrew Lang was re-valuing the reports concerning native capacities to effect such startling intimacies and occult communications. The colonial contexts that informed the categories of psychical research were not, then, propped in a simply parasitical way on the popular support of empire at the *fin de siècle*. The collection of *doxai* regarding clairvoyance, visiting phantasms or telepathic contacts certainly did shadow imperial routes of communication, just as the Theosophical astral plane offered conveniently fast and direct deliveries between Madras and London. At the edges of Western rule, the supernatural clearly did function as a useful currency to articulate encounters, an economy that only fitfully surfaced in official records, bubbling up as gossip and rumour. But in an interesting way theorisations of telepathy and the disputes over the nature of evidence from the margins became bound up in an important transvaluation of the anthropological field. This suggests that the blurred locations between knowledge and *doxa* are productive sites in which to pursue the continuing cultural uses of the supernatural in the late Victorian world.

NOTES

1   Standard histories are Alan Gauld, *The Founders of Psychical Research* (London: Routledge and Kegan Paul, 1968) and Janet Oppenheim, *The Other World: Spiritualism and Psychical Research in England 1850–1914* (Cambridge: Cambridge University Press, 1985).

2   An exception is John Cerullo's analysis of a number of upper- and middle-class general members in *The Secularisation of the Soul: Psychical Research in Modern Britain* (Philadelphia: Institute for the Study of Human Issues, 1982).

3   All from Frederic Myers, 'The Subliminal Consciousness': case P.253, Chapter 9, *Proceedings of the Society for Psychical Research (PSPR)* 11 (1895), p. 448; case L.619, Chapter 4 *PSPR* 8 (1892), p. 398; case M.54, Chapter 5, *PSPR* 8 (1892), p. 522.

4   Case M.54, Chapter 5, *PSPR* 8 (1892) p. 522.

5   Case L.841, Chapter 4 *PSPR* 8 (1892), p. 399.

6   For commentary on the servant, see Anne McClintock, *Imperial Leather: Race, Gender and Sexuality in the Colonial Contest* (London: Routledge, 1995).

7   Morell Theobald, cited in Alex Owen, *The Darkened Room: Women, Power and Spiritualism in Late Victorian England* (London: Virago, 1989), p. 98.

8   I will use *doxa* throughout in the sense of 'opinion' or 'belief'. *Doxai* can still feature as the horrifying other of critical thought. Roland Barthes, for instance, states of his own mode of critical thinking: 'Reactive formations: a *Doxa* (a popular opinion) is posited, intolerable; to free myself of it, I postulate a paradox.' Roland Barthes, *Roland Barthes*, trans. Richard Howard (London: Macmillan, 1977), p. 71.

9   Michel Foucault, 'Two Lectures', in *Power/Knowledge: Selected Interviews & Other Writings*, trans. Colin Gordon *et al.* (New York: Pantheon, 1980), pp. 78–108; p. 82.

10   Ibid., p. 82.

11   Hans-Joachim Neubauer, *The Rumour: A Cultural History*, trans. Christian Braun (London: Free Association Books, 1999), pp. 93, 21.

12   Ibid., pp. 45–6.

13   The phrase 'centres of calculation' derives from Bruno Latour, *Science in Action: How to Follow Scientists and Engineers through Society* (Cambridge, MA: Harvard University Press, 1987).

14   Alison Winter, *Mesmerized: Powers of Mind in Victorian Britain* (Chicago: University of Chicago Press, 1998), p. 187.

15   John Seeley, *The Expansion of England* (London: Macmillan, 1883), p. 342.

16   Lewis D. Wurgraft, *The Imperial Imagination: Magic and Myth in Kipling's India* (Middletown, CT: Wesleyan University Press, 1983), pp. xix, 58.

17   Andrew Lang, 'Ghosts Up to Date', *Blackwood's Magazine* 155 (1894), 47–58; p. 47.

18   James Knowles, 'The Hypothesis of Brain-Waves', *Spectator*, 30 January 1869, 133–4; p. 133. William Barrett, Edmund Gurney and F. W. H. Myers jointly wrote 'Thought-Reading', *Nineteenth Century* 11 (1882), 890–902.

19   James Knowles, 'Brain-Waves: a Theory', *Spectator*, 30 January 1869, 134–6; p. 135.

20   Ibid., p. 136.

21   Ibid., p. 136.

22   For commentary, see Ronald Robinson and John Gallagher with Alice Denny, *Africa and the Victorians: The Official Mind of Imperialism* (London: Macmillan, 1981).

23   See the entries in Henry Sidgwick's diary in which he shifts from a Liberal to Liberal Unionist position on questions of empire. Arthur and Eleanor Sidgwick, *Henry Sidgwick: A Memoir* (London: Macmillan, 1906).

24   Owen, *The Darkened Room*.

25   Patrick Brantlinger, *Rule of Darkness: British Literature and Imperialism, 1830–1914* (Ithaca: Cornell University Press, 1998).

26   *Medium and Daybreak*, 6 September 1872, p. 368; 6 October 1876, p. 626.

27   Théodore Flournoy, *From India to Planet Mars* (1899) (Princeton, NJ: Princeton University Press, 1994), p. 175.

28   A. P. Sinnett, *The Occult World* (London: Trubner, 1881), p. 1.

29   Gauri Viswanathan, 'The Ordinary Business of Occultism', *Critical Inquiry* 27(2000), 1–20; p. 3.

30   Lord Roberts, cited in *JSPR* 9 (1899–1900), p. 128.

31   Marchioness of Dufferin and Ava, cited in *JSPR* 8 (1898–9), p. 329.

32   Dr Felkin, cited as a case in *JSPR* 9 (1899–1900), pp. 60–1.

33   Dr J. Shepley Part, 'A Few Notes on Occultism in West Africa', *PSPR* 14 (1898–9), 343–7; p. 344.

34   Ibid., p. 346.

35   Zulus discussed in Andrew Lang, *The Making of Religion* (London: Longman's, Green, 1898), p. 76. *Review of Reviews* report in news paragraph (August 1898), p. 157.

36   Lang, *Making of Religion*, pp. 75, 76, 79.

37   Frederick George Lee, *Glimpses of the Supernatural, Being Various Notes, Records, and Examples of The Supernatural* (London: Blackwood, 1885), p. 370.

38   Jan B. Gordon, *Gossip and Subversion in Nineteenth-century British Fiction: Echo's Economies* (Basingstoke: Macmillan, 1996), p. 57.

39   Harry Kellar, 'High Caste in Indian Magic', *North American Review* 46 (1893), 75–86; p. 81.

40   Charles Bray, *On Force, its Mental and Moral Correlates; and on That Which is Supposed to Underlie all Phenomena: With Speculations on Spiritualism, and Other Abnormal Conditions of Mind* (London: Longmans, 1866), p. 84.

41   H. S. Drayton, *Human Magnetism: Its Nature, Physiology and Psychology* (New York: Fowler and Wells, 1889), p. 105.

42   C. A. Bayly, *Empire and Information: Intelligence-Gathering and Social Communication in India 1780–1870* (Cambridge: Cambridge University Press, 1996), p. 143.

43 Ibid., p. 6.

44 Neubauer, *The Rumour*, p. 22.

45 Bayly, *Empire and Information*, p. 372.

46 The subtitle of Robinson and Gallagher, *Africa and the Victorians*.

47 Myers, *Human Personality*, vol. I, p. II.

48 Ibid., pp. 16, 38.

49 R. S. Rait, Salomon Reinach, Gilbert Murray and J. H. Millar, 'Andrew Lang', *Quarterly Review* 218 (1913), 299–329. R. S. Rait wrote on Lang's history writing, Salomon Reinach on his folklore and mythology studies, Gilbert Murray on his Classical translations and Homeric scholarship, and J. H. Millar on his poetry, fiction and critical essays. The main studies of Andrew Lang are Roger Lancelyn Green, *Andrew Lang: A Critical Biography* (Leicester: E. Ward, 1946) and Antonius de Cocq, *Andrew Lang: A Nineteenth-Century Anthropologist* (Amsterdam: Uitg Zwijsen Tilburg, 1968).

50 Andrew Lang, 'Realism and Romance', *Contemporary Review* 52 (1887), 683–93; p. 688.

51 Ibid., p. 689.

52 Edward Tylor, *Primitive Culture: Researches into the Development of Mythology, Philosophy, Religion, Art, and Custom*, 2 vols. (London: John Murray, 1871), vol. I, p. 15.

53 Andrew Lang, 'Mythology and Fairy Tales', *Fortnightly Review*, New Series, 8 (1873), 618–31; p. 620. Obituarists emphasised Lang's refutation of Müller as Lang's contribution to knowledge. Lang's exposure to Tylor's *Primitive Culture* at Oxford in March 1872 is discussed in Robert Crawford, 'Pater's *Renaissance*, Andrew Lang, and Anthropological Romanticism', *ELH* 53 (1986), 849–79.

54 Andrew Lang, *Adventures in Books* (London: Longmans, 1905), p. 37.

55 Salomon Reinach in Rait *et al.*, 'Andrew Lang', p. 310.

56 Lang, 'Ghosts Up to Date', pp. 56–7.

57 Tylor, *Primitive Culture*, vol. II, p. 453.

58 Andrew Lang, *Cock Lane and Common-Sense* (London: Longmans, 1894), p. 22.

59 Andrew Lang, 'The Comparative Study of Ghost Stories', *Nineteenth Century* 17 (1885), 623–32; p. 627.

60 Andrew Lang, 'Savage Spiritualism', *Longman's Magazine* 23 (1894), 482–95; p. 483.

61 Lang, 'Comparative Study', p. 624.

62 Andrew Lang, 'Literature', *New Review* 8 (1893), 710–14; p. 710.

63 Lang, *Cock Lane*, p. ix.

64 Ibid., pp. x, 4.

65 Ibid., pp. 99–100.

66 James George Frazer, *The Golden Bough: A Study in Magic and Religion Part One: The Magic Art*, vol. I (1890), 3rd edn (London: Macmillan, 1932), p. 237. The first edition appeared in 1890.

67 Lang, *Cock Lane*, p. 131.

68 Spencer's theory was developed in his *Study of Sociology* (1870) and developed by Allen in *The Evolution of the Idea of God: An Inquiry into the Origin of Religions* (1897).
69 See Frazer's preface to the second edition (1900), which explains the opposition of magic and religion, absent from the first version of *The Golden Bough*.
70 Lang, *Cock Lane*, p. 338.
71 Edward Clodd, 'Presidential Address', *Folk-Lore* 6 (1895), 54–81; pp. 78, 79.
72 Andrew Lang, 'Protest of a Psycho-Folklorist', *Folk-Lore* 6 (1895), 236–48; p. 242.
73 Ibid., p. 247.
74 Ibid., pp. 246, 243.
75 Edward Clodd, 'A Reply to the Foregoing "Protest"', *Folk-Lore* 6 (1895), 248–58; p. 258.
76 Edward Clodd, 'The Making of Religion', *The Academy* 53 (18 June 1898), 651–2; p. 651.
77 Lang, *Making of Religion*, p. 2.
78 Ibid., p. 7.
79 Ibid., p. 111.
80 Ibid., p. 111.
81 Ibid., p. 73.
82 See Andrew Lang, 'Psychical Research of the Century' in *The Nineteenth Century: A Review of Progress* (New York: G. P. Putnam's Sons, 1901), pp. 358–69. His defence of Myers, which *Nineteenth Century* refused to publish, was presented as '"The Nineteenth Century" and Mr F. Myers', *PSPR* 18 (1903–4), 62–76.
83 Andrew Lang, 'Presidential Address', *PSPR* 25 (1911), 364–76; pp. 364, 368.
84 Ibid., pp. 370, 375.
85 Frazer, *Golden Bough*, p. 119.
86 W. H. R. Rivers, 'In Memoriam: Andrew Lang', *Folk-Lore* 23 (1912), 369–71; p. 370.
87 Lang stated that 'We need persons trained in the psychological laboratories of Europe and America as members of anthropological expeditions' in the Preface to the second edition of *The Making of Religion* (London: Longmans, 1900).
88 George Stocking, *Victorian Anthropology* (New York: Free Press, 1987), p. 266.
89 See Henrika Kuklick and Robert E. Kohler, 'Introduction' to special issue on fieldwork, *Osiris* 11 (1996), 1–14.
90 See Mary Kingsley, 'Black Ghosts', *Cornhill Magazine*, New Series, 1 (1896), 79–92. She also lectured to the SPR on 'Forms of Apparitions in West Africa', *PSPR* 14 (1898–9), 331–42. For Malinowski see James Clifford, *The Predicament of Culture* (Cambridge, MA: Harvard University Press, 1988).
91 Clifford, *Predicament of Culture*, pp. 40–1.

CHAPTER 10

Romance, reincarnation and Rider Haggard

Carolyn Burdett

A growing public interest in archaeological finds in the last decades of the nineteenth century was echoed in the appearance of archaeological themes in popular fiction. Henry Rider Haggard frequently drew on the discipline, for example.[1] Haggard's interest in archaeology was largely a consequence of his passion for Ancient Egypt, a passion fostered in boyhood by visits to a fine amateur collection belonging to a near-neighbour in Norfolk. He made the first of many trips to see archaeological sights in Egypt shortly after the book publication of *She* in 1887, and over the course of his life he became a well-regarded amateur Egyptologist.[2] Like many others, Haggard was especially fascinated by the excavation of ancient burial sites and the discovery of their extraordinary human remains.

Many enthusiasts, including Haggard, were nevertheless increasingly troubled by the hunt for the secrets of Egyptian burial practices. The desecrated mummy and its revenges became a favourite topic for fictional and non-fictional writing.[3] Haggard addressed the issue on several occasions, including the following, published in the *Daily Mail*:

It does indeed seem wrong that people with whom it was the first article of religion that their mortal remains should lie undisturbed until the Day of Resurrection should be hauled forth, stripped and broken up . . . How should we like our own bodies to be treated in such a fashion . . . If one puts the question to those engaged in excavation, the answer is a shrug of the shoulders and a remark to the effect that they died a long while ago. But what is time to the dead? To them, waking or sleeping, ten thousand years or a nap after dinner must be one and the same thing.[4]

But time is, surely, nothing to the dead at all, unless the dead live again? Throughout his work, but with increasing intensity, Haggard explored the idea that the dead do indeed live again via the process of reincarnation, an idea contemporaneously being described and espoused by the emerging Theosophical movement. That Haggard's fictions suggest a keen interest in occult phenomena has long been acknowledged.[5] Patrick Brantlinger, for example, explores the role played by the occult in what he calls the 'imperial Gothic', a term meant to capture 'that blend of adventure story with Gothic elements' which became a significant popular literary form at the *fin de siècle*, and which is exemplified by Haggard's work. For Brantlinger, the occult, together with imperial ideology and the subjectivism of the romance genre as such, are all signs of an atavism that is symptomatic of a profound anxiety about the specific forms of late nineteenth-century modernity.[6] Recent research, however, has shown how interest in the supernatural was woven through the culture of the *fin de siècle* in ways which cannot simply be described as atavistic.[7] In this essay, I examine the idea of reincarnation in Haggard's work and its relation to the romance. The supernatural played its part in the political culture of the period, and threw together some unlikely bedfellows: in the case of Haggard, a belief in the doctrine of reincarnation aligned him with the radical socialist Annie Besant. At the same time Haggard was using his popular romances to consolidate an image of the modern future based on the values of Toryism and Anglicanism.

ABOUT FICTION

Haggard's first successful adventure story, *King Solomon's Mines*, was inspired by Robert Louis Stevenson's *Treasure Island*.[8] It secured for him the friendship of the critic Andrew Lang, already an admirer of Stevenson's, and, in Lang, Haggard found a spokesman for the imaginative scope of the romance, and for its cultural importance. In *King Solomon's Mines*, the supernatural powers claimed by the witch-like Gagool are exposed as a sham; Lang, however, confirmed that supernatural happenings were very much to be welcomed in stories. In a short essay on 'The Supernatural in Fiction', for example, he mocks the idea that in a positivist age the 'power of learning to shudder' must inevitably die out. Instead, 'as this visible world is measured, mapped, tested, weighed, we seem to hope more and more that a world of invisible romance may not be far from us'.[9] As Roger Luckhurst shows in his essay, Lang certainly took ghost stories seriously. His particular mix of anthropology, folklore and psychical research, especially as exemplified in his investigations of occult phenomena gathered from places where pre-modern powers supposedly held sway, contributed to significant realignments of anthropology's positivist underpinnings.

In *Cock Lane and Common-Sense*, published in 1894, Lang collected stories about ghosts and other strange happenings from the past and present, and from a wide range of cultures. Anthropologists understand occult practices as 'survivals' from an earlier age, Lang explains, and as such the latter were viewed in a negative light as the source of harmful superstition. But what is striking to Lang is that apparently spontaneous happenings, attested to by all sorts of people, over time, are 'undeniably all "in the same tale"':

Now we can easily devise an explanation of the stories told by savages, by fanatics, by peasants, by persons under ecclesiastical influence, by witches and victims of witches. That is simple, but why are sane, scientific, modern sceptics, in a tale, and that just the old savage tale? What makes them repeat the stories they do repeat? We do not so much ask: 'Are the stories true?' as '*Why are these stories told?*'[10]

Lang's modest conclusion is that, contrary to the insistence that belief in everything from fairies to the miracles of the Gospel declines as rationalism and Enlightenment advance, the evidence shows that: 'The last forty enlightened years gives us more bogles than all the ages between St Augustine and the Restoration . . . In the face of all these facts, it does not seem easy to aver that one kind of age, one sort of "culture" is more favourable to an occurrence of, or belief in, these phenomena than another.'[11] In other words, far from defining the difference between primitive and civilised peoples and cultures, the supernatural seems to muddy it.

In writing merely fictional romances, Haggard might seem to avoid the risks Lang encountered in trying to reroute anthropology and folklore through psychical research.[12] In his account of the writing of *She* – the manuscript which he recalls taking to his literary agent and throwing on the table, saying 'There is what I shall be remembered by' – Haggard enshrines the vision of the romance writer possessed by his fantastic imaginative world and needing, for the duration, to inhabit no other: 'The whole romance', he explains, 'was completed in a little over six weeks . . . The fact is that it was written at white heat, almost without rest, and that is the best way to compose.'[13] Not long after the first appearance of *She*, Haggard published a short article called 'About Fiction' in the *Contemporary Review*. In it, he claims romance fiction writing as the height of literary art ('really good romance writing is perhaps the most difficult art practised by the sons of man'), seemingly because it taps, or mirrors, some primordial human quality:

The love of romance is probably coeval with the existence of humanity. So far as we can follow the history of the world we find traces of it and its effects among every people, and those who are acquainted with the habits and ways of thought of savage races will know that it flourishes as strongly in the barbarian as in the cultural breast. In short, it is like the passions, an innate quality of mankind.[14]

This makes similar claims for the provenance of romance to those Lang will later make for the recording of supernatural experiences in *Cock Lane*. It is striking, though, that whereas the burden of Lang's rhetoric is to suggest that practices and beliefs associated with 'primitive' cultures are also to be found in the civilised and scientific world, Haggard stresses that the lust for imaginative stories is at least as great 'in the barbarian as in the cultural breast'. In other words, romance is not merely a 'survival', a make-believe version of things once *truly* believed in, and still embraced as real occurrences by so-called savage peoples. In insisting that the love of romance is a common feature of all people, Haggard blurs the distinction not just between 'primitive' and 'civilised' humanity, but also between representation (storytelling and make-believe) and what is claimed as real event (belief in occult phenomena).

In *King Solomon's Mines*, certainly, the 'supernatural' powers of the witch-like Gagool are a fake, and the Africans superstitious dupes whom she manipulates for political ends. The Englishmen are generally immune to the lure of the supernatural, merely exploiting the natural occurrence of an eclipse as proof of their extraordinary powers in order to negotiate a sticky moment of danger. In *She*, Ayesha too knows that her rule is based upon what she can make her subjects believe. As she says to Holly: 'How thinkest thou that I rule this people? ... it is not by force ... My empire is of the imagination' (175).[15] Ayesha's capacity to manipulate what others believe is not based on trickery, however, nor is she revealed as a charlatan by the Englishmen who find her. Instead, it is they that come to believe in her immortality and her deathless beauty.

Ayesha is not literally reincarnated in *She* – her glory and her punishment is that she cannot die – but Haggard wrote three further romances featuring She, all of which are saturated with the theme of reincarnation. Haggard's fascination with the oriental doctrine of reincarnation in Buddhism is made explicit in the setting of the sequel to *She, Ayesha: The Return of She*, published in 1905, in which Holly and Leo travel to Tibet. There they stay at a Lamasery, to which they are admitted in part because of Holly's knowledge of Buddhist teaching, and where they are welcomed as 'brethren'. The importance of Tibet as a centre for occult philosophy and practice had been widely popularised, both through the notoriety of Helena Petrovna Blavatsky and by Alfred Sinnett's influential books, *The Occult World* and *Esoteric Buddhism*, published in the early 1880s.[16] These works set out the tenets of Theosophy and, in part, chart Sinnett's relations with Madame Blavatsky and the 'Masters' with whom she communed. In 1880, Koot Hoomi, Master of the Great White Brotherhood (a secret order of enlightened masters in Tibet with whom Blavatsky had reputedly been an initiate), describes Tibet thus:[17]

For centuries we have had in Thibet a moral, pure hearted, simple people, unblest with civilization, hence – untainted by its vices. For ages has been Thibet the last corner of the globe not so entirely corrupted as to preclude the mingling together of the two atmospheres – the physical and the spiritual.[18]

In his work on Western perceptions of Buddhism, Donald S. Lopez explains that leading nineteenth-century British orientalists saw Buddhism as a rationalist and humanist creed based on reason and restraint, and free of ritual and superstition. They found early Buddhism attractive in part because it seemed to mirror the Western, Protestant, rejection of Roman Catholicism.[19] By contrast, the esoteric wing of the occult movement associated with Blavatsky emphasised the importance of Tibet (rather than India) as the original source of Buddhism. Tibetan Buddhism was thus associated with sacerdotalism, and hence with Catholicism rather than Protestantism.[20]

The Tibetan setting for Holly and Leo Vincey's next quest is crucial in its ability culturally to carry the following, sometimes contradictory, meanings. First, it signifies the ideal of a religion, philosophy and subjectivity untouched by the spiritually deadening effects of western rationalism and materialism. Just as importantly, though, it signals an esoteric order in which the strictest hierarchies exist. Such hierarchies are unquestioned and unquestionable because they are authentically based on the most fundamental values of spiritual wisdom. Haggard's interest in Buddhism and the doctrine of reincarnation draws on both meanings. The former affords a familiar critique of the spiritually moribund nature of industrial modernity. The second, though, suggests a more covert ideological agenda. For Haggard, English society was increasingly prey to the values of both a liberal metropolitan elite and the vulgar masses. Its culture lauded material over spiritual value, and the life of the city over the agricultural land Haggard strove to protect.[21] The metropolitan critic preferred abstruse psychological speculations over the robust plots of adventure fiction, and heaped derision on Haggard's literary pretensions, while the masses pruriently enjoyed vulgar naturalistic detail. Haggard thus found himself an anti-populist who became one of the most popular authors of his day. Repelled by the dominance of the commercial motive, he was a key player in the increasing commercialisation of the literary market. The Tory values to which Haggard was strongly attached were thoroughly inadequate to deal with these contradictions. Reincarnation and the concept of spiritual evolution with which it was associated in Theosophical doctrine provided a model of harmony and hierarchy capable of shoring up Haggard's crumbling faith in a democratising Britain and a struggling empire.

Haggard wrote his autobiography in 1912, though it was published only posthumously in 1927. *The Days of My Life* is strikingly full of references to occult phenomena. As a young man of eighteen, Haggard attended séances in London and, after its inception, followed with interest the *Proceedings* of the Society for Psychical Research. Indeed, he provided a case for the Society's journal in 1904, concerning a dream in which a family dog was in distress and trying to speak to him. He later discovered the dog to have been killed by a train at the moment, or just before, the dream took place and he firmly believed that the dog had communicated with him.[22] In a chapter on 'Romance-Writing', Haggard lists a series of events invented in his romances that later occurred in exactly the same manner in real life, and he returns again and again to comment on reincarnation. He hints that the strange intimacy he feels with certain peoples and periods – the Ancient Egyptians and the Zulus, for example – stems from the fact that in previous lives he had lived as a Zulu and an Egyptian.[23]

   These narratives of strange happenings are, however, always hedged about with disclaimers. Thus, Haggard describes dream-like visions of his own previous incarnations as 'a curiosity in which I have no personal faith', saying, 'it is not worth while to waste time in discussing them' – before going on to discuss them in detail.[24] 'And now farewell to the occult', he writes, later. 'Mysticism in moderation adds a certain zest to life and helps to lift it above the commonplace. But it is at best a dangerous sea to travel before the time' (vol. II, 172). Haggard was horrified by the prospect of being associated with vulgar, decadent or primitive interests – all charges frequently levelled at Spiritualism, for example – let alone being thought irrational and superstitious. Apparently to clarify his position, Haggard added to the end of *The Days of My Life* 'A Note on Religion', in which he restates his Anglican faith. He characterises those without faith and with questioning spirits as damagingly caught in 'wild searches' among 'alien religions' or Spiritualism, and ultimately lost without the 'sure, anchored rocks' of a home-grown Christianity. This 'unsatisfied, unsettled, hungry' and frightened searcher may be Haggard in earlier years, but it is a portrait of doubt the older man wishes to confirm himself rid of (vol. II, 236).

What comes next, though, would surprise at least some of Haggard's co-religionists who had learned, since the publication of *Essays and Reviews*, to make some accommodation between Christ and reason. Haggard insists that it is mistaken to deny the miracles of the New Testament, and most mistaken of all to deny the literal resurrection of Jesus Christ. He adds:

This may be a convenient place to state my private opinion . . . to the effect that we, or at any rate some of us, already have individually gone through this process of coming into active Being and departing out of Being more than once – perhaps very often indeed . . . In short, like the Buddhists, I am strongly inclined to believe that the Personality which animates each of us is immeasurably ancient . . . there is no proof and yet reason comes to support these imaginings. Unless we have lived before . . . [our present existence is comparable to] a great ball-room wherein a Pucklike Death acts as Master of Ceremonies. Here the highly born, the gifted and successful are welcomed with shouts of praise, while the plain, the poorly dressed, the halt, are trodden underfoot; here partners, chosen at hazard, often enough seem to be dancing to a different time and step, till they are snatched asunder to meet no more . . . But if we admit that every one of these has lived before and danced in other rooms, and will live again and dance in other rooms, then meaning informs the meaningless. (vol. ɪɪ, 241–2)

However much Haggard proclaims Anglicanism, the rhetoric here is instead markedly Theosophical: it accounts for human difference by reference to reincarnation.[25] Haggard insists that the religious world he evokes is fundamental for the survival of 'civilised and thoughtful man'. While admitting that his convictions are personally consoling (Haggard was shattered by the death in 1891 of his only son), he is convinced that they are also the sound and moral basis on which rests the future of both nation and empire. His beliefs 'may be right or wrong', Haggard writes, 'that the future of the white races will reveal' (vol. ɪɪ, 45).

When Haggard eventually settled in Norfolk with his family, he clearly aspired to the life of a Tory squire. His hatred of Gladstone, his ardent and lifelong support for empire, mark him as a certain brand of Victorian patriot, while his Toryism was manifested in a dislike of industrialism, and consequent work to defend the rights of agricultural workers. A sense of civic duty meant that he was active in the bureaucracy of social reform and served on various Royal Commissions, and, as an ecumenical Anglican, he reported on the success of the social programmes of the Salvation Army. Haggard wanted desperately for the Church of England to function as a spiritual anchor capable of sustaining the 'future of the white races'; he was also, as I have already suggested, profoundly uncertain as to whether it could do so. Perhaps this is why, in his fictions and elsewhere, Haggard often seems to be trying to convert to Theosophy. In a letter to William J. Horton, Haggard writes: 'If only one could get the real hang of this reincarnation business: if only one could be *sure*. It seems reasonable, a quarter of the inhabitants of the world believe in it to this day, it explains things, there is nothing against it (and one or two things for it) in the Bible, and yet if one could be sure!'[26]

The Theosophical Movement, founded in America in 1875 by Helena Petrovna Blavatsky and Henry Steele Olcott, had its origins in Spiritualism.[27] Olcott was an early convert to Spiritualism, and also, from the 1850s through to the 1870s, distinguished himself as a social reformer. He was part of New York's new urban intelligentsia, and became a member of the prestigious Lotus Club, the hub of Manhattan's artistic and literary elite. Stephen Prothero argues that when the patrician Olcott met the aristocratic Blavatsky, they set about transforming the plebeian basis of Spiritualism, a movement that insisted on its appeal to the common people and its opposition to a priestly caste. As Prothero puts it, 'Early Theosophy represented an attempt by elites like Blavatsky and Olcott to reform Spiritualism by "uplifting" its masses out of their supposed philosophical and moral vulgarities – to transform the masses of prurient ghostseeking Spiritualists into ethically exemplary theorists of the astral plane.'[28] Under Olcott's tutelage, the séance was no longer conceptualised as mediums speaking to the disembodied spirits of the dead. Instead, spirit manifestation was the result of 'adepts' who were able to manipulate occult forces, because of their initiation into secret knowledge of occult laws.

A. P. Sinnett, an early and influential Anglo-Indian supporter of Blavatsky and, later, President of the London Lodge of the Theosophical Society, explains that 'Occult phenomena must not be confused with the phenomena of Spiritualism. The latter, whatever they may be, are manifestations which mediums can neither control nor understand. The former are achievements of a conscious, living operator comprehending the laws with which he works. If these achievements appear miraculous that is the fault of the observer's ignorance.'[29] Prothero points out that this entailed a shift from the tradition of predominantly female and often lower-class mediums, working in darkened rooms, to a tradition of adepts and 'Masters'. The latter were predominantly male (the most notable exception being Blavatsky, whom Olcott described as 'a most learned and wonderful man . . . a Hindu man')[30] and they worked in strict accordance with ancient and esoteric law.[31]

The Theosophical Society's aims were threefold: to form a universal brotherhood of humanity free from distinctions of race, creed, sex, caste or colour; to support and encourage the study of comparative religion,

philosophy and science; and to investigate occult laws.[32] It saw itself as ush-
ering in 'a new epoch for Science and Religion'.[33] Sinnett, like many other
enthusiasts, was concerned to establish Theosophy's scientific credentials,
and to demonstrate that occult science was as rigorous as physical. His aim,
in *The Occult World*, is to

record with exactitude the experimental proofs I have obtained that occult science
invests its adepts with a control of natural forces superior to that enjoyed by
physicists of the ordinary type . . . Modern science has discovered the circulation
of the blood; occult science understands the circulation of the life-principle.[34]

Annie Besant, who became Blavatsky's favoured successor, sought to represent Theosophy as an evolutionary science, with the concept of reincarnation at its centre. She contended that civilisation, or evolved life, is
the product of rebirths. Evolutionary science has shown the workings of
physical heredity, but: 'There is no mental or moral heredity, genius does
not descend; it is the death-knell of human progress, unless reincarnation
be true.' Besant utilises the notion of evolutionary forces elaborated by
Herbert Spencer as a means of transcending the bleaker implications of
Darwin. Thus, the brutal and competitive world, where only self-interest
wins out, is replaced by a vision of the just rewards of 'karma', the moral
account which each individual accrues during their life. Through reincarnation 'nothing is lost, nothing is wasted. And how perfectly this agrees
with the scientific view of the conservation of energy, the indestructibility
of force, in the lower world.'[35] The pucklike death is banished, and reincarnation is properly understood as the mechanism of moral evolution.

SHE

In *She*, reincarnation is a central plot device whereby Leo Vincey is linked
to Ayesha's lost love, the Greek Kallikrates. Reincarnation promises a literal version of the continuity promised by archaeology. The potsherd with
which Holly and Leo begin their adventure is, as Shawn Malley points out,
the book's first archaeological site and the material sign of a continuity from
the ancient past to contemporary Cambridge. The chests within chests that
contain the sherd, and the wrapped sherd itself, contribute to a motif of
unveiling: of the sherd, of Ayesha, of history and of truth. The sherd is an
archaeological motif, of histories buried under histories, which saturates
every aspect of the story, and informs its narrative structure.[36] At its most
literal, archaeological unveiling meant unwrapping mummies, thus inten-
sifying further the associations between death and rebirth (of knowledge,

empire, history and self) permeating the narrative. The text, like the caves of the ruined city of Kôr, is littered with bodies: death is omnipresent. Many are the mummified bodies of the inhabitants of imperial Kôr. 'Like the Egyptians, they thought more of the dead than the living', Ayesha tells Holly (177–8). They populate the caves of Kôr in their thousands, in a honeycomb of sepulchres. It is an empire awaiting resurrection.

Throughout *She*, Haggard draws on his active interest in archaeology and Ancient Egypt. The 'horrors and wonders' which infect Holly's dreams after viewing with Ayesha the vaults of imperial Kôr's dead, are inspired by finds in Egypt of burial grounds containing up to a thousand corpses. Even the most Gothic scene, in which mummified bodies are used as blazing torches to illuminate an Amahagger dance, may have been inspired by the commonly believed rumour that the Egyptians used mummies as locomotive fuel. Holly describes 'the awful and hideous grandeur of the spectacle' as 'a satire, both on the living and the dead'. Although he notes the irony of the fact that 'the function of these dead Caesars of the past was to light up a savage fetish dance' (218), it is an irony no more marked than that the bodies of the ancients might fuel modern means of transportation. Elsewhere, the 'editor' explicitly cautions readers against a too swift condemnation of 'savage' Amahagger practice. The latter habitually use fragments of mummy remains as tinder, but 'after all we are not in advance of the Amahagger in these matters. "Mummy", that is pounded ancient Egyptian, is, I believe, a pigment much used by artists' (261–2).

When he first arrives at the caverns of Kôr, Holly enjoys a 'wash and brush up' and the sensory pleasure of clean flannels. In this, he confirms solid English values, before being called to his first interview with the 'savage, dusky queen' he expects to encounter (134, 138). Instead, he experiences 'nameless terror' as he comes into 'the presence of something that was not canny' (141, 142). On the first of many occasions on which she corrects Holly's partial understanding of the world, Ayesha says, 'I tell thee naught really dies. There is no such thing as Death, though there be a thing called Change' (149). Holly's first lesson is thus of reincarnation. Initially, he understands Ayesha's evocation of the 'great race' of Kôr as simply an imaginative response to its material remains (some sculptures on a rocky wall), and reminds her that 'to the world they are dead'. No, she replies, 'even to the world they are born again and again' (149).

Ayesha is a materialist: here, as throughout the book, she is depicted as a scientist, not a mystic. She is a linguist, a chemist, a geologist, an astronomer and a practical eugenicist. She is, above all, an adept, a knower of occult law. In her encounters with the sceptical Holly, she pits her materialism against both his empiricist common sense and his terror of supernatural forces. 'Nay, nay; oh Holly', she says, as Holly reels with shock at the scenes she shows him in a font of water, 'it is no magic; that is a fiction of ignorance. There is no such thing as magic, though there is such a thing as a knowledge of the secrets of Nature' (151–2). Later, when the superstitious Job is horrified by seeing images of his long-scattered family in the water's surface, Holly has come to accept the sight as 'nothing more than an instance of glorified and perfected telepathy' (216). Writing in *The Occult World*, Sinnett notes:

The important point which occultism brings out is that the soul of man, while something enormously subtler and more ethereal and more lasting than the body, is itself a *material* reality. Not material as chemistry understands matter, but as physical science *en bloc* might understand it if the tentaculae of each branch of science were to grow more sensitive and were to work more in harmony.[37]

Theosophists such as Sinnett claimed scientific credibility but also sought to refine and regenerate science as a holistic enterprise: the soul can only be properly understood in its material dimension via a transformed notion of physics. Haggard's romances are founded on archaeological discovery, but also draw on contemporary ideas about the occult associated with Theosophy.[38] Central to these ideas is the role of the Master or adept. In the next 'She' story, *Ayesha: The Return of 'She'*, Ayesha's role as an adept is continually emphasised, not least by her mastery of the most celebrated of occult practices – namely alchemy. The gold she makes will ostensibly fund her plans for a global domination beginning in China, but it also provides an opportunity for a critique of market economy and commodification (156).

At the beginning of *Ayesha: The Return of 'She'*, Leo Vincey, heartbroken with loss, and suicidal, has a dream in which Ayesha leads him to a volcanic mountain 'far past the furthest borders of Thibet' (9). Holly, hearing that Leo intends immediately to depart for India to find this mysterious place, says incredulously: 'Do you suggest that Ayesha is reincarnated in Central Asia – as a female Grand Lama or something of that sort?' Leo replies:

Do you remember a certain scene in the Caves of Kôr yonder, when the living looked upon the dead, and dead and living were the same? And do you remember what Ayesha swore, that she would come again – yes, to this world; and how could that be except by re-birth, or, what is the same thing, by the transmigration of spirit? (10)

The vision, of course, is accurate, and Holly and Leo journey to Central Asia via Tibet, where they study 'the laws and traditions of the Lamas' (10). The first sign that they are nearing their goal is a colossal yellow stone Buddha, which replaces the Ethopian's head in *She*. Instead of being populated by a hybrid African people, this is a world populated by characters that seem like 'survivals' of Ancient Egypt.[39]

Much romance fiction depends on a structure of ordeal through which the hero passes, and here the idea of initiation is explicitly flagged in chapters headed 'The Second Ordeal', 'The Third Ordeal' and so on. Holly and Leo are being prepared for esoteric knowledge, a knowledge which turns out to be the supplementation (and thus regeneration) of Christianity with reincarnation. The Ayesha they find, first appearing to them as a ghost-like mummy-figure, swathed in linen, is the Priestess – the Hes or Hesea or Mother – of the mysterious fire-mountain. Her transformation from aged and wizened mummy back to immortal beauty is suggestively confused with the process by which the Priestess of the Mountain is succeeded or reborn. Holly finds himself perplexed not by the idea of a woman who has lived for two thousand years, but the idea of one who has lived through several incarnations. Ayesha herself refers to the time 'when I last was born' (163) and rebukes Holly for doubting her: 'Know, foolish man, that when I said the Macedonian Alexander lived before me, I meant before this present life of mine' (163).

In *She*, Ayesha mocks Holly for his Christian belief in an afterlife. The eye of faith, she says, is a painted-glass of imagination: 'Strange are the pictures of the future that mankind can thus draw with this brush of faith and this many-coloured pigment of imagination! Strange, too, that no one of them doth agree with another!' (252). In *Ayesha*, however, when Leo refuses to compromise his own Christian belief by joining in the religious rituals over which she presides, Ayesha is not concerned. She tells Leo that 'all great faiths are the same, changed a little to suit the needs of passing times and peoples. What taught that of Egypt, which, in a fashion, we still follow here? That hidden in a multitude of manifestations, one Power, great and good, rules all the universes' (134). Like the Theosophists, Ayesha has studied comparative religions and, like them, she challenges the exceptionalism of Christian doctrine. Holly describes the religion of the mountain as 'harmless enough': 'It was but a diluted version of the Osiris and Isis worship of old Egypt, from which it had been inherited, mixed with the central Asian belief in the transmigration of souls and the possibility of drawing near to the ultimate Godhead by holiness of thought and life' (144).

Ayesha provides a narrative of Christian salvation supplemented by the hybrid forms of religion to which Holly alludes. Ayesha first appears to

Holly and Leo in this story as an Egyptian mummy-figure, swathed in bandages. When she unveils, it is to reveal the hideous, shrunken figure marked
'with the stamp of unutterable age' last encountered by the men in the cave
of the Pillar of Life in *She*. Leo proves his faith to his love, however, by kiss-
ing the wizened figure, and thereby restoring Ayesha to her former beauty.
This act of Leo's is explicitly interpreted as an act of redemption and atone-
ment for sin: 'Therefore merciful Mother that bore me, to Thee I make my
prayer. I let this true love atone my sin' (121). Later, Ayesha says: 'Know that
in mercy it is given to us to redeem one another' (136). When he eventually persuades Ayesha to kiss him, Leo dies in her unearthly embrace. Leo's
death, however, is merely a sign of the defeat of flesh and triumph of spirit –
the final image is of Leo and Ayesha ascending, presumably heavenwards,
together. This death, represented as a form of resurrection, folds the narrative back to the book's beginning and Holly's own end. When the doctor
who discovers Holly's body describes him as paradoxically 'beautiful . . . a
wise and benevolent but rather grotesque spirit' (4), it is clear that Holly,
too, has learned a transcendent message. It is Christian, certainly, but it is a
Christianity revitalised and reanimated by the doctrine of reincarnation. As
with *She*, *Ayesha* begins with a manuscript sent on Holly's instructions to the
same 'editor'. In an accompanying letter, Holly tells the 'editor' 'As soon as I
came into touch with civilisation again I found a copy of your book, "She",
or, rather, of my book, and read it – first of all in a Hindostani translation'
(2). What in effect is being translated by Haggard, however, is a construction of 'the East': its religions, its philosophy and, as E. D. Walker puts it, in
Reincarnation: A Study of Forgotten Truth, 'the secret of Eastern superiority to
materialism'.[40]

Andrew Lang professed himself pleased with *Ayesha*, but Haggard was
profoundly disillusioned with romance writing, especially after the death
of his son. It remained, though, his main source of income – he had of
necessity to keep writing – and successful formulaic plots were increasingly
manipulated as vehicles for religious and spiritual speculation. Thus, the
unlikely pairing of Allan Quatermain, the white hunter who appears in
many of Haggard's romances, and Ayesha, in the 1921 *She and Allan*, is
explicitly framed as a spiritual quest. Allan Quatermain is melancholically
obsessed by the wish to know if love survives death. He attends a séance and
talks to a clergyman, all to no avail; eventually, he seeks aid from the dwarf
wizard, Zikali, an African witch doctor who appears in other Quatermain
adventures. Zikali, though, confirms that magic is racially choosy: 'Only
black feet travel on the road which I can open; over those in which ran
white blood I have no power.'[41] Instead, Zikali directs Allan to Ayesha.

What is striking in the story, however, is the emphasis on the similarity between Ayesha and Zikali as knowers of occult law: Ayesha's superiority comes not from her colour but her greater esoteric knowledge. Similarly, the capacity to pass temporarily to the side of death is not granted to the white hero Allan Quatermain alone, but also to his Zulu companion, the warrior Umslopogaas. The supernatural does not secure a racial hierarchy in which 'white' spirituality is contrasted with 'black' witchery. What is confirmed, again and again, is rather a hierarchy of elites – a hierarchy that includes Zulu nobility as easily as the priestess of Isis or the sceptical and educated Englishman.

The final 'She' book, *Wisdom's Daughter: The Life and Love Story of She-Who-Must-Be-Obeyed*, published in 1925, is narrated by Ayesha herself and tells the story of her origins, her vows as the high priestess of Isis and her love for a Greek converted to Isis worship, Kallikrates.[42] Much of the book is fictionalised ancient history, drawing on Haggard's study of ancient civilisations, especially Egypt. The wise man, Noot, who guards the place of Life in *She*, is here Ayesha's teacher and Master, and the lesson Ayesha has to learn is that there is a universal God who unifies and reconciles all religions, a 'God beyond the gods' (137).[43] That Ayesha cannot quite learn this lesson and still be the Ayesha who has waited for Kallikrates for two thousand years was clearly apparent to Haggard, and accounts for odd inconsistencies in the narrative. In the main, though, Haggard probably did not care. He had reached an end-point with the fictional form that had provided his living for forty years – so at least his friend Rudyard Kipling suggests. He wrote to Haggard after reading *Wisdom's Daughter*:

The more I went through it the more I was convinced that it represented the whole sum and substance of your convictions along certain lines...the book is miles above the head of the reader at large. It will not come to its own for a long time, but to those to whom it is a message or a confirmation it will mean more than the rest of your work.

'In that book is my philosophy – or rather some of it. The Eternal War between Flesh and Spirit, the eternal loneliness and search for unity', Haggard responded.[44] *Wisdom's Daughter* was published in 1923; it was one of the last things Haggard wrote before his death in 1925. It is a narrative about crumbling civilisations, and the end of empires, but it strives nevertheless to depict a faith in continuity and meaning via the spiritual and occult knowledge Ayesha gains.

After Haggard's death, his nephew wrote the following:

Rider had grown slowly into the soil like a native oak tree . . . Not quite hidden in the dark foliage . . . was an offshoot of another shade . . . his mysticism . . . The bizarre growth became a part of him, more prominent towards his later years. It developed undismayed by the tempests of hard facts which our wondering eyes saw whistling round it. How a person so precise in statement, and so severe on others who were not, could allow his judgement wholly to abdicate to his imagination in matters of spirit, was an anomaly which had to be accepted.[45]

Theosophy sees no such anomaly – even for a Tory imperialist. Discussing a Theosophist whose politics are seemingly at an opposite extreme from Haggard's – the socialist and atheist Annie Besant – Gauri Viswanathan asserts that: 'The definers of British imperialism . . . also included anti-establishment figures like Annie Besant.'[46] Viswanathan shows how Theosophists developed the idea of a universal brotherhood of man alongside theories of racial hierarchy. For example, the notion of a commonwealth was enthusiastically embraced as an ideal of benevolent relations between states. In practice, however, the commonwealth served to maintain and perpetuate the empire and its relations of dominance and subordination in the face of increasing demands for national independence.[47]

The experts of the modern world – its scientists and its literary elites – seemed to Haggard to have little to say about the spiritual heart of humanity. Theosophy, by contrast, proposed the existence of other 'experts'. These adepts or 'Masters' had, by long struggle and study, discovered secret and esoteric laws which restored moral and spiritual meaning. In his diary for 7 September 1920, Haggard reports seeing notices posted by refreshment places between Lowestoft and London refusing to serve 'brake, char-a-banc or omnibus parties'. This ban results, so the notices reveal, from the conduct of these parties, including unpaid bills, pilfering of glasses and jugs, insults to women members of staff and general rowdiness. 'Here is a strange development of our advanced civilisation', Haggard comments:

The average European, especially if he be English, looks down upon Easterns and natives of all sorts whom he names 'niggers'. But would savages behave in such a way as this? So far as my rather extended experience of them goes, I should say 'No!' At any rate they have a culture of sorts, they have manners – often quite distinguished manners – they have breeding and they have traditions. Lastly they are not vulgar. Can we say as much of our 'charrybangers', excursionists, sea-side crowds and others?[48]

Haggard was well aware that romance writing was part of a crude commercial world, one in which an expanding reading public mirrored the
democratisation of other public spaces, including the refreshment places
between Lowestoft and London. Fiction itself is both an escape from, and
part of, capitalist modernity: 'A weary public calls continually for books,
new books to make them forget, to refresh them, to occupy minds jaded
with the toil and emptiness and vexation of our competitive existence',
Haggard wrote in 'About Fiction'.[49] In trying to occupy minds with adventure, Haggard more and more tried also to occupy them with the urgency
of spiritual evolution in a world threatened with the deadening effects of
materialism, secularism and rationalism. His imagined worlds seek to rein-
carnate the past, and to reimpose a world in which authentic hierarchy holds
fast against the vulgarising forces of democracy. But the 'charrybangers' and
seaside crowds are exactly the kind of readers who devoured Haggard's romances. These daytrippers, clutching their Rider Haggard books, are out
for an adventure, but they also receive a lesson about order, hierarchy
and meaning: values against which they, paradoxically, pose the greatest
threat.

NOTES

1   This has begun to be explored by critics. See, for example, Shawn Malley,
'"Time Hath No Power Against Identity": Historical Continuity and Archaeological Adventure in H. Rider Haggard's *She*', *English Literature in Transition
1880–1920* 40 (1997), 275–97; Richard Pearson, 'Archaeology and Gothic Desire:
Vitality Beyond the Grave in H. Rider Haggard's Ancient Egypt' in *Victorian Gothic*, eds. Ruth Robbins and Julian Wolfreys (London: Palgrave, 2001)
pp. 218–44.
2   See Shirley M. Addy, *Rider Haggard and Egypt* (Suffolk: AL Publications, 1998).
3   See, for example, John Richard Stephens (ed.), *Into the Mummy's Tomb* (New
York: Berkley Books, 2001). This collection includes Haggard's short story
about a man whose passion for Egypt, and archeological activities there, come
literally to life when he has to spend a night alone in the Cairo Museum. There,
the mummified remains of the ancient kings and queens walk and talk again,
and arraign him for the violation of their tombs. ('Smith and the Pharaohs',
pp. 137–78.) This story was first published in the *Strand Magazine* in 1913, and
is also included in Peter Haining (ed.), *The Best Short Stories of Rider Haggard*
(London: Michael Joseph, 1981), pp. 148–91. Stephens's collection also has
'mummy' stories by Kipling, Stoker and Conan Doyle, as well as non-fictional
extracts on raiding tombs by various nineteenth- and early twentieth-century
Egyptologists. The mummy story in the period of the *fin de siècle* is analysed in
Nicholas Daly, *Modernism, Romance and the fin de siècle 1880–1914* (Cambridge:
Cambridge University Press, 1999).

4 H. Rider Haggard, *The Days of My Life: An Autobiography*, 2 vols. (London: Longmans and Co., 1926), vol. II, p. 158. Further citations will appear in the text.

5 Glen St John Barclay includes a chapter on Haggard in *Anatomy of Horror: The Masters of Occult Fiction* (London: Weidenfeld and Nicolson, 1978), for example.

6 Patrick Brantlinger, *Rule of Darkness: British Literature and Imperialism, 1830–1914* (Ithaca: Cornell University Press, 1988), pp. 227–53.

7 See Roger Luckhurst, *The Invention of Telepathy, 1870–1901* (Oxford: Oxford University Press, 2002).

8 For accounts of his life and career, see Haggard, *Days of My Life*; Lilias Rider Haggard, *The Cloak That I Left* (Ipswich: Boydell Press, 1976); Morton Cohen, *Rider Haggard: His Life and Work* (London: Macmillan, 1968); Norman Etherington, *Rider Haggard* (Boston: Twayne, 1984).

9 Andrew Lang, 'The Supernatural in Fiction', *Adventures Among Books* (London: Longmans and Co., 1905), pp. 273–80; p. 279.

10 Andrew Lang, *Cock Lane and Common-Sense* (London: Longmans, 1894), pp. 7–8.

11 Ibid., pp. 30–1.

12 This formula is, again, drawn from Luckhurst's essay in this volume.

13 Haggard, *Days of My Life*, vol. I, p. 245.

14 H. Rider Haggard, 'About Fiction', *Contemporary Review* 51 (1887), 172–80; p. 172.

15 H. Rider Haggard, *She* (1887), ed. Daniel Karlin (Oxford: Oxford University Press World's Classics, 1991), p. 175. Further references will appear in the text.

16 Blavatsky was investigated by Richard Hodgson for the Society for Psychical Research; his findings, published in 1885, concluded that she 'has achieved a title to permanent remembrance as one of the most accomplished, ingenious, and interesting imposters in history'. See Sylvia Cranston, *The Extraordinary Life and Influence of Helena Blavatsky, Founder of the Modern Theosophical Movement* (New York: G. P. Putnam's Sons, 1993), p. xvii.

17 Supposedly in a letter which materialised in Blavatsky's cabinet, a favoured means by which the Mahatmas communicated their teachings to Blavatsky and to Sinnett. The cabinet featured prominently in the various scandals and exposés of Blavatsky. Many people claimed Koot Hoomi and others to be fictions of Blavatsky's devising.

18 Quoted in Donald S. Lopez, Jr, *The Prisoners of Shangri-La: Tibetan Buddhism and the West* (Chicago and London: University of Chicago Press, 1998), p. 201.

19 For an example, see E. D. Walker, *Reincarnation: A Study of Forgotten Truth* (Boston and New York: Houghton, Mifflin and Co., 1888), p. 241: 'Buddhism, the later Protestant phase of the old faith [of Brahmanism], which abolished its abuses of priesthood and caste and spread its reformation broadcast through Asia, did not alter the original teaching of re-birth.'

20 Lopez, *Prisoners of Shangri-La*, pp. 30–2, 37, 50. Lopez claims that this orientalist view was mistakenly constructed on the basis of only a restricted knowledge of texts.
21 Haggard wrote extensively on the decline of agriculture, including *Rural England* (1902) and *The Poor and the Land* (1905).
22 Haggard also wrote about the incident in a letter to *The Times* (21 July 1904). The episode made a profound effect. He writes: 'It does seem to suggest that there is a more intimate ghostly connection between all members of the animal world, including man, than has hitherto been believed, at any rate by Western peoples.' He claims to have been converted to a belief in the oneness of all life and, from that moment, gave up his hitherto favourite recreation of shooting. See *Days of My Life*, vol. II, pp. 159–65.
23 This belief is well documented in writing about Haggard, although not explicit in *Days of My Life*. Haggard's nephew links the idea of Haggard's former lives as an Ancient Egyptian and as a Zulu to his 'completely convincing' rendering of Egyptian and Zulu speech and emotion in *Cleopatra* and the Zulu tale *Nada the Lily*. Godfrey Haggard, 'Foreword', Lilias Haggard, *The Cloak That I Left*, p. 20.
24 Haggard gives three possible explanations of these 'visions': they are memories of incidents in a previous incarnation; they are 'racial' memories of events that happened to forefathers; or they are subconscious invention. His comment that 'Personally I favour – indeed I might almost say that I accept – the last' is unpersuasive; the vivid descriptions which follow indicate that Haggard finds the scenes compellingly real as forms of personal memory.
25 There were, of course, significant alignments between Christianity and Theosophy. See, for example, Professor Francis Bowen, 'Christian Metempsychosis', quoted in Walker, *Reincarnation*, pp. 102–19; and, for an account of Theosophical claims about the esoteric origins of Christianity, see Gauri Viswanathan, *Outside the Fold: Conversion, Modernity and Belief* (Princeton: Princeton University Press, 1998), pp. 182–3.
26 See Cohen, *Rider Haggard*, p. 50.
27 Anne Taylor, *Annie Besant: A Biography* (Oxford: Oxford University Press, 1992), p. 224.
28 Stephen Prothero, 'From Spiritualism to Theosophy: "Uplifting" a Democratic Culture', *Religion and American Culture: A Journal of Interpretation* 3 (1993), 197–216; p. 198.
29 A. P. Sinnett, *The Occult World* (London: Trubner, 1881), p. 12.
30 Quoted in Taylor, *Annie Besant*, p. 249.
31 Prothero, 'From Spiritualism to Theosophy', pp. 203–4. The similarities between this and Haggard and Lang's wish to masculinise 'unmanly' literature are obvious.
32 Josephine Ransom, *The Direction of the Theosophical Society by Masters of Wisdom* (London: Theosophical Publishing House, 1942), p. 1.
33 Quoted in Prothero, 'From Spiritualism to Theosophy', p. 206.
34 Sinnett, *Occult World*, pp. 2, 4.

35 Annie Besant, *Reincarnation: Its Necessity* (Madras: Theosophical Publishing House, 1915), pp. 18, 21. Spencerian evolution was frequently evoked in support of reincarnation. See, for example, Walker, *Reincarnation*, p. 25: 'The law of the conservation of energy holds in the spiritual realm as in physics . . . [science] recognises the universality of resurrection throughout all nature . . . The idea of the soul as a phoenix, eternally continuing through myriad embodiments, is adapted to the whole spirit of modern science.'
36 Malley, 'Time Hath No Power', pp. 278–80.
37 Sinnett, *Occult World*, p. 19.
38 This phrase is Malley's, in 'Time Hath No Power', p. 283.
39 This effect is intensified in Maurice Greiffenhagen's illustrations for the serial edition, which represent the Queen Atene as an Egyptian queen, and the mountain peoples as shaven-headed monks.
40 Walker, *Reincarnation*, p. 242.
41 H. Rider Haggard, *She and Allan* (1921) (Hastings: Pulp Fictions, 1998), p. 4. Further citations will appear in the text.
42 H. Rider Haggard, *Wisdom's Daughter: The Life Story and Love Story of She-Who-Must-Be-Obeyed* (London: Hutchinson, 1923).
43 It is tempting to think that Haggard named Noot after Koot Hoomi, the most famous of Blavatsky's 'Masters', who featured prominently in the various scandals about her authenticity. Sinnett's *The Mahatma Letters* were supposedly written by Koot Hoomi and relayed to Sinnett. For a fascinating reading of *The Mahatma Letters*, the bureaucratisation of the occult, and the relation of Western initiates to Eastern adepts, see Gauri Viswanathan, 'The Ordinary Business of Occultism' *Critical Inquiry* 27(2000), 1–20.
44 Both in Morton Cohen (ed.), *Rudyard Kipling to Rider Haggard: The Record of a Friendship* (London: Hutchinson, 1965), pp. 124–5.
45 Godfrey Haggard, 'Foreword', in Lilias Haggard, *The Cloak That I Left*, p. 20.
46 Viswanathan, *Outside the Fold*, p. 188.
47 Ibid., p. 187.
48 H. Rider Haggard, *The Private Diaries of Sir Rider Haggard, 1914–1925*, ed. D. S. Higgins (London: Cassell, 1980), p. 202.
49 Haggard, 'About Fiction', p. 174.

PART VI

Haunted modernism

CHAPTER II

The origins of modernism in the haunted properties of literature

Geoffrey Gilbert

One of the first things the Society for Psychical Research did after its foundation in 1882 was to set up a committee to investigate haunted houses. It ran into problems almost immediately. It was not just, as they later discovered, that ghosts were notoriously shy of their investigative machineries, but that the houses themselves behaved strangely when approached by psychic investigators.

The Society aimed to resituate the supernatural: to take it away from shadier spaces and replace it within relatively positivistic scientific discourses. There is nothing inherently disastrous to such a project in a failure to record supernatural phenomena: ghosts have a right to be tricky, and that kind of difficulty can be understood as merely a spur to further creativity in experimental design. What is more difficult for an experimental science to absorb is the reflection on the material conditions – the houses as properties – which are not easy to separate from the phenomena – the ghosts – themselves.

The first report of the committee acknowledges the problem:

The owners of houses reputed to be haunted are reluctant to make the general public, or even a select portion of it, partakers in the privileges which they themselves enjoy. The man who admits the possibility of any house being haunted runs the risk of being regarded as a visionary; but the hint of such a possibility in the case of a man's own house is, none the less, commonly regarded by him as impairing the value of his property.[1]

This worry is confirmed by another member, writing about the reluctance of one informant to say too much about his house and its ghost: he 'was for a time unwilling to give further accounts, lest the house, which belonged to a friend of his, should again become depreciated in value; as it appears from Miss Morton's record that it has previously been [it was rented for £60, less than half its market value, in 1879–80]'.[2] Somewhere before the problem of recording unstably material phenomena, then, another materiality insists. A ghost in the house affects its value; a privilege recognised by risky visionaries is undervalued by the common regard. This problem cannot be seen as merely the irruption of an extraneous and singular anomaly, because there is no more articulate ground for property values *than* that of the common regard. That is, within a free market, price is the point of operation of the invisible hand; exchange value is the immanent expression of a harmonious social totality. And the search for ghosts stumbles on incoherencies within this consensus.

The committee responds with a reactive overvaluation:

We would earnestly entreat our members and friends who are so fortunate as to inhabit haunted houses, to afford us an opportunity of visiting them ... we are willing to incur much trouble and expense for the chance.[3]

Several years later the committee has investigated much inflated rumour, but still no measured ghosts. Their labours are not entirely without product, though. They have 'gained some experience in a rather difficult art, the negotiation of leases for "haunted houses"'.[4]

Tracking apparitions has taken a detour into the heart of market operations. This chapter will follow this lead towards a reading of a short story which, I argue, is placed at one programmatic origin of British modernism: Henry James's 'The Jolly Corner', published in Ford Madox Hueffer's *English Review* in 1908. My reading of this text concentrates on one central figuration: where a ghost arises from the echoing emptiness of a house, and the house's emptiness – or perhaps its simultaneous emptiness and overcrowding with meaning – signals something already present in the materiality of the property market. This will be an essay in reduction, then, pushing stolidly on through ghostly apparitions towards the material ground they so flimsily obscure. The Victorian supernatural has no place in modernism. But, as the experience of the Society for Psychical Research suggests, the material *as* property is no stable base from which to determine superstructural or symptomatic effects like ghosts.

I want to take this pattern – where the ghost keeps re-appearing within the material explanations which would aim to exorcise or to regularise it as a phenomenon – as a model for what to do with another kind of reductive ambition. In the claim for origination, modernism disavows its relationship to the literary marketplace; imagines itself as free and autonomous in relation to its economic conditions. That freedom is conceived as alternately serene or critical, as disinterested or determinedly negating. Much recent work has usefully debunked this conception in the name of social history. Lawrence Rainey, for example, argues that 'modernism, among other things, is a strategy whereby the work of art invites and solicits its commodification, but does so in such a way that it becomes a commodity of a special sort'.[5] But in concentrating on the story of the integration of modernism within a socio-economic story, this body of work has been in danger of misreading disavowal – the break for freedom – as simply disingenuousness, and thus losing the charged ambitions of this odd trajectory of writing.[6] That charge has a historical resonance that will not be contained by literary history, and I suggest that the history of the urge to autonomy may be best approached through the strangenesses of properties, and the ghosts that they breed.

AS CLEAR AS THE FIGURE ON A CHEQUE

Virginia Woolf, in 'Mr Bennett and Mrs Brown', her by turns retrospective and prospective account of the origination of modernism, sees a properly autonomous modern fiction as requiring the wholesale destruction of houses. The problem with the fiction which has gone before – specifically that of Bennett, Wells and Galsworthy – is that it has depended upon a dodgy synecdoche: they 'have laid an enormous stress upon the fabric of things. They have given us a house in the hope that we may be able to deduce the human beings who live there.'[7] For Woolf, this does not work. Character has been obscured by the details of property and the rattle of narration. In Bennett's *Hilda Lessways*, for example: 'We cannot hear her mother's voice, or Hilda's voice; we can only hear Mr Bennett's voice telling us facts about rents and freeholds and copyholds and fines.'[8] There is a failure of integrity which betrays a lack of 'interest in character in itself; or in the book in itself . . . Their books, then, were incomplete as books, and required that the reader should finish them, actively and practically, for himself.' We are led back outside into the world, where to complete the activity of reading we may have 'to join a society, or, more desperately, to write a cheque'.[9]

Modern fiction has as its object, for Woolf, to save in one swoop the autonomy of the artwork and the autonomy of the person from the Victorian and Edwardian world of societies and cheques. So the buildings have to go. 'At whatever cost to life, limb, and damage to valuable property Mrs Brown must be rescued, expressed, and set in her high relations to the world . . . And so the smashing and the crashing began. Thus it is that we hear all round us, in poems and novels and biographies, even in newspaper articles and essays, the sound of breaking and falling, crashing and destruction.'[10] This noisy clearing of the ground may be something she hears as problematic and strained in other modernists, but it is a scene of which Woolf is fond.

When 'Time Passes' in *To the Lighthouse*, darkness floods into the Hebridean holiday home of the Ramsays:

Nothing, it seems, could survive the flood, the profusion of darkness which, creeping in at keyholes and crevices, stole round window blinds, came into bedrooms, swallowed up here a jug and basin, there the sharp edges and firm bulk of a chest of drawers. Not only was furniture confounded; there was scarcely anything left of body and mind by which one could say 'This is he' or 'This is she'.[11]

The confounding of furniture and the approach to an effacement of personhood looks set to take the whole house with it, to the point where 'some trespasser, losing his way, could have told only by a red-hot poker among the nettles, or a scrap in the hemlock, that here once some one had lived; there had been a house'.[12] This uncertainly motivated wanderer, at once actively trespassing and passively lost, light himself of property, reads personhood – against the Mr Bennetts – elegiacally from the effacement of property. 'And so the smashing and crashing began.'

Of course, the house does not go this way. Through the sniffily valued efforts of Mrs McNab and Mrs Bast, described as 'a force working; something not highly conscious; something that leered, something that lurched', the house is restored to its holiday distinction.[13] But the movement which would have levelled it to the undifferentiating ground is continued. The redemptive aesthetic enclosure, and the corresponding rescuing and expressing of Mrs Ramsay is heavily and pointedly dramatised in the simultaneous solution to the formal problems of Lily Briscoe's painting and completion of the long-postponed trip to the lighthouse. But that resounding closure is far from satisfying; or perhaps far *too* satisfying. There persists an alignment of the vision of the novel with those 'destructive elements' which would have our houses and our forms collapse.[14] Lily herself articulates it:

One wanted fifty pairs of eyes to see with, she reflected. Fifty pairs of eyes were not enough to get round that woman with, she thought. Among them must be one that was stone blind to her beauty. One wanted most some secret sense, fine as air, with which to steal through keyholes and surround her where she sat knitting, talking, sitting silent in the window alone; which took to itself and treasured up like the air which held the smoke of the steamer, her thoughts, her imaginations, her desires.[15]

This secret sense, ghostly in its vacancy and profusion, follows closely the path of the flood of darkness which had earlier effaced body and furniture together. The sense that getting rid of the house will give us 'the person' and the 'complete' artwork is a disavowal of this alignment, where the aesthetic sense necessary to give us the person is the same destructive dark force that will cause the house to crumble. The movement of disavowal is complete when it imagines writing as founded on the inheritance of a 'room of one's own', protected from all propertied interferences, or when it forgets about the cheque presented at the moment of purchasing the novel in its eagerness to imagine that the autonomous artwork has nothing to do with the writing of cheques.

What is, I think, most powerful about Woolf is the way that the *movement* of disavowal on which the autonomy of the individual or the artwork depends is given noisy and destructive agency. Escaping from the Edwardian novel of property places its own 'enormous stress upon the fabric of things'. What Woolf imagines as being programmatically and metaphorically done to properties from outside – the crashing, the stress on the fabric, the breaking of windows – is already ramifying within the physical, civic and economic structure of housing. Low interest rates in the 1890s led, in London, to a building boom of unstoppable momentum, which met a fall in real wages and a substantial rise in interest rates from the beginning of the century.[16] The result was a visible juxtaposition of unoccupied and overcrowded properties. This pressure on central London property lent further momentum to the expansion of urbanisation outwards into cheaper land. Part of the effect of this was to produce a substantial random and unstable 'unearned dividend' for those who happened to own these areas. And none of these processes was easily either predicted or controlled. Banks would not lend to landowners on the promise of urban expansion, so the development of suburbs proceeded irregularly, according to speculative investments: 'There is not a town in England where you may not find secluded plots of building land, which the tide of building has passed by on either side, from no apparent cause, and left in abandoned sterility.'[17] The rent-gradient – property getting cheaper as it becomes distant from urban centres – did not reduce pressure on the centres, because, public transport still being relatively expensive, the very or even moderately poor were unable to afford to commute.

These contradictory stresses on the fabric of property should be understood in the context of changes in the structure of wealth in Britain through the long *fin de siècle*. The value of British agricultural land plummeted. In 1878, according to José Harris, land constituted one quarter of the national wealth; in 1914, less than one twelfth.[18] Land had been the ground, both material and symbolic, of social hierarchy in Britain: wealth, power and land ownership had circumscribed relatively congruent constituencies. So we might expect the collapse in land values to have led to a dramatic confounding of economic and social distinction. But access to property in Britain at the end of this period was probably more unequal than at any time in national history (and, incidentally, than in any comparable European country). The dematerialisation of capital did not have democratising effects.

The liberal government of the latter part of the Edwardian period tried repeatedly to rationalise this situation. This is the preoccupation of the Edwardians that worries Woolf, with 'rents and freeholds and copyholds and fines', although it is also a preoccupation shared by Paul and Minta in *To the Lighthouse*, whose relationship looks like the clearest version in the novel of the 'change in human character' for which Woolf's essay demands representation. They no longer love one another, but their relationship has somehow been 'righted' by a social sense that can absorb his affair with another woman who shares his position on the 'taxation of land values'.[19] That tax was proposed to normalise the unearned dividend from urban expansion and to level out the rent-gradient, and, along with new rating policies to pay for the amelioration of human conditions from the rise in urban property prices, to humanise the movements of exchange value. But the phenomena themselves were perhaps too odd, local and rapidly changing to be covered by any rationalising plan at the level of the state. The limits here of humanist, reformist and politically consensual policy (the limits, I would say, of liberalism), are marked by their baffled confrontation with the details of a spectralised economy of property. J. A. Hobson, an influential left-liberal thinker, realised that 'nothing less [than the beginnings of an unceasing and an enlarging attack on the system of private property and private industrial enterprise] can fulfil the demand, which Mr Churchill has expressed, that "property be associated in the minds of the mass of the people with ideas of reason and justice"'.[20]

WAS THE WHOLE HOUSE CROWDED FROM FLOOR TO CEILING?

Algernon Blackwood, in his first published story, 'The Empty House', fictionalises the situation of the Society for Psychical Research. The story concerns the investigation of a building which, although it 'seemed precisely similar to its fifty ugly neighbours, was as a matter of fact entirely different – horribly different'.[21] Its difference results in its collapsed market value, expressed in the haunted emptiness of a house which cannot be rented or sold.

Two psychic researchers, Geoffrey Shorthouse, and his aged but intrepid aunt, investigate the house and attempt to get rid of the ghost, in order to make the house habitable, and thus to normalise its value. The ghosts in the

empty house embody a glitch in the operations of the market. Their apparition is clearly class-marked. They arise from downstairs in the kitchen and
scullery (20), and descend from upstairs 'somewhere among those horrid
gloomy servant's rooms with their bits of broken furniture, low ceilings, and
cramped windows' (25). Within the representation of an abnormal house,
they are excessively present manifestations of the properly invisible servants
who maintain propriety, a registration of the different kinds of inhabiting
that maintain an idea of 'home'. But the details of Blackwood's scene are
very slightly skewed from a simple expression of the repressed materiality
of the domestic. What these ghosts object to is what makes them manifest
as ghosts: the fact of representation or rationalisation. They do not want
to be measured or evoked, but to be left alone. 'The whole dark interior
of the old building seemed to become a malignant Presence that rose up,
warning them to desist and mind their own business' (14).

   This subtilisation of the problem of class occurs through a full identification of the ghosts with the property, with the 'whole dark interior of
the old building'. This is not just an evasion: as Churchill and Hobson
suggest, a crisis of legitimation appears in the form of a malignant –
irrational – something undermining the ambition to represent property.
It is also a move which, as Sharon Marcus has argued, is determined itself
by the generic demands on the story.[22] This articulation of the particular
demands of *literary* property with the relations between houses and their
ghosts is taken up again in Blackwood's third book, *John Silence: Physician
Extraordinary* (1908).[23]

   John Silence is called in to solve the case of Felix Pender, an increasingly successful humorous writer, living in an increasingly pricey district of
London. Under the effects of 'psychical invasion', by a previous – long dead,
proletarian – occupant of the house, Pender has lost his marketable facility.
After a battle of psychic and moral wills, Silence exorcises the ghost, and
Pender's talent is restored. Pender's problem is not productivity: in fact 'he
works like a fury'. What is wrong with the writing, what makes it 'nothing',
unthinkable, is that it is not saleable. 'He can no longer write in the old
way that was bringing him success.' '"[He] produces nothing" – [Pender's
wife] hesitated a moment – "nothing that he can use or sell."' The fear is
economic. 'Unless something competent is done, he will simply starve to
death'; starve to death, and lose his hold on the house (7).

   It is a problem of value, then. But not a simple one. The story covertly ad-
mires this new production: it is 'most damnably clever in the consummate
way the vile suggestions are insinuated under cover of high drollery' (29).
These 'vile, debased tragedies, the tragedies of broken souls' (12), products

of 'the kind of bad imagination that so far has been foreign, indeed impossible, to [Pender's] normal nature' (25), and productive of laughter that
is 'bizarre, horrible, disturbing' (24), in their effectiveness, their ability
to evince a different sort of response from the reader, are rather a challenge to than an evacuation of Pender's sense of literary value. Pender is
becoming a proto-modernist. The right of Pender to occupy this house
and to participate in its capital growth depends upon his relation to a literary marketplace. This happy situation is fraught with instabilities. The
ghost, and the writing practice it incites in Pender, expresses something
of the logic of this instability. Through its agency the house threatens to
become empty or overcrowded. While the aetiology of only one ghost is
given in the story, it appears as multiplied excessively: 'Was, then, even
the staircase occupied? Did *They* stand also in the hall? Was the whole
house crowded from floor to ceiling?'(59). And within this scene, an
unnameable and unsaleable creativity – the production of nothing – is
imagined.

John Silence solves the case in two stages. First, and quietly, he takes
over Pender's rental payments.[24] Then, he exorcises the ghost, and with it
the spectre of modernism. In the relay between property value and literary values, both within the fiction and around it in the relation between
Blackwood and his readers, the ghost and the writing it dictates are a pressing anomaly. Without them, a consensus about value can be produced and
maintained. But the reproduction of the ideal of that consensus in the representations and in the action of the successful generic ghost story require
that the threat be invoked.

Writing about the production of these early stories, Blackwood suggested: 'Something in me, doubtless, sought a natural outlet.' This 'something', he claims, is the 'accumulated horror of his years in New York'.[25] As
he describes it, the horror was of life among the lumpenproletariat, living
as a casual labourer among criminals and bohemians. On the other hand,
this horror is of ambition, of the speed of American capitalism. 'I realised
how little I desired this [speed, display, advertisement] and glittering brilliance, this frantic rush to be at all costs sharper, quicker, smarter than one's
neighbour ... I missed tradition, background, depth.'[26] He is looking for
a practice which will evade these two horrors, the two faces of homeless
capital, and he finds it in writing. The books sold well enough to support
Blackwood's subsequent retreat into a compensatory rural fantasy: 'With
my typewriter and kit-bag, [I took] my precious new liberty out to the Jura
Mountains where, at frs. 4.50 a day, I lived in reasonable comfort and wrote
more books.'[27] But at the same time his writing needs its implication in the

economies that it helps him to escape. *John Silence: Physician Extraordinary* was itself part of a speculative literary market: it was, for instance, the first book to be advertised on roadside billboards.[28]

In one of the many new manuals for authors which are both symptoms of the new literary business and attempts to control its implications, Walter Besant, president of the Society of Authors, estimates, wildly, that since the middle of the nineteenth century, due to the Education Act of 1870 and the opening up of colonial markets, the potential readership for a novel in English has risen from around 50,000 to more than 120 million.[29] With this massive inflation in the powers and rewards of fiction, there were considerable shifts in the economies of authorship. The royalty system opened authorship to freedom of labour (or latent pauperism).[30] The census of 1881 included 3,400 self-identified authors; by 1891 the number had risen to 6,000; by 1901 to 11,000.[31] These new speculators are offered the kind of status which went with landed properties. Besant argues that 'it is now well known that a respectable man of letters may command an income and a position quite equal to those of the average lawyer or doctor. It is also well known that one who rises to the very top may enjoy as much social consideration as a Bishop and as good an income.'[32] But the new and marginal readers who make this status possible bring with them the ghost of the mob, the negation of the consensus which secures the stabilities on which the social consideration of a bishop depends.[33] 'Writing fiction . . . becomes a wild gamble instead of a moderately remunerative occupation.'[34]

Modernism is an effect of and a response to this. David Trotter, for one, has pointed to the way that a mass market opens up the possibility for specialised market fractions to be defined against it.[35] But the sense of the anarchic threat of market expansion and literary speculation is lost in his immensely productive account of the relation between the textual development of modernism and the structure of the reading public. This, I think, is to lose the dialectical relations between a consolidated mass market and its implausible fractions, a hope for wholeness both signalled and mourned in the withdrawal of modernism to an immaterially stable room of its own, while the buildings crash down around it. Trotter saves a liberal accommodation of individuals to the texts which please them, against the haunting sense that liberalism is not in control of the forces building and destroying its world. This is to deny – or to relegate to a space *within* representation – the excesses and vacancies of agency that crowd and abandon the liberal individual; to get rid too quickly of the ghost.

248   GEOFFREY GILBERT

NOT THE GHOST OF A REASON

Ford Madox Hueffer (later Ford) set up the *English Review* in 1908. Its aim
was to inaugurate a new standard and frame for literary value, one that has
been seen as making a place for British modernism, and to consolidate a
function for valued literature. Its professionalism is defined against the marketplace, through disavowal. The first issue quotes with pride from a letter
from Shaw, which it glosses as 'at once . . . a benediction and . . . a prophecy
of [financial] disaster'.[36] Douglas Goldring, Hueffer's assistant, describing
the care with which Hueffer and Conrad worked and reworked the statement of the journal's mission, complained that 'with my experience of
"commercial journalism" gained in the well-run office of *Country Life*, it all
seemed rather babyish'.[37] In one of the constructions of affiliation through
which the idea of 'modernism' is immanently produced, Ezra Pound described the *Little Review* as continuing in exactly this anti-market tradition. 'The *Little Review* is now the first effort to do comparatively what the
English Review did in its first year and a half: that is, to maintain the rights
and position of literature, I do not say in contempt of the public, but in
spite of the curious system of trade and traders which has grown up with the
purpose or result of interposing itself between literature and the public.'[38]

But the claimed exemption from market rationalities – rights and positions maintained 'in spite of' the market, the value of the autonomous
posited against the curious system of the mediated – was not conceived
only for art's sake. The journal had a substantial political section, analysing
for instance the structure of British unemployment, the intractable problems of the Balkan crisis, the possibility of a National Insurance scheme.
To these problems, the journal offered 'The Critical Attitude': an attitude
fostered by the literature which it aimed to print. The icons throughout
were Flaubert and Henry James, and to their work is ascribed considerable
political potential: not through moral or ideological compulsion – the last
thing one would associate with the reading of either author is a strongly
unifying or an uplifting idea – but through the spectacle of disinterested
literary value itself, and through the notion of 'really reading'. 'Flaubert said
that had the French really read his "Education Sentimentale" France would
have avoided the horrors of the *Débâcle*. Mr James might say as much for
his own country and for the country he has so much benefited by making
his own.'[39]

Aside from the unexamined 'quality' exemplified by James and Flaubert,
the journal had some difficulty in defining the new literature it sought.
When it comes to embodying its project, the journal publishes literature about property. The first issue started the serialisation of Wells's *Tono*

Bungay. The novel begins with the collapse of the world organised around the great estate; the disintegration of a spatial organisation of distinction. This is the property plot I outlined earlier: a vision of property consolidated by its relation to land and signalling social organisation gives way catastrophically onto an era of speculation. The novel plots the movements of a fortune based on a drug, 'Tono Bungay', described as 'nothing coated in advertisements' which is the – absent – centre of an advertising and financial industry.[40] Riches proliferate through this wild gamble, but they will not consolidate. Specifically, the house the newly paper-wealthy protagonist attempts to build sprawls and hesitates and will not take form. '[Financiers] all seem to bring their luck to the test of realisation, try to make their fluid opulence coagulate out as bricks and mortar . . . Then the whole fabric of confidence and imagination totters, and down they come.'[41] This is much closer to Woolf's vision than the schematics of 'Mr Bennett and Mrs Brown' will admit: a new-liberal stress on the fabric of things is entirely consonant with the modernist 'sound of breaking and falling'.

Pride of place in the first issue was given to Henry James's story 'The Jolly Corner'.[42] As Michael Anesko demonstrates, James had already shown himself sensitive to the details of the literary marketplace; and in at least one late story he displays intimacy with the kinds of property terms that dismayed Woolf. The two female cousins in Henry James' story 'The Third Person' (1900) have unexpectedly inherited a house that is haunted.[43] The ghost – a hanged smuggler ancestor, 'third person' to their strange couple – both enables and troubles their intimacy; certainly it adds a kind of frisson and interest and history to their ownership. They describe this interest as an 'unspeakable unearned increment': referring again to the 'unearned dividend' which provoked attempts at liberal tax reform.[44] Like Pender in the Blackwood ghost story, they find this anomaly increasingly difficult to live with: they strive to exorcise the ghost. And there is something pointed, if schematic and jokey, about the logic through which they do finally normalise and quiet their house: one of the cousins replays the ancestral crime, smuggling in her case a Tauschnitz paperback across from Paris. This strange – if lightly touched – transfer between the details of the literary marketplace and those of the terms of anarchic property values is telling. And it is much more profoundly at the heart of 'The Jolly Corner'.

'The Jolly Corner' is the story of Spencer Brydon, returned to his native New York after thirty-three redemptive years of refinement in Europe. He is shocked; and shocked by the manner in which he is shocked.

Proportions and values were upside-down; the ugly things he had expected, the ugly things of his far-away youth, when he had too promptly waked up to a sense of the ugly – these uncanny phenomena placed him rather, as it happened, under the charm; whereas the 'swagger' things, the modern, the monstrous, the famous things, those he had more particularly, like thousands of ingenuous inquirers every year, come over to see, were exactly his sources of dismay . . . It was interesting, doubtless, the whole show, but it would have been too disconcerting hadn't a certain finer truth saved the situation. He had distinctly not, in this steadier light, come over *all* for the monstrosities; he had come, not only in the last analysis but quite on the face of the act, under an impulse with which they had nothing to do. He had come – putting the thing pompously – to look at his 'property', which he had thus for a third of a century not been within four thousand miles of; or, expressing it less sordidly, he had yielded to the humour of seeing again his house on the jolly corner.[45]

The 'house on the jolly corner' will be the site of a process of refinement. It signs the less sordid, the less pompous than 'property'. It signals – both as object and title – the ideal of a motivation which can face up to this inversion of values and proportions, an impulse (both in the last analysis and on the face of things) with which the monstrous speculative architecture has 'nothing to do'. And it is the finer truth which will, with the mysterious agency craved by the *English Review*, 'save' the undefined situation; which will defeat the horrors that Blackwood also associated with New York.

But the separation of kinds of value is unstable. Brydon's refinement – exactly that which recoiled from all that 'swagger' – is and always has been built upon his happily disavowed implication in the crazy financial logic which drives New York up. And he is about to become considerably richer as a result of a market in which a house that has fallen down is worth more than one standing:

He could live in 'Europe,' as he had been in the habit of living, on the product of these flourishing New York leases, and all the better since, that of the second structure, the mere number in its long row, having within a twelve-month fallen in, renovation at a high advance had proved beautifully possible . . . The house within the street . . . was already in course of reconstruction as a tall mass of flats. (162–3).

Like Blackwood's 'Empty House', this 'structure' is unmarked; it is a 'mere number in its long row'. Only its collapse allows the singularities and anomalies which reside within the empty space of the commodity, and within the space of the social consensus upon which exchange values depend, to be expressed. This monstrosity is harder for Brydon to separate his impulses from.

No longer hygienically distanced from the tainted sources of his dividend, Brydon turns to Alice Staverton in order to learn a new and adequate way of relating to his property, and particularly of possessing and valuing the empty house on the jolly corner. She is

the delicately frugal possessor and tenant of the small house in Irving Place to which she had subtly managed to cling through her almost unbroken New York career. If he knew the way to it now better than to any other address among the dreadful numberings which seemed to him to reduce the whole place to some vast ledger-page, overgrown, fantastic, of ruled and criss-crossed lines and figures – if he had formed, for his consolation, that habit, it was really not a little because of the charm of his having encountered and recognised, in the vast wilderness of the wholesale, breaking through the mere gross generalisation of wealth and force and success, a small still scene where items and shades, all delicate things, kept the sharpness of the notes of a high voice perfectly trained, and where economy hung about like the scent of a garden. (163–4)

She has managed a resistance to the economy which is unaccountable; which escapes absolutely any mapping in money. This is the voice of Mrs Brown, perhaps, heard across and despite the noises of Mr Bennett. Perhaps it is not surprising that her relation to the property is vague – she is 'possessor and tenant', subtly clinging to it, rather than either exclusively owning or renting it.

Brydon's first response to Alice's example is to keep his preferred property empty and unsold, and indeed to display its emptiness to Alice. 'He only let her see for the present, while they walked through the great blank rooms, that absolute vacancy reigned' (166). He refuses to capitalise on the house as property. This is an interruption of market value through the production of a significant nothing.

The beauty of it – I mean of my perversity, of my refusal to agree to do a 'deal' – is just in the total absence of a reason. Don't you see that if I had a reason about the matter at all it would *have* to be the other way, and would then be inevitably a reason of dollars? There are no reasons here *but* of dollars. Let us therefore have none whatever – not the ghost of one. (168)

This is disavowal at its most absolute, denying *interest* all the way through to the ghost. He drives this perverse singularity further, and the narration checks him, free-indirect discourse providing the juice in which he is to stew: 'He had found the place, just as it stood and beyond what he could express, an interest and a joy. There were values other than the beastly rent values, and in short, in short – !' Alice Staverton follows up: her interjection is brutal, and absolutely to the point:

It was thus Miss Staverton took him up. 'In short you're to make so good a thing of your sky-scraper that, living in luxury on *those* ill-gotten gains, you can afford to be sentimental here!' . . . He explained that even if never a dollar were to come to him from the other house he would nevertheless cherish this one; and he dwelt, further, while they lingered and wandered, on the fact of the stupefaction he was already creating, the positive mystification he felt himself create.

He spoke of the value of all he read into it. (167)

This explanation is indeed a 'positive mystification' – frankly whitewashing the failure to respond to Alice's audit of his sentimental construction of value. And it is significant that the move towards blatant mystification and stupefaction is imagined and experienced as creative; is valued as an exorbitant act of reading. Any reader who enjoys late James must share this baffling sense of value.

She suggests further, having seen him surprisingly competently 'stand up' to the representative of the firm which is turning the 'other' property into a skyscraper, that if he had stayed in New York he would have 'discovered his genius in time really to start some new variety of awful architectural hare and run it till it burrowed into a goldmine' (165). This is the trigger for the rest of the plot, which fairly romps onwards from this point. Brydon haunts his own empty house, attempting to find out what he would have been like had he stayed, and finally meets the ghostly figure of his counterfactual possibility. The frisson is in a confusion of pronouns, the possibility of their identity, or the interrogation of the mode of his identity with this other self.[46]

But I think that there is a sense in which this line of analysis is an extension of the creative mystification. Alice Staverton's brutal question was not about identity but about relation; not about whether he could have *been* a New York property speculating billionaire, but about the fact that his refined difference is already implicated in the monstrosities of the world of property. I am suggesting that the story is at least partially reflexive: that it is interested in the relation between an achieved textual refinement and the sordid implication of the story as literary property in the spaces of domestic property, and that it figures this refinement as positive mystification; as a valuable and creative disavowal. In his autobiography, James speaks about the mutually exclusive physicality of writing and money; here he describes his first payment:

I see before me, in the rich, the many-hued light of my room . . . the very green-backs, to the total value of twelve dollars, into which I had changed the cheque representing my first earned wage. I had earned it, I couldn't but feel, with fabulous felicity: a circumstance so strangely mixed with the fact that literary composition of a high order had, at that table where the greenbacks were spread out, quite viciously declined, and with the air of its being also once for all, to 'come' on any save its own essential terms, which it seemed to distinguish in the most invidious manner conceivable from mine.[47]

The claim here is of absolute spatial exclusion: money, with its 'queer ... rather greasy complexion', cannot be on the desk at the same time as writing.[48] And the agency of the writing subject is baffled before both: money arrives with fabulous felicity; literary composition has its own vicious and inscrutable terms. But this was also the scene in which James discovers his vocation. Michael Anesko, discussing this moment, has suggested that:

We should recognise that money alone is not the primary vehicle for reconciling James' attitudes toward art and the marketplace. What renders 'literary composition of a high order' compatible with 'sordid gain' is precisely the 'positive consecration to letters' James experienced ... his signal commitment to the literary vocation.[49]

'Positive consecration' fulfils here the same function as the 'positive mystification' that Brydon dwells on and feels himself create. It is a sort of disavowal: imagining literature happening in a place which has 'nothing to do' with the desk that in turns the money and the writing paper occupy. Within 'The Jolly Corner' we can trace, I think, the movement of that disavowal: a leaving behind of rather than a response to or a refinement of, Alice's brutal acknowledgement of a structural dependence between the two realms. As in Woolf, the presentation of the person requires a moving away from property, but, again like Woolf, the interest in James's story is less in the achieved stillness at the end of the process – an achieved autonomy of person and of artwork – than in the less easy movement of disavowal itself.

This movement is inscribed in the particular mode of textual refinement – the convolutions of figurality – that marks James's high distinction. This is the economically implausible writing of a risky visionary, too expensive of readerly attention to sell simply, to become the happy commodity, the 'ghost story'. But its condition of possibility – its exploitation of the new market fractions thrown up in reactive response to a speculatively consolidated world of the literary commodity – is as tied to the logic of the commodity as the value of the house on the jolly corner is to the monstrously coining 'other structure'.

The 'real' ghost, that is, is the wrong kind of figure. It is given, generically, in advance, as that which the plot will produce. Brydon knows all along 'what he meant and what he wanted: it was as clear as the figure on a cheque presented in demand for cash' (175). The distinctly Jamesian haunting stands at a refined distance from this blatancy.

It had begun to be present to him after the first fortnight, it had broken out with the oddest abruptness, this particular wanton wonderment: it met him there – and this was the image under which he himself judged the matter, or at least, not a little, thrilled and flushed with it – very much as he might have been met by some strange figure, some unexpected occupant, at a turn of one of the dim passages of an empty house. The quaint analogy quite hauntingly remained with him, when he didn't indeed rather improve it by a still intenser form: that of his opening a door behind which he would have made sure of finding nothing, a door into a room shuttered and void, and yet so coming, with a great suppressed start, on some quite erect confounding presence, something planted in the middle of the place and facing him through the dusk. (165)

The persistent haunting is by the literary figure, by the 'quaint analogy', as it was the figure of positive mystification, rather than its content, that Brydon dwelt on. The ghostliness which the story realises settles at one remove from the fictional world, within the world of figures. Haunting is performed by the value of prose, inflated by a strangely creative force of positive mystification; the ghost figures whatever it is that seeks an absolute distinction between that value and its massy sustenance. However hard the severance is wished, what is figured is also propertied, and is no more literal – no less spectral – for that.

I have suggested that this story is placed at one of the programmatic origins of modernism, charged there with instancing a mode of 'really reading' which is adequate to its conditions in liberal crisis. It is the charge itself, the demand that writing extricate itself from the conditions that grossly generalise without at the same time disappearing into thin air, that appears as a ghost. It is troubling to Blackwood's ambitions of producing a writing on which one can live; it competes as a darkly erosive force with Woolf's luminous enclosing of the autonomous person and her artwork; it survives as a movement inhabiting, but in no sense at home in, the very fabric of literary and domestic property.

NOTES

1 'First Report of the Committee on Haunted Houses', *Proceedings of the Society for Psychical Research* 1 (1882), 101–15; p. 115.
2 R. C. Morton, 'Record of a Haunted House', *Proceedings of the Society for Psychical Research* 8 (1892), 311–32; p. 315.
3 'Report of the General Meeting', *Journal for the Society for Psychical Research* 16 (1884), p. 35.

4   *Journal for the Society for Psychical Research* 16 (1884), p. 52.
5   Lawrence Rainey, *Institutions of Modernism: Literary Elites and Public Culture* (New Haven: Yale University Press, 1998), p. 3.
6   Throughout, I follow critically Pierre Bourdieu's account of the role of disavowal as a relay between the general economy and restricted – relatively autonomous – fields such as that of cultural production. See particularly 'The Field of Cultural Production, or: The Economic World Reversed' and 'The Production of Belief: Contribution to an Economy of Symbolic Goods' in Pierre Bourdieu, *The Field of Cultural Production* (Cambridge: Polity, 1993), pp. 29–63, 74–111.
7   Virginia Woolf, 'Mr Bennett and Mrs Brown' (1924), *A Woman's Essays*, ed. Rachel Bowlby (London: Penguin, 1992) pp. 69–87; p. 82.
8   Ibid., p. 80. Henry James's objection to Bennett is couched in similar terms: his work is 'a monument exactly not to an idea, a pursued and captured meaning, or in short *to* anything whatsoever, but just simply *of* the quarried and gathered material it happens to contain, the stones and bricks and rubble and cement and promiscuous constiutents of every sort that have been heaped in it and thanks to which it quite massively piles itself up. Our perusal and our enjoyment are our watching of the growth of the pile and of the capacity, industry, energy with which the operation is directed.' 'The New Novel' (1914), in *The Critical Muse: Selected Literary Criticism*, ed. Roger Gard (Harmondsworth: Penguin, 1987) pp. 595–614; p. 604.
9   Woolf, 'Mr Bennet and Mrs Brown', p. 77.
10   Ibid., p. 84.
11   Virginia Woolf, *To the Lighthouse* (1927), ed. Stella McNichol (London: Penguin, 1992), p. 137.
12   Ibid., p. 151.
13   Ibid.
14   I borrow this notion from Lyndsey Stonebridge, *The Destructive Element: British Psychoanalysis and Modernism* (Basingstoke: Macmillan, 1998), especially Chapter 3.
15   Woolf, *To the Lighthouse*, p. 214.
16   See, for example, Forest Capie and Geoffrey Wood, 'Money in the Economy, 1870–1939', *The Economic History of Britain Since 1700*, vol. II, *1860–1939*, 2nd edition, eds. Roderick Floud and D. N. McCloskey (Cambridge: Cambridge University Press, 1994), pp. 217–46.
17   Rae, *The Country Banker*, quoted in Avner Offer, *Property and Politics* (Cambridge: Cambridge University Press, 1981), p. 115.
18   José Harris, *Private Lives, Public Spirit: A Social History of Britain, 1870–1914* (Oxford: Oxford University Press, 1993), p. 97.
19   Woolf, *To the Lighthouse*, p. 189.
20   J. A. Hobson, *The Crisis of Liberalism: New Issues of Democracy* (London: P. S. King and Son, 1909), p. vi. Hobson published one piece, 'The Extension of Liberalism', in Hueffer's *English Review* in November 1909.

21 Algernon Blackwood, 'The Empty House', *The Empty House and Other Ghost Stories* (London: Eveleigh Nash, 1906) pp. 1–31; p. 2. Further references are included in the text.

22 Sharon Marcus, *Apartment Stories: City and Home in Nineteenth-Century Paris and London* (Berkeley: University of California Press, 1999), especially pp. 116–27.

23 Algernon Blackwood, *John Silence: Physician Extraordinary* (London: Eveleigh Nash, 1908). Further references are included in the text.

24 'Being at heart a genuine philanthropist' (3), Silence does not charge his clients. But neither does he rid the very poor of their ghosts, reckoning rather oddly that they can make use of charitable agencies. His interest is solely with that 'very large class of ill-paid, self respecting workers, often followers of the arts' (3), to which Blackwood's target reader will also belong.

25 Algernon Blackwood, *Episodes Before Thirty* (London: Cassell, 1923), p. 222.

26 Ibid., p. 303.

27 Ibid., p. 224.

28 According to the *Book Monthly* 6, no. 1 (October 1908), p. 12.

29 Walter Besant, *The Pen and the Book* (London: Thomas Burleigh, 1899), p. 30. See also, for example, Arnold Bennett, *Fame and Fiction* (London: Grant Richards, 1901).

30 See Peter Keating, *The Haunted Study: A Social History of the English Novel 1875–1914* (London: Fontana, 1991), p. 15.

31 Michael Anesko, *'Friction with the Market': Henry James and the Profession of Authorship* (New York: Oxford University Press, 1986), p. 34.

32 Besant, *The Pen and the Book*, p. vi.

33 On the 'courting' and 'management' of the 'mob' by the author, see Arnold Bennett, *How to Be an Author* (London: C. Arthur Pearson, 1903), p. 26.

34 'Light and Leading, New Fact and Current Opinion Gathered from the Book World', *Book Monthly* 6, no. 8 (May 1909), p. 651, quoting the *Observer.*

35 David Trotter, *The English Novel in History, 1895–1920* (London: Routledge, 1993), especially pp. 62–79.

36 Ford Madox Hueffer, 'The Function of the Arts in the Republic', *The English Review* 1 (1908), pp. 157–60; p. 157.

37 Douglas Goldring, *South Lodge: Reminiscences of Violet Hunt, Ford Madox Ford and the English Review Circle* (London: Constable, 1943), p. 23.

38 Ezra Pound, 'Editorial on Solicitous Doubt'. First printed in the suppressed edition of October 1917 (suppressed by the US post office because of an 'obscene story by Wyndham Lewis'), then reprinted in the *Little Review* 1, no. 8 (December 1917), p. 54.

39 Hueffer, 'The Function of the Arts', p. 160.

40 H. G. Wells, *Tono Bungay* (London: Macmillan, 1909). Perhaps it should not be too surprising that the serialisation of Wells's novel was not completed, due, it seems, to Wells's discomfort with the financial operation of the journal.

41   Ibid., p. 341. This, of course, is the image that Galsworthy, another contributor to the first issue of the *English Review*, made central to *The Forsyte Saga* in general and *Man of Property* (1906) in particular.

42   The other story James published in the *English Review* was 'The Velvet Glove' (March 1909), which charts the refusal of John Berridge to consecrate the work of the mediocre but socially fabulous Princess; a refusal to allow anything – social success, sexual desire, even the recognition of the fabulous refinement of the Princess – to cash in the value of his writing.

43   Leon Edel notes the relations between this story and James's purchase of Lamb House in Rye, in *Henry James*, vol. IV, *The Treacherous Years: 1895–1901* (New York: Avon Books, 1978), pp. 317–28.

44   Henry James, 'The Third Person' (1900), in *The Jolly Corner and Other Tales*, ed. Roger Gard (Harmondsworth: Penguin, 1990), pp. 15–46; p. 30.

45   Henry James, 'The Jolly Corner', *The English Review* I (December 1908), reprinted in *The Jolly Corner and Other Tales* (pp. 161–93), p. 162. Further references will be included in the text.

46   Strangely, the billionaire ghost is sensed first in the servants' quarters: 'The rear of the house affected him as the very jungle of his prey. The place was there more subdivided; a large "extension" in particular, where small rooms for servants had been multiplied, abounded in nooks and corners, in closets and passages' (176).

47   Henry James, *Autobiography* (1954), ed. Frederick Dupee (Princeton: Princeton University Press, 1983) p. 476.

48   Ibid.

49   Michael Anesko, *'Friction With the Market'*, p. 27.

CHAPTER 12

Afterword

Steven Connor

The 'supernatural' was no alternative or other world, but rather an image, annex or extension of the imposing, ceaselessly volatile real world of the nineteenth century. In this collection, Roger Luckhurst and Richard Noakes explore the intimate and sustained relations between science and the supernatural, Carolyn Burdett reads Rider Haggard's supernatural romances in the context of anxieties about the spiritual effects of modernity, and Geoff Gilbert finds that, in the 1890s, 'Ghostliness is correlated with the intricacies of property.' We can expect the strong and somewhat surprising associations between the occult and the politics of socialism, feminism, Irish nationalism, war and antivivisection to come increasingly under scrutiny. Just as Freud desublimates possession, the uncanny and other kinds of supernatural terror by revealing their basis in mechanisms of repression and delusion, so our contemporary concern with the Victorian supernatural is governed by the principle that the Other Worlds of Victorian speculation were no mere fantasy retreats or anomalous excrescences from the exigencies of power and money and violence. We can clearly expect for some time to see the Victorian supernatural taken seriously.

However, our way of taking the supernatural seriously must inevitably be oblique to the way in which (at least some) Victorians took it seriously. Few literary and cultural historians writing today are likely to be interested in the evidential value experiments and testimonies collected by the Society for Psychical Research, or the truth of the phenomena produced in the séance. We keep a cautious knight's move away from the primary concerns of Victorian mesmerists, mediums and occultists, and their opponents, as we set ourselves not to establish the truth of the supernatural, but to trace out the shape and space of their curiosity. Now it happens that questions of space, place, shape, position and location seem to nag with a particular intensity in Victorian dealings with the supernatural. This is suggested by the plethora of prepositions that Spiritualists and occultists generated, with which to suggest the place of the other world relative to this. The 'other world' was envisaged as above, beyond, beneath, beside, alongside and even within this world. The *Illustrated London News*, quoted by Richard Noakes, warned that it could be 'a bottomless deep'. It was on the other side, or the 'night-side of nature', beyond the veil, beyond the vale, across the boundary. It was supernatural, praeternatural. There were gateways, doors, paths, veils, curtains. By the end of the nineteenth century, the cartography of the supernatural was being reduplicated by the mapping out of mental life, usually in terms of an archaeology of depths and gulfs, but also sometimes, for instance in the work of Pierre Janet and others influenced by the epistemology of the Salpêtrière school, in the terms of adjacent and collateral forms of displacement and 'co-consciousness'.

Perhaps questions of space seem to bulk large in considerations of the Victorian supernatural because the supernatural came up close during the course of the nineteenth century, and became intimate and domestic. The yawning vaults, pits and turrets, the cavernous castles and catacombs and cataracts of the Gothic novel became progressively more pent, urban, petit bourgeois. As Eve M. Lynch observes, the ghost stories which multiplied from the 1850s onwards 'most frequently take place in the bounded space of the home'. In the middle of the century, Dickens's Mrs Rouncewell announced that a ghost was a necessity for the best houses; but, as the century wore on, haunting began to be a feature of less exclusive addresses. Charles Maurice Davies's *Mystic London*, a gazetteer of his occult experiences in the dubious drawing rooms of the capital, is another mark of the identification of the occult with urban space, and the occult powers of city space as such.[1] By the end of the century, Stevenson and Machen and Blackwood had consolidated the position of the urban ghost. The period also saw tourist versions of what Jacques Derrida has called a 'hauntology'; for this is the century of the 'homes and haunts' album. The opening up from mid-century of country houses to crowds of class tourists made them vulnerable to new kinds of 'visitation', as well as perhaps stimulating the manufacture of more ancestral spooks than ever before. The earthly visitors who came to see or hear tell of the ghosts in the house were liable to be identified with them. The story is told in many country houses of the pale visitor left behind in the drawing room who, when reminded that it is closing time, takes her leave calmly through the wall.

The spirit of place infects the century, during which, we might say, not only did more and different kinds of spaces and places start to develop occult potential, but, as Anthony Vidler has suggested, space itself started to become a haunted category.[2] Essays in this present collection home in repeatedly on the question of the spaces of the supernatural. Nicola Bown explores how opposing theories of the origin of dreams – from the mind of the dreamer, or from some extrasubjective source of knowledge – are distributed across Victorian paintings' theatre of the eye. The place of the dream is closely linked to the question of the status of the supernatural, dreams being an interesting problem for those who would wish to confine subjectivity to the boundaries of the mind. As Richard Noakes observes, medical arguments against supernaturalism often turned on a similar effort at spatial reassignment, since 'for physiologists and medical practitioners, what Spiritualists attributed to agencies outside of the body were well known to medical practitioners as consequences of agencies within the body.' Where the eighteenth century had witnessed a stand-off between rational enquiry and magical belief, the nineteenth century saw the beginning of an uneasy alliance that is still with us, between an orthodox science that was busy bedding itself down in universities, associations and quarterly journals and the supernaturalist pseudo-science that irritatingly shadowed it, hijacking its theories, mimicking its language and authoritative style and seducing its audiences. As Richard Noakes writes, science and supernaturalism engaged in continual border skirmishes, as Victorian popularisers of science 'helped represent Spiritualism as beyond the domain of natural enquiry'.

Freud adopted from Schelling the formula that the uncanny is that which should have been forgotten, but comes back. Rotated into spatial terms (and if, as Freud instructs us, time has no meaning in the unconscious, then space is everything for it) this might be read as 'something which should be distant comes up close.' Essays in this collection frequently bring forward evidence of this abrupt, Alice-like shutting up of the telescope. 'Occult relation oscillates between distance and touch', writes Roger Luckhurst of accounts of overseas psychic events, 'restoring and dissolving boundaries in the same moment'. Moments 'in which the boundaries of self and other become ecstatically or terrifyingly permeable' are thrilling precisely because they bring up against the body and therefore make literal the abstract mapping of social or symbolic spaces. Eve M. Lynch observes this process being enacted in terms of the class politics of the home, as the employing and servant classes were brought uncomfortably together in houses that got steadily smaller during the suburban expansions of the 1870s and onwards. 'Like the ghost, the servant was in the house but not of it', Lynch says. (As I write these words in a pokey upper room of one such North London house, I imagine the single live-in maid whom its first occupant, solicitor or insurance clerk, might just have run to for a time, lying here in the dark, neck-hair bristling, listening to the ashes shift.) Pamela Thurschwell's *Literature, Technology and Magical Thinking* similarly finds that the idea of the supernatural mediates an uncomfortable but also exciting concern with the paradoxically intimate relations established and exercised over distances.[3] Both Pamela Thurschwell's and Roger Luckhurst's essays in this collection show how phantasms of the supernatural were generated, as in our own era, by the increased speed of communications and the passage of information.

One can easily find analogies to the involution of far and near in the topographies of Victorian social space at the end of the nineteenth century, during which things that for the mid-century seemed to be kept safely at arm's (or telegraph's) length in Bombay and Borioboola-Gha started to pop up in Bayswater and Bermondsey. In the last two decades of the century, London was subject to large and enlivening influxes of Jews, East Europeans, Irish, Chinese and other Oriental peoples. The 1890s saw the beginning of a process of immigration, reverse colonisation, or feeding back into the metropolitan centre that would be renewed at intervals through the following century. It is almost too easy for us to recognise the symptoms of unease and even panic that this induced; we are perhaps less well attuned to reactions of curiosity, arousal, expansion, desire, fascination. The stories of Doyle and Stoker harness the thrill and forensic possibilities of an urban space haunted by people, objects and events that had their origins in the other side of the world.

One of our ways of bringing the Victorian supernatural down to earth is to map out what Roger Luckhurst calls 'the topography of the supernatural'. We are at home in topographic explanations, which give us the sense of being able to see for ourselves what the Victorians could not for themselves, the specific shape marked out by their concerns with space and place. We take it for granted that 'the Victorian supernatural', like any other of those things we call historical 'topics', has its own specific shape, and occupies its own determinate kind of space, with specifiable boundaries, dimensions and vectors. Though complex and knotted, this shape somewhere lies stable and complete, and needs only to have the resolution turned up for it to jump into full, stereoscopic focus, foreground and background clearly distinguished. What, though, if our contemporary activity of mapping out the Victorians' concern with the supernatural and finding lines of connection between that concern and larger, more familiar historical questions, of power, gender, class and empire, was being conducted in terms of the very kind of topography that was beginning to come under strain in nineteenth-century mathematics and geometry?

The heightened concern with the shape of space has its beginnings in the new non-Euclidean geometry and the beginnings of topology of the nineteenth century, developments which not only occurred contemporaneously with the growing attempts to provide a scientific rationale for the supernatural from the late 1860s onwards, but also provided metaphorical resources for thinking and writing about the supernatural. While we occupy ourselves in spatialising the spiritual, many in the later nineteenth century became consciously concerned with spiritualising the spatial. Geometry began to nourish supernaturalism from the 1880s onwards, precisely because experiences of and speculations about the uncanny, the Gothic, the otherworldly and the supernatural seemed to involve so much complication of the sense of the here and now. At the same time, the supernaturalist mood may itself have been propitious for scientific speculation, helping it to stretch and skew its own conceptions of space and matter.

Nevertheless, it is surprising that geometry should have become implicated with supernaturalism. For over 2,000 years, the Euclidean principles of geometry had represented the claim of the human mind to be able to form an absolute understanding of the conditions of its world. Although Kant speculated on the possibility, even the probability, of there being more than three dimensions, his arguments about the epistemological guarantees secured by the mutually confirming fit between the human mind and the three-dimensional conditions of space were influential and often-cited during the nineteenth century. The truths of geometry were at once empirical, presented to and interpreted by the senses, and transcendental, appearing to apply without exception throughout the known and unknown universe. Geometry was the meeting point of mind and world, spirit and matter, sense and intellect, fact and truth, the practical and the theoretical, the unextended and the extended, the local and the universal. As such, geometry supplied a kind of epistemological cement for other areas of intellectual life. There are reasons why this was particularly the case in England. As Joan L. Richards observes, the very condition that made England something of a mathematical backwater in the nineteenth century, the fact that mathematics was regarded as a subject of general utility to be taught across the entire curriculum rather than a specialist subject in which advanced research could develop, ensured that the reverberations of new ideas in this area were violent.[4]

A number of exceptions and anomalies in the postulates and axioms of Euclid had been investigated in the first decades of the nineteenth century by Nicholai Lobachevski, János Bólyai and Carl Friedrich Gauss, though their work only really became known when it was taken up by the German

Bernhard Riemann to assist in his formulation of the geometry of manifolds, or multi-dimensional spaces.[5] Riemann's central propositions were
announced at the beginning of his 'On the Hypotheses which Lie at the
Bases of Geometry', which appeared in 1867 in German and in an English
translation by W. K. Clifford in 1873:

The propositions of geometry cannot be derived from general notions of
magnitude . . . the properties that distinguish space from other conceivable triply
extended magnitudes are only to be deduced from experience. Thus arises the
problem, to discover the simplest matters of fact from which the measure-relations
of space may be determined; a problem which from the nature of the case is not
completely determinate, since there may be several systems of matters of fact which
suffice to determine the measure-relations of space – the most important system
for our present purpose being that which Euclid has laid down as a foundation.
These matters of fact are – like all matters of fact – not necessary, but only of
empirical certainty; they are hypotheses.[6]

English readers might have encountered Riemann's arguments some years
earlier, in two articles by Hermann von Helmholtz, entitled 'The Axioms of
Geometry', which appeared in *The Academy* in 1870 and 1872.[7] Four years
later, Helmholtz would assist at the inauguration of another new journal,
Mind, with the first of two further articles in which he repeated and extended the arguments of the first.[8] Drawing on Riemann, Hermann von
Helmholtz argued in the first of his *Academy* articles that: 'The axioms on
which our geometrical system is based, are no necessary truths, depending
solely on irrefragable laws of our thinking.'[9] Rather, our understanding of
space is contingent upon the conditions under which we regularly experienced. The central feature of our space is that bodies may be moved from
place to place without altering their forms. This allows us reasonably to
infer that the space in which we exist is either flat, or of a constant curvature, for a patch cut out of the surface of a sphere can be made to fit
on any other part of the sphere without tearing or distortion. However, a
being who lived in a space of variable curvature – an ellipse, the inside of
a wine glass, or some more capriciously undulating surface in which some
parts of the space were more steeply curved than others – would find that
objects which had one set of dimensions and angles in one part of the space
would undergo distortion of shape when transferred to another part of it.
In an area of positively curved space, a triangle will be plumped out, so that
its three angles will add up to slightly more than 180°; moved to an area
of flat, or negatively curved space, the sum of the angles will reduce, thus
changing the shape of the triangle. Helmholtz follows Riemann in drawing
from this the somewhat startling conclusion that the axioms of Euclid may

be, perhaps, 'only approximately true'.[10] How entirely true they were, or how far their truth reached, would depend upon the value of the curvature of the space we inhabit, which can only be established by actual measurement, not by abstract reasoning. The geometrical rules which apply in our space will depend on the kind of space it turns out to be.

It is a striking illustration of how much mathematics mattered in late Victorian England that it was not just specialist mathematicians who rallied to the defence of the absolute space of Euclid. It was an economist, W. S. Jevons, who responded to Helmholtz in *Nature*, arguing that even inhabitants of environments in which angles and dimensions of objects fluctuated rather than remaining constant would be able to project themselves out of their localised apprehensions to a full understanding of absolute Euclidean principles, just as we have been. So the very conceivability of other spaces, as demonstrated by Riemann and Helmholtz, and the possibility of developing other, entirely self-consistent systems of geometry to go with them, were actually proofs that geometry is not dependent on particular physical conditions.[11] It is a neat argument, but not as decisive as Jevons would have wished it to be, so much did it have to concede to those who no longer saw the propositions of Euclid as absolute and universal.

Perhaps the most powerful proponent of the new or expanded geometry was the mathematician W. K. Clifford. Clifford's account of the non-Euclidean principles developed in the work of Bernhard Riemann announced a revolution in conceptions of geometrical space, though one which depended upon the drastic abridgement of the reach of human understanding. Whatever it may have promised in the way of new horizons, the new non-Euclidean geometry made suddenly and heart-stoppingly evident the presumptuousness of the views of space, according to which 'the Universe was a known thing', which had held sway for over 2,000 years:

You see, there is a real parallel between the work of Copernicus and his successors on the one hand, and the work of Lobatchewsky and his successors on the other. In both of these the knowledge of Immensity and Eternity is replaced by knowledge of Here and Now. And in virtue of these two revolutions, the idea of the Universe, the Macrocosm, the All, as subject of human knowledge, and therefore of human interest, has fallen to pieces.[12]

The expansiveness of Clifford's sensibility, along with his remarkable rhetorical gifts and genius at conveying the implications of complex mathematical reasoning to a general readership, combined to make the orthodox four-square world postulated by Euclid and his defenders seem very dreary indeed. Clifford concluded his remarkable essay on the postulates of space with some speculations on the possibility that we might inhabit a positively curved rather than a uniformly flat universe, a universe, that is, in which the shortest distance between two points would not necessarily be a straight line, parallel lines would meet, and proceeding constantly in any direction would eventually lead you back to where you started. Only some such hypothesis permits the universe which had come asunder in geometrical speculation once more to be, as Clifford drily has it, a 'valid conception'. The conclusion of Clifford's essay looks forward into twentieth-century physics, even beyond Einstein's assumptions of the positive curvature of space, to Alan Guth's arguments about the apparent flatness of cosmic space in the early 1990s.[13]

Upon this supposition of a positive curvature, the whole of geometry is far more complete and interesting; the principle of duality, instead of breaking down over metric relations, applies to all propositions without exception. In fact, I do not mind confessing that I personally have often found relief from the dreary infinities of homaloidal space in the consoling hope that, after all, the other may be the true state of things.[14]

Curvature of space may have provided intellectual consolation for Clifford, but it comported no spiritual hope. Clifford saw no promise of an afterlife or alternative sphere of existence encoded in the variable geometries of higher space. As the marvellously serene, self-authored epitaph on his tomb in Highgate cemetery suggests, Clifford saw an individual earthly life on earth as no more than a lucid parenthesis pinched out of a featureless nescience extending infinitely on either side of it:

> I was not and was born.
> I loved, and did a little work.
> I am not, and grieve not.[15]

On the face of it, nothing could seem more unpromising for appropriation by the often idealistic, sentimental, narcissistic, credulous and highly charged discourses of the supernatural than the detailed technical explications of the different conditions of shape and magnitude obtaining in planar and curved space, or less likely to offer the glimpses of other worlds than speculations about beings of implausible tenuity eking out their existences on the surfaces of whimsical ellipsoids or in the groins of vastly enlarged champagne glasses. And yet the speculations of Clifford and others do seem to have provided unexpected imaginative and rhetorical resources for religious and supernaturalist believers.

The most important idea thrown up by the discussion of the mysteries of non-Euclidean space was the possibility of a fourth dimension of space.

For geometricians in the Riemann tradition, of course, there was no reason to tarry at the fourth dimension, since n-dimensional manifolds were quite conceivable and mathematically manipulable, but supernaturalists found quite enough to delight and arrest them in the idea of four-dimensional space. The supernatural possibilities of 'the fourth dimension', as four-dimensional space soon came inaccurately and uncomprehendingly to be called, seem first to have been broached by the German physicist Friedrich Zöllner, who reported in his *Transcendental Physics* of 1880 on the experiments he had undertaken between 1877 and 1879 with the medium (and conjuror) Henry Slade. Despite the fact that Slade had already been publicly rumbled as a trickster at least once, Zöllner was convinced by Slade's capacity to perform tricks like unknotting a rope without releasing either of the ends secured against two walls that the fourth dimension of space was being employed. Zöllner also used the hypothesis of four-dimensional space to explain the intermittence of ghosts and spiritual manifestations, for we should not expect to be able to see the whole of the four-dimensional profile of the beings who occasionally graze against or butt into our 3-D world.[16]

Despite the hum that Zöllner's work caused in the early 1880s, he seems to have been less influential in spreading awareness of the idea of the fourth dimension than the headmaster of City of London school, Edwin A. Abbott, whose short, witty mathematical fable *Flatland* appeared in 1884. Abbott was only an amateur mathematician, and would devote the rest of his writing career to theology and Shakespearian studies. *Flatland*, first published under the pseudonym of 'A. Square', responds to the climate of geometrical speculation by telling the story of a race of beings who inhabit an entirely flat world.[17] Up and down are entirely unknown and inconceivable in this world, until one day a strange and terrifying being mysteriously intersects it. In a recapitulation in spatial terms of Scrooge's temporal journey between past, present and future in *A Christmas Carol*, the narrator is taken by his three-dimensional guide not only into the solid world of three dimensions, revealing to him the alarming fact that the lines which impede and enclose in Flatland offer no kind of barrier to a three-dimensional visitor, who is able to move at will in and out of prisons, and even to watch food being digested, but also into a one-dimensional world consisting of a single line, and even into a no-dimensional world consisting of a single, hilariously solipsistic point.

Abbott's *Flatland* was written with an eye on the child reader, and looks back at least partly to the conspicuously planar sensibility, as well as the intricate topologies, of Carroll's *Alice* books. Dodgson was himself a mathematician, who wrote geometrical squibs like 'The Dynamics of a Part-icle', and his *Alice Through the Looking Glass* had appeared in 1871, just at the moment when awareness of non-Euclidean geometry was stirring in England. The sale-catalogue of books in his library on his death also indicates an interest in the supernatural and psychic phenomena. This might lead one to suspect that the Lewis Carroll side of Dodgson saw relations between spectrality and the complexities of shape and space. Oddly, however, for all the stretching, contraction, twisting and inversion in the *Alice* books, which resemble both the spatial paradoxes of geometricians like Felix Klein, whose work began to be reported in England in the early 1870s[18] and the 'reeling and writhing' of mediums and mesmeric subjects, the daylight Dodgson side remained a staunch defender of Euclid, publishing a critique in dialogue form of alternative theories entitled *Euclid and His Modern Rivals* in 1885.[19] Francine F. Abeles rightly judges that, though Dodgson knew of non-Euclidean geometry, he could not accept the idea that geometry was not an absolute science.[20] In this Dodgson followed Augustus de Morgan, who stubbornly held the line for traditional geometry at University College London until his death in 1871, just as the bad news for Euclideans was breaking from Germany. The fact that his wife, Sophia de Morgan, was one of the most prominent and respected mediums of the mid-century seems in no way to have impinged upon de Morgan's fierce foundationalism. There are clearly limits to the shapes into which one can bend cultural and intellectual life.

Nevertheless, Carroll's dream-geometries may have helped form the climate in which *Flatland* flourished. Amid some mildly Swiftian satire about the class prejudice and the foolishness of social convention Abbott offers a lucid and influential tutorial about the process whereby one can extrapolate from the spatial conditions of one's own world to worlds with larger numbers of dimensions. The hint is as broad as it can be: if a two-dimensional creature could be brought to grasp the nature of three-dimensional space, then what is to prevent three-dimensional creatures from exploring the possibility of four-dimensional space?

It was at this particular chink in absolute space that C. H. Hinton, a writer on popular science, had already begun to chip, with an article on the fourth dimension published in the *Dublin University Magazine* in 1880. Hinton was also a teacher, first at Cheltenham Ladies' College and then as science master at Uppingham School, where Abbott may have encountered him. Hinton was to be dismissed from his post after confessing to bigamy, and spent much of the remainder of his life abroad, first as a headmaster of a school in Yokohama, then as a teacher at the Universities of Princeton and Minnesota and employee of the US Patents Office.[21] In 1884, he published the first of a series of what he called *Scientific Romances*, entitled 'What Is The Fourth Dimension?', followed in 1888 by a book, grandly entitled *A New Era of Thought*, and many other mathematical papers, fables and novels. Hinton saw space neither as neutral, nor as confining with respect to human intelligence. Rather, space was a dynamic 'instrument of the mind'.[22] The aim of *A New Era of Thought* was to use the mind's own capacity to generate new understandings of space to lift itself into a mathematically inflected version of the higher kinds of understanding traditionally promised by mystics, in which one looks 'not away from matter to spiritual existences, but towards the discovery of conceptions of higher matter, and thereby of those material existences whose definite relations to us are apprehended as spiritual intuitions. Thus, "material" would simply mean "grasped by the intellect, become known and familiar".'[23]

Hinton tirelessly explained in a series of essays, stories and books how a four-dimensional space might not only be extrapolable from the mathematics of three-dimensional space, but might also throw light on physical phenomena such as electricity.[24] Hinton was an important mediating figure because, like some of the physical scientists who investigated Spiritualism, his grasp of scientific principles was extensive and subtle. It was usual for those who considered the fourth dimension in mathematical or philosophical journals to pour scorn on the Spiritualistic and supernaturalist appropriations of the idea: Hinton, however, remained open to such ideas and was therefore the best ally of supernaturalist 4D-ers.

One of the earliest spiritualised, if not precisely Spiritualist, appropriations of the fourth dimension in England was A. T. Schofield's *Another World, or, The Fourth Dimension* (1888). Schofield offered bold renderings of spiritual conditions in mathematical terms:

Let, for example, the body, material and solid, be represented fairly enough by x^3, and the spirit, higher and possessing an unknown power, by x^4. Then $(x^3 + x^4)$ represents the man in life, while $(x^3 + x^4) - x^4$ represents the departure of the spirit (x^4) at death, which returns to its own dimension, while the body (x^3), which is left, returns to the earth to which *it* belongs.[25]

Schofield believed, as many others began to, that the visitations of angels and other supernatural beings were crossings of the fourth dimension into this world. The leading theme in his predominantly Christian argument is the mathematical demonstration of the literal truth that 'we are everywhere surrounded by another world', and the fact that: 'Though the glorious material universe extends beyond the utmost limits of our vision, even artificially aided by the most powerful telescopes, that does not prevent the spiritual world and its beings, and heaven and hell being by our very side.'[26]

One might expect the idea of the fourth dimension to appeal to the more esoteric and highly organised forms of supernaturalism, such as Theosophy, especially given the geometrical cast of Theosophy's favourite metaphor, that of spiritual or astral 'planes'. Indeed, the use of the word 'plane' in this sense, to signify a level of spiritual development, seems to be uncommon before the middle of the nineteenth century, and may have been given some considerable lift by the geometrical speculations of the 1870s onwards. This geometrical context might also have played its part in suggesting to the otherwise conspicuously non-mathematical W. B. Yeats the gyres, cones and other more complex geometrical figures which he would develop for his magical system in *A Vision* (1920). In fact, Theosophists were slower than one might have expected to see the possibilities of the fourth dimension, perhaps because they were discouraged by H. P. Blavatsky's dismissal of the idea. Writing in Theosophy's house journal, *Lucifer*, Herbert Coryn saw speculation about higher dimensions as merely an oblique way of registering the more fundamental truth of the growing spiritualisation or transparency of matter:

We are becoming a degree more sensitive, and matter is about to become transparent visually and practically. Visual and practical transparence is the 'Fourth Dimension'; not the taking on by matter of any stature in some inconceivable direction, but the taking on by human consciousness of a new sense and power. The term 'Fourth Dimension' is therefore, as H. P. B. points out, incorrect . . . we need not make the theory of a 'Fourth Dimension' to account for inrecognisable and unsuspected facts. It is enough that we are about to climb upon a new plane of the hitherto unknown.[27]

But the absorptiveness of Theosophy meant that it was not long before others in the movement started to look more favourably on the idea of spiritual geometry, of whom the most important is C. W. Leadbeater. By the second decade of the following century, buoyed up by the prominence of Einsteinian relativity, the fourth dimension had become a central feature of the intellectual gadgetry of Theosophy.

The more absurd accounts of the fourth dimension tended to represent it confidently as a region of hyperspace inhabited by spirits in a perfect state of being. What some saw as the 'fairyland' view of the fourth dimension became more and more apparent in the first and second decades of the twentieth century. It is illustrated at one kind of extreme by Charles Brodie Patterson's *A New Heaven and a New Earth* (1909), which described the fourth dimension recklessly as 'a world of infinite variety of colour and sound' and as 'nature's great vacation ground', in which there is 'no night, no sickness, no death, as we understand any of these things'.[28] It is always light there, and it is filled with forms 'more ethereal and more beautiful than those we see in the body'. It has the most advanced transport systems, for 'locomotion is a question of thought; one in which one goes at will where he wills to go, and in the going seems to fly, yet not with wings; and where natural form offers no resistance to the going or the coming'.[29] Silly and sad though this vision of a happy otherworld might seem, the late nineteenth- and early twentieth-century notion of the fourth dimension as a sort of place, or demarcated region of space, predicts the fascination and power to arouse of 'cyberspace' in the late twentieth century. Indeed, the word that nineteenth-century mathematicians began to use to report on their speculative spaces, 'hyperspace', has a direct link to the spaces of information that began to be constructed and experienced a century later.

Other conceptions of higher space among supernaturalists were considerably more demanding, and used the idea of the fourth dimension to reflect intelligently on the permeability and interpenetration of different spaces. Abbott's *Flatland* had pointed to the odd fact that beings inhabiting one dimension can only comprehend their spatial status from the outside. So the nature of existence as a point can only be appreciated from the point of view of someone who understands what a line is, but the nature of a line can only fully be apprehended by one capable of grasping the nature of a plane surface, while a Flatlander can only understand the nature of a planar existence from a condition of three-dimensional existence. It looks from this that the different levels of dimensions existence may be looped, or chained together, with each higher dimension as it were implied in the level below it. This encouraged the second claim of fourth-dimension supernaturalism, namely that we are able to conceive of higher dimensions than our own because we ourselves are partially four-dimensional creatures, caught between worlds. As the Theosophist C. W. Leadbeater put it in a lecture of 1900:

There may be, then, as I believe to be the case, much more in each than we can see. You might be, here on this plane, only a very common person, but one who could see in the fourth dimension the unknown part, that which we call 'soul', might see a much higher development.[30]

The question repeatedly posed in discussion of the new geometry is, could these new spaces or possibilities of space actually exist? As Rosemary Jann observes: 'Far from reinforcing empiricist limits on the knowable, the

concept of a fourth and higher dimensions furnished many believers with
new ways of urging the reality of the supernatural.'[31] Used to defending the
absoluteness of scientific truth by means of arguments based on verifiable
material fact, mathematicians found themselves fending off the literalism
of Spiritualist visions of the fourth dimension with the argument that the
mathematics of higher dimensions were abstract extrapolations, and need
not imply the actuality of the spaces they described. As Claude Bragdon
would explain, 'the mind finds itself still at home in regions where the
senses do not operate'.[32] Hermann Schubert devoted the forty-eight pages
of his article 'The Fourth Dimension: Mathematical and Spiritualistic' to
distinguishing, not without the occasional flare of exasperation, the use
of the fourth dimension by mathematicians, who 'though they have for-
saken the path of actual representability . . . have never left that of the truth'
from the notion 'which has passed into the heads of lay persons who have
used it as a catchword, ordinarily without having any clear idea of what
they or anyone else mean by it'.[33] Schubert laments the fact that

The knowledge of a four-dimensioned space did not reach the ears of cultured
non-mathematicians until the consequences which the Spiritualists fancied it was
possible to draw from this mathematical notion were publicly known. But it is a
tremendous step from the four-dimensioned space of the mathematicians to the
space from which the spirit-friends of the Spiritualistic mediums entertain us with
rappings, knockings, and bad English.[34]

Yet the important point about four-dimensional space seems to have been
not its inconceivability, but the fact that it could not but be conceived,
however provisionally or projectively, in the terms of an experiential space,
which entails a kind of phenomenology, a corporeal reach into abstraction.
Samuel Roberts affirmed at the London Mathematical Society in November
1882 that 'the progress of analysis has in no way affected the philosophical
status of our notions of space and time'; though, in going on to reassure
his audience that 'metaphysicians need feel no alarm at what is going on
behind the veil of mathematical symbolism', his language seems to hint at
the sense of occult embodiment that thickened speculation about manifold
space.[35]

So the positions of supernaturalism and geometry regarding the reality
of the four-dimensional space represent an inversion of the positions one
might expect the two sides to occupy. Geometry, which was accustomed
to represent itself as the grounding of mathematical truth in the actual-
ities of space-experience, the foot on the ground that mathematics used
to keep its balance, found itself having to recognise that the subjects of

its reasoning were unearthly. Supernaturalist appropriations of the idea of
hyperspace and higher dimensions borrowed from the materiality that had
previously underpinned geometry's claims. The increasing disembodiment
of the physical and mathematical sciences, as they began to explore the
nature of an astronomical and sub-atomic world that it was never likely
human eyes could see or hands touch, gave both warrant and necessity
for the more vulgarly embodied sorts of fantasy, delivering the power of
manifestness and experimental proof that had once been part of science's
arsenal over to supernaturalism.

But perhaps there is a further twist in this tale. For, in its urge to provide
irrefutable evidence of the materiality of the geometricians' abstract conceptions, supernaturalist argument and experiment belonged to and perhaps
even helped to condition the further development of the mathematics of
shapes and spatial relations known as projective geometry, or topology, that
was already underway by the 1870s. Though just as abstract and unworldly
as analytic geometry, topology, as the study not of absolute measures of
dimension and direction, but of the relations of transformability between
shapes, can be seen as a refined form of that corporeal imagination which is
so vulgarly on display in the transformations of objects and the arts of what
Mr Micawber somewhere calls 'personal contortion' in the séance. Even
ectoplasm, that crazy dreamstuff, or embodied dream of higher matter,
somewhere between matter and space, can be seen as a corporeal image for
a topologised conception of the world, in which what mattered most were
not fixed quantities, but relations. It was sometimes suggested in this period that each dimension had its characteristic state of matter. Where solid
materials tend, if force is applied to them, to move in straight lines, fluids
tend to spread out in planes, and gases tend to diffuse in three dimensions.
It was suggested the matter appropriate to the fourth dimension was ether,
that impalpable universal medium allowing for the transmission of gravity
and electromagnetic energy, the long career of which in scientific thinking
was then, and is now, far from over. Ectoplasm helps image the specifically
topological, as opposed to topographical conception of space which, for
Michel Serres, has become characteristic of contemporary sciences from
physics to ecology and genetics. What matters is not the shape things come
in, but how they may be folded. The stubborn and vulgar insistence on the
materiality of the virtual in the late Victorian period predicts and prepares
for the virtuality of the real in this early twenty-first century.

For Serres, every philosophy or metaphysics is governed by an implicit
physics, or theory of matter; in his book *Atlas*, he argues for the possibility of a new understanding of space, governed not by either of the usual

alternatives of solidity (say, Comte) or fluidity (say, Bergson), but by the labile, intermediary form of the textile:

Now, between the so-called rigorous hardness of crystal, geometrically configured, and the fluidity of soft and sliding molecules, there is an intermediary material which tradition leaves to the female, and is thus thought little of by philosophers, with the exception perhaps of Lucretius: veil, canvas, tissue, chiffon, fabric, goatskin and sheepskin, known as parchment, the flayed hide of a calf, known as vellum, paper, supple and fragile, linens and silks, all the forms of planes or twists in space, bodily envelopes or writing supports, able to flutter like a curtain, neither liquid nor solid, to be sure, but participating in both conditions. Pliable, tearable, stretchable . . . topological.[36]

Serres supplies a very specific anticipation of the topological sensibility of the later twentieth century in an example of nineteenth-century su-pernaturalist fantasy. Guy de Maupassant's story 'The Horla' concerns a man haunted by an invisible familiar, who causes him terrifying vampiric dreams, drinks milk and water from the carafes on his bedside table, plucks flowers and causes them to hover in the air. Driven to the point of madness, the narrator traps his double, as he believes, in his house, and burns it to the ground.[37] Rather than accounting for, or mapping out the story, Serres adopts it as a model, the contours of which indicate the multiplicity and thick interpenetration of spaces that any fully specified atlas of contempo-rary space will need to supply. Serres observes how the theme of place is interwoven with that of identity in the story, which moves back and forth between enclosure and expansion, neighbourhood and far distance. The narrator tells us that 'there can be no doubt that everything depends on places and settings' but is unable to maintain that separation of spaces upon which all of the theories of the 'horla' – haunting, hallucination, mesmeric influence, dual consciousness – continue to depend.[38] Serres's attention is caught in particular by the account given by the narrator of how he wraps the carafes in white muslin cloths, ties down the stoppers and coats his lips and hands in black lead, in order to test whether it is he himself who has been drinking the contents. In the morning, the bottles are intact and the muslin immaculate, but the contents of the carafes have again van-ished. The paradoxical topology of this event seems to make unconscious reference to the Klein bottle, a Möbius strip in three dimensions with no interior or exterior, which is almost contemporary with Maupassant's story.[39]

The narrator of 'The Horla' ends up in terrified despair, unsure whether or not his shadow self has really been destroyed in the fire. Serres reverses the valences of Maupassant's story, urging us to embrace positively what it projects as pathology. This involves acknowledging the principle of the 'included third', that which lies between the mutually incompatible locations of the inside and outside, the intimate and the foreign, the proximate and the far removed.[40] In this new topology of the self, identity does not reside securely in itself, and it is no act of bad faith to acknowledge that one includes what one is not within oneself, that the self is always beside itself. Serres recommends an expansion of categories and dimensions in philosophical writing, to take account of the emerging topological conditions and sensibilities of the modern world. It comes down to, or perhaps, rather moves out from, prepositions, as it did for nineteenth-century supernaturalism:

Has not philosophy restricted itself to exploring – inadequately – the 'on' with respect to transcendence, the 'under', with respect to substance and the subject and the 'in' with respect to the immanence of the world and the self? Does this not leave room for expansion, in following out the 'with' of communication and contract, the 'across' of translation, the 'among' and 'between' of interferences, the 'through' of the channels through which Hermes and the Angels pass, the 'alongside' of the parasite, the 'beyond' of detachment . . . all the spatio-temporal variations preposed by all the prepositions, declensions and inflections?[41]

The list Serres gives us alludes characteristically to a number of his own works, *L'interférence* (the second volume of his *Hermès* sequence), *The Parasite, Detachment* and *Angels*, thereby looping together his topologised history of spatial thought with his own efforts to open up the oblique and branching 'North-West passage' between culture and science. Serres's mode of reading history topologically, looking for irregularities in the continuum of history, places where the fabric of time may be folded or pleated or stretched, provides a model for the way in which we might find our own spatio-temporal predicaments and exhilarations implied in those of the later nineteenth century, and our acts of attention prefigured in theirs. The concern with shape and space of Victorian supernaturalism is continuous with the question of the shape and space of 'the Victorian supernatural' itself. Rather than the latter being at a higher level than the former, each is the other's inside. Do cats eat bats? Do bats eat cats? We cannot fully specify the shape of the Victorian supernatural, because it is not an inert and finished shape in space, but a continuing potential for reshaping of the space it is in, and so partly includes us. Maupassant's narrator names his second self the 'horla' because it seems to combine the senses of the two prepositions *hors* and *là*, 'out', or 'beyond' and 'there'. One possible translation of the name might therefore be 'the out-with', the one who is both beyond and beside me. In claiming the historian's traditional prerogative of distance, in assuming that the Victorian supernatural has finished happening, we hope to be able to make more of it than it could make of itself. But we may thereby render ourselves less able to see that these particular 'Victorians' could be beside themselves, in a way that finds them at our shoulder, makes them an 'opaque transparency', a turbulence in the eye or glass, which troubles our image in the mirror.[42] The Victorian supernatural was, and is, *fort* and *da*, *hors-là* (not all there).

NOTES

1   Charles Maurice Davies, *Mystic London: Or, Phases of Occult Life in the Metropolis* (London: Tinsley Bros, 1875).
2   Anthony Vidler, *The Architectural Uncanny: Essays in the Modern Unhomely* (Cambridge, MA and London: MIT Press, 1992).
3   Pamela Thurschwell, *Literature, Technology and Magical Thinking 1880–1920* (Cambridge: Cambridge University Press, 2001).
4   Joan L. Richards, *Mathematical Visions: The Pursuit of Geometry in Victorian England* (San Diego and London: Academic Press, 1988), p. 7.
5   See János Bólyai, 'The Science of Absolute Space' and Nicholai Lobachevski, 'The Theory of Parallels', trans. George Bruce Halstead, in Roberto Bonola (ed.), *Non-Euclidean Geometry: A Critical and Historical Study of Its Development*, trans. H. S. Carslaw (New York: Dover Publications, 1955); *Disquisitiones generales circa superficies curvas* (1828), in Carl Friedrich Gauss, *Werke*, 12 vols. (Göttingen: Königlichen Gesellschaft der Wissenschaften zu Göttingen, 1880), vol. IV, pp. 217–58.
6   Bernhard Riemann, 'On the Hypotheses which Lie at the Bases of Geometry', trans. W. K. Clifford, *Nature* 8 (1873), 14–17, 36–7; p. 14.
7   Hermann von Helmholtz, 'The Axioms of Geometry', *The Academy* 1 (1870), 128–31; 3 (1872), 52–3.
8   Hermann von Helmholtz, 'The Origin and Meaning of Geometrical Axioms: I', *Mind* 1 (1876), 301–32, and 'The Origin and Meaning of Geometrical Axioms: II', *Mind* 3 (1878), 212–25.
9   Helmholtz, 'The Axioms of Geometry', p. 130.
10 Ibid., p. 131.
11 William Stanley Jevons, 'Helmholtz on the Axioms of Geometry', *Nature* 4 (1871), 481–2.
12 W. K. Clifford, 'The Philosophy of the Pure Sciences: II: The Postulates of the Sciences of Space', *Contemporary Review* 25 (1878), 360–76; p. 363.
13 Alan H. Guth, *The Inflationary Universe: The Quest For a New Theory of Cosmic Origins* (London: Jonathan Cape, 1997).
14 Clifford, 'Postulates of the Sciences of Space', p. 376.
15 Highgate Cemetery, London, grave no. 23181, quoted in Richards, *Mathematical Visions*, p. 113.

16 Friedrich Zöllner, *Transcendental Physics*, trans. Charles Carleton Massey (London: Massey, 1880).
17 Edwin A. Abbott, *Flatland: A Romance of Many Dimensions* (London: Seeley, 1884).
18 Richards, *Mathematical Visions*, pp. 143–8.
19 Charles Lutwidge Dodgson, *Euclid and his Modern Rivals* (London: Macmillan and Co., 1885).
20 Charles Lutwidge Dodgson, *The Pamphlets of Lewis Carroll*: vol. II: *The Mathematical Pamphlets of Charles Lutwidge Dodgson and Related Pieces*, ed. Francine F. Abeles (Charlottesville: University Press of Virginia, for the Lewis Carroll Society of America, 1994), pp. 17–18.
21 Thomas F. Banchoff, 'From Flatland to Hypergraphics: Interacting with Higher Dimensions', *Interdisciplinary Science Reviews* 15 (1990), 364–72, and http://www.geom.umn.edu/~banchoff/ISR/ISR.html.
22 C. H. Hinton, *A New Era of Thought* (London: Swann, Sonnenschein and Co., 1888), p. 2.
23 Ibid., p. xiv.
24 The most important of Hinton's many works are *Scientific Romances*, 2 vols. (London: Swann, Sonnenschein and Co., 1884–5); 'The Recognition of the Fourth Dimension', *Bulletin of the Philosophical Society of Washington* 14 (1900–4), 179–203; *The Fourth Dimension* (London: Swann, Sonnenschein and Co., 1904); and *An Episode of Flatland: Or, How a Plane Folk Discovered the Third Dimension* (London: Swann, Sonnenschein and Co., 1907).
25 A. T. Schofield, *Another World, or, The Fourth Dimension* (London: Swann, Sonnenschein and Co., 1888), pp. 68–9.
26 Ibid., pp. 82, 86.
27 Herbert Coryn, 'The Fourth Dimension', *Lucifer* 12 (1893), 326–32; pp. 331–2.
28 Charles Brodie Patterson, *A New Heaven and a New Earth: Or, The Way to Life Eternal (Thought Studies of the Fourth Dimension)* (London: George G. Harrap and Co., 1909), p. 91.
29 Ibid., pp. 95–6.
30 C. W. Leadbeater, *The Fourth Dimension* (San Francisco: Mercury Publishing Office, 1900), p. 21.
31 Rosemary Jann, 'Christianity, Spiritualism, and the Fourth Dimension in Late Victorian England', *Victorian Newsletter* 70 (1986), 124–8; p. 124.
32 Claude Bragdon, 'Space and Hyperspace', *The Fourth Dimension Simply Explained: A Collection of Essays Selected From Those Submitted in the Scientific American's Prize Competition*, ed. Henry P. Manning (New York: Munn and Co., 1910), pp. 91–110; p. 97.
33 Hermann Schubert, 'The Fourth Dimension: Mathematical and Spiritualistic', *The Monist* 3 (1892–3), 402–49; p. 403.
34 Ibid., pp. 427–8.
35 Samuel Roberts, 'Remarks on Mathematical Terminology, and the Philosophic Bearing of Recent Mathematical Speculations Concerning the Realities of Space', *Proceedings of the London Mathematical Society* 14 (1882–3), 5–15; p. 11.

36 Michel Serres, *Atlas* (Paris: Editions Julliard, 1994), p. 45.
37 Guy de Maupassant, 'The Horla', in *Selected Short Stories*, trans. Roger Colet (Harmondsworth: Penguin, 1971), pp. 313–44.
38 Ibid., p. 329.
39 Serres, *Atlas*, p. 77.
40 Ibid., pp. 81–2.
41 Ibid, p. 83.
42 Maupassant, 'The Horla', p. 341.

Bibliography

PERIODICALS

Athenaeum
Journal of the Society for Psychical Research
Medium and Daybreak
Proceedings of the Society for Psychical Research
Review of Reviews
Spiritual Magazine

BOOKS AND ARTICLES

Abbott, Edwin A., *Flatland: A Romance of Many Dimensions* (London: Seeley, 1884).

Abraham, Nicholas and Maria Torok, *The Shell and the Kernel*, vol. I, ed. and trans. Nicholas Rand (Chicago: University of Chicago Press, 1994).

The Wolf-Man's Magic Word: A Cryptonomy, trans. Nicholas Rand, introd. Jacques Derrida (Minneapolis: University of Minnesota Press, 1986).

Addy, Shirley M., *Rider Haggard and Egypt* (Suffolk: AL Publications, 1998).

Aguirre, Michael, *The Closed Space: Horror Literature and Western Symbolism* (Manchester and New York: Manchester University Press, 1990).

Altholz, Joseph L., *Anatomy of a Controversy: the Debate over Essays and Reviews 1860–1864* (Aldershot: Scolar Press, 1994).

'The Mind of Victorian Orthodoxy: Anglican Responses to *Essays and Reviews*, 1860–1864' in *Religion in Victorian Britain*, vol. IV, *Interpretations*, ed. Gerald Parsons (Manchester University Press / Open University, 1988).

Anderson, Benedict, *Imagined Communities: Reflections on the Origin and Spread of Nationalism* (London: Verso, 1983).

Anesko, Michael, *'Friction with the Market': Henry James and the Profession of Authorship* (New York: Oxford University Press, 1986).

Anon., *Astounding Disclosures in Connection with Spiritualism and the Spirit World! Supernatural Visits at the House of a Clergyman in Bayswater* (London: J. Onwhyn, 1864).

'The British Association and Spiritualism', *Saturday Review*, 16 September 1876, 345–7.

'The Catholics and Spiritualism', *Spiritualist Magazine*, New Series, 1 (1866), 12–16.

The Countess of Blessington's True Interpreter of Dreams, Visions and Omens of the Wedding Day (London: H. Elliott, 1861).

'Divination for the Drawing Room', *Englishwoman's Domestic Magazine*, New Series, 3 (1867), 141–3, 205–5.

'Dreams', *Once a Week* 7 (1862), 543–5.

Essays and Reviews (London: John W. Parker, 1860).

'An Experimental Investigation of a New Force', *Spiritual Magazine* 6 (1871), 337–54.

'First Report of the Committee on Haunted Houses', *Proceedings of the Society for Psychical Research* 1 (1882), 101–15.

Footsteps of Spirits: A Collection of Upwards of Seventy Well-Authenticated Stories of Dreams, Impressions, Sounds and Appearances (London: Burns and Lambert, 1859).

'Light and Leading, New Fact and Current Opinion Gathered from the Book World', *Book Monthly* 6, no. 8 (May 1909), p. 651.

'The Literature of Dreams', *Bentley's Miscellany* 59 (1866), 267–71.

'The Mystery of the Tables', *Illustrated London News*, 18 June 1853, 481–2.

'The Night-Side of Nature', *Blackwood's Edinburgh Magazine* 66 (1850), 265–70.

'The Nude in Photography: With Some Studies Taken in the Open Air', *Studio* 1 (1893), 105–6.

'On the Scarcity of Good Maidservants', *Englishwoman's Review: A Journal of Woman's Work* 1 (1866), 12–26.

'A Physician's Dreams', *All the Year Round* 2 (1859), 109–13.

'A Physician's Ghosts', *All the Year Round* 1 (1859), 346–50.

'Psychic Force', *Saturday Review*, 18 July 1871, 82–3.

'Report of the General Meeting', *Journal for the Society for Psychical Research* 16 (1884), 35.

'The Royal Society Professors and Spiritualism', *Spiritual Magazine* 3 (1868), 254–81.

'A Scientific Testing of Mr Home', *Spectator*, 8 July 1871, 827–8.

'Spiritualism', *Saturday Review*, 21 October 1871, 518–19.

'Spiritualism and the Newspapers', *Spiritualist* 1 (1871), 189.

'Spiritualism Tested', *British Medical Journal*, 15 July 1871, 71–2.

'Such Stuff as Dreams are Made of', *Eclectic Review*, New Series, 9 (1865), 516–30.

Argyll, Duke of (George Douglas Campbell), *The Reign of Law*, 19th edn (London: John Murray, 1890).

Armstrong, Isobel, *Victorian Poetry: Poetry, Poetics and Politics* (London: Routledge, 1993).

Bailyss, Wyke, *Five Great Painters of the Victorian Era: Leighton, Millais, Burne-Jones, Watts, Holman Hunt* (London: Sampson, Low, Marston and Co., 1902).

Banchoff, Thomas F., 'From Flatland to Hypergraphics: Interacting with Higher Dimensions', *Interdisciplinary Science Reviews* 15 (1990), 364–72, and http://www.geom.umn.edu/~banchoff/ISR/ISR.html.

Barclay, Glen St John, *Anatomy of Horror: The Masters of Occult Fiction* (London: Weidenfeld and Nicolson, 1978).

Barker, A. Trevor (ed.), *The Letters of Helena Blavatsky to A. P. Sinnott* (Pasadena, CA: Theosophical University Press, 1973).

Barnum, P. T., *Humbugs of the World: An Account of the Humbugs, Delusions, Impositions, Deceits, and Deceivers Generally, in all Ages* (New York: Carleton, 1866).

Barrett, William, 'Pseudo Thought-Reading', *Journal of the Society for Psychical Research* 1 (1884), 10.

Barrett, William, Edmund Gurney and F. W. H. Myers, 'Thought-Reading', *Nineteenth Century* 11 (1882), 890–902.

Barrow, Logie, *Independent Spirits: Spiritualism and the English Plebeians, 1850–1910* (London: Routledge and Kegan Paul, 1986).

Barthes, Roland, 'The Rhetoric of the Image', *Image, Music, Text*, ed. and trans. Stephen Heath (London: Flamingo, 1984), pp. 32–51.

Roland Barthes, trans. Richard Howard (London: Macmillan, 1977).

Baudrillard, Jean, *Symbolic Exchange and Death* (1976), introd. Mike Gane, trans. Iain Hamilton Grant (London: Sage Publications, 1993).

Bayly, C. A., *Empire and Information: Intelligence-Gathering and Social Communication in India 1780–1870* (Cambridge: Cambridge University Press, 1996).

Beer, Gillian, *Arguing with the Past: Essays in Narrative Form from Woolf to Sidney* (London: Routledge, 1989).

'"Authentic Tidings of Invisible Things": Secularizing the Invisible in Late Nineteenth-Century Britain' in *Vision in Context*, eds. Teresa Brennan and Martin Jay (New York and London: Routledge, 1996), pp. 83–98.

Benkowitz, Miriam, *Frederick Rolfe: Baron Corvo* (New York: Putnam, 1977).

Bennett, Arnold, *Fame and Fiction* (London: Grant Richards, 1901).

How to Be an Author (London: C. Arthur Pearson, 1903).

Bernard, Catherine A., 'Dickens and Victorian Dream Theory' in *Victorian Science and Victorian Values: Literary Perspectives*, eds. James Paradis and Thomas Postletwait (New York: Annals of the New York Academy of Sciences vol. 360, 1981), pp. 197–216.

Besant, Annie, *Reincarnation: Its Necessity* (Madras: Theosophical Publishing House, 1915).

Besant, Walter, *The Pen and the Book* (London: Thomas Burleigh, 1899).

Blackwood, Algernon, 'The Empty House' in *The Empty House and Other Ghost Stories* (London: Eveleigh Nash, 1906), pp. 1–31.

Episodes Before Thirty (London: Cassell, 1923).

John Silence: Physician Extraordinary (London: Eveleigh Nash, 1908).

Bonola Roberto (ed.), *Non-Euclidean Geometry: A Critical and Historical Study of Its Development*, trans. H. S. Carslaw (New York: Dover Publications, 1955).

Bourdieu, Pierre, *The Field of Cultural Production* (Cambridge: Polity, 1993).

Bown, Nicola, *Fairies in Nineteenth-Century Art and Literature* (Cambridge: Cambridge University Press, 2001).

Braddon, Mary Elizabeth, 'At Chrighton Abbey' in *Victorian Ghost Stories: An Oxford Anthology*, eds. Michael Cox and R. A. Gilbert (Oxford: Oxford University Press, 1991).

The Doctor's Wife (London: J. Maxwell and Co., 1864).

The Fatal Marriage and Other Stories, ed. Chris Willis (Hastings: Sensation Press, 2000).

The Lady's Mile (London: Ward, Lock and Tyler, 1866).

Ralph the Bailiff and Other Stories (London: Ward, Lock and Tyler, 1867).

'The Shadow in the Corner', *All the Year Round*, New Series, 23 (1879), Extra Summer Number, 1–11.

Bragdon, Claude, 'Space and Hyperspace' in *The Fourth Dimension Simply Explained: A Collection of Essays Selected From Those Submitted in the Scientific American's Prize Competition*, ed. Henry P. Manning (New York: Munn and Co., 1910), pp. 91–110.

Brand, C. P., *Italy and the English Romantics* (Cambridge: Cambridge University Press, 1957).

Brandon, Ruth, *The Spiritualists* (New York: Alfred Knopf, 1983).

Brantlinger, Patrick, *Rule of Darkness: British Literature and Imperialism, 1830–1914* (Ithaca: Cornell University Press, 1988).

'What is Sensational about the Sensation Novel?', *Nineteenth-Century Fiction* 37 (1982), 1–28.

Bray, Charles, *On Force, its Mental and Moral Correlates; and on That Which is Supposed to Underlie All Phenomena: With Speculations on Spiritualism, and Other Abnormal Conditions of Mind* (London: Longmans, 1866).

Brewster, David, *Letters on Natural Magic, Addressed to Sir Walter Scott* (London: John Murray, 1832).

Briggs, Julia, *Night Visitors: The Rise and Fall of the Ghost Story* (London: Faber, 1977).

Britten, Emma Hardinge, 'Science and Spiritualism', *Spiritualist* 1 (1870), 124–7.

Browne, Alice, 'Dreams and Picture-writing: Some Examples of this Comparison from the Sixteenth to the Eighteenth Century', *Journal of the Warburg and Courtauld Institutes* 44 (1981), 90–100.

Browning, Robert, *The Oxford Authors: Robert Browning*, ed. Adam Roberts, introd. Daniel Karlin (Oxford: Oxford University Press, 1997).

The Ring and the Book, ed. Richard D. Altick (Harmondsworth: Penguin, 1971).

The Ring and the Book, Books I–IV, vol. VII of *The Complete Works of Robert Browning*, ed. Roma King (Athens, GA: Ohio University Press, 1985).

Burns, James, 'About Scientific Spiritualism', *Medium and Daybreak* 1 (1870), 201–2.

Editorial note, *Medium and Daybreak* 2 (1871), 231.

'The Philosophy of the Spirit Circle', *Medium and Daybreak* 1 (1870), 308.

'Professor Tyndall and the Spiritualists', *Human Nature* 2 (1868), 454–6.

'Spiritualism and Science', *Medium and Daybreak* 1 (1870), 108.

Buse, Peter and Andrew Stott (eds.), *Ghosts: Deconstruction, Psychoanalysis, History* (London: Macmillan, 1999).

Bushnell, Horace, *Nature and the Supernatural as Together Constituting the One System of God* (Edinburgh: Alexander Strahan, 1862).

Busst, A. J. L., 'Scottish Second Sight: The Rise and Fall of a European Myth', *European Romantic Review* 5 (1995), 149–77.

Byatt, A. S., *Angels and Insects* (New York: Vintage, 1994).

Byrde, Pamela, *Nineteenth-Century Fashion* (London: Batsford, 1992).

Capie, Forest, and Geoffrey Wood, 'Money in the Economy, 1870–1939' in *The Economic History of Britain Since 1700*, vol. II, *1860–1939*, 2nd edn., eds. Roderick Floud and D. N. McCloskey (Cambridge: Cambridge University Press, 1994), pp. 217–46.

Carnell, J., *The Literary Lives of Mary Elizabeth Braddon* (Hastings: Sensation Press, 2000).

Caron, James, 'The Rhetoric of Magic in *Daniel Deronda*', *Studies in the Novel* 15 (1983), 1–9.

Carpenter, Mary Wilson, '"A bit of her flesh": Circumcision and "The Signification of the Phallus" in *Daniel Deronda*', *Genders* 1 (1989), 1–23.

Carpenter, William Benjamin, 'Mesmerism, Odylism, Table-Turning and Spiritualism, Considered Historically and Scientifically', *Fraser's Magazine* 15 (1877), 135–57, 382–405.

  'On the Fallacies of Testimony in Relation to the Supernatural', *Contemporary Review* 27 (1876), 279–95.

  'The Radiometer and its Lessons', *Nineteenth Century* 1 (1877), 242–56.

  'Spiritualism and its Latest Converts', *Quarterly Review* 131 (1871), 301–53.

Cassels, Walter, *Supernatural Religion: An Inquiry into the Reality of Divine Revelation*, 3 vols. (London: Green and Co., 1874).

Castle, Terry, *The Female Thermometer: Eighteenth-Century Culture and the Invention of the Uncanny* (Oxford: Oxford University Press, 1995).

Cerullo, John, *The Secularization of the Soul: Psychical Research in Modern Britain* (Philadelphia: Institute for the Study of Human Issues, 1982).

Chadwick, Owen, *The Secularisation of the European Mind in the Nineteenth Century* (Cambridge: Cambridge University Press, 1975).

  The Victorian Church, 2 vols. (London: A. & C. Black, 1966–70).

Chambers, Robert, *Testimony: Its Posture in the Scientific World* (London and Edinburgh: W. and R. Chambers, 1859).

Chase, Cynthia, *Decomposing Figures* (Baltimore: Johns Hopkins University Press, 1986).

Clifford, James, *The Predicament of Culture* (Cambridge, MA: Harvard University Press, 1988).

Clifford, W. K., 'On Some of the Conditions of Mental Development' in *Lectures and Essays*, ed. Leslie Stephen and Frederick Pollock, 2 vols. (London: Macmillan, 1879), vol. I, pp. 75–108.

  'The Philosophy of the Pure Sciences: II: The Postulates of the Sciences of Space', *Contemporary Review* 25 (1878), 360–76.

Clodd, Edward, 'The Making of Religion', *The Academy* 53 (18 June 1898), 651–2.
'Presidential Address', *Folk-Lore* 6 (1895), 54–81.
'A Reply to the Foregoing "Protest"', *Folk-Lore* 6 (1895), 248–58.
de Cocq, Antonius, *Andrew Lang: A Nineteenth-Century Anthropologist* (Amsterdam: Uitg Zwijsen Tilburg, 1968).
Cohen, Morton, *Rider Haggard: His Life and Work* (London: Macmillan, 1968).
(ed.), *Rudyard Kipling to Rider Haggard: The Record of a Friendship* (London: Hutchinson, 1965).
Collins, H. M. and T. J. Pinch, *Frames of Meaning: The Social Construction of Extraordinary Science* (London: Routledge and Kegan Paul, 1982).
Collins, Phillip, 'Dickens on Ghosts: An Uncollected Article', *Dickensian* 59 (1963), 5–14.
Cooter, Roger, *The Cultural Meaning of Popular Science: Phrenology and the Organisation of Consent in Nineteenth-Century Britain* (Cambridge: Cambridge University Press, 1984).
Corvo, Baron, (Frederick Rolfe), *Hadrian the Seventh* (London: Chatto and Windus, 1904).
In His Own Image (London: John Lane, 1901).
Coryn, Herbert, 'The Fourth Dimension', *Lucifer* 12 (1893), 326–32.
Cox, Michael, and R. A. Gilbert (eds.), *Victorian Ghost Stories: An Oxford Anthology* (Oxford: Oxford University Press, 1991).
Cranston, Sylvia, *The Extraordinary Life and Influence of Helena Blavatsky, Founder of the Modern Theosophical Movement* (New York: G. P. Putnam's Sons, 1993).
Crawford, Robert, 'Pater's *Renaissance*, Andrew Lang, and Anthropological Romanticism', *ELH* 53 (1986), 849–79.
Crookes, William, 'Another Lesson from the Radiometer', *Nineteenth Century* 1 (1877), 879–87.
'Experimental Investigation of a New Force', *Quarterly Journal of Science*, New Series 1(1871), 339–49.
'Notes of an Enquiry into the Phenomena Called Spiritual, During the Years 1870–1873', *Quarterly Journal of Science*, Second Series, 3 (1874), 77–97.
'Notes on Séances with D. D. Home', *Journal of the Society for Psychical Research* 6 (1889–1890), 98–127.
Psychic Force and Modern Spiritualism: A Reply to the 'Quarterly Review' and other Critics (London: Longmans, Green, and Co., 1871).
'Spiritualism Viewed by the Light of Modern Science', *Quarterly Journal of Science* 7 (1870), 316–21.
Crowe, Catherine, *The Night-Side of Nature, or Ghosts and Ghost-Seers* (1848), 3rd edn. (London: George Routledge, 1852).
Cumberland, Stuart, 'Pin-Finding and Thought-Reading at Charing Cross', *Pall Mall Gazette* 39 (1884), 10.
The Rabbi's Spell: A Russo-Jewish Romance (London and New York: Frederick Warne and Co., 1886).
That Other World: Personal Experiences of Mystics and their Mysticism (London: Grant Richards Ltd, 1918).

A Thought-Reader's Thoughts: Being the Impressions and Confessions of Stuart Cumberland (London: Sampson, Row, Marston, Searle and Rivington, 1888).

'D. C.' (De Morgan, Sophia), *From Matter to Spirit: The Result of Ten Years' Experience in Spirit Manifestations* (London: Longman, Green, Longman, Roberts and Green, 1863).

D'Albe, E. E. Fournier, *The Life of Sir William Crookes* (London: T. Fisher Unwin, 1923).

Dalby, Richard (ed.), *The Cold Embrace and Other Ghost Stories* (Ashcroft, BC: Ash-Tree Press, 2000).

Daly, Nicholas, *Modernism, Romance and the Fin de Siècle 1880–1914* (Cambridge: Cambridge University Press, 1999).

Dante Alighieri, *The Vision; or Hell, Purgatory and Paradise*, trans. Rev. Henry Francis Cary (London: Henry G. Bohn, 1860).

Daston, Lorraine, 'Preternatural Philosophy' in *Biographies of Scientific Objects*, ed. Lorraine Daston (Chicago: Chicago University Press, 2000), pp. 14–41.

Davies, Charles Maurice, *Mystic London: Or, Phases of Occult Life in the Metropolis* (London: Tinsley Bros, 1875).

Dawes, Edwin A., *The Great Illusionists* (Secaucus, NJ: Chartwell Books, 1978).

Day, W. P., *In the Circles of Fear and Desire: A Study of Gothic Fantasy* (Chicago: University of Chicago Press, 1985).

Dendy, Walter C., *On the Phenomena of Dreams and Other Transient Illusions* (London: Whittaker, Treacher and Co., 1832).

Derrida, Jacques, *The Gift of Death*, trans. David Wills (Chicago: University of Chicago Press, 1995).

Specters of Marx: the State of the Debt, the Work of Mourning and the New International, trans. Peggy Kamuf (London and New York: Routledge, 1994).

Dickens, Charles, *American Notes* (1842) (Oxford University Press, 1957).

Barnaby Rudge (1841), ed. Donald Hawes (London: Dent Everyman, 1996).

Bleak House (1854) (New York: W. W. Norton, 1977).

The Christmas Books, Centenary Edition of the Works of Charles Dickens, 36 vols. (London: Chapman and Hall, 1910).

Dombey and Son (1848) (London: Mandarin, 1991).

The Haunted House, All the Year Round Extra Christmas Number, 1 (1859), 1–48.

The Lazy Tour of Two Idle Apprentices, Chapter the Fourth, *Household Words* 16 (1857), 385–93.

The Letters of Charles Dickens, ed. Kathleen Tillotson *et al.*, 11 vols. (Oxford: Clarendon, 1965–99).

'No. 1 Branch Line: The Signal-man', *Mugby Junction, All the Year Round*, Extra Christmas Number, 16 (1866), 20–5.

'The Spirit Business', *Household Words* 7 (1853), 217–20.

'To Be Read at Dusk', *Reprinted Pieces*, ed. Andrew Lang (London: Chapman & Hall, 1903), pp. 303–18.

'To Be Taken with a Grain of Salt', *Dr Marigold's Prescriptions, All the Year Round* Extra Christmas Number, 14 (1865), 33–8.

The Uncommercial Traveller and Reprinted Pieces (Oxford: Oxford University Press, 1958).

Dickerson, Virginia, *Victorian Ghosts in the Noontide: Women Writers and the Supernatural* (Columbia and London: University of Missouri Press, 1996).

Dircks, Henry, 'Spiritualism and Science', *The Times*, 2 January 1873, 12.

'Science versus Spiritualism', *The Times*, 27 December 1872, 10.

Dodgson, Charles Lutwidge, *Euclid and his Modern Rivals* (London: Macmillan and Co., 1885).

The Pamphlets of Lewis Carroll, vol. II, *The Mathematical Pamphlets of Charles Lutwidge Dodgson and Related Pieces*, ed. Francine F. Abeles (Charlottesville: University Press of Virginia, for the Lewis Carroll Society of America, 1994).

Donne, John, *Selected Poetry*, ed. John Carey (Oxford: Oxford University Press World's Classics, 1996).

Drayton, H. S., *Human Magnetism: Its Nature, Physiology and Psychology* (New York: Fowler and Wells, 1889).

Eagles, John, 'A Few Passages Regarding Omens, Dreams, etc.', *Blackwood's Edinburgh Magazine* 48 (1840), 194–204.

Edel, Leon, *Henry James*, vol. IV, *The Treacherous Years: 1895–1901* (New York: Avon Books, 1978).

Eliot, George, *Adam Bede* (1859), ed. Leonee Ormond (London: Everyman's Library, 1992).

Daniel Deronda (1878), ed. John Rignall (London: Dent Everyman, 1999).

The Lifted Veil (1859), ed. Beryl Gray (London: Virago, 1985).

Ellis, Ieuan, *Seven Against Christ: A Study of 'Essays and Reviews'* (Leiden: E. J. Brill, 1980).

Engen, Rodney, *Richard Doyle* (Stroud: Catalpa Press, 1983).

Enright, D. J. (ed.), *The Oxford Book of the Supernatural* (Oxford: Oxford University Press, 1994).

Etherington, Norman, *Rider Haggard* (Boston: Twayne, 1984).

Faber, Geoffrey Cust, *Jowett: A Portrait with Background* (London: Faber and Faber, 1957).

'F. I. S.', 'Dreams', *Tinsley's Magazine* 2 (1868), 268–83.

Flint, Kate, *The Victorians and the Visual Imagination* (Cambridge: Cambridge University Press, 2000).

Flournoy, Théodore, *From India to Planet Mars* (1899) (Princeton, NJ: Princeton University Press, 1994).

Fodor, Nándor, *Encyclopaedia of Psychic Science* (London: Arthurs Press, 1934).

Ford, Jennifer, *Coleridge on Dreaming: Romanticism, Dreams and the Medical Imagination* (Cambridge: Cambridge University Press, 1998).

'Samuel Taylor Coleridge and the Pains of Sleep', *History Workshop Journal* 48 (1999), 170–86.

Forster, John, *The Life of Charles Dickens*, 3 vols. (London: Chapman & Hall, 1874).

Foucault, Michel, 'Two Lectures' in *Power/Knowledge: Selected Interviews & Other Writings*, trans. Colin Gordon *et al.* (New York: Pantheon, 1980).

Frazer, James George, *The Golden Bough: A Study in Magic and Religion Part One: The Magic Art*, vol. 1 (1890), 3rd edn. (London: Macmillan, 1932).
Freud, Sigmund, 'Mourning and Melancholia' (1917). *Standard Edition of the Complete Psychological Works of Sigmund Freud*, trans. and ed. James Strachey *et al.*, 23 vols. (London: Hogarth Press, 1957), vol. XIV, pp. 237–58.
'The Uncanny' (1919), *Penguin Freud Library* vol. XIV: *Art and Literature*, ed. Albert Dickerson (London: Penguin, 1985).
Gallagher, Catherine, 'George Eliot and *Daniel Deronda*: The Prostitute and the Jewish Question' in *Sex, Politics and Science in the Nineteenth-Century Novel*, ed. Ruth Bernard Yeazell, *Selected Papers from the English Institute*, New Series 10 (1983–4), 39–62.
Gauld, Alan, *The Founders of Psychical Research* (London: Routledge and Kegan Paul, 1968).
Gauss, Carl Friedrich, *Werke*, 12 vols. (Göttingen: Königliche Gesellschaft der Wissenschaften zu Göttingen, 1880).
Gilley, Sheridan, 'Supernaturalised Culture: Catholic Attitudes and Latin Lands 1840–60' in *The Materials, Sources and Methods of Ecclesiastical History*, ed. Derek Baker (Oxford: Blackwell, 1975), pp. 309–23.
Gilmour, Robin, *The Victorian Period: the Intellectual and Cultural Context of English Literature 1830–1890* (London and New York: Longman, 1993).
Ginzburg, Carlo, 'Morelli, Freud, Sherlock Holmes: Clues and Scientific Method' in *The Sign of Three: Dupin, Holmes, Pierce*, eds. Umberto Eco and Thomas Sebeok (Bloomington: Indiana University Press, 1983), pp. 81–118.
Glancy, Ruth, 'To Be Read at Dusk', *Dickensian* 83 (1987), 40–7.
Godfrey, N. S., *Table-Moving Tested, and Proved to be the Result of Satanic Agency* (London: Sealeys, 1853).
Goldring, Douglas, *South Lodge: Reminiscences of Violet Hunt, Ford Madox Ford and the English Review Circle* (London: Constable, 1943).
Goodwin, C. W., 'On the Mosaic Cosmogony' in *Essays and Reviews* (London: John W. Parker, 1860), pp. 94–144.
Gordon, Jan B., *Gossip and Subversion in Nineteenth-Century British Fiction: Echo's Economies* (Basingstoke: Macmillan, 1996).
Gosse, Edmund, *Father and Son*, 3rd edn. (Harmondsworth: Penguin Books, 1972).
Gray, B. M., 'Pseudoscience and George Eliot's "The Lifted Veil"', *Nineteenth-Century Fiction* 36 (1992), 407–23.
Green, Roger Lancelyn, *Andrew Lang: A Critical Biography* (Leicester: E. Ward, 1946).
Greenblatt, Stephen, *Shakespearean Negotiations: The Circulation of Social Energy in Renaissance England* (Oxford: Clarendon Press, 1988).
Grixti, John, *Terrors of Uncertainty: The Cultural Contexts of Horror Fiction* (London and New York: Routledge, 1989).
Guth, Alan H., *The Inflationary Universe: The Quest For a New Theory of Cosmic Origins* (London: Jonathan Cape, 1997).

Haggard, H. Rider, 'About Fiction', *Contemporary Review* 51 (1887), 172–80.
Ayesha: The Return of 'She' (1905) (New York: Dover, 1978).
The Best Short Stories of Rider Haggard, ed. Peter Haining (London: Michael
    Joseph, 1981).
The Days of My Life: An Autobiography, 2 vols. (London: Longmans and Co.,
    1926).
The Private Diaries of Sir Rider Haggard, 1914–1925, ed. D. S. Higgins (London:
    Cassell, 1980).
She (1887), ed. Daniel Karlin (Oxford: Oxford University Press World's Classics,
    1991).
She and Allan (1921) (Hastings: Pulp Fictions, 1998).
*Wisdom's Daughter: The Life Story and Love Story of She-Who-Must-Be-
    Obeyed* (London: Hutchinson, 1923).
Haggard, Lilias Rider, *The Cloak That I Left* (Ipswich: Boydell Press, 1976).
Hall, Trevor H., *The Spiritualists. The Story of Florence Cook and William Crookes*
    (London: Gerald Duckworth and Co., 1962).
Hardinge, Emma, 'Rules to be Observed for the Spirit Circle', *Human Nature* 2
    (1868), 48–52.
Harris, José, *Private Lives, Public Spirit: A Social History of Britain, 1870–1914*
    (Oxford: Oxford University Press, 1993).
Harrison, Frederic, 'Art. 1 – Neo-Christianity – *Essays and Reviews*. Second Edition.
    London: J. W. Parker and Son. 1860', *Westminster Review*, New Series, 17
    (1860), 293–332.
Harrison, William Henry, 'Miracles', *Spiritualist* 1 (1870), 117.
'Opening Address', *Spiritualist* 1 (1869), 5.
'Professor Tyndall at a Spirit Circle', *Spiritualist* 1 (1871), 156–7.
'The Scientific Investigation of Spiritual Phenomena', *Spiritualist* 1 (1869), 5.
'Spiritualism', *Spiritualist* 3 (1873), 306.
Hatton, Joseph, 'On Some Notable Dreams', *Argosy* 5 (1867–8), 462–6.
Hayward, Rhodri, 'Policing Dreams: History and the Moral Uses of the Uncon-
    scious', *History Workshop Journal* 49 (2000), 142–60.
Heaphy, Thomas, 'Mr H.'s Own Narrative', *All the Year Round* 6 (1861),
    36–43.
Heller, T., *The Delights of Terror: An Aesthetics of the Tale of Terror* (Urbana:
    University of Illinois Press, 1987).
von Helmholtz, Hermann, 'The Axioms of Geometry', *The Academy* 1 (1870),
    128–31; 3 (1872), 52–3.
'The Origin and Meaning of Geometrical Axioms: I', *Mind* 1 (1876), 301–32.
'The Origin and Meaning of Geometrical Axioms: II', *Mind* 3 (1878),
    212–25.
Henson, Louise, 'Charles Dickens, Elizabeth Gaskell and Victorian Science', PhD
    thesis, University of Sheffield (2000).
Hertz, Neil, 'George Eliot's Pulse', *Differences* 6 (1994), 28–45.
Hibbert, Samuel, *Sketches of the Philosophy of Apparitions; or, an Attempt to Trace
    such Illusions to their Physical Causes* (London: Whittaker, 1824).

Hill, J. Arthur, *Spiritualism: Its History, Phenomena and Doctrine* (London: Cassell, 1918).

Himmelfarb, Gertrude, *The Idea of Poverty: England in the Early Industrial Age* (New York: Vintage, 1985).

Hinton, C. H., *An Episode of Flatland: Or, How a Plane Folk Discovered the Third Dimension* (London: Swann Sonnenschein and Co., 1907).

The Fourth Dimension (London: Swann Sonnenschein and Co., 1904).

A New Era of Thought (London: Swann Sonnenschein and Co., 1888).

'The Recognition of the Fourth Dimension', *Bulletin of the Philosophical Society of Washington* 14 (1900–1904), 179–203.

Scientific Romances, 2 vols. (London: Swann Sonnenschein and Co., 1884–5).

Hobson, J. A., *The Crisis of Liberalism: New Issues of Democracy*, (London: P. S. King and Son, 1909).

Holland, Henry, *Chapters on Mental Physiology* (London: Longman, Orme, Brown, Green and Longman, 1852).

Hook, Phillip, and Mark Poltimore, *Popular Nineteenth-Century Painting: A Dictionary of European Genre Painters* (Woodbridge, Suffolk: Antique Collectors' Club, 1986).

Howitt, William, *The History of the Supernatural*, 2 vols. (London: Longman, Green, Roberts and Green, 1863).

Hueffer, Ford Madox, 'The Function of the Arts in the Republic', *English Review* 1 (1908), pp. 157–60.

Hughes, Winifred, *The Maniac in the Cellar: Sensation Novels of the 1860s* (Princeton: Princeton University Press, 1980).

Hunt, Frederick Knight, 'Wings of Fire', *Household Words* 2 (1850), 241–5.

Hunt, William Holman, *Pre-Raphaelism and the Pre-Raphaelite Brotherhood*, 2 vols. (London: Macmillan and Co., 1905).

Huxley, T. H., 'On the Method of Zadig: Retrospective Prophecy as a Function of Science' (1880) in *Collected Essays*, vol. IV (London: Macmillan and Co., 1893), pp. 1–23.

Ilie, Paul, 'Goya's Teratology and the Critique of Reason', *Eighteenth-Century Studies* 18 (1984–5), 35–56.

Inglis, Brian, *Natural and Supernatural: A History of the Paranormal from Earliest Times to 1914* (London: Hodder and Stoughton, 1977).

Jacobus, Mary, 'Hysterics Suffer Mainly from Reminiscences' in *Reading Woman: Essays in Feminist Criticism* (London: Methuen, 1986), pp. 249–74.

James, Henry, *Autobiography* (1954), ed. Frederick Dupee (Princeton: Princeton University Press, 1983).

'The New Novel' (1914) in *The Critical Muse: Selected Literary Criticism*, ed. Roger Gard (Harmondsworth: Penguin, 1987), pp. 595–614.

The Jolly Corner and Other Tales, ed. Roger Gard (Harmondsworth: Penguin, 1990).

James, William, 'What Psychical Research has Accomplished' in *The Will to Believe: and Other Essays in Popular Philosophy* (New York, London and Bombay, Longman's, Green and Co., 1897), pp. 299–327.

Jann, Rosemary, 'Christianity, Spiritualism, and the Fourth Dimension in Late Victorian England', *Victorian Newsletter* 70 (1986), 124–8.

Jevons, William Stanley, 'Helmholtz on the Axioms of Geometry', *Nature* 4 (1871), 481–2.

Jones, John, *The Natural and Supernatural, or Man Physical, Apparitional and Spiritual* (London: H. Bailliere, 1861).

Jowett, Benjamin, 'On the Interpretation of Scripture' in *Essays and Reviews* (London: John W. Parker, 1860), pp. 330–443.

Kaplan, Fred, *Dickens and Mesmerism: The Hidden Springs of Fiction* (Princeton: Princeton University Press, 1975).

Keating, Peter, *The Haunted Study: A Social History of the English Novel 1875–1914* (London: Fontana, 1991).

Kellar, Harry, 'High Caste in Indian Magic', *North American Review* 46 (1893), 75–86.

King, John H., *The Supernatural: Its Origin, Nature and Evolution*, 2 vols. (London: Williams and Norgate, 1892).

Kingsford, Anna, *Clothed with the Sun* (London: Redway, 1889).

Kingsley, Charles, *His Letters and Memories of his Life, Edited by his Wife*, 2 vols. (London: Henry S. King and Co., 1877).

Kingsley, Mary, 'Black Ghosts', *Cornhill Magazine*, New Series, 1 (1896), 79–92.

'Forms of Apparitions in West Africa', *PSPR* 14 (1898–9), 331–42.

Knight, David M., *The Age of Science* (Oxford: Blackwell, 1986).

Knowles, James, 'Brain-Waves: A Theory', *Spectator* (30 January 1869), 134–6.

'The Hypothesis of Brain-Waves', *Spectator* (30 January 1869), 133–4.

Kottler, Malcolm Jay, 'Alfred Russel Wallace, the Origin of Man, and Spiritualism', *Isis* 65 (1972), 145–92.

Kuklick, Henrika and Robert E. Kohler, 'Introduction', *Osiris* 11 (1996), 1–14.

Londow, George P., *William Holman Hunt and Typological Symbolian* (New Haven and London: Yale University Press, 1979).

Lang, Andrew, *Adventures Among Books* (London: Longmans and Co., 1905).

Cock Lane and Common-Sense (London: Longmans, 1894).

'The Comparative Study of Ghost Stories', *Nineteenth Century* 17 (1885), 623–32.

'Ghosts Up to Date' *Blackwood's Magazine* 155 (1894), 47–58.

'Literature', *New Review* 8 (1893), 710–14.

The Making of Religion (London: Longman's, Green, 1898).

'Mythology and Fairy Tales', *Fortnightly Review*, New Series, 8 (1873), 618–31.

'"The Nineteenth Century" and Mr F. Myers', *PSPR* 18 (1903–4), 62–76.

'Presidential Address', *PSPR* 25 (1911), 364–76.

'Protest of a Psycho-Folklorist', *Folk-Lore* 6 (1895), 236–48.

'Psychical Research of the Century' in *The Nineteenth Century: A Review of Progress* (New York: G. P. Putnam's Sons, 1901), pp. 358–69.

'Realism and Romance', *Contemporary Review* 52 (1887), 683–93.

'Savage Spiritualism', *Longman's Magazine* 23 (1894), 482–95.

Latour, Bruno, *Science in Action: How to Follow Scientists and Engineers through Society* (Cambridge, MA: Harvard University Press, 1987).

Leadbeater, C. W., *The Fourth Dimension* (San Francisco: Mercury Publishing Office, 1900).

Lee, Frederick George, *Glimpses of the Supernatural. Being Facts, Records and Traditions Relating to Dreams, Omens, Miraculous Occurrences, Apparitions, Wraiths, Warnings, Second-Sight, Witchcraft, Necromancy, etc.* (London: H. S. King and Co., 1875).

Glimpses of the Supernatural, Being Various Notes, Records, and Examples of the Supernatural (London: Blackwood, 1885).

Leslie, Duncan, *Leslie's Tourist Guide to the Scottish Highlands* (Perth: D. Leslie; Edinburgh and Glasgow: John Menzies and Co.; London: Simpkin, Marshall and Co., 1888).

Lewes, G. H., *The Physiology of Common Life*, 2 vols. (Edinburgh: Blackwood, 1859).

Linton, Eliza Lynn, *The Second Youth of Theodora Desanges* (London: Hutchinson, 1900).

Locke, John, *Essay Concerning Human Understanding* (1690), ed. John Yolton (London: Dent Everyman, 1993).

Lombroso, Cesare, *After Death: What?* (London and Manchester: Sherratt and Hughes, 1910).

Lopez, Donald S. Jr, *The Prisoners of Shangri-La: Tibetan Buddhism and the West* (Chicago and London: University of Chicago Press, 1998).

Luckhurst, Roger, *The Invention of Telepathy, 1870–1901* (Oxford: Oxford University Press, 2002).

'Passages in the Invention of the Psyche: Mind-Reading in London, 1881–4' in *Encounters: Transactions between Science and Culture in the Nineteenth Century*, eds. Josephine McDonagh and Roger Luckhurst (Manchester: Manchester University Press, 2002), pp. 117–50.

Lytton, Earl of (Victor Alexander George Robert Lytton), *The Life of Edward Bulwer Lytton, First Lord Lytton*, 2 vols. (London: Macmillan and Co., 1913).

Macaulay, Charles Babington, 'History. The Romance of History. England. By Henry Neele. London. 1828. (May 1828)' in *The Works of Lord Macaulay*, ed. Lady Trevelyan, 8 vols. (London: Longmans, Green and Co., 1866), vol. v, pp. 122–61.

McClintock, Anne, *Imperial Leather: Race, Gender and Sexuality in the Colonial Contest* (London: Routledge, 1995).

Macnish, Robert, *The Philosophy of Sleep* (Glasgow: W. R. M'Phun, 1830).

Malley, Shawn, '"Time Hath No Power Against Identity": Historical Continuity and Archaeological Adventure in H. Rider Haggard's *She*', *English Literature in Transition 1880–1920* 40 (1997), 275–97.

Marcus, Sharon, *Apartment Stories: City and Home in Nineteenth-Century Paris and London* (Berkeley: University of California Press, 1999).

Marshall, David, *The Figure of Theater* (New York: Columbia University Press, 1986).

Martin, Loy, *Browning's Dramatic Monologues and the Post-Romantic Subject* (Baltimore and London: Johns Hopkins University Press, 1985).

Martin, Martin, *A Description of the Western Islands CIRCA 1695, Including a Voyage to St Kilda by the Same Author and a Description of the Western Islands of Scotland by Sir Donald Munro*, ed. Donald J. Macleod (Stirling: Aeneas Mackay, 1934).

Marx, Karl, *The Eighteenth Brumaire of Louis Napoleon* (London: Lawrence & Wishart, 1954).

Mathers, Samuel Liddell Macgregor, *The Book of Sacred Magic of Abra-Melin the Mage* (London: J. M. Watkins, 1897).

The Kabbalah Unveiled (London: Routledge and Kegan Paul, 1926).

Maudsley, Henry, *Natural Causes and Supernatural Seemings* (1886) (London: Watts and Co., 1939).

de Maupassant, Guy, *Selected Short Stories*, trans. Roger Colet (Harmondsworth: Penguin, 1971).

M'Cosh, James, *The Natural in Relation to the Supernatural* (Cambridge: Macmillan, 1862).

Menke, Richard, 'Fiction as Vivisection: G. H. Lewes and George Eliot', *ELH* 67 (2000), 617–53.

Messent, P. (ed.), *The Literature of the Occult: A Collection of Critical Essays* (Englewood Cliffs, NJ: Prentice Hall, 1981).

Milbank, Alison, *Dante and the Victorians* (Manchester: Manchester University Press, 1998).

Miller, Hugh, *Sketch-book of Popular Geology; Being a Series of Lectures Delivered Before the Philosophical Institution of Edinburgh* (Edinburgh: Thomas Constable and Co.; London: Hamilton, Adams and Co., 1859).

Millington, Rev. Thomas, *A Lecture on Dreams, Mesmerism, Clairvoyance & c.* (London: H. Bailliere, 1852).

Moore, James R., 'Geologists and Interpreters of Genesis in the Nineteenth Century' in *God and Nature: Historical Essays on the Encounter Between Christianity and Science*, eds. David C. Lindberg and Ronald L. Numbers (Berkeley and London: University of California Press, 1986), pp. 322–50.

Moore, R. Laurence, *In Search of White Crows: Spiritualism, Parapsychology, and American Culture* (New York: Oxford University Press, 1977).

Morley, Henry, 'New Discoveries in Ghosts', *Household Words* 4 (1852), 403–6.

Morley, Henry and W. H. Wills, 'The Ghost of the Cock Lane Ghost', *Household Words* 6 (1853), 217–23.

Morton, R. C., 'Record of a Haunted House', *Proceedings of the Society for Psychical Research* 8 (1892), 311–32.

Murray, Gilbert, *et al.*, 'Andrew Lang', *Quarterly Review* 218 (1913).

Myers, Frederick William Henry, *Human Personality and its Survival of Bodily Death*, 2 vols. (London: Longmans, Green and Co., 1915).

Human Personality and its Survival of Bodily Death, edited and abridged by S. B. and L. H. M. (London: Longmans, Green and Co., 1927).

'Rossetti and the Religion of Beauty' in *Essays Modern* (London: Macmillan, 1897), pp. 312–34.

Neubauer, Hans-Joachim, *The Rumour: A Cultural History*, trans. Christian Braun (London: Free Association Books, 1999).

Newnham, W., *Essay on Superstition, Being an Inquiry into the Effects of Physical Influence on the Mind* (London: Hatchard and Son, 1830).

Noakes, Richard J., '"Cranks and Visionaries": Science, Spiritualism, and Transgression in Victorian Britain', PhD thesis, University of Cambridge (1998).

'Telegraphy is an Occult Art: Cromwell Fleetwood Varley and the Diffusion of Electricity to the Other World', *British Journal for the History of Science* 32 (1999), 421–59.

O'Connor, Maura, *The Romance of Italy and the English Political Imagination* (London: Macmillan, 1998).

Offer, Avner, *Property and Politics* (Cambridge: Cambridge University Press, 1981).

Oldroyd, David R., 'The Geologist from Cromarty' in *Hugh Miller and the Controversies of Victorian Science*, ed. Michael Shortland (Oxford: Clarendon Press, 1996), pp. 76–102.

Ollier, Charles, *Fallacy of Ghosts, Dreams and Omens* (London: Charles Ollier, 1848).

Olsen, Donald J., 'Victorian London: Specialisation, Segregation and Privacy', *Victorian Studies* 17 (1974), 265–78.

Oppenheim, Janet, *The Other World: Spiritualism and Psychical Research in England 1850–1914* (Cambridge: Cambridge University Press, 1985).

Ostry, Elaine, '"Social Wonders": Fancy, Science, and Technology in Dickens's Periodicals', *Victorian Periodicals Review* 34 (2001), 54–78.

Owen, Alex, *The Darkened Room: Women, Power and Spiritualism in Late Victorian England* (London: Virago, 1989).

Owen, Robert Dale, *Footfalls on the Boundary of Another World* (London: Trübner and Sons, 1860).

Palfreman, Jon, 'William Crookes: Spiritualism and Science', *Ethics in Science and Medicine* 3 (1976), 211–27.

Part, Dr J. Shepley, 'A Few Notes on Occultism in West Africa', *Proceedings of the Society for Psychical Research* 14 (1898–9), 343–7.

Patterson, Charles Brodie, *A New Heaven and a New Earth: Or, The Way to Life Eternal (Thought Studies of the Fourth Dimension)* (London: George G. Harrap and Co., 1909).

Paulson, Ronald, *Representations of Revolution (1789–1920)* (New Haven and London: Yale University Press, 1983).

Pearce, C. W., 'Mr. Crookes's Experiments', *Spiritualist* 1 (1871), 190.

Pearson, Richard, 'Archaeology and Gothic Desire: Vitality Beyond the Grave in H. Rider Haggard's Ancient Egypt' in *Victorian Gothic*, eds. Ruth Robbins and Julian Wolfreys (London: Palgrave, 2001), pp. 218–44.

Penzoldt, P., *The Supernatural in Fiction* (New York: Humanities Press, 1965).

Perkins, Maureen, 'The Meaning of Dream Books', *History Workshop Journal* 48 (1999), 102–13.

Peterson, M. J., 'The Victorian Governess: Status Incongruence in Family and Society' in *Suffer and Be Still: Women in the Victorian Age*, ed. Martha Vicinus (Bloomington: Indiana University Press, 1972), pp. 3–19.

Podmore, Frank, *Modern Spiritualism: A History and a Criticism*, 2 vols. (London: Methuen and Co., 1902).

The Naturalisation of the Supernatural (New York and London: G. P. Putnam's Sons, 1908).

The Newer Spiritualism (London: T. Fisher Unwin, 1910).

Pointon, Marcia, 'Geology and Landscape Painting in Nineteenth-Century England' in *Images of the Earth: Essays in the History of the Environmental Sciences*, eds.Ludmilla Jordanova and Roy S. Porter (Chalfont St Giles: British Society for the History of Science, 1979), pp. 84–108.

William Dyce 1806–1864: A Critical Biography (Oxford: Clarendon Press, 1979).

'William Dyce as a Painter of Biblical Subjects', *Art Bulletin* 58 (1976), 260–8.

Pound, Ezra, 'Editorial on Solicitous Doubt', *Little Review* 1, no. 8 (December 1917), p. 54.

Powell, Baden, 'On the Study of the Evidences of Christianity' in *Essays and Reviews* (London: John W. Parker, 1860), pp. 94–144.

The Order of Nature Considered in Reference to the Claims of Revelation (London: Longman, Brown, Green, Longmans, & Roberts, 1859).

Powell, Nicolas, *Fuseli: The Nightmare* (London: Allen Lane, 1973).

Praz, Mario, *The Romantic Agony*, trans. A. Davidson, 2nd edn (London and New York: Oxford University Press, 1970).

Press, Jacob, 'Same-Sex Unions in Modern Europe: *Daniel Deronda, Altneuland*, and the Homoerotics of Jewish Nationalism' in *Novel-Gazing: Queer Readings in Fiction*, ed. Eve Kosofsky Sedgwick (Durham, NC: Duke University Press, 1997), pp. 249–68.

Prothero, Stephen, 'From Spiritualism to Theosophy: "Uplifting" a Democratic Culture', *Religion and American Culture: A Journal of Interpretation* 3 (1993), 197–216.

Rabaté, Jean Michel, *The Ghosts of Modernity* (Gainesville: University Press of Florida, 1996).

Radcliffe, John Netten, *Fiends, Ghosts and Sprites, Including an Account of the Origin and Nature of Belief in the Supernatural* (London: Richard Bentley, 1854).

Rainey, Lawrence, *Institutions of Modernism: Literary Elites and Public Culture* (New Haven: Yale University Press, 1998).

Rait, R. S., Salomon Reinach, Gilbert Murray and J. H. Millar, 'Andrew Lang', *Quarterly Review* 218 (1913), 299–329.

Ransom, Josephine, *The Direction of the Theosophical Society by Masters of Wisdom* (London: Theosophical Publishing House, 1942).

Raymond, William, *The Infinite Moment* (Toronto: University of Toronto Press, 1950).

Richards, Joan L., *Mathematical Visions: The Pursuit of Geometry in Victorian England* (San Diego and London: Academic Press, 1988).

Riemann, Bernhard, 'On the Hypotheses which Lie at the Bases of Geometry', trans. W. K. Clifford, *Nature* 8 (1873), 14–17, 36–7.

Rivers, W. H. R., 'In Memoriam: Andrew Lang', *Folk-Lore* 23 (1912), 369–71.

Roberts, Adam, 'The Ring and the Book: the Mage, the Alchemist, and the Poet', *Victorian Poetry* 36 (1998), 37–46.

Roberts, Samuel, 'Remarks on Mathematical Terminology, and the Philosophic Bearing of Recent Mathematical Speculations Concerning the Realities of Space', *Proceedings of the London Mathematical Society* 14 (1882–3), 5–15.

Robinson, Ronald and John Gallagher with Alice Denny, *Africa and the Victorians: The Official Mind of Imperialism* (London: Macmillan, 1981).

Robinson, Solveig C., 'Editing *Belgravia*: M. E. Braddon's Defense of "Light Literature"', *Victorian Periodicals Review* 28 (1995), 109–22.

Rossetti, Dante Gabriel, *Dante and his Circle: With the Italian Poets Preceeding Him (1100–1200–1300)* (London: Ellis and White, 1874).

Royle, Nicholas, *Telepathy and Literature* (Oxford: Basil Blackwell, 1990).

Ruskin, John, *The Complete Works of John Ruskin* (Library Edition), eds. E. T. Cook and Alexander Wedderburn, 39 vols. (London: George Allen, 1903–12).

Rutherford, John, 'Dreams', *Cornhill Magazine* 29 (1874), 720–6.

Rylance, Rick, *Victorian Psychology and British Culture 1850–1880* (Oxford: University Press, 2000).

Salmonson, J. A. (ed.), *What Did Miss Darrington See?* (New York: Feminist Press, 1988).

Schiller, Gertrud, *Iconography of Christian Art*, trans. Janet Seligman, 2 vols. (London: Lund Humphreys, 1972).

Schofield, A. T., *Another World, or, The Fourth Dimension* (London: Swann, Sonnenschein and Co. 1888).

Schubert, Hermann, 'The Fourth Dimension: Mathematical and Spiritualistic', *The Monist* 3 (1892–3), 402–49.

Scott, Walter, *Letters on Demonology and Witchcraft Addressed to J. G. Lockhart Esq.* (London: John Murray, 1830).

Scrope, William, *The Art of Deer-Stalking* (1838) (London and New York: Edward Arnold, 1897).

Seeley, John, *The Expansion of England* (London: Macmillan, 1883).

Seibold-Bultmann, Ursula, 'Monster Soup: the Microscope and Victorian Fantasy', *Interdisciplinary Science Reviews* 25 (2000), 211–19.

Serres, Michel, *Atlas* (Paris: Editions Julliard, 1994).

Sharp, William, *Papers Critical and Reminiscent* (London: Heinemann, 1912).

Shelley, Percy Bysshe, *Complete Poetical Works*, ed. Thomas Hutchinson (Oxford: Oxford University Press, 1971).

Sheppard, John, *On Dreams, in Their Mental and Moral Aspects* (London: Jackson and Walford, 1847).

Shortt, S. E. D., 'Physicians and Psychics: The Anglo-American Response to Spiritualism, 1870–1890', *Journal for the History of Medicine* 39 (1984), 339–55.

Shuttleworth, Sally, *Charlotte Brontë and Victorian Psychology* (Cambridge: Cambridge University Press, 1996).

'The Malady of Thought: Embodied Memory in Victorian Psychology and the Novel', *Memory and Memorials 1789–1914: Literary and Cultural Perspectives*, eds. Matthew Campbell, Jacqueline M. Labbe and Sally Shuttleworth (London: Routledge, 2000), pp. 46–59.

Sidgwick, Arthur and Eleanor, *Henry Sidgwick: A Memoir* (London: Macmillan, 1906).

Sinnett, A. P., *The Occult World* (London: Trubner, 1881).

(ed.), *The Mahatma Letters* (London: T. Fisher Unwin, 1924).

Slinn, Warwick, *The Discourse of the Self in Victorian Poetry* (London: Macmillan, 1991).

Smith, Timothy d'Arch, *Love in Earnest* (London: Routledge and Kegan Paul, 1970).

Sokolsky, Anita, 'A Dark Inscription: Questions of Representation in *Daniel Deronda*', PhD thesis, Cornell University (1983).

Staley, Allen, *The Pre-Raphaelite Landscape* (Oxford: Clarendon Press, 1973).

Stein, Gordon, *The Sorcerer of Kings: The Case of Daniel Dunglas Home and William Crookes* (New York: Prometheus Books, 1993).

Stephen, Leslie, 'The Scepticism of Believers', *Fortnightly Review* 22 (1877), 355–76.

Stephens, F. G., *William Holman Hunt and his Works: A Memoir of the Artist's Life, with Descriptions of his Pictures* (London: James Nisbet and Co., 1860).

Stephens, John Richard (ed.), *Into the Mummy's Tomb* (New York: Berkley Books, 2001).

Stewart, Garrett, *Death Sentences: Styles of Dying in British Fiction* (Cambridge, MA: Harvard University Press, 1984).

Stocking, George, *Victorian Anthropology* (New York: Free Press, 1987).

Stone, Harry, 'The Unknown Dickens', *Dickens Studies Annual* 1 (1971), 1–22.

Stonebridge, Lyndsey, *The Destructive Element: British Psychoanalysis and Modernism* (Basingstoke: Macmillan, 1998).

Sullivan, J., *Elegant Nightmares: The British Ghost Story from Le Fanu to Blackwood* (Athens, GA: Ohio University Press, 1978).

Surtees, Viriginia, *Dante Gabriel Rossetti 1828–1882: The Paintings and Drawings: A Catalogue Raisonné* (London: Oxford University Press, 1971).

Swedenborg, Emmanuel, *Spiritual Diary: A Brief Record, During Twenty Years, of his Supernatural Experience*, vol. 1, trans. J. H. Smithson (London: Newbery / The Swedenborg Society, 1846).

Symonds, John Addington, *Sleep and Dreams: Two Lectures* (London: John Murray, 1851).

Symons, A. J. A., *Essays and Biograpies* (London: Cassell, 1969).

The Quest for Corvo (London: Cassell, 1934).

Taylor, Anne, *Annie Besant: A Biography* (Oxford: Oxford University Press, 1992).

Taylor, Jenny Bourne, 'Obscure Recesses: Locating the Victorian Unconscious' in *Writing and Victorianism*, eds. Alice Jenkin and Juliet John (London: Longmans, 1998), pp. 137–79.

Taylor, Jenny Bourne and Sally Shuttleworth (eds.), *Embodied Selves: An Anthology of Nineteenth-Century Psychological Writings* (Oxford: Clarendon, 1998).

Temple, Frederick, 'The Education of the World' in *Essays and Reviews* (London: John W. Parker and Son, 1860), pp. 1–49.

Thackeray, William Makepeace, *Roundabout Papers* (1846) (London: Blackie and Son, Ltd, n.d.).

Thomas, Keith, *Religion and the Decline of Magic: Studies in Popular Beliefs in Sixteenth- and Seventeenth-Century England* (Harmondsworth: Penguin, 1973).

Thomson, William, 'Six Gateways of Knowledge [1883]' in *Popular Lectures and Addresses*, 2nd edn., 3 vols. (London: Macmillan and Co, 1889–94), I, pp. 253–99.

Thurschwell, Pamela, *Literature, Technology and Magical Thinking 1880–1920* (Cambridge: Cambridge University Press, 2001).

Todorov, Tsvetan, *The Fantastic: A Structural Approach to a Literary Genre*, trans. R. Howard (Cleveland, OH: Case Western Reserve University Press, 1973).

Tomlinson, Janis, *Graphic Evolutions: the Prints of Francisco Goya* (New York: Columbia University Press, 1989).

Torok, Maria and Nicholas Rand, *Questions for Freud: The Secret History of Psychoanalysis* (Cambridge, MA: Harvard University Press, 1997).

Townshend, Chauncy Hare, *Mesmerism Proved True and the Quarterly Reviewer Reviewed* (London: Thomas Bosworth, 1854).

Tromp, Marlene, Pamela K. Gilbert and A. Haynie (eds.), *Beyond Sensation: Mary Elizabeth Braddon in Context* (New York: State University of New York Press, 2000).

Tropp, Martin, *Images of Fear: How Horror Stories Helped Shape Modern Culture, 1818–1918* (Jefferson, NC and London: McFarland, 1990).

Trotter, David, *The English Novel in History, 1895–1920* (London: Routledge, 1993).

Tucker, Herbert, *Browning's Beginnings: the Art of Disclosure* (Minneapolis: University of Minnesota Press, 1980).

Turner, Frank M., *Between Science and Religion: The Reaction to Scientific Naturalism in Victorian Britain* (New Haven: Yale University Press, 1974).

Contesting Cultural Authority: Essays in Victorian Intellectual Life (Cambridge: Cambridge University Press, 1993).

Tylor, Edward, *Primitive Culture: Researches into the Development of Mythology, Philosophy, Religion, Art, and Custom*, 2 vols. (London: John Murray, 1871).

Uglow, Jenny, 'Introduction', *Victorian Ghost Stories by Eminent Women Writers*, ed. Richard Dalby (New York: Carroll and Graf, 1988).

Vaughan, William, 'Realism and Tradition in Religious Art' in '*Sind Briten hier?*' *Relations between British and Continental Art 1680–1880*, ed. Zentralinstitut für Kunstgeschichte (Munich: Wilhelm Fink Verlag, 1981), pp. 207–23.

Vicinus, Martha, 'The Adolescent Boy: Fin-de-Siècle Femme Fatale?' in *Victorian Sexual Dissidence*, ed. Richard Dellamora (Chicago and London: University of Chicago Press, 1999), pp. 83–108.

Victorian Fairy Painting, exhibition catalogue (London: Royal Academy of Arts, 1997).

Vidler, Anthony, *The Architectural Uncanny: Essays in the Modern Unhomely* (Cambridge, MA and London: MIT Press, 1992).

Viswanathan, Gauri, 'The Ordinary Business of Occultism', *Critical Inquiry* 27 (2000), 1–20.

Outside the Fold: Conversion, Modernity and Belief (Princeton: Princeton University Press, 1998).

Walker, E. D., *Reincarnation: A Study of Forgotten Truth* (Boston and New York: Houghton, Mifflin and Co., 1888).

Wallace, Alfred Russel, *My Life: A Record of Events and Opinions*, 2 vols. (London: Chapman and Hall, 1905).

The Scientific Aspect of the Supernatural (London: F. Farrah, 1866).

'Spiritualism and Science', *The Times*, 5 January 1873, 10.

Weeks, Donald, *Corvo* (London: Michael Joseph, 1971).

Wells, H. G., *Tono Bungay* (London: Macmillan, 1909).

Wilberforce, Samuel, 'Art. VIII – *Essays and Reviews*. London. 1860', *Quarterly Review* 109 (1861), 248–305.

Winter, Alison, *Mesmerized: Powers of Mind in Victorian Britain* (Chicago: University of Chicago Press, 1998).

Wolff, Robert L., *Sensational Victorian: The Life and Fiction of Mary Elizabeth Braddon* (New York: Garland, 1979).

Woolf, Cecil, *A Bibliography of Frederick Rolfe, Baron Corvo* (London: Rupert Hart Davis, 1972).

(ed.), *Without Prejudice: One Hundred Letters from Frederick Rolfe 'Baron Corvo' to John Lane* (London: Allen Lane, 1963).

Woolf, Virginia, 'Mr Bennett and Mrs Brown' (1924) in *A Woman's Essays*, ed. Rachel Bowlby (London: Penguin, 1992), pp. 69–87.

Orlando A Biography (London: The Hogarth Press, 1928).

To the Lighthouse (1927), ed. Stella McNichol (London: Penguin, 1992).

Wurgraft, Lewis D., *The Imperial Imagination: Magic and Myth in Kipling's India* (Middletown, CT: Wesleyan University Press, 1983).

Wynne, Catherine, 'Mesmeric Exoticism, Idolatrous Beliefs, and Bloody Rituals: Mesmerism, Catholicism and Second Sight in Bram Stoker's Fiction', *Victorian Review* 26 (2000), 43–63.

Zöllner, Friedrich, *Transcendental Physics*, trans. Charles Carleton Massey (London: Massey, 1880).

Index

CAMBRIDGE STUDIES IN NINETEENTH-CENTURY
LITERATURE AND CULTURE

General editor
Gillian Beer, *University of Cambridge*

Titles published

Printed in Great Britain
by Amazon